Microsoft®

Expression® Web 3
Complete

Gary B. Shelly
Jennifer T. Campbell
Ollie Rivers

Shelly Cashman Series®

An imprint of Course Technology, Cengage Learning

COURSE TECHNOLOGY
CENGAGE Learning™

Australia • Brazil • Japan • Korea • Mexico • Singapore • Spain • United Kingdom • United States

Microsoft® Expression® Web 3 Complete

Gary B. Shelly, Jennifer T. Campbell, Ollie Rivers

Vice President, Publisher: Nicole Pinard

Executive Editor: Kathleen McMahon

Product Manager: Jon Farnham

Associate Product Manager: Aimee Poirier

Editorial Assistant: Lauren Brody

Director of Marketing: Cheryl Costantini

Marketing Manager: Tristen Kendall

Marketing Coordinator: Stacey Leasca

Senior Print Buyer: Julio Esperas

Director of Production: Patty Stephan

Content Project Manager: Jennifer Feltri

Development Editor: Susan Whalen

Copyeditor/Proofreader: Suzanne Huizenga

Indexer: Sharon Hilgenberg

QA Manuscript Reviewers: John Freitas, Danielle Shaw

Art Director: Marissa Falco

Cover Designer: Lisa Kuhn, Curio Press, LLC

Cover Photo: Tom Kates Photography

Compositor: PrePress, PMG

All photos are property of the author. The art in Chapter 4 is included with the permission of Mimei Thompson.

For product information and technology assistance, contact us at
Cengage Learning Customer & Sales Support, 1-800-354-9706

For permissions to use material from this text or product, submit all request online at www.cengage.com/permissions Futher permissions questions can be emailed to **permissionrequest@cengage.com**

Library of Congress Control Number: 2010925123

International Student Edition:
ISBN-13: 978-0-8400-5478-4
ISBN-10: 0-84005-478-5

Cengage Learning International Offices

Asia
www.cengageasia.com
tel: (65) 6410 1200

Brazil
www.cengage.com.br
tel: (55) 11 3665 9900

Latin America
www.cengage.com.mx
tel: (52) 55 1500 6000

Australia/New Zealand
www.cengage.com.au
tel: (61) 3 9685 4111

India
www.cengage.co.in
tel: (91) 11 4364 1111

UK/Europe/Middle East/Africa
www.cengage.co.uk
tel: (44) 0 1264 332 424

Represented in Canada by Nelson Education, Ltd.
tel: (416) 752 9100 / (800) 668 0671
www.nelson.com

Cengage Learning is a leading provider of customized learning solutions with office locations around the globe, including Singapore, the United Kingdom, Australia, Mexico, Brazil, and Japan. Locate your local office at: **www.cengage.com/global**

For product information: **www.cengage.com/international**
Visit your local office: **www.cengage.com/global**
Visit our corporate website: **www.cengage.com**

AVAILABILITY OF RESOURCES MAY DIFFER BY REGION. Check with your local Cengage Learning representative for details.

Printed in the United States of America
1 2 3 4 5 6 7 15 14 13 12 11 10

Contents

Preface   ix

Microsoft EXPRESSION WEB 3

CHAPTER ONE
Creating an Expression Web Site

Objectives	EW 1
What Is Microsoft Expression Web?	EW 2
Project — Home Page	EW 2
Overview	EW 4
Starting Expression Web	EW 5
To Start Expression Web	EW 6
Expression Web Workspace	EW 7
The Workspace Window	EW 7
Toolbars	EW 8
To Reset Workspace Layout	EW 9
Creating a Web Site	EW 10
To Create a Web Site	EW 10
To Open a Web Page	EW 14
Setting Page Properties	EW 14
To Set Page Properties	EW 15
Entering Text	EW 20
To Add a <Div> Tag	EW 20
To Add Paragraph Text	EW 23
To Add a Bulleted List	EW 25
To Complete Page Content	EW 28
Saving Individual Web Pages	EW 30
To Save a Web Page	EW 30
Applying Formatting and Styles	EW 30
To Use the Quick Tag Selector	EW 31
To Apply a Heading Style	EW 33
To Center Text	EW 36
Applying Font Characteristics	EW 36
To Change Font Color	EW 37
Changing Font Sizes	EW 38
To Change Font Size	EW 39
To Indent Text	EW 41
To Italicize Text	EW 42
Choosing a Font	EW 43
To Change a Font	EW 44

Spell Checking Pages	EW 45
To Spell Check a Page	EW 46
Switching Views	EW 48
To Show Code and Split Views	EW 49
To View the Page in the Snapshot Panel	EW 51
Visual Aids and Quick Tags	EW 52
To Hide and Display Visual Aids	EW 52
Previewing in Browsers	EW 54
To Preview in a Browser	EW 54
Printing a Web Page	EW 55
To Print a Web Page	EW 56
Closing Expression Web	EW 57
To Close a Web Page	EW 57
To Quit Expression Web	EW 58
Chapter Summary	EW 58
Learn It Online	EW 59
Apply Your Knowledge	EW 59
Extend Your Knowledge	EW 61
Make It Right	EW 62
In the Lab	EW 63
Cases and Places	EW 68

CHAPTER TWO
Working with Images and Links

Objectives	EW 71
Introduction	EW 72
Project — Enhancing the Boon Mountain Resort Web Site	EW 72
Overview	EW 73
Choosing Images and File Types	EW 74
Technical Considerations for Image Files	EW 74
Accessibility Properties	EW 75
Inserting an Image	EW 76
To Start Expression Web	EW 77
To Open a Web Site	EW 77
To Insert an Image	EW 80
Adjusting the Workspace Layout	EW 84
Panels	EW 84
To Close a Panel	EW 85
To Display the Ruler	EW 87
Adjusting Proportions	EW 89
To Resize an Image	EW 89

Positioning an Image   **EW 93**
   To Align an Image   EW 94
   Adding Borders and Spacing   EW 95
   To Add a Border to an Image   EW 95
   To Modify Image Margins   EW 97
Enhancing an Image   **EW 98**
   To Add Transparency to an Image   EW 99
   The Clipboard   EW 103
   To Copy an Image to Other Pages   EW 103
   To Crop an Image   EW 106
Controlling Image Files   **EW 111**
   Thumbnail Images   EW 111
   To Create a Thumbnail   EW 112
   To Create a Folder for Images   EW 116
Adding Navigational Links to a Site   **EW 120**
   To Add an Internal Link   EW 121
   To Test Internal Links   EW 125
   To Copy and Paste Internal Links   EW 127
   To Add an External Link   EW 129
   To Test External Links   EW 132
   To Add a Bookmark   EW 134
   To Add an E-Mail Link   EW 137
   To Add a ScreenTip   EW 138
   To Preview the Site   EW 139
   To Close a Site and Quit Expression Web   EW 140
Chapter Summary   **EW 141**
Learn It Online   **EW 141**
Apply Your Knowledge   **EW 142**
Extend Your Knowledge   **EW 143**
Make It Right   **EW 145**
In the Lab   **EW 146**
Cases and Places   **EW 150**

CHAPTER THREE
Working with Templates and Styles
Objectives   **EW 151**
Introduction   **EW 152**
Project — Personal Portfolio   **EW 152**
   Overview   EW 153
Starting a New Web Site Using a Template   **EW 154**
   To Start Expression Web and Reset the
      Workspace Layout   EW 156
   Placeholders   EW 156
   To Create a New Web Site from a Template   EW 157
Specifying the Structure of the Site   **EW 160**
   To Rename a Folder   EW 161
   To Rename a Web Page   EW 162
Modifying the Structure of a Web Site   **EW 163**
   To Delete a Web Page   EW 164
   To Delete a Folder   EW 166
   To Add a Folder   EW 167
   To Add a Web Page   EW 169
Entering and Editing Text   **EW 172**
   To Replace Template Placeholder Text   EW 172
   Pasting Text   EW 177
   To Paste Text   EW 177

   To Close Microsoft Word   EW 182
   Editing Text   EW 182
   To Edit Text   EW 183
   To Find and Replace Text   EW 186
Dynamic Web Page Template Pages   **EW 189**
   To Make Global Changes to a Template   EW 190
Defining Styles and Style Sheets   **EW 193**
   Style Sheet Types   EW 194
   Style Rule Syntax   EW 194
   To Modify a Style   EW 195
   To Create a Style   EW 198
   To Apply a Style   EW 201
   To Preview the Site   EW 203
   To Close a Site and Quit Expression Web   EW 204
Chapter Summary   **EW 204**
Learn It Online   **EW 205**
Apply Your Knowledge   **EW 205**
Extend Your Knowledge   **EW 207**
Make It Right   **EW 209**
In the Lab   **EW 210**
Cases and Places   **EW 215**

EXPRESSION WEB DESIGN FEATURE
Web Design Basics
Objectives   **EW 217**
Introduction   **EW 218**
**Web Site Purpose, Target Audience, and
    Structure**   **EW 218**
   Establishing Your Site's Purpose   EW 219
   Identifying Your Site's Target Audience   EW 220
   Types of Web Pages   EW 220
   Site Structure   EW 222
Site Navigation System   **EW 224**
Color Schemes and Page Layout   **EW 227**
   Color Schemes   EW 228
   Page Length and Content Positioning   EW 230
   Balance, Proximity, Alignment, and Focus   EW 232
Writing Web Page Text   **EW 234**
Web-Ready Images and Multimedia   **EW 236**
Pre- and Post-Publishing Testing   **EW 237**
Feature Summary   **EW 237**
In the Lab   **EW 238**

CHAPTER FOUR
Creating Styles and Layouts with CSS
Objectives   **EW 241**
Introduction   **EW 242**
Project — Gallery Web Site   **EW 242**
   Overview   EW 243
Using CSS to Control Formatting and Layout   **EW 244**
   CSS Syntax   EW 244
Using CSS to Prioritize Rules   **EW 246**
   To Start Expression Web and Reset the
      Workspace Layout   EW 246
   To Open a Web Site and Web Page   EW 247

Microsoft®

Expression® Web 3
Complete

Gary B. Shelly

Jennifer T. Campbell

Ollie Rivers

To Define an ID-Based Style   EW 249
To Position Content Using a Class-Based Style   EW 254
To Use the CSS Properties Panel   EW 256
Creating and Attaching Style Sheets   **EW 259**
To Create an External Style Sheet   EW 260
Font Families   EW 262
To Create a Font Family   EW 262
Entering CSS Code   EW 265
To Modify a Page in Code View   EW 266
To Attach a Style Sheet   EW 268
Pre-Built CSS Layouts   EW 271
To Use Pre-Built CSS Layouts   EW 271
To Copy and Paste Elements   EW 274
To Complete Page Content   EW 276
To Attach Multiple Style Sheets   EW 280
To Add a Hyperlink   EW 283
To Organize Style Sheets   EW 284
To Create a CSS Report   EW 286
To Preview the Site   EW 288
To Close a Site and Quit Expression Web   EW 289
Chapter Summary   **EW 289**
Learn It Online   **EW 290**
Apply Your Knowledge   **EW 290**
Extend Your Knowledge   **EW 292**
Make It Right   **EW 294**
In the Lab   **EW 295**
Cases and Places   **EW 299**

CHAPTER FIVE

Working with Data Tables and Inline Frames

Objectives   **EW 301**
Introduction   **EW 302**
Project — Hair Salon   **EW 302**
Overview   EW 304
To Start Expression Web and Reset
  Workspace Layout   EW 305
To Create a New Web Site and Web Page   EW 305
Using a Preformatted Style Sheet   **EW 309**
To Create a New Style Sheet   EW 310
To Create a New Page and Attach a Style Sheet   EW 315
Creating Data Tables   **EW 316**
Working with Data Tables   EW 317
To Insert a Data Table   EW 317
Table and Cell Properties   **EW 319**
To Change Table and Cell Properties   EW 320
Entering Text into Cells   **EW 323**
To Add Text to a Table   EW 323
Adding Images into Cells   **EW 326**
To Add Images to a Table   EW 327
Adding Rows and Columns   **EW 329**
The Tables Toolbar   EW 329
To Add Rows and Columns   EW 330
Table Fill   EW 333
To Use Table Fill   EW 334

Merging and Splitting Cells   **EW 336**
To Merge Table Cells   EW 337
To Split Table Cells   EW 338
Formatting Table Text   **EW 340**
To Apply Styles to Table Text   EW 340
Converting Text to a Table   **EW 342**
To Convert Text to a Table   EW 342
To Distribute Rows and Columns   EW 345
Table AutoFormat   **EW 346**
To Use Table AutoFormat   EW 347
About Inline Frames   **EW 348**
To Create an I-Frame   EW 349
To Target Links in an I-Frame   EW 352
Using Frames and Tables to Lay Out a Web Page **EW 354**
To Close a Site and Quit Expression Web   EW 354
Chapter Summary   **EW 354**
Learn It Online   **EW 355**
Apply Your Knowledge   **EW 355**
Extend Your Knowledge   **EW 358**
Make It Right   **EW 359**
In the Lab   **EW 360**
Cases and Places   **EW 365**

CHAPTER SIX

Adding Interactivity

Objectives   **EW 367**
Introduction   **EW 368**
Project — Farm Stand Web Site   **EW 368**
Overview   EW 370
To Start Expression Web and Reset
  Workspace Layout   EW 371
To Open a Web Site and Web Page   EW 371
Creating an Interactive Navigation Bar   **EW 372**
Interactivity and Web Browsers   EW 372
To Create an Interactive Button   EW 373
To Duplicate an Interactive Button   EW 379
Editing and Organizing Interactive Buttons   **EW 379**
To Edit an Interactive Button   EW 380
To Test Interactive Buttons   EW 382
To Copy and Paste the Navigation Bar   EW 385
To Organize the Button Images into Folders   EW 387
Defining Behaviors   **EW 390**
Creating a Jump Menu   EW 391
To Add a Jump Menu Behavior   EW 391
Creating a Status Bar Behavior   EW 396
To Add a Status Bar Behavior   EW 397
Creating a Swap Image Behavior   EW 398
To Add a Swap Image Behavior   EW 399
To Modify a Swap Image Behavior   EW 402
Creating Image Maps   **EW 405**
To Add an Image Map   EW 405
To Close a Site and Quit Expression Web   EW 409
Chapter Summary   **EW 409**
Learn It Online   **EW 410**
Apply Your Knowledge   **EW 410**

Extend Your Knowledge | EW 413
Make It Right | EW 414
In the Lab | EW 416
Cases and Places | EW 420

E-COMMERCE FEATURE
E-Commerce
Objectives | EW 423
The Role of E-Commerce in Today's Business
   Environment | EW 424
E-Commerce Business Models | EW 424
  Business-to-Consumer (B2C) | EW 425
  Business-to-Business (B2B) | EW 425
  Consumer-to-Consumer (C2C) | EW 426
  Consumer-to-Business (C2B) | EW 427
  Business-to-Government (B2G) | EW 427
  Business-to-Employee (B2E) | EW 428
Web Site E-Commerce Elements | EW 429
  Product Catalog | EW 429
  Shopping Cart | EW 430
  Payment Processors, Payment Gateways, and
    Merchant Accounts | EW 432
  Order Fulfillment | EW 434
  Customer Support | EW 435
  Transaction Security | EW 435
Adding E-Commerce Capability to a Web Site | EW 436
  Third-Party Payment Processor Solution | EW 436
  All-in-One E-Commerce Solution | EW 437
Feature Summary | EW 439
In the Lab | EW 439

APPENDIX A
Using the Microsoft Expression Web User Guide
Introduction | APP 1
  To Open the Microsoft Expression
    Web User Guide Window | APP 2
The Microsoft Expression
   Web User Guide Window | APP 3
  The Toolbar | APP 3
  Finding a Specific Help Topic by Searching
    the Index Tab | APP 4
  Browsing Help Topics by Category Using
    the Contents Tab | APP 4
  To Browse Help Topics by Category | APP 5
  To Search for a Help Topic Using the Index Tab | APP 6
  Searching for a Specific Help Topic Using
    the Search Tab | APP 8

  To Search for a Specific Help Topic Using
    the Search Tab | APP 8
Getting Help with the User Guide | APP 10

APPENDIX B
Web Standards and Accessibility
Introduction | APP 11
Web Standards | APP 11
Web Accessibility | APP 13

APPENDIX C
Publishing Content to the Web
Introduction | APP 15
Publishing Your Site Using Expression Web | APP 18
  Connection Settings | APP 18
  Publishing View | APP 20
Publishing Your Site Using FTP Client Software | APP 22

APPENDIX D
Microsoft Expression Studio 3
Introduction | APP 24
Expression Web | APP 24
Expression Design | APP 24
Expression Blend | APP 25
Expression Encoder | APP 27

APPENDIX E
Using Expression Web in Windows XP
  To Start Expression Web | APP 29
  To Open an Existing Web Site | APP 30
  To Close a Web Site | APP 32

APPENDIX F
Using Expression Web in Windows Vista
  To Start Expression Web | APP 34
  To Open an Existing Web Site | APP 35
  To Close a Web Site | APP 37

APPENDIX G
Changing Screen Resolution
  To Change the Screen Resolution | APP 39

Index | IND 1

Quick Reference Summary | QR 1

Preface

Shelly Cashman Series® offers the finest textbooks in computer education. We are proud of the fact that our textbooks have been the most widely used books in education. *Microsoft® Expression® Web 3: Complete* continues with the innovation, quality, and reliability that you have come to expect from the Shelly Cashman Series.

Microsoft Expression Web is known as the standard in Web authoring and enhances the work experience for users by providing a WYSIWYG design environment that can be used to create complex, standards-compliant, multi-page Web sites using tools such as dialog boxes, task panes, and dynamic Web templates without needing to enter HTML or CSS code.

In this Microsoft Expression Web 3 book, you will find an educationally sound and easy-to-follow pedagogy that combines a step-by-step approach with corresponding screens. All projects and exercises in this book are designed to take full advantage of the Expression Web 3 enhancements. The Other Ways feature offers in-depth knowledge of Expression Web. The popular Q&A feature provides answers to common questions students have about the Web design processes. The Learn It Online page presents a wealth of additional exercises to ensure your students have all the reinforcement they need. The project material is developed carefully to ensure that students will see the importance of learning Expression Web for future coursework.

Objectives of This Textbook

Microsoft® Expression® Web 3: Complete is intended for a course that includes an introduction to Expression Web 3. A basic understanding of the Internet, computers, data entry, and program tools such as dialog boxes and menu bars is assumed. The objectives of this book are:

- To teach the fundamentals of Microsoft Expression Web 3

- To expose students to the planning and decision-making process involved in creating Web pages, Web sites, and style sheets

- To acquaint students with the proper procedures to create Web pages and Web sites that include text, images, and hyperlinks, and are suitable for coursework, professional purposes, and personal use

- To help students use the Expression Web tools and user interface to create Web pages, Web sites, and style sheets that are easy to create, maintain, and use

- To develop an exercise-oriented approach that allows learning by doing

Distinguishing Features

A Proven Pedagogy with an Emphasis on Project Planning Each chapter presents a practical problem to be solved, within a project planning framework. The project orientation is strengthened by the use of Plan Ahead boxes that encourage critical thinking about how to proceed at various points in the project. Step-by-step instructions with supporting screens guide students through the steps. Instructional steps are supported by the Q&A, Experimental Step, and BTW features.

A Visually Engaging Book that Maintains Student Interest The step-by-step tasks, with supporting figures, provide a rich visual experience for the student. Callouts on the screens that present both explanatory and navigational information provide students with information they need when they need to know it.

Supporting Reference Materials (Quick Reference, Appendices) The appendices provide additional information about Expression Web 3, such as the Help Feature and customizing the application. With the Quick Reference, students can quickly look up information about a single task, such as keyboard shortcuts, and find page references of where in the book the task is illustrated.

Integration of the Web The World Wide Web is integrated into the Expression Web 3 learning experience by (1) BTW annotations; and (2) the Learn It Online section for each chapter.

End-of-Chapter Student Activities Extensive end-of-chapter activities provide a variety of reinforcement opportunities for students where they can apply and expand their skills through individual and group work.

Instructor Resources CD-ROM

The Instructor Resources include both teaching and testing aids.

INSTRUCTOR'S MANUAL Includes lecture notes summarizing the chapter sections, figures and boxed elements found in every chapter, teacher tips, classroom activities, lab activities, and quick quizzes in Microsoft Word files.

SYLLABUS Easily customizable sample syllabi that cover policies, assignments, exams, and other course information.

FIGURE FILES Illustrations for every figure in the textbook in electronic form.

POWERPOINT PRESENTATIONS A multimedia lecture presentation system that provides slides for each chapter. Presentations are based on chapter objectives.

SOLUTIONS TO EXERCISES Includes solutions for all end-of-chapter and chapter reinforcement exercises.

TEST BANK & TEST ENGINE Test Banks include 112 questions for every chapter, featuring objective-based and critical thinking question types, and including page number references and figure references, when appropriate. Also included is the test engine, ExamView, the ultimate tool for your objective-based testing needs.

DATA FILES FOR STUDENTS Includes all the files that are required by students to complete the exercises.

ADDITIONAL ACTIVITIES FOR STUDENTS Consists of Chapter Reinforcement Exercises, which are true/false, multiple-choice, and short answer questions that help students gain confidence in the material learned.

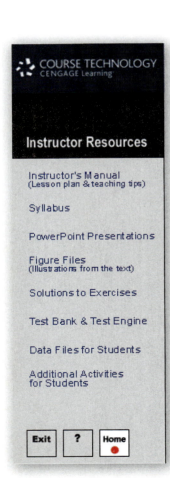

COURSE TECHNOLOGY
CENGAGE Learning

Instructor Resources

Instructor's Manual
(Lesson plan & teaching tips)

Syllabus

PowerPoint Presentations

Figure Files
(Illustrations from the text)

Solutions to Exercises

Test Bank & Test Engine

Data Files for Students

Additional Activities
for Students

Exit   ?   Home

Content for Online Learning

Course Technology has partnered with the leading distance learning solution providers and class-management platforms today. To access this material, instructors will visit our password-protected instructor resources available at www.cengage.com/coursetechnology. Instructor resources include the following: additional case projects, sample syllabi, PowerPoint presentations per chapter, and more. For additional information or for an instructor username and password, please contact your sales representative. For students to access this material, they must have purchased a WebTutor PIN-code specific to this title and your campus platform. The resources for students may include (based on instructor preferences), but are not limited to: topic review, review questions, and practice tests.

CourseNotes

Course Technology's CourseNotes are six-panel quick reference cards that reinforce the most important concepts and features of a software application in a visual and user-friendly format. CourseNotes serve as a great reference tool during and after the student completes the course. CourseNotes are available for software applications, such as Microsoft Office 2007, Word 2007, PowerPoint 2007, Excel 2007, Access 2007, and Windows 7. There are also topic-based CourseNotes available for Best Practices in Social Networking, Hot Topics in Technology, and Web 2.0. Visit www.cengage.com/ct/coursenotes to learn more!

Guided Tours

Add excitement and interactivity to your classroom with the "*A Guided Tour*" product line. Play one of the brief mini-movies to spice up your lecture and spark classroom discussion. Or, assign a movie for homework and ask students to complete the correlated assignment that accompanies each topic. The "*A Guided Tour*" product line takes the prep work out of providing your students with information on new technologies and software applications and helps keep students engaged with content relevant to their lives — all in under an hour!

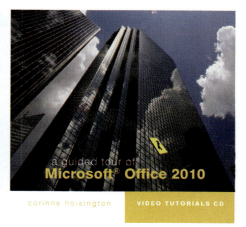

Textbook Walk-Through

The Shelly Cashman Series Pedagogy:
Project-based — Step-by-step — Variety of assessments

Plan Ahead boxes prepare students to create successful projects by encouraging them to think strategically about what they are trying to accomplish before they begin working.

- Format text on the page.
- Use visual aids and tags.
- Save the page.
- Preview the page.
- Print the page.

Plan Ahead

General Project Guidelines

When creating an Expression Web site, the actions you perform and decisions you make will affect the pages and links included in the site. As you create a Web site, such as the project shown in Figure 1–1, you should follow these general guidelines:

1. **Choose a Web site structure to use as the starting point for the site.** A Web site consists of one or more Web pages. Determine the purpose of the site, such as commercial or personal, then determine the number of pages and how site users will navigate to the pages.

2. **Determine folder structure and location and file naming conventions for the Web site files.** You must save all of the related files and folders for the Web site in one location.

3. **Determine the page properties or settings that will apply to the pages.** You can choose page settings, such as page title and keywords, using the Page Properties dialog box.

4. **Decide what the page layout will look like.** Page layout, which is the placement of text and objects, contributes to the look and consistency of a site. Well-arranged elements, such as a company logo or a navigation bar with links to the main pages of a site, keep the visitor interacting with the site longer and give the site a professional look.

5. **Determine the text content for the page.** Use text to convey the message with as few words as possible. Easy-to-read content encourages visitors to consider your product or service.

6. **Design the format for the text elements on the page.** The use of headings, fonts, lists, and color helps to identify important content and assists the visitor when scanning the page for specific content.

When necessary, specific details about these guidelines are presented at appropriate points in the chapter. The chapter also will identify the tasks performed and decisions made during the creation of the Web site shown in Figure 1–1.

Step-by-step instructions now provide a context beyond the point-and-click. Each step provides information on why students are performing each task, or what will occur as a result.

To Start Expression Web

The following steps, which assume Windows 7 is running, start Expression Web based on a typical installation. You may need to ask your instructor how to start Expression Web for your computer.

Note: If you are using Windows XP, see Appendix E for alternate steps. If you are using Windows Vista, see Appendix F for alternate steps.

❶
- Click the Start button on the Windows 7 taskbar to display the Start menu.

- Click All Programs at the bottom of the left pane on the Start menu to display the All Programs list.

- Click the Microsoft Expression folder on the All Programs list to display the Microsoft Expression list (Figure 1–3).

❷
- Click Microsoft Expression Web 3 to start Expression Web and display a new blank Web page in the Expression Web editing window (Figure 1–4).

Q&A Why does Expression Web sometimes open a Web site and other times open with a blank Web page named Untitled_1.html?

When you quit Expression Web without closing the Web site you are working on, Expression Web remembers the site and automatically opens it the next time Expression Web starts. If no previous site is in Expression Web's memory, it starts with a blank page named Untitled_1.html.

Q&A Sometimes when opening Expression Web, a server error message displays. What does that error mean?

If you quit Expression Web without closing a Web site first, Expression Web will try to open that site the next time Expression Web is started. If the site was saved on an external drive such as a USB flash drive, Expression Web looks for that drive address; if the location is not available (such as when the USB flash drive has been removed), the server error is generated. Just click OK to proceed.

Microsoft Expression Web 3 command

Microsoft Expression folder

All Programs list is displayed in left pane of Start menu

Figure 1–3

Folder List

Untitled_1.html

<body>

Toolbox

Tag Proper...   CSS Properties

<body>

Figure 1–4

Other Ways
1. Double-click the Microsoft Expression Web 3 icon on the desktop, if one is present
2. Click Microsoft Expression Web 3 on the Start menu

project in this chapter, and you want your ...uld change your screen's resolution to ... change a computer's resolution, read

File Extensions
HTML files can be saved with either the .html or .htm file extension. DOS-based operating systems restricted file extensions to three letters, necessitating the abbreviation of .html to .htm. All of today's browsers recognize both file extensions.

Navigational callouts in red show students where to click.

Explanatory callouts summarize what is happening on screen.

Screen Shots
Callouts in screen shots give students information they need, when they need to know it. The Series has always used plenty of callouts to ensure that students don't get lost. Now, we use color to distinguish the content in the callouts to make them more meaningful.

Textbook Walk-Through

Experiment Steps within our step-by-step instructions encourage students to explore, experiment with, and take advantage of the features of Expression Web 3. These steps are not necessary to complete the projects, but are designed to increase students' confidence with the software and build problem-solving skills.

4
- Click Computer in the Navigation pane to display a list of available drives (Figure 1–12).
- If necessary, scroll until FLASH DRIVE or USB (G:) appears in the list of available drives.

Q&A Do I have to use a USB flash drive?
No. You can save to any device or folder. Use the same process, but select your device or network folder from the Computer list.

- Double-click FLASH DRIVE (G:) to select the USB flash drive, drive G in this case, as the new save location.

Figure 1–12

5
- If necessary, navigate to or create a folder on your drive into which you will save your Data Files.
- Click the Open button to return to

Figure 1–13

2
- Click the <li> tag on the Quick Tag Selector to select the entire bullet (Figure 1–46).

Q&A Why did a menu appear when I clicked the <li> tag?
Be sure to click the tag, not the arrow to its right.

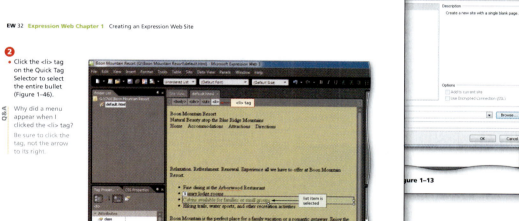

Figure 1–46

3
- Click the <ul> tag on the Quick Tag Selector to select the entire bulleted list (Figure 1–47).

Experiment
- Use the Quick Tag Selector to select other tags, such as <body>, to see how many nested elements are selected. The farther left you click on the Quick Tag Selector, the higher you are in the hierarchy of tags on the page.

Figure 1–47

Textbook Walk-Through

Other Ways boxes that follow many of the step sequences explain the other ways to complete the task presented.

④
- Click groups in the Suggestions box.
- Click the Change button to correct the word (Figure 1–71).

Figure 1–71

⑤
- Click the Ignore button to skip the name of the town, Redhat (Figure 1–72).

Figure 1–72

⑥
- Click the OK button to close the message box indicating that spell checking is complete (Figure 1–73).
- Click the Save button on the Common toolbar to save the page.

Figure 1–73

Other Ways
1. As you are typing, right-click a flagged word to display a short-cut menu that includes a list of suggested spelling corrections
2. Press the F7 key to start the spell checker

16. Press ENTER a second time after the last line to end the bulleted list.
17. Select the <ul> tag of the bulleted list and change the font color to the red co navigation text. Press the Increase Indent button eight times to indent the list
18. Add a div at the bottom of the page for the footer.
19. Press ENTER twice at the beginning of the div to add some space.
20. Type the company address and phone number in the div as follows: 14 Emer Exeter, NH 03833, (603) 555-1743.
21. Select the footer div, center and bold the div, and then change the font color previously used teal color, and then bold the div.
22. Select the body tag, then change the font family to Gill Sans, Gill Sans MT, G sans-serif.
23. Save the default.html Web page.
24. Spell check the Web page.
25. Preview the site in two different browsers or resolutions.
26. Use Print Preview to view the site.
27. Print the site.
28. Change the site properties, as specified by your instructor.
29. Close the default.html Web page and the site.
30. Rename the site using the filename, Apply 1-1 Jewelry Site using Windows Explorer.
31. Submit the revised site in the format specified by your instructor.

Extend Your Knowledge

Extend the skills you learned in this chapter and experiment with new skills. You may need to use Help to complete the assignment.

Formatting a Web Site

Instructions: Start Expression Web. Open the Web site, Extend 1-1 Music Festival, from the Data Files for Students. See the inside back cover of this book for instructions for downloading the Data Files for Students, or see your instructor for information about accessing the required files.
Enhance the Web page to match the one shown in Figure 1–93.

Perform the following tasks:
1. Use Help to learn about changing the default font color and how to insert a horizontal line.
2. Print the default.html page.
3. Make notes on the hard copy as to how you will change the Web page to more closely match Figure 1–93.
4. Use the Page Properties dialog box to change the page background to orange (255, 204, 102) and the default font color to blue (0, 51, 153). (*Hint:* Click Custom in the More Colors dialog box to enter Red, Green, and Blue values.)
5. Change the font family of the masthead div using a font family containing Gill Sans (or another font family of your choice) and the font color to red. Bold and center the masthead text and change the font size to x-large.

Continued >

Extend Your Knowledge projects at the end of each chapter allow students to extend and expand on the skills learned within the chapter. Students use critical thinking to experiment with new skills to complete each project.

Textbook Walk-Through

Extend Your Knowledge *continued*

6. Click at the end of the masthead text and press ENTER. Double-click the Horizontal Line tag in the Toolbox to insert a horizontal line under the masthead.

7. Change the font family of both the bulleted list and the paragraph to one containing Arial.

8. Increase the font size of the bulleted list text to large and apply the bold attribute.

9. Select the text, Incoming Flight, then click the Italic button on the Common toolbar.

10. On a separate piece of paper, draw a mock-up of the final page, identifying each part of the page. Make two suggestions for changes based on your own design preferences.

11. Change the site properties, as specified by your instructor.

12. Save and close the default.html page and the Web site. Using Windows Explorer, rename the Extend 1-1 Music Festival site folder as Extend 1-1 Music Site.

13. Submit the revised site in the format specified by your instructor.

Fourth Annual Oxbow Music Festival

- **Friday June 10 through Sunday June 12, 2011**
- **Nightly concerts**
- **Afternoon open mic sessions**
- **Street fair**

Join us in downtown Oxbow for the Fourth Annual Music Festival. We will have nightly concerts in three venues, featuring performances by new and old favorites, such as Oxbow's own *Incoming Flight*. Sign up daily for the afternoon open mic sessions, open to all! The street fair includes booths for performers, recording studios, t-shirt vendors, and food. Stop by Beaumill Park with your old and new CDs to take part in the largest free music swap around.

Figure 1–93

Make It Right projects call on students to analyze a file, discover errors in it, and fix them using the skills they learned in the chapter.

Make It Right

Analyze a site and correct all errors and/or improve the design.

Increasing Readability and Correcting Spelling Errors

Instructions: Start Expression Web. Open the Web site, Make It Right 1-1 Swim Club, from the Data Files for Students. See the inside back cover of this book for instructions on downloading the Data Files for Students, or see your instructor for information about accessing the required files.

The site's font colors and sizes do not provide enough contrast to be easily readable from the screen, and the Expression Web dictionary has flagged several words as being erroneous. Using Figure 1–94 to guide you, change the background color of the page, bullet and indent the list, change the text alignment, and then change the font sizes and colors to make the text more readable and to show a hierarchy of information. Apply a font family with Franklin Gothic Medium in it to the entire page. Correct each spelling error by right-clicking the flagged text and clicking the appropriate correction or option on the shortcut menu, then run the spelling checker to make sure there are no other errors. Change the page title in the Page Properties dialog box to Macon Waves Swim Club.

Cases and Places

Apply your creative thinking and problem-solving skills to

• EASIER ••MORE DIFFICULT

• 1: Work with the Expression Web Window

You want to practice working with the Expression Web window. Chapter 1, then open that site's default.html page. Use the Page word. Switch to Code view, then split the view. Select text in Co to the HTML code. Switch to Design view. Insert a new paragra graph, create a numbered list with three items, and include one Expression Web identifies as a misspelling. Check the spelling o and ignore the name. Select one item using the Quick Tag Selec select the entire list. Close the default.html page without saving quit Expression Web.

• 2: Design and Plan a School Web Site

You have just finished a class on Web design. The school administration of Pinkham Academy, a private high school, would like to plan a Web site that will include a home page, and eventually it will add other pages. Sketch a plan on a piece of paper for the home page of the Web site that you can present to the administration and use to gather its feedback. Include a masthead that lists the school name and a navigation bar with links to the library, administration, and calendar. The administration wants to include the school logo on the home page. Include an area for a letter from the principal and a footer for the address. The school's colors are blue and white; indicate on the Web site sketch how you will incorporate the school's colors.

•• 3: Format a One-Page Alumni Web Site

You have recently joined the Connecticut branch of your college alumni association. You have been working on a home page that can tell other local graduates of Gulliver College about upcoming alumni events. You have already entered the text for the home page. Open the site Cases and Places 3 Alumni, then open the page default.html. Use the page properties to add a title, a description, and four appropriate keywords. Use the heading style and other formatting techniques to apply italics, bold, center alignment, and indentations to make the home page easy to read.

•• 4: Create a Job Search Home Page

Make It Personal ◄

When you are looking for a job, it is helpful to have a résumé or list of your skills that you can share with potential employers. What is your dream job? Imagine yourself a decade from now—what amazing skills and job experiences will you have collected? Will you have won any awards, made a scientific discovery, learned a foreign language, or gone to art school? Create a one-page Web site that you can use to show potential employers all of the things that you might have learned and done over the next 10 years that would qualify you for your dream job. Include a masthead, bulleted list, footer, and any other information you think is relevant. Format the Web site attractively, including adding a background color, changing the fonts, and applying effects such as bold and italics. Add a page title, a description, and keywords.

Found within the Cases and Places exercises, the **Make It Personal** exercises call on students to create an open-ended project that relates to their personal lives.

1 | Creating an Expression Web Site

Objectives

You will have mastered the material in this chapter when you can:

- Start and quit Expression Web
- Describe the features of Expression Web's main window
- Create a new Expression Web site
- Set page properties
- Enter and format text
- Create headings and lists

- Switch views
- Spell check a page
- Save a page
- Show and hide visual aids
- Use Quick Tag Selectors
- Display a page in a browser
- Close an Expression Web site

1 | Creating an Expression Web Site

What Is Microsoft Expression Web?

Microsoft Expression Web 3 is a full-featured Web site authoring program that allows you to create professional looking Web sites. A **Web site** is a collection of connected Web pages that contain text, images, or video. With Expression Web, you can create any type of Web site, from a one-page personal site to a sophisticated professional site consisting of hundreds of pages. Expression Web provides a **What You See Is What You Get (WYSIWYG)** design interface; in Design view, you can see exactly how the layout and formatting will appear in a browser and make necessary changes while editing. Expression Web provides automated tools for creating Web pages and Web sites.

You can use Expression Web to create and edit HTML files that contain the content of a page, and Cascading Style Sheets (CSS) files that control the formatting and layout of text and objects on a page or on multiple pages. Expression Web tools such as the design interface, panel, and dialog boxes assist you in entering content and defining the style rules, without you having to know CSS and HTML codes. Expression Web also provides a full-featured HTML/XHTML editor for viewing and entering code, and allows you to view and modify the CSS code.

Expression Web is part of the **Microsoft Expression Studio 3** program suite. Appendix D provides more information on the various products in Expression Studio and describes how they work together.

Project Planning Guidelines

Before you can begin to create a Web site, you must do some initial planning and get approval on the plan from your client or colleagues. You will need to establish the goal or purpose of the Web site and the type of site (such as informational or e-commerce), and identify the target users you want to attract to your site. Next, you should conduct research to learn how comparable sites are designed. With these elements defined, you should create a plan that specifies the content and layout of your site. After establishing the basic structure and content of your site, you will be ready to develop the site and test it with multiple browsers. Finally, after the site is complete, you can publish it to a Web server and begin marketing your site to attract visitors. Each project in this book provides practical applications of these guidelines.

Project — Home Page

Boon Mountain Resort is located in Redhat, Georgia. The resort has been in business for one year and now would like to have a Web site to promote its many features. The resort has an excellent restaurant, luxury lodge rooms, and individual cabins located throughout the property. Nearby hiking trails and water sports are available for guests. The resort intends to promote itself to potential guests through a Web site with pages for accommodations, attractions, and directions, along with a home page.

The project in this chapter follows general guidelines and uses Expression Web to create the home page shown in Figure 1–1. This home page is the entry to the Boon Mountain Resort Web site, and will need text and formatting, and, eventually, graphics and hyperlinks. You will create a navigation bar to which you will add links to other site pages in the next chapter. In Chapter 1, you will create the text for the Boon Mountain Resort home page, and in the next chapter, you will enhance your Web site by adding pages, images, and links.

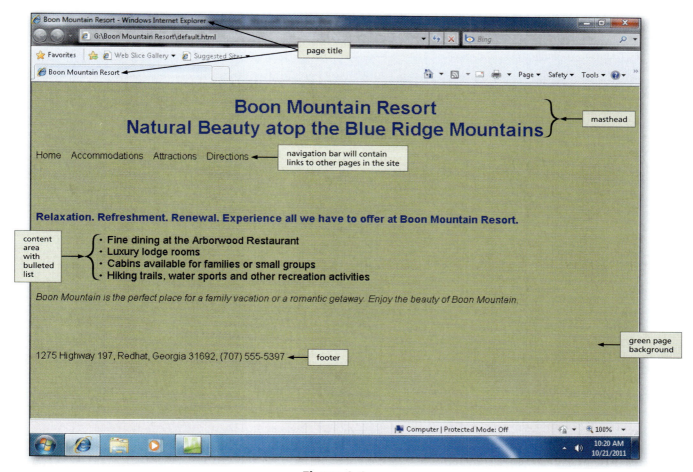

Figure 1–1

Figure 1–2 illustrates a plan for the layout and content of the default.html page of the Boon Mountain Resort Web site.

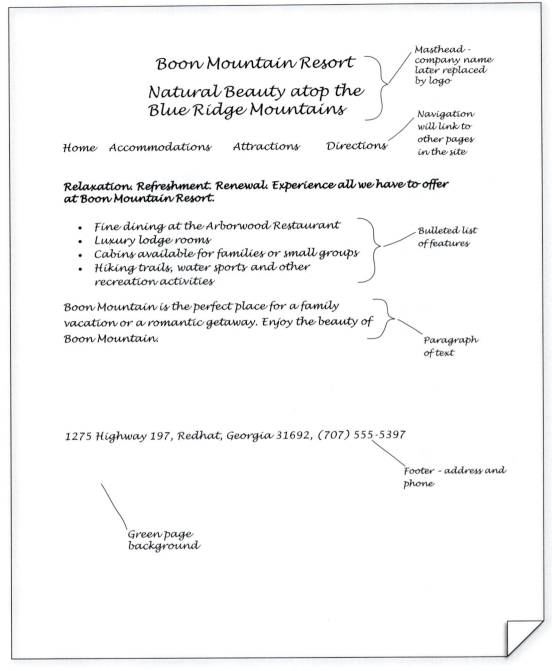

Boon Mountain Resort

Natural Beauty atop the Blue Ridge Mountains

Masthead - company name later replaced by logo

Home   Accommodations   Attractions   Directions

Navigation will link to other pages in the site

Relaxation. Refreshment. Renewal. Experience all we have to offer at Boon Mountain Resort.

- *Fine dining at the Arborwood Restaurant*
- *Luxury lodge rooms*
- *Cabins available for families or small groups*
- *Hiking trails, water sports and other recreation activities*

Bulleted list of features

Boon Mountain is the perfect place for a family vacation or a romantic getaway. Enjoy the beauty of Boon Mountain.

Paragraph of text

1275 Highway 197, Redhat, Georgia 31692, (707) 555-5397

Footer - address and phone

Green page background

Figure 1–2

Overview

As you read this chapter, you will learn how to create the Web site shown in Figure 1–1 by performing these general tasks:

- Open the Expression Web program.
- Create an Expression Web site.
- Set page properties.
- Add page divisions.
- Enter text on the page.

- Format text on the page.
- Use visual aids and tags.
- Save the page.
- Preview the page.
- Print the page.

Plan Ahead

General Project Guidelines

When creating an Expression Web site, the actions you perform and decisions you make will affect the pages and links included in the site. As you create a Web site, such as the project shown in Figure 1–1, you should follow these general guidelines:

1. **Choose a Web site structure to use as the starting point for the site.** A Web site consists of one or more Web pages. Determine the purpose of the site, such as commercial or personal, then determine the number of pages and how site users will navigate to the pages.

2. **Determine folder structure and location and file naming conventions for the Web site files.** You must save all of the related files and folders for the Web site in one location.

3. **Determine the page properties or settings that will apply to the pages.** You can choose page settings, such as page title and keywords, using the Page Properties dialog box.

4. **Decide what the page layout will look like.** Page **layout**, which is the placement of text and objects, contributes to the look and consistency of a site. Well-arranged elements, such as a company logo or a navigation bar with links to the main pages of a site, keep the visitor interacting with the site longer and give the site a professional look.

5. **Determine the text content for the page.** Use text to convey the message with as few words as possible. Easy-to-read content encourages visitors to consider your product or service.

6. **Design the format for the text elements on the page.** The use of headings, fonts, lists, and color helps to identify important content and assists the visitor when scanning the page for specific content.

   When necessary, specific details about these guidelines are presented at appropriate points in the chapter. The chapter also will identify the tasks performed and decisions made during the creation of the Web site shown in Figure 1–1.

Starting Expression Web

If you are using a computer to step through the project in this chapter, and you want your screen to match the figures in this book, you should change your screen's resolution to 1024×768. For more information about how to change a computer's resolution, read Appendix G.

BTW

File Extensions
HTML files can be saved with either the .html or .htm file extension. DOS-based operating systems restricted file extensions to three letters, necessitating the abbreviation of .html to .htm. All of today's browsers recognize both file extensions.

To Start Expression Web

The following steps, which assume Windows 7 is running, start Expression Web based on a typical installation. You may need to ask your instructor how to start Expression Web for your computer.

Note: If you are using Windows XP, see Appendix E for alternate steps. If you are using Windows Vista, see Appendix F for alternate steps.

- Click the Start button on the Windows 7 taskbar to display the Start menu.

- Click All Programs at the bottom of the left pane on the Start menu to display the All Programs list.

Figure 1–3

- Click the Microsoft Expression folder on the All Programs list to display the Microsoft Expression list (Figure 1–3).

- Click Microsoft Expression Web 3 to start Expression Web and display a new blank Web page in the Expression Web editing window (Figure 1–4).

Q&A Why does Expression Web sometimes open a Web site and other times open with a blank Web page named Untitled_1.html?

When you quit Expression Web without closing the Web site you are working on, Expression Web remembers the site and automatically opens it the next time Expression Web starts. If no previous site is in Expression Web's memory, it starts with a blank page named Untitled_1.html.

Q&A Sometimes when opening Expression Web, a server error message displays. What does that error mean?

If you quit Expression Web without closing a Web site first, Expression Web will try to open that site the next time Expression Web is started. If the site was saved on an external drive such as a USB flash drive, Expression Web looks for that drive address; if the location is not available (such as when the USB flash drive has been removed), the server error is generated. Just click OK to proceed.

Figure 1–4

Other Ways
1. Double-click the Microsoft Expression Web 3 icon on the desktop, if one is present   2. Click Microsoft Expression Web 3 on the Start menu

Expression Web Workspace

Expression Web opens with a menu, a toolbar, a status bar, an editing window, and four panels for adding components and managing site content. When you first open Expression Web, a new blank HTML page displays with the name, Untitled_1.html.

The Workspace Window

The workspace window shown in Figure 1–5 is where you build your Web site. The **workspace** contains the tools necessary to edit and manage Web pages. You can customize the workspace to contain the tools you use most often.

Figure 1–5

Title Bar   The **title bar** at the top of the screen shows the application name and filename of the current Web page.

Menu Bar   The **menu bar** at the top of the workspace contains all of the Expression Web commands.

Common Toolbar   The **Common toolbar** is located below the menu bar and contains buttons for the most commonly used commands.

Editing Window The **editing window** is where you create your Web page using the various Expression Web tools.

Web Page Tab The **Web page tab** shows the filename of the page being edited as well as any other open pages.

Quick Tag Selector The **Quick Tag Selector**, located just below the Web page tab, shows the underlying HTML tags generated as you add content to the page.

Panels There are four default **panels:** two on the left (Folder List and Tag Properties) and two on the right (Toolbox and Apply Styles). Panels are moved or replaced to reflect the current task.

View Buttons The **view buttons** are located at the lower left of the editing window and change depending on which tab is active (Web Site tab or Web page tab). When a Web page is open, the available view buttons are Design, Split, and Code. Design view is the WYSIWYG view. Split view shows the HTML tags at the top of the screen and the WYSIWYG page on the bottom. Code view shows only the HTML code.

Status Bar The right side of the **status bar** shows HTML incompatibilities and code errors, XHTML version, the status of visual aids, page size dimensions, and the XHTML and CSS versions Expression Web is using to code your pages.

Toolbars

Expression Web's default toolbar is the Common toolbar. To display the menu of toolbar options, right-click a toolbar (Figure 1–6). In addition to the Common toolbar, Expression Web has 10 other task-specific toolbars that you can display when needed to perform a specific task, such as working with a table. When Expression Web opens for the first time, the Common toolbar is the only one visible. When you open a toolbar, it remains open each time the program is started, until you close it manually. Depending on past usage, your toolbar buttons may differ slightly. A check mark next to the toolbar name indicates it is visible. To show a toolbar, click the toolbar name to add a check mark. To hide a toolbar, click the name that contains the check mark to remove the check mark.

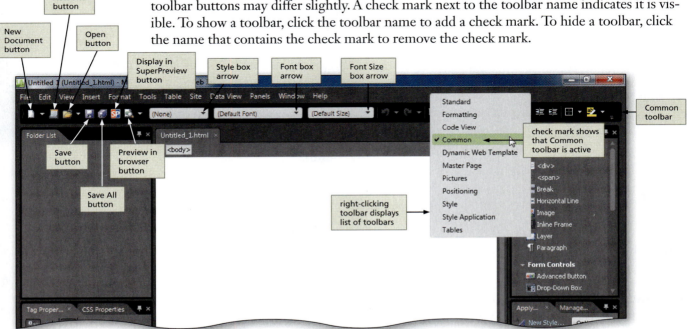

Figure 1–6

To Reset Workspace Layout

As you work with Expression Web, you may rearrange the toolbars and panels by opening, moving, maximizing, or closing them. To make your screen match the figures in this book and to ensure that you start from the same point during each work session, you should reset the workspace to the default layout, and close any open sites. The following steps restore all panels and content areas to the default sizes and locations, and close any open sites.

- Click Panels on the menu bar to open the Panels menu and then point to Reset Workspace Layout (Figure 1–7).

Figure 1–7

2

- Click Reset Workspace Layout to restore the panels to their default layout.

- If a site is open, click Site on the menu bar to open the Site menu, and then click Close to close the site (Figure 1–8).

Figure 1–8

Naming Files and Folders

The site name, which is the folder that contains the site contents, can include spaces. Within the site, folders and filenames cannot contain uppercase letters, spaces, or certain characters, such as the pound sign (#) or an asterisk (*). You can separate words in a filename by using an underscore (_), such as in the folder name assets_images or the filename web_page2.html.

Creating a Web Site

A Web site consists, at minimum, of a folder and an HTML file. Once these two basic components are created, you can enhance the site with additional HTML files, embed images and style sheets, and organize the files into folders and subfolders. The first Web page in the site is the **home page**. The home page provides access to the other Web pages in the site by including hyperlinks in a navigation bar.

When creating an Expression Web site, you are actually creating a root folder to store all the files and subfolders for your site. When you create a new one-page Web site, Expression Web creates a root folder and a file named default.html, which serves as the home page for the site. Expression Web uses the default.html name because the Web servers on which Web pages are stored look for a home page named default.html or index.html.

Plan Ahead

Choose the Web site structure to use as the starting point for the site.
You must first decide whether to begin your Web site by using a blank Web site, modifying an existing Web site, using a template, or importing an existing site from the Internet or other location into Expression Web.

Determine folder structure and location and file naming conventions for the Web site files.
Saving an Expression Web site is different from saving an individual file created in another program. A site consists of HTML files that store content, style sheets that indicate how formatting is applied, and elements such as graphics and media files. It is important to plan how you will name and organize the files and folder structure where you will store the site's pages, style sheets, and graphics and media files.

To Create a Web Site

If you need your site to be portable so that you can work on it on different computers, you should store the site on an external storage device such as a USB flash drive. The following steps create the Web site folder for the Boon Mountain Resort site and a one-page blank HTML file, and save them to the USB flash drive.

- With a USB flash drive connected to one of the computer's USB ports, click Site on the menu bar to open the Site menu, then point to New Site (Figure 1–9).

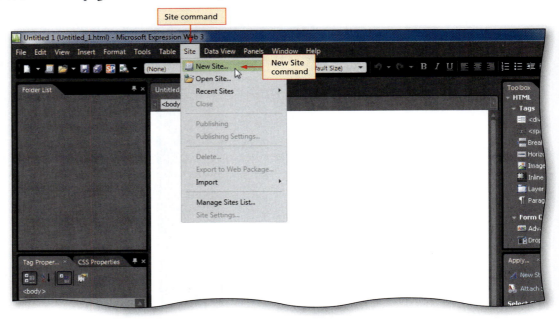

Figure 1–9

2

• Click New Site on the Site menu to display the New dialog box (Figure 1–10).

Figure 1–10

3

• In the middle pane, click One Page Site.

• Click the Browse button to open the New Site Location dialog box (Figure 1–11).

Figure 1–11

4

- Click Computer in the Navigation pane to display a list of available drives (Figure 1–12).

- If necessary, scroll until FLASH DRIVE or USB (G:) appears in the list of available drives.

Q&A Do I have to use a USB flash drive?

No. You can save to any device or folder. Use the same process, but select your device or network folder from the Computer list.

- Double-click FLASH DRIVE (G:) to select the USB flash drive, drive G in this case, as the new save location.

Figure 1–12

5

- If necessary, navigate to or create a folder on your drive into which you will save your Data Files.

- Click the Open button to return to the New dialog box (Figure 1–13).

Q&A What if my USB flash drive has a different name or letter?

It is likely that your USB flash drive will be named differently and be connected to a different lettered port. Use the device, folder, or drive where you save your files.

Figure 1–13

6

- Click in the Location text box, then click after the text to position the insertion point to create a new Web site folder.
- Type Boon Mountain Resort to specify the site folder name (Figure 1–14).

Figure 1–14

7

- Click the OK button to close the New dialog box, open the Web site folder for the site, and create the default.html page (Figure 1–15).

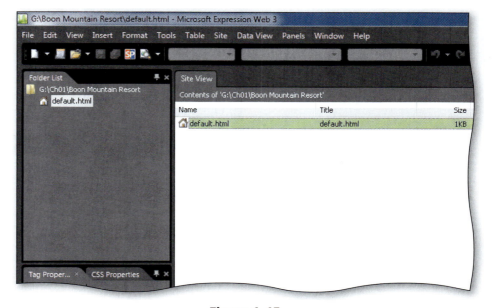

Figure 1–15

To Open a Web Page

Now that you have created the Web site, you are ready to add content to the home page. The home page will contain links to the other pages in the site and information about the Boon Mountain Resort. The following step opens the HTML file that will contain the home page content.

- Double-click default.html in the Folder List panel to open the page (Figure 1–16).

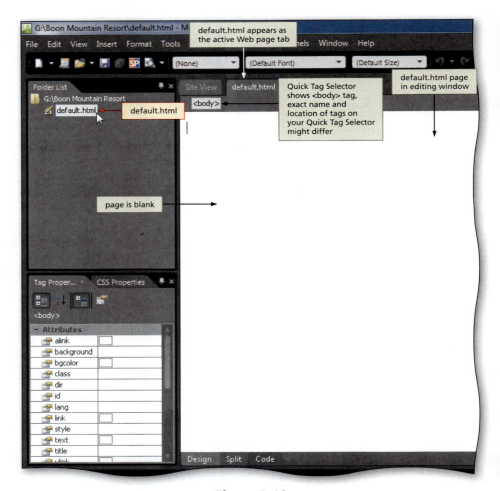

Figure 1–16

Other Ways		
1. Double-click the filename in the Site View tab	2. Click File on the menu bar, then click Open to open the Open File dialog box. Click the filename, then click the Open button	3. Press CTRL +O to open the Open File dialog box. Click the filename, then click the Open button

Setting Page Properties

Each page in the site can have unique page properties. These properties include file location, page title, page description, keywords, background sound, background image, hyperlink colors, and margins. Such properties can add visual interest, increase readability, and reflect a company's identity, in addition to making your site easier for search engines to find. You can use a predefined color for the page background, or define characteristics to create a custom color.

The **page title** displays on the title bar of a browser and should be meaningful to a visitor. If the visitor adds the page to his or her browser Favorites or Bookmarks list, the page title is often what appears in the Favorites list, depending on the browser. Search engines display the **page description** in search results, and use **keywords** to place your page in search results by matching the keywords listed in the site with the user's search criteria.

Determine the page properties or settings that will apply to the page.
You can set page properties at any time, but it is a good design strategy to set them before you enter text onto the page. These page specifications should be determined during the planning and design stage while you are making decisions about the site color scheme and layout.

When deciding on a background color or graphic, keep in mind that the text on the page should be easy to read. A dark background or busy graphic might distract from the content and could cause your site visitors to miss important information.

Plan Ahead

BTW

Misspellings
If some of your keywords include common misspellings, or British and American English spelling variations (such as *colour* and *color*), be sure to include them in the Page Properties dialog box.

To Set Page Properties

To enter or change the page description and keywords, you use the General, Formatting, and other tabs in the Page Properties dialog box. The following steps change the page properties and add a custom color background to the page.

- Click File on the menu bar to display the File menu, then click Properties to display the Page Properties dialog box (Figure 1–17).

Figure 1–17

2

- On the General tab, type `Boon Mountain Resort` in the Title text box to specify the page title.

- Press the TAB key to move to the Page description text box.

- Type `Magnificent resort atop the majestic Blue Ridge Mountains.`

- Press the TAB key to move to the Keywords text box.

- Type `resort, cabins, mountains, romantic getaway, family vacation, Blue Ridge Mountains, Redhat, Georgia` (Figure 1–18).

Figure 1–18

3

- Click the Formatting tab to display the background options (Figure 1–19).

Figure 1–19

4

• In the Colors area, click the Background color button arrow to display the color palette (Figure 1–20).

Figure 1–20

5

• Click More Colors to display the More Colors dialog box (Figure 1–21).

Q&A

What is a custom color?

A custom color is created by using numbers to define characteristics such as hue, saturation, and luminosity or red, green, and blue.

Figure 1–21

6

- Click the Custom button to open the Color dialog box.

- Double-click in the Hue box, then type 40.

- Press TAB and then type 80 in the Sat box.

- Press TAB, and then type 137 in the Lum box to define a green custom color (Figure 1–22).

Figure 1–22

7

- Click the OK button to close the Color dialog box (Figure 1–23).

Q&A

What is a hex color value?

A hex color value is a number that represents color in the format that is used in HTML code.

Figure 1–23

8

- Click the OK button to close the More Colors dialog box.

- Click the OK button to close the Page Properties dialog box and view the green page background (Figure 1–24).

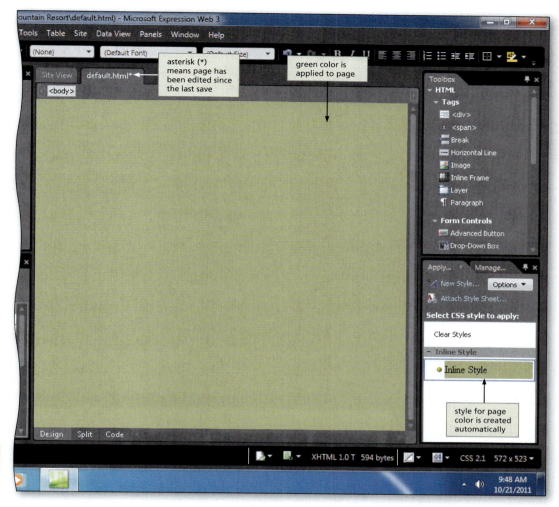

Figure 1–24

Decide what the page layout will look like.
Most pages on the Internet follow similar layout rules because of the restrictions of HTML. Using a layout with which users feel comfortable allows them to focus on the content and message of your site.

- Some common elements found on each page of most professionally developed Web sites include a masthead or page banner, one or more navigational systems, a content section divided into one or more columns, and a footer area. Minor variations of page layouts throughout the site can add interest and variety to the site to enhance the visitor experience, but the overall structure should be consistent.

- A page mockup for each page, either hand drawn or computer generated, indicates what a finished page will look like.

- Select font families, color schemes, or palettes to provide contrast, set the mood, and maintain consistency throughout the site.

Determine the text content for the page.
Avoid long paragraphs of text. Use short sentences, bulleted lists, and boldface key terms to show the main points of a page without bogging down the reader. Divide content among site pages to avoid having visitors scroll to read all information on a page.

Plan Ahead

BTW

Web Standards
Web standards are guidelines for Web development, defined by the World Wide Web Consortium (W3C), an international organization of Web developers (www.w3c.org). Web standards ensure that viewers of a Web site who are using different browsers have a common experience.

Entering Text

Faster Downloading
Another advantage of using a division-based layout is that it reduces the number of lines of code needed to create a page, resulting in faster downloading from the Internet.

A basic Web page layout typically contains four sections: masthead, navigation, content, and footer. These sections are usually enclosed within division containers made up of <div>…</div> tag elements. This method of layout is called **division-based layout**. The purpose of using <div> </div> tags, or **divs**, is to define an area of the page that you can format using **styles**, which are collections of formatting attributes.

Using the page layout mockup shown in Figure 1–2, the home page shows the company name and tagline at the top of the page, called the **masthead**. The **navigation bar** includes the names of the other site pages, each of which will contain information relating to a specific topic, and to which you will later add links. The body of the home page, called the content area, contains a bulleted list that highlights important features of the resort. The page is visually appealing and easy to read because of the varying font colors used for emphasis and the green page background.

Once the layout is defined, you can start entering text by clicking in a div and typing.

To Add a <Div> Tag

As shown in Figure 1–1, the final page will include four text areas: a masthead, a navigation bar, a page content area, and a footer. To define the masthead section of the page where the company name and tagline will appear, you will insert a <div> tag before typing text. You will also need to add a <div> tag, to define the navigation bar of the page, into which you will type the names of the other site pages. In a later chapter, you will add links to those pages. The following steps create the first two tags and their content.

- If necessary, click at the top of the page to position the insertion point where you want the <div> tag to appear (Figure 1–25).

Figure 1–25

- Double-click the <div> tag in the Toolbox to place a <div> division container on your page at the insertion point's location (Figure 1–26).

Q&A What if I double-click too many times and get more than one tag on my page?

Click the Undo button on the Common toolbar.

Q&A What should I do if I cannot see the new div?

Point to Visual Aids on the View menu, and then click Show.

Other Ways

1. Click the <div> tag in the Toolbox, then drag the <div> tag to where you want it on the page
2. Click the <div> button on the Common toolbar

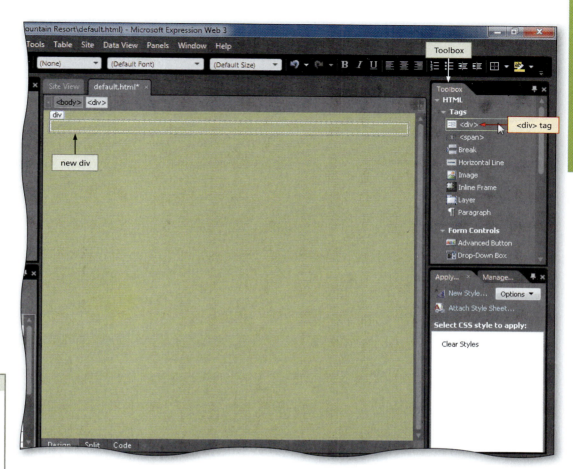

Figure 1–26

❸

- Type Boon Mountain Resort, then press the ENTER key to move the insertion point to the next line (Figure 1–27).

Q&A What if my insertion point is not inside the <div> container?

Click inside the <div> container.

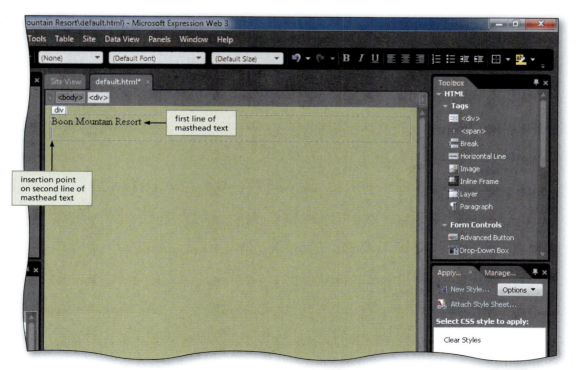

Figure 1–27

4

• Type Natural Beauty atop the Blue Ridge Mountains, then click a blank spot on the page outside of the <div> tag to indicate you are finished entering data into it (Figure 1–28).

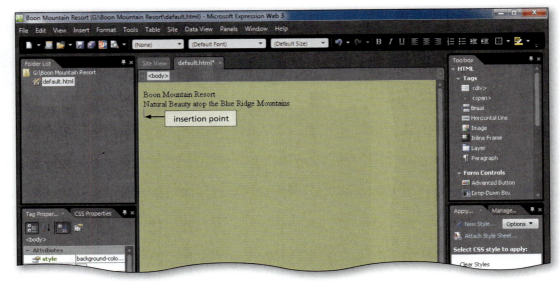

Figure 1–28

5

• Double-click the <div> tag in the Toolbox to place a division container at the insertion point's location (Figure 1–29).

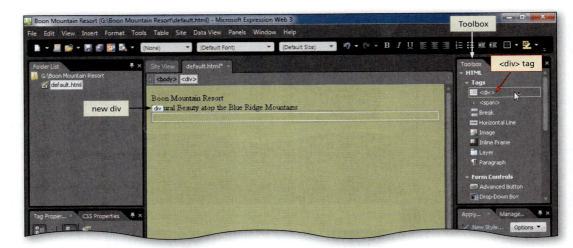

Figure 1–29

6

• Be sure the insertion point is inside the <div> tag. Type Home, then press TAB to enter the text for the first navigational link (Figure 1–30).

Q&A

Why do I press TAB instead of the SPACEBAR?

Pressing TAB inserts more space than pressing the SPACEBAR. TAB is used to insert a consistent amount of space between words.

Figure 1–30

7

- Type Accommodations as the text for the second link, then press TAB.

- Type Attractions as the text for the third link, then press TAB.

- Type Directions as the text for the final navigational link, then click a blank spot on the page outside of the <div> to indicate you are finished entering data into it (Figure 1–31).

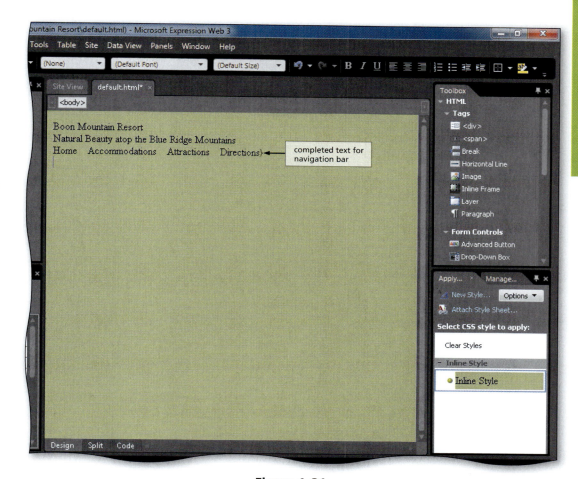

Figure 1–31

To Add Paragraph Text

A paragraph is specified by using the <p> tag, and is used to contain text. When you press ENTER in a <p> tag, a new paragraph is inserted, with line space between the two paragraphs. The following steps add another <div> . . . </div> container to hold the rest of the page content, then add space between divs on the page. Within the new <div> tag you will embed a paragraph <p> tag and enter content. When Expression Web 3 inserts <p></p> tags they are represented in Design view by a <p> on the Quick Tag Selector and a p tab and container in the editing window.

1

- Double-click the <div> tag in the Toolbox to place a division container at the insertion point's location (Figure 1–32).

Figure 1–32

● With the insertion point still inside
the <div> tag, press the ENTER
key four times to add line spacing inside the <div> tag container
(Figure 1–33).

Figure 1–33

● Double-click the
Paragraph tag in the
Toolbox to place a
paragraph <p> tag on
the page inside of the
<div> tag container
(Figure 1–34).

Q&A

Why should I add
extra lines on
the page?

Using generous
blank areas, or white
space, helps to avoid
a cluttered page.

Figure 1–34

● With the insertion
point inside the
Paragraph tag,
type Relaxation.
Refreshment.
Renewal. Experience
all we have to
offer at Boon
Mountain Resort.,
then press ENTER to
insert a new <p> tag
(Figure 1–35).

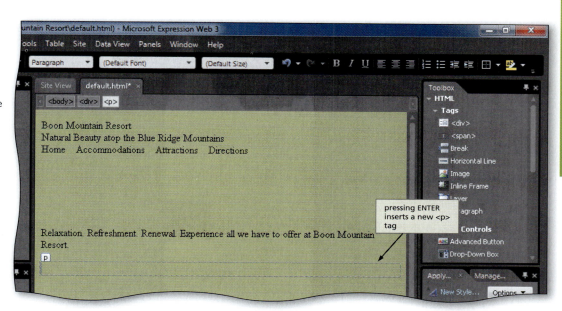

Figure 1–35

To Add a Bulleted List

A **bulleted list** is used to portray several points that do not need to appear in any specific order. The following steps add features to extol the benefits of the Boon Mountain Resort by creating a bulleted list.

● Be sure the insertion
point is inside the
new <p> tag and
then click the Bullets
button on the
Common toolbar to
create the first bul-
let (Figure 1–36).

Q&A

What happened to
the <p> tag?

The <p> tag was
replaced with the
<ul> tag when the
Bullets button was
clicked.

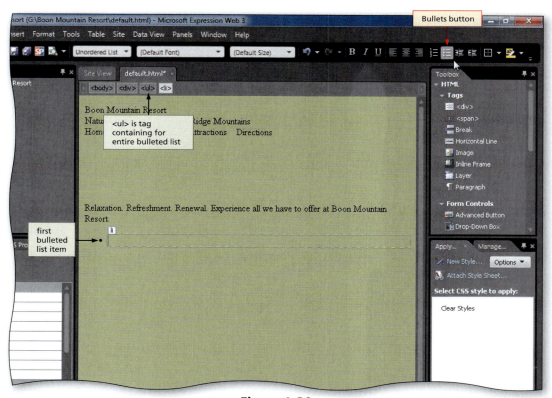

Figure 1–36

2

- Type `Fine dining at the Arborwood Restaurant`, then press ENTER to start a new bullet (Figure 1–37).

What is the red, wavy line under Arborwood?

Words with a red, wavy line are not in the Expression Web dictionary. If you don't see the line, click Tools on the menu bar, point to Spelling, click Spelling Options to open the Spelling Options dialog box, click the 'Check spelling as you type' check box to select it, then click the OK button to close the dialog box. You will check spelling later in Chapter 1.

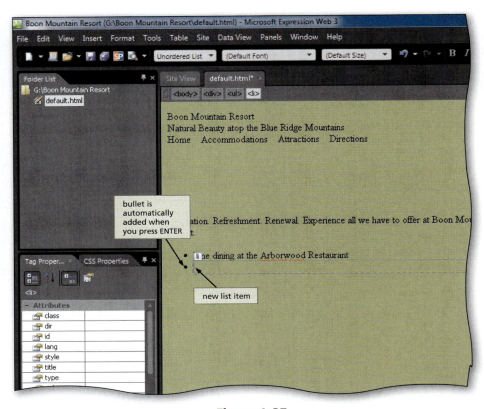

Figure 1–37

3

- Type `Luxury lodge rooms` as the text for the second bullet, then press ENTER.

- Type `Cabins available for families or small groups` as the third list item, then press ENTER.

- Type `Hiking trails, water sports and other recreation activities`, then press ENTER to start a new line (Figure 1–38).

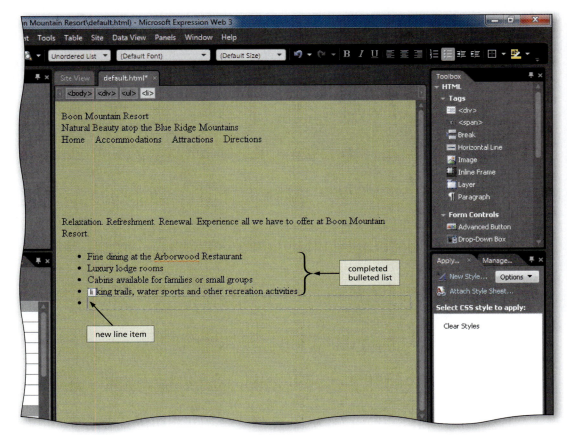

Figure 1–38

• Click the Bullets button on the Common toolbar to end the bulleted list. Expression Web starts a new paragraph by inserting a <p> tag (Figure 1–39).

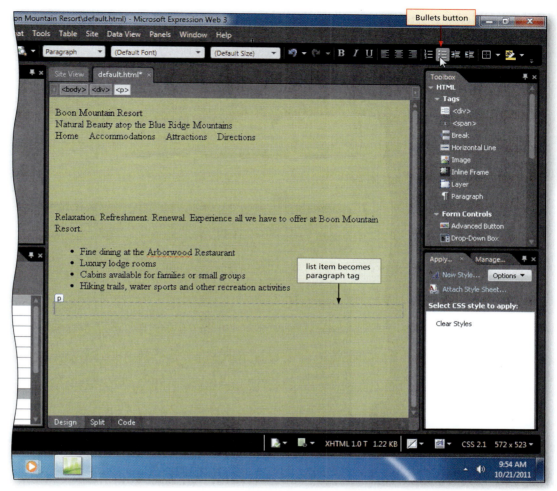

Figure 1–39

To Complete Page Content

The last <p> tag in the content area on the default page will contain the resort's advertising slogan. The final <div> tag, which you add in the following steps, will be used as the footer area on the page. The following steps enter the content for the slogan and add the footer.

1

- With the insertion point inside the new <p> tag, type Boon Mountain is the perfect place for a family vacation or a romantic getaway. Enjoy the beauty of Boon Mountain., but do not press ENTER (Figure 1–40).

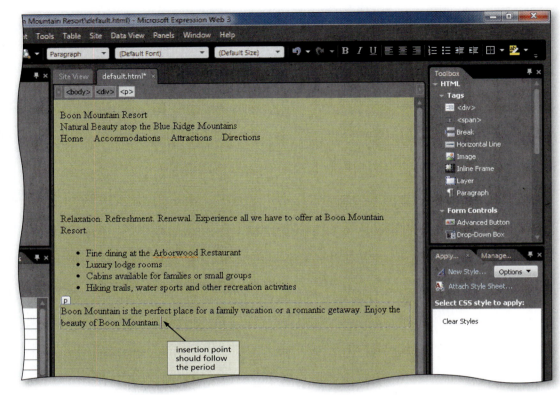

Figure 1–40

2

- Click a blank area under the <p> tag, then press ENTER twice to add white space to the page (Figure 1–41).

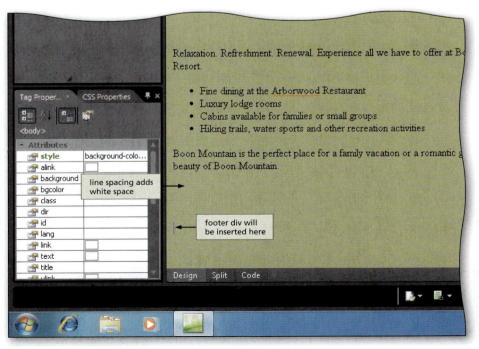

Figure 1–41

3

- Double-click the \<div> tag in the Toolbox to place a division container at the insertion point's location (Figure 1–42).

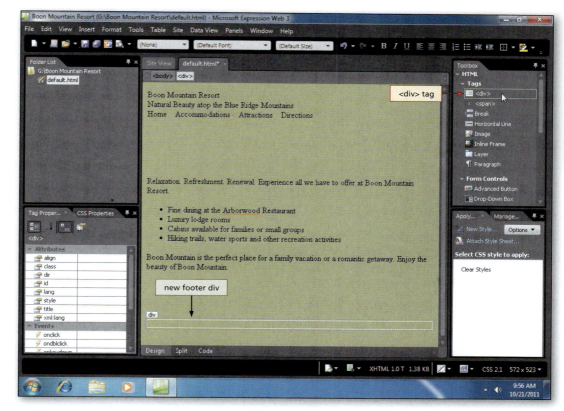

Figure 1–42

4

- **Type** 1275 Highway 197, Redhat, Georgia 31692, (707) 555-5397 **(Figure 1–43).**

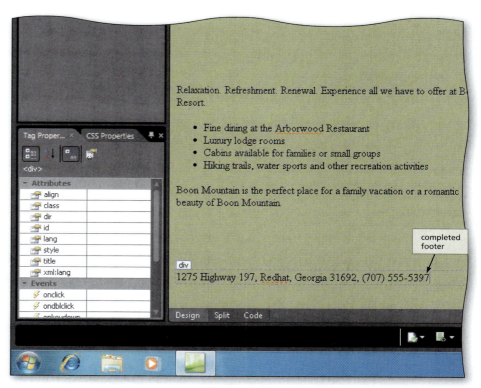

Figure 1–43

BTW

AutoSave
Depending on your system settings, Expression Web may save pages automatically as you work. If you get an error message indicating that a more recent version of the file was saved to the server, click Yes to overwrite the file.

Saving Individual Web Pages

As you make changes to a page, an asterisk (*) appears next to the page name on the tab at the top of the editing window, indicating that it needs to be saved before your changes will be reflected in a browser. You should save your pages frequently while editing so that you do not lose any content, layout, or other work you have done on your site.

To Save a Web Page

It is a good habit to save your page often as you are creating it. The following step saves the page you are working on.

- Click the Save button on the Common toolbar (Figure 1–44).

Figure 1–44

Other Ways

1. Right-click the page tab at the top of the Editing window, then click Save

2. Click File on the menu bar, then click Save

3. Press CTRL+S

BTW

Web Accessibility
See Appendix B for more information about accessibility and assistive technology.

Applying Formatting and Styles

Formatting is the combination of design characteristics that are applied to text, specifying a hierarchy of headings and text levels. Consistently applied formatting can guide the reader through the content on your site. Formatting techniques include changing fonts and font sizes, applying font attributes such as bold and italics, and changing the alignment and indentation of lines and paragraphs of text. To emphasize just one word or a series of words in a paragraph, you can apply the bold or italic font attribute by using formatting buttons or keyboard shortcuts.

You can apply formatting such as bold as you enter text (just as you would in a word processing program) or apply predefined or custom styles that combine a variety of attributes.

Heading and subheading styles indicate the relative importance of each line of text. HTML supports six levels of heading style tags: <h1>, the largest, through <h6>, the smallest. All heading styles apply the bold attribute automatically but use different font sizes to show the level. Using styles, as opposed to applying formatting directly, ensures consistency in a large site so that if you change an attribute of a style, it applies automatically to other elements that share that style.

As you apply various formatting to text on the page, Expression Web creates a style in the Apply Styles panel. The styles are given a default number as they are applied and that number becomes part of the HTML tag. You can then apply these styles to different areas of the page or site, such as for bulleted lists. You will work with the Apply Styles panel in Chapter 3.

Design the format for the text elements on the page.
Plan Ahead

When formatting fonts, you should select font families and assign formatting characteristics for headings, captions, and lists that help make your page attractive and easy to read.

- Readability is the first consideration for text formatting. Font size should be neither too small, which is difficult to read, nor too large, which looks unprofessional and wastes screen space.

- Use headings and subheadings to emphasize important words and to draw the reader's eye to that location of the screen.

- Limit the number of fonts used in your site to two or three. Choose common fonts or font families that will be recognizable to many browsers. Avoid ornate fonts, such as handwriting or scroll fonts, because they are difficult to read and are not recognized by many browsers. If your company uses a custom or fancy font in its logo, create the logo as a graphic element rather than text to ensure that it appears the same in all browsers.

- Use font color as emphasis on important words within a paragraph or bulleted text rather than applying a color to the entire text section. Consider the background of the page and make sure that the font color you choose provides contrast.

- Avoid using underlined text, which usually represents a hyperlink.

To Use the Quick Tag Selector

Use the Quick Tag Selector to confirm that you have selected an entire element before applying formatting or making changes to the text. The following step selects a list item and a list using the Quick Tag Selector.

1

- Click in the text of the third bullet to display the <li> tag for the list item (Figure 1–45).

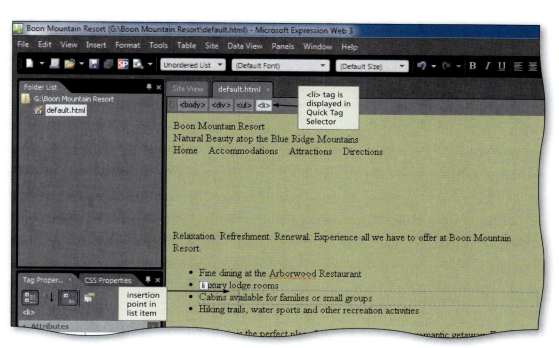

Figure 1–45

2

- Click the <li> tag on the Quick Tag Selector to select the entire bullet (Figure 1–46).

Q&A

Why did a menu appear when I clicked the <li> tag?

Be sure to click the tag, not the arrow to its right.

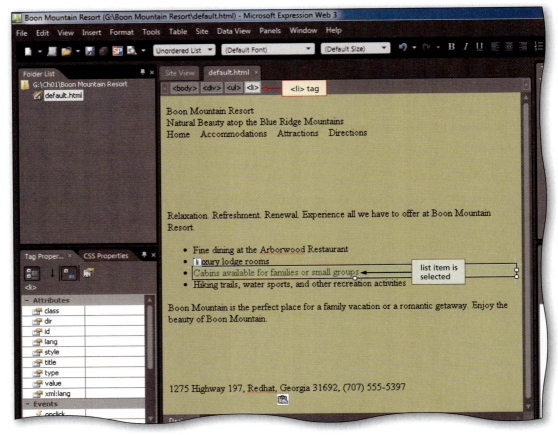

Figure 1–46

3

- Click the <ul> tag on the Quick Tag Selector to select the entire bulleted list (Figure 1–47).

Experiment

- Use the Quick Tag Selector to select other tags, such as <body>, to see how many nested elements are selected. The farther left you click on the Quick Tag Selector, the higher you are in the hierarchy of tags on the page.

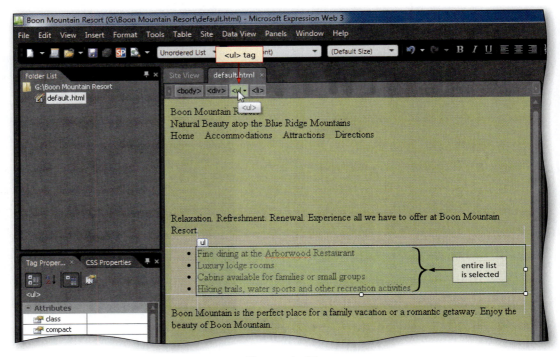

Figure 1–47

To Apply a Heading Style

In addition to providing a visual cue as to a heading's relative importance, using the heading style ensures that assistive technology can distinguish how the text has been formatted, to accurately represent it to vision-impaired site visitors. The following steps use heading styles to change the font size and apply the bold attribute.

1
- Click after the words, Blue Ridge Mountains, at the top of the page inside the first <div> tag (Figure 1–48).

Q&A Can I still apply the heading style if only a few words of the div are selected?

To ensure that the heading style is applied to all of the text, click the <div> tag on the Quick Tag Selector to select all of the text at once.

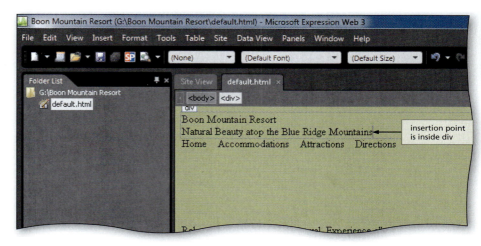

Figure 1–48

2
- With the insertion point inside the first div, click <div> on the Quick Tag Selector to select the entire two lines of text inside the <div> tag container (Figure 1–49).

Q&A Can I select the individual words rather than the entire <div> tag container?

Yes, but Expression Web will assign the code to only the selected text, which will cause problems if you later attempt to apply styles using CSS.

Figure 1–49

3
- Click the Style box arrow on the Common toolbar to display the Style menu (Figure 1–50).

Figure 1–50

- Click Heading 1 <h1> to apply it (Figure 1–51).

Figure 1–51

- Click in the word, Relaxation, to position the insertion point.

- Click the <p> tag on the Quick Tag Selector to select the paragraph tag (Figure 1–52).

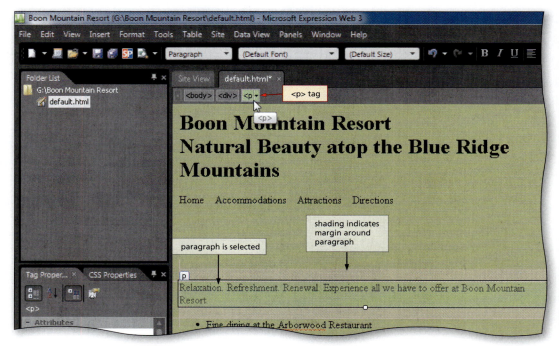

Figure 1–52

6

- Click the Style box arrow on the Common toolbar to display the menu.

- Click Heading 2 <h2> to apply it (Figure 1–53).

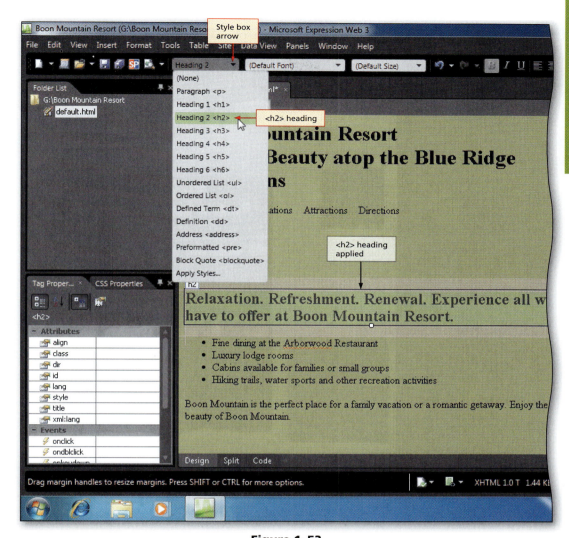

Figure 1–53

To Center Text

When all of the text is aligned to the left side of a Web page, it is difficult for the visitor to scan the page. Using centered text draws the eye to certain headings and paragraphs, and improves the overall look of the page. In the following steps, you will apply center alignment to the company name and tagline.

- Click in the masthead, then click the <div> tag on the Quick Tag Selector to select the div.

- Click the Center button on the Common toolbar to center the selected text (Figure 1–54).

- Click the Save button on the Common toolbar to save the page.

Experiment

- Click the Align Text Right button to see the effect. Press CTRL+Z to undo the change.

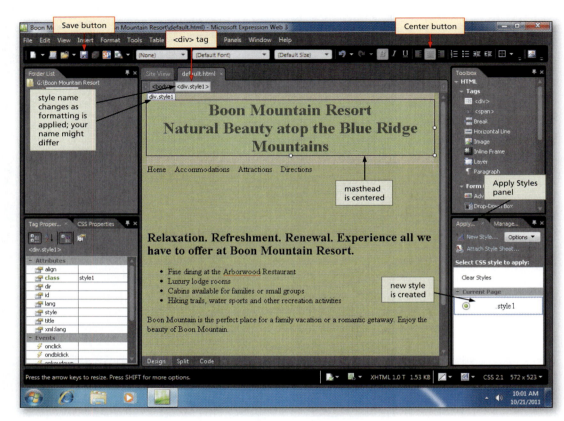

Figure 1–54

Centering Usage
Centering, like all formatting techniques, should not be overdone. Apply centering to headings or elements such as footers. Paragraphs and lists are usually left-aligned.

Applying Font Characteristics

Text attributes can include the font family (such as Arial or Times New Roman), as well as the size, color, alignment, and other attributes of individual characters or words, such as blinking or small capital letters.

Fonts help establish the mood of the site. Clean, simple fonts convey professionalism and clarity, whereas ornate fonts can provide a feeling of excitement or creativity. Fonts with serifs (strokes at the ends of lines that make up letters) are considered easier to read in paragraphs of text. Fonts without serifs, called sans serif fonts, are often used for headings. For more information on fonts, see Special Feature 1.

Font color is also an important consideration. Most sites use a dark font on a light background, or vice versa, which provides good contrast and is easy to read. Royal blue or purple underlined text often indicates a hyperlink, so avoid using this combination of characteristics unless it is for a link.

To Change Font Color

Many sites use colored fonts to distinguish headers but use black for paragraphs of text. The following steps add font colors to selected text to contrast with the green page background.

1

- With the company name and tagline div still selected, click the Font Color button arrow on the Common toolbar to display the Font Color palette (Figure 1–55).

Q&A

The Font Color button is not on my Common toolbar.

Depending on your screen resolution and toolbar setup, you may have to click the More button to the right of the Common toolbar to access additional buttons, as shown in Figure 1–55.

Figure 1–55

2

- Click the #000080 button on the Standard Colors palette, then click Apply to make the masthead text navy blue (Figure 1–56).

 Experiment

- Select a lighter font color to see how difficult it is to see a color that does not contrast with the page background. Press CTRL+Z to undo the change.

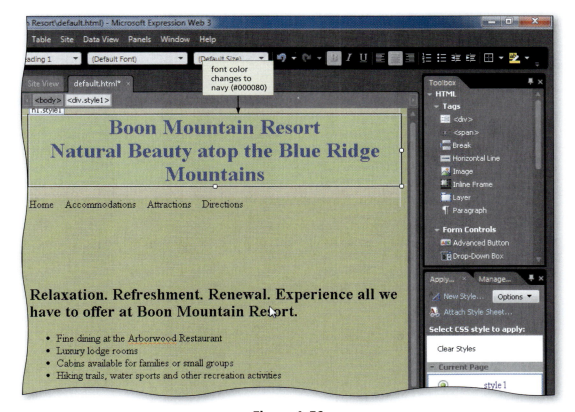

Figure 1–56

3

- Click at the end of the word, Relaxation, to place the insertion point inside the <h2> tag.

- Click the <h2> tag on the Quick Tag Selector to select the tag.

- Click the Common toolbar More button if necessary, then click the Font Color button on the Common toolbar to format the text with blue (Figure 1–57).

- Click the Save button on the Common toolbar to save the page.

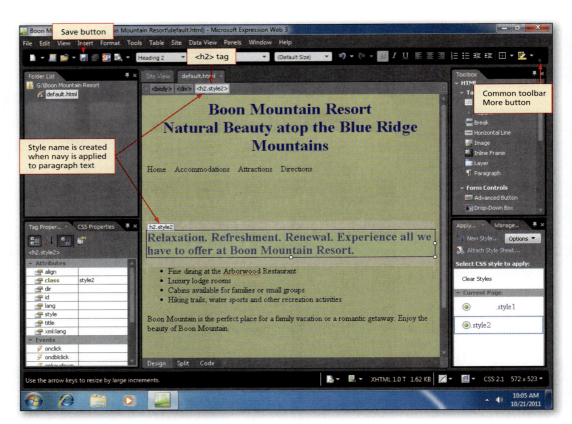

Figure 1–57

Quick Reference
For a table that lists how to complete the tasks covered in this book using the mouse, shortcut menu, and keyboard, see the Quick Reference Summary at the back of this book, or visit the Expression Web 3 Quick Reference Web page (scsite.com/ew3/qr).

BTW

Changing Font Sizes

Unlike in printed documents, the appearance of the actual point size of fonts in a Web page depends on the screen size and resolution of the viewer's computer setup and browser resolution. Using text that is too small might cause you to lose visitors with poor eyesight. Avoid text that is too large to conserve space and retain a professional look. Using all capital letters, except in a heading, is difficult to read and is the Web equivalent of SHOUTING.

Font size options use a relative system of increments, such as xx-small, which is approximately 8 points, to xx-large, which is approximately 36 points.

To Change Font Size

The default font size for the <h2> heading style is x-large. The default font size of plain text is medium. The following steps change the font size of the bulleted list and the paragraph above it.

1
- With the h2 tag still selected, click the Font Size box arrow on the Common toolbar to display the Font Size menu (Figure 1–58).

Figure 1–58

2
- Click large (18 pt) to decrease the size of the text (Figure 1–59).

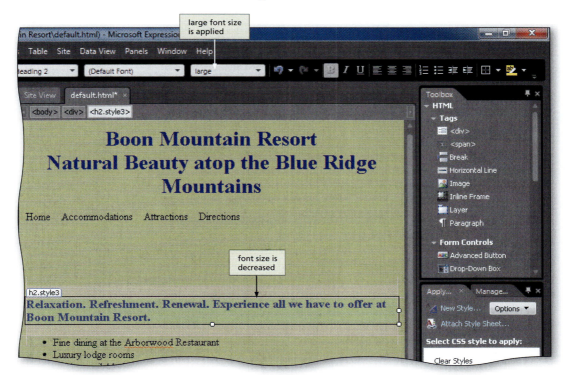

Figure 1–59

3

- Click at the end of the first bulleted item after the word, Restaurant.

- Click the <ul> tag on the Quick Tag Selector to select all four lines of the bulleted list (Figure 1–60).

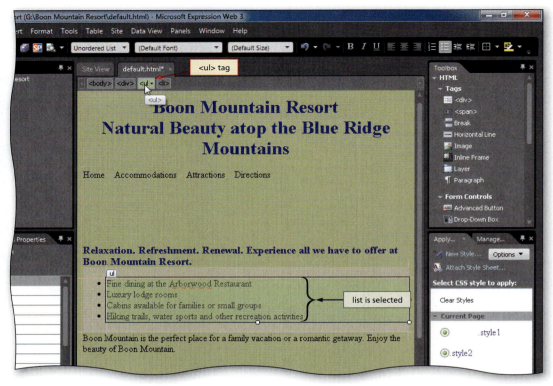

Figure 1–60

4

- Click the Font Size box arrow on the Common toolbar to display the menu.

- Click large (18 pt) to apply it (Figure 1–61).

Why does my Apply Styles task pane show different styles?

Depending on the exact steps you perform, your Apply Styles task pane might show more, fewer, or differently numbered styles. Follow the figures in the text to make sure you are applying formatting to the correct tag.

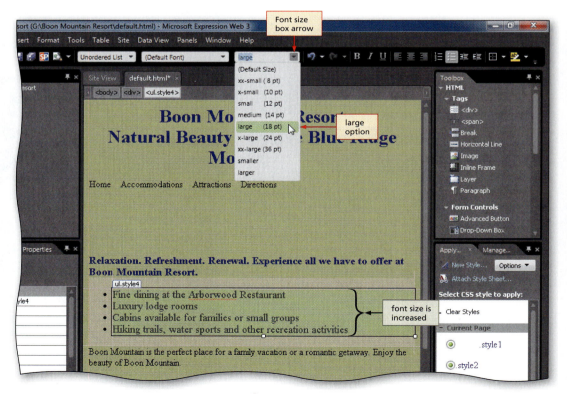

Figure 1–61

To Indent Text

Indenting text moves it away from the margin. Usually, you will see text indented from the left margin, such as at the beginning of the first line of a paragraph of text. You can also indent multiple lines at once to nest them below a heading. The following step indents the bulleted list.

1
• With the bulleted list still selected, click the Increase Indent Position button on the Common toolbar to move the list to the right (Figure 1–62).

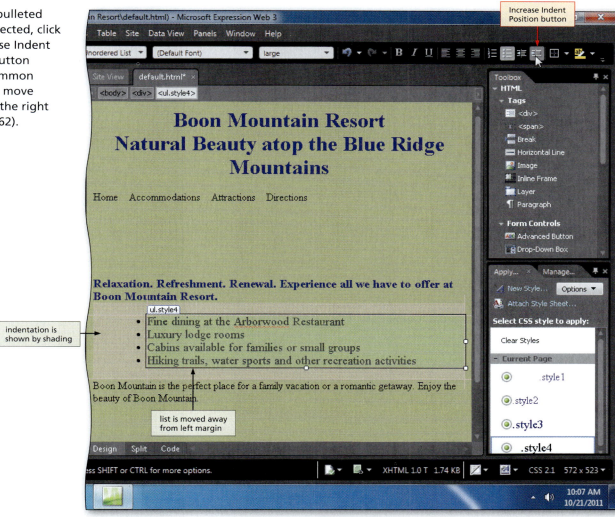

Figure 1–62

BTW

Indent Size
To indent further, click the Increase Indent Position button until you reach the desired indentation. Click the Decrease Indent Position button to move closer to the left margin. Clicking Paragraph on the Format menu opens the Paragraph dialog box, where you can specify indentation from the left and right margins, or for the first line of text only.

To Italicize Text

Italicized text appears slanted and is another type of font attribute. The following steps italicize the text below the bulleted list.

- Click anywhere in the first sentence below the bulleted list.

- Click the <p> tag on the Quick Tag Selector to select both sentences in the tag (Figure 1–63).

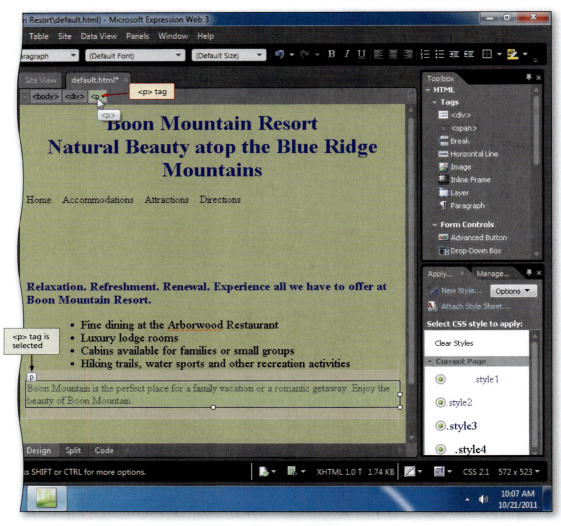

Figure 1–63

2

- Click the Italic button on the Common toolbar to apply the italic attribute to the selected text (Figure 1–64).

- Click the Save button on the Common toolbar to save the page.

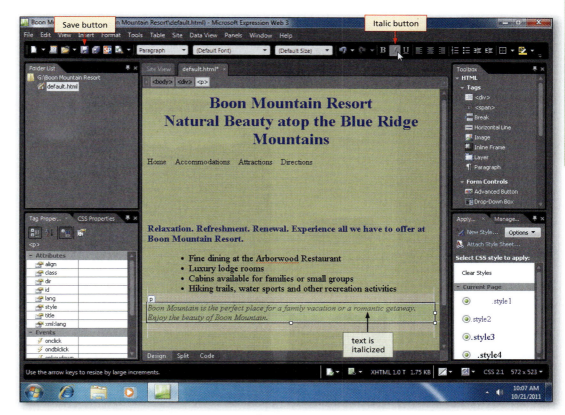

Figure 1–64

Choosing a Font

The fonts that appear on a Web page in the visitor's browser depend on the fonts installed on his or her computer. Expression Web provides font families (groups of similar fonts) to control how your pages appear. If your pages use font families, the page will default to the next available font in the family if the first font choice is not available to your visitor's browser.

BTW

Microsoft Expression Web User Guide
The best way to become familiar with the Microsoft Expression Web User Guide is to use it. Appendix A includes detailed information about the Microsoft Expression Web User Guide and exercises that will help you gain confidence in using it.

To Change a Font

The following steps change the font family from the default to a sans serif font family.

 • Click the <body> tag on the Quick Tag Selector to select all of the page content (Figure 1–65).

Figure 1–65

 • Click the Font box arrow to display the Font gallery (Figure 1–66).

🔎 **Experiment**

• Scroll in the list of fonts to view the various fonts and font families available.

Figure 1–66

3

- Click the Arial, Helvetica, sans-serif font family to apply it (Figure 1–67).

- Click the Save button on the Common toolbar to save the page.

Q&A What if my list of fonts differs?

Depending on your installation, you may have different fonts and font families available to you. Choose a similar font family or one that appeals to you.

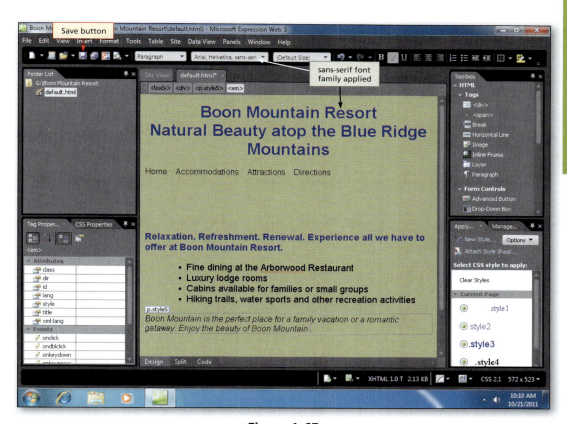

Figure 1–67

Spell Checking Pages

Spelling and grammar errors can distract a reader and make your site look unprofessional. Expression Web has a built-in **spell checker** that displays a red wavy line below words that are not included in the Expression Web dictionary. Words that Expression Web flags as being misspelled are not necessarily incorrect; for example, Expression Web's spell checker does not recognize some proper nouns. Using the spell checker, you can correct misspelled words and choose to ignore words that are proper nouns, or that are otherwise acceptable.

To Spell Check a Page

It is a good idea to check for spelling errors when you are finished entering text. The following steps introduce a spelling error, then correct that error as well as any others you might have made while entering text.

- Select the word, groups, in the third line of the bulleted list.

- Type gourps, then press the SPACEBAR to make the word appear with a red wavy line below it (Figure 1–68).

Figure 1–68

- Click a blank area of the page to deselect all text.

- Click Tools on the menu bar to open the Tools menu and then point to Spelling to display the Spelling submenu. Point to Spelling on the Spelling submenu (Figure 1–69).

Figure 1–69

- Click the Spelling command to start the spell checker and open the Spelling dialog box.

- Click the Ignore button to skip the name of the restaurant, Arborwood, because it is correct (Figure 1–70).

Figure 1–70

4

- Click groups in the Suggestions box.

- Click the Change button to correct the word (Figure 1–71).

Figure 1–71

5

- Click the Ignore button to skip the name of the town, Redhat (Figure 1–72).

Figure 1–72

6

- Click the OK button to close the message box indicating that spell checking is complete (Figure 1–73).

- Click the Save button on the Common toolbar to save the page.

Other Ways

1. As you are typing, right-click a flagged word to display a short-cut menu that includes a list of suggested spelling corrections

2. Press the F7 key to start the spell checker

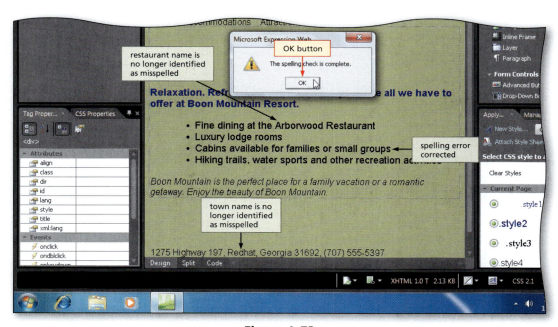

Figure 1–73

Switching Views

Learning HTML
Working in Split view is an excellent way to learn HTML, as you can see how the changes you make in Design view translate into HTML.

A Web page is created using **Hypertext Markup Language (HTML)** and **Extensible Hypertext Markup Language (XHTML)** tags. HTML and XHTML tags consist of the code within a Web page that instructs a browser where formatting is to be applied, how the layout should appear, and where images should be placed. A **browser** is software that is used to display Web pages. HTML and XHTML are the markup languages used to create Web documents. You do not need to know how to write or use HTML/XHTML codes to create Web pages in Expression Web, because as you enter and format content onto your page, Expression Web inserts the appropriate **HTML tags** to define position and formatting attributes.

Expression Web provides four views for working with Web pages. Thus far in this chapter, you have used **Design view**, which gives you a general idea of what your page will look like when viewed in a browser. **Code view** displays the underlying HTML code, which is the data that the browser will use to interpret the content, formatting, and layout when displaying your site on the Internet. In **Split view**, you can see the underlying HTML code in the top half of the Editing window and your page in the bottom half of the editing window. A fourth view, **Snapshot view**, which is available from the Panels menu, displays the page as it would appear in Internet Explorer. Snapshot view is used to do a quick check to make sure the layout of your page appears as intended; you cannot edit the page or test any hyperlinks using Snapshot view.

Looking at the code generated by Expression Web will help you become more familiar with how HTML tags are applied to your page. Figure 1–74 shows part of the code for the Boon Mountain Resort home page.

Figure 1–74

To Show Code and Split Views

Now that you have added content to the page, the following steps use the various view buttons to display the HTML code Expression Web has generated.

1

• Click the Show Code View button at the bottom of the editing window to see the HTML tags and the assigned styles (Figure 1–75).

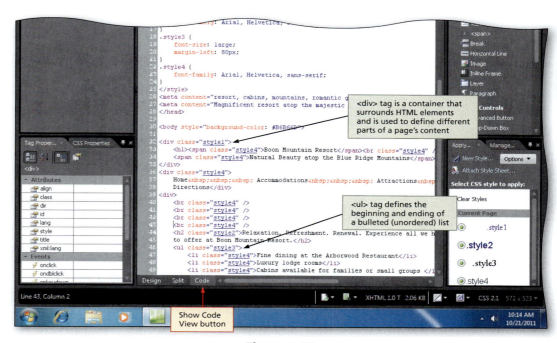

Figure 1–75

2

• Click the Show Split View button at the bottom of the Editing window to show both Code and Design views simultaneously. In Code view, drag the scroll box up to show the head area of the code as shown in the figure (Figure 1–76).

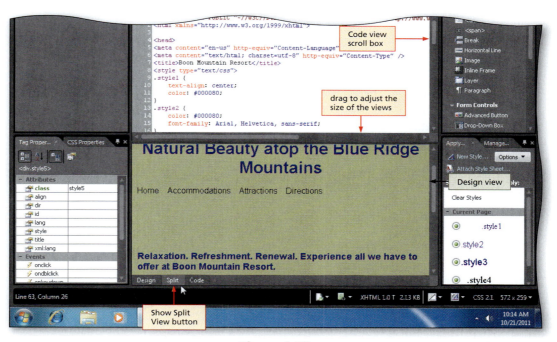

Figure 1–76

3

- Drag the separator that divides the two sections up to display more of the Design view window (Figure 1–77).

I am having trouble moving the separator up.

Make sure you are pointing to the underside of the separator so that the pointer shown in the figure appears. Then drag the separator up.

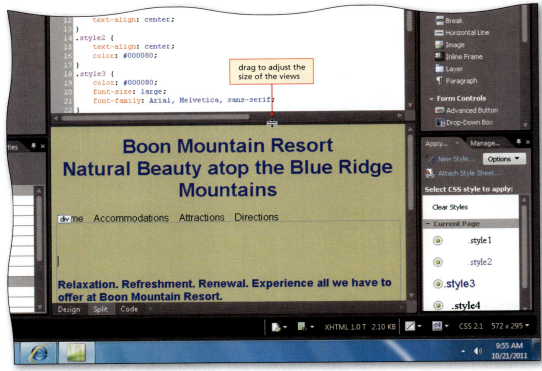

Figure 1–77

4

- Select the words, Natural Beauty, in the Design view window. Expression Web will also select them in the Code view window (Figure 1–78).

- Click anywhere in the Design view window to deselect the text.

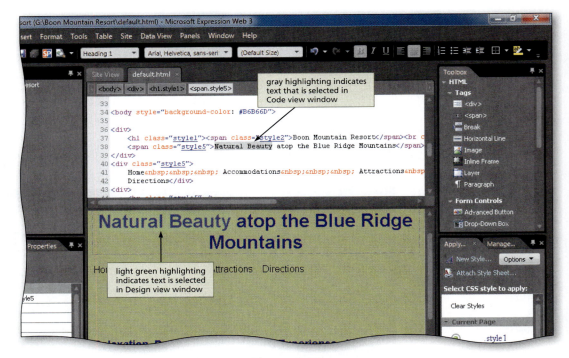

Figure 1–78

5

• Click the Show Design View button to close Code view (Figure 1–79).

Q&A Why would I want to learn HTML if Expression Web generates the code for me?

As you become a more experienced Web designer, you will find it easier to make changes and troubleshoot errors by editing the HTML code directly.

Figure 1–79

To View the Page in the Snapshot Panel

The following steps display the default.html Web page in Snapshot view, which demonstrates how it will appear in Internet Explorer 8.

1

• Click Snapshot on the Panels menu to open the Snapshot panel (Figure 1–80).

Q&A The panel opens, but I only see a clock.

You may have to wait a few moments while Expression Web generates a snapshot of the Web page and checks compatibility.

Figure 1–80

2

• Drag the Snapshot panel scroll box down to see the rest of the default.html page (Figure 1–81).

• Click the Close button to close the Snapshot panel.

Figure 1–81

BTW

Toggle Commands
Visual aids are a toggle command, meaning that you click the same command to turn them both on and off.

Visual Aids and Quick Tags

Expression Web uses visual aids to make it easier to work with page elements, such as layers, borders, and padding, while in Design View. **Visual aids** are onscreen labels that do not appear on the actual Web page, but in Expression Web, they allow you to see the HTML tags and sizing information for elements in order to better work with them. Visual aids can also help make sure that you are selecting an entire div, or tag, before applying formatting or making other changes. By default, visual aids are turned on. You can turn them off to have a better sense of how your final page will look, then turn them back on to fine-tune elements.

Quick tags are a type of visual aid that display labels for the HTML elements on a Web page, such as paragraphs, tables, and headers. When a page element is selected, a box with a label appears around the element; this box is the selected element's visual aid. The tag for the item also appears on the Quick Tag Selector. With some page elements, such as an item in a bulleted list, you can select just one line (the tag <li> for line item), or click the tag to the left of it (the tag <ul> for unordered list) to select the entire list. Use the Quick Tag Selector to make sure that you have selected the correct item before applying formatting or making other changes.

To Hide and Display Visual Aids

You can choose to show only certain types of visual aids, such as margins or padding, or choose to show or hide all types. The visual aid settings are shown as On or Off on the status bar. The following step uses the View menu to turn off all visual aids to view the page as it would appear when finished, then turns them back on.

1
• Click in the first line of the bulleted list to select the first item, and notice that the <li.style5> tag name appears on a tab above the element (Figure 1–82).

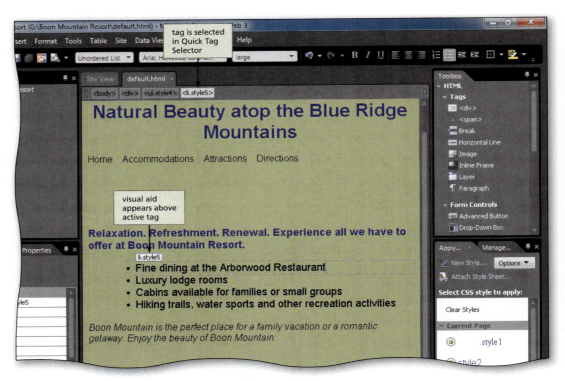

Figure 1–82

2

• Click View on the menu bar to open the View menu, point to Visual Aids to display the Visual Aids submenu, and then click Show to turn off visual aids.

• Click the second line of the bulleted list, and notice that no tag name appears above the line (Figure 1–83).

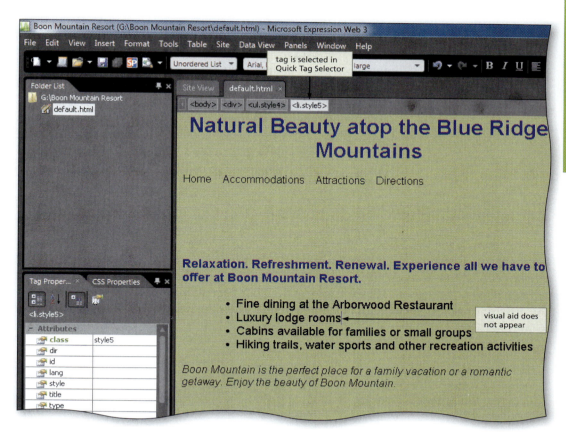

Figure 1–83

3

• Click View on the menu bar to open the View menu, point to Visual Aids to display the Visual Aids menu, then click Show to display visual aids.

• If necessary, click the second line of the bulleted list and notice that the <li> tag name appears above the line (Figure 1–84).

Other Ways

1. Click the Visual Aids button arrow on the status bar and then click Show to turn visual aids off and on

2. Press CTRL+/ to turn visual aids off and on

Figure 1–84

Publishing a Site
See Appendix C for more information about publishing to the Web.

Previewing in Browsers

Web surfers use a variety of browsers. The most popular are Windows Internet Explorer, Mozilla Firefox, Opera, Google Chrome, and Apple Safari. Variations among browsers can cause your pages to appear slightly differently from browser to browser, so it is important to test your pages in as many different browsers as possible before publishing your site to a Web server. Expression Web uses Windows Internet Explorer as the default browser, but you can add others to the browser list. Although you can view a page as it would appear in Internet Explorer using Snapshot view, it is always best to also view the page in a browser window. Browsers allow you to see a full view of your page as it will appear to visitors to your site, as well as allow you to test any hyperlinks, such as to other site pages.

To Preview in a Browser

Although the WYSIWYG interface of Expression Web and Snapshot view give a reasonable sense of how the page will look in a browser, it is still a good idea to preview the page from within the browser program to check for any obvious errors. You can also simulate various page sizes that represent a range of screen resolutions to get a better idea of how the visitor's browser will render your page. If your browser was maximized the last time you used it, the different resolutions will not be demonstrated when the page is previewed. The following steps preview the site in Internet Explorer.

1
- Click the Preview in Windows Internet Explorer 8.0 button arrow to display the browser list (Figure 1–85).

Experiment
- Choose different browser programs and/or resolutions to view any differences in how the site appears.

Q&A
Why did a dialog box appear?

If a Microsoft Expression Web dialog box appears instructing you to save your changes, then you've made a change to your page since the last save. Click OK to save your changes and preview the page.

Figure 1–85

- Click Windows
  Internet Explorer 8.0
  in the menu to
  view the page
  in a browser
  (Figure 1–86).

- If the Maximize
  button appears,
  click it to view the
  browser window
  maximized.

3

- When you are
  finished looking
  at your page in the
  browser, click the
  Close button on
  the browser's title
  bar to return to
  Expression Web.

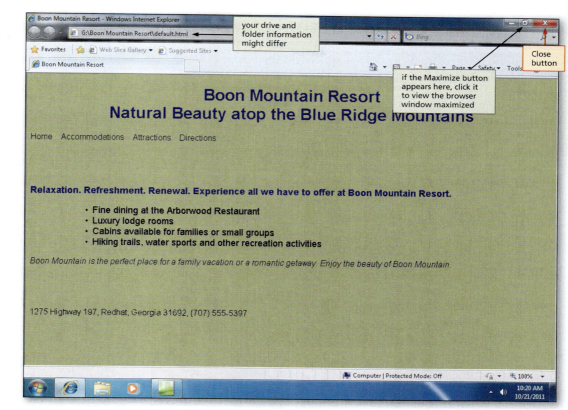

Figure 1–86

Other Ways
1. Press the F12 key to preview the site using the most recently used browser   2. Click the Preview button on the Common toolbar

Printing a Web Page

Expression Web allows you to print a page that looks just like it will appear in a browser. You might want a printout or hard copy of your site pages for proofreading or design markup. Printouts can also be used as archive copies and for distributing to clients.

BTW

Conserving Ink and Toner

You can print a Web page in black-and-white to conserve ink or toner by clicking the Properties button in the Print dialog box to open the properties dialog box. Click the tab and select any option(s) necessary to print in grayscale using black ink, then click OK to close the properties dialog box.

To Print a Web Page

To save ink and paper, use the Print Preview feature before printing a page to make sure that it fits on a reasonable number of pages. Expression Web adds the page title and a page number to the printed page. Web page background images or colors do not appear on the printed output. The following steps preview and then print the Boon Mountain Resort home page.

- Click File on the menu bar to open the File menu, and then point to Print to display the Print submenu.

- Click Print Preview on the Print submenu to see what the page will look like before printing it (Figure 1–87).

Figure 1–87

- Click the Close button at the top of the Print Preview window to close Print Preview.

- Click File on the menu bar to open the File menu, and then point to Print to display the Print submenu.

- Click Print to open the Print dialog box (Figure 1–88).

- Click the OK button in the Print dialog box to begin printing.

Q&A What if I do not want to print at this time?

Click the Cancel button to close the Print dialog box.

Figure 1–88

Other Ways

1. Press CTRL+P, then press the ENTER key

Closing Expression Web

If you quit Expression Web without closing the Web page, Expression Web will attempt to open the page when the program is restarted. If you are not the next user of the program, others might have access to your work. If you are storing your Web page files on a portable device such as a flash drive, Expression Web will display an error message if the portable device is not connected. To avoid these pitfalls, it is a good policy to save and close your files before you exit the Expression Web program.

BTW

Saving Before Closing
If you have made changes since the last time a page was saved, you will be prompted to save the page before closing the site.

To Close a Web Page

Now that you are finished working on the Boon Mountain home page, the following steps close the page, then close the site.

- Right-click the default.html tab at the top of the editing window and then point to Close (Figure 1–89).

Figure 1–89

❷
- Click Close on the shortcut menu.

- Click Site on the menu bar to open the Site menu, then click the Close command (Figure 1–90).

Other Ways

1. Click the Close button in the upper-right corner of the Editing window

Figure 1–90

To Quit Expression Web

You have finished the initial text design and formatting for the Boon Mountain Resort Web site. The following step closes Expression Web.

- Click File on the menu bar to open the File menu and then point to Exit (Figure 1–91).

- Click the Exit command to quit Expression Web.

Figure 1–91

Other Ways

1. Click the Close button on the Expression Web title bar to close the program

Chapter Summary

In this chapter, you have learned how to use Expression Web to open a Web site, enter text, modify text, apply styles, and preview and print a Web page. The items listed below include all the new Expression Web skills you have learned in this chapter.

1. Start Expression Web (EW 6)
2. Reset Workspace Layout (EW 9)
3. Create a Web Site (EW 10)
4. Open a Web Page (EW 14)
5. Set Page Properties (EW 15)
6. Add a <Div> Tag (EW 20)
7. Add Paragraph Text (EW 23)
8. Add a Bulleted List (EW 25)
9. Complete Page Content (EW 28)
10. Save a Web Page (EW 30)
11. Use the Quick Tag Selector (EW 31)
12. Apply a Heading Style (EW 33)
13. Center Text (EW 36)
14. Change Font Color (EW 37)
15. Change Font Size (EW 39)
16. Indent Text (EW 41)
17. Italicize Text (EW 42)
18. Change a Font (EW 44)
19. Spell Check a Page (EW 46)
20. Show Code and Split Views (EW 49)
21. View the Page in the Snapshot Panel (EW 51)
22. Hide and Display Visual Aids (EW 52)
23. Preview in a Browser (EW 54)
24. Print a Web Page (EW 56)
25. Close a Web Page (EW 57)
26. Quit Expression Web (EW 58)

For current SAM information, including versions and content details, visit SAM Central (http://samcentral.course.com). If you have a SAM user profile, you may have access to hands-on instruction, practice, and assessment of the skills covered in this chapter. Since various versions of SAM are supported throughout the life of this text, check with your instructor for the correct instructions and URL/Web site for accessing assignments.

Learn It Online

Test your knowledge of chapter content and key terms.

Instructions: To complete the Learn It Online exercises, start your browser, click the Address bar, and then enter the Web address `scsite.com/ew3/learn`. When the Expression Web Learn It Online page is displayed, click the link for the exercise you want to complete and then read the instructions.

Chapter Reinforcement TF, MC, and SA

A series of true/false, multiple choice, and short answer questions that test your knowledge of the chapter content.

Flash Cards

An interactive learning environment where you identify chapter key terms associated with displayed definitions.

Practice Test

A series of multiple choice questions that test your knowledge of chapter content and key terms.

Who Wants To Be a Computer Genius?

An interactive game that challenges your knowledge of chapter content in the style of a television quiz show.

Wheel of Terms

An interactive game that challenges your knowledge of chapter key terms in the style of the television show *Wheel of Fortune*.

Crossword Puzzle Challenge

A crossword puzzle that challenges your knowledge of key terms presented in the chapter.

Apply Your Knowledge

Reinforce the skills and apply the concepts you learned in this chapter.

Modifying Text and Formatting a Web Site

Instructions: Start Expression Web. Open the Web site, Apply 1-1 Jessica's Jewels, from the Data Files for Students. See the inside back cover of this book for instructions for downloading the Data Files for Students, or see your instructor for information about accessing the required files.

The Web site you open contains an unformatted home page. Open the default.html file and modify and format the text so it looks like Figure 1–92.

Continued >

Apply Your Knowledge *continued*

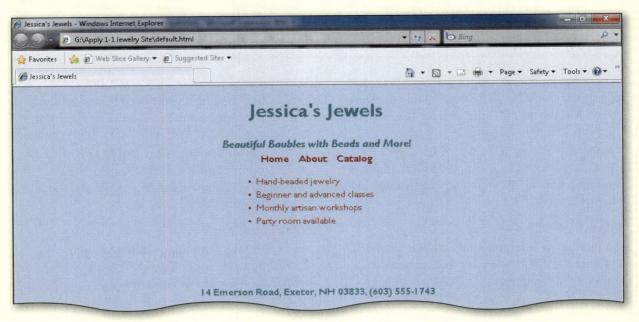

Figure 1–92

Perform the following tasks:

1. Open the Page Properties dialog box, then add the text, Jessica's Jewels, as the page title.

2. Add a page description: Beautiful Baubles with Beads and More!

3. Add the following as keywords: beads, bauble, jewels, jewelry, necklace, bracelet.

4. Change the page background to light blue (140, 240, 192), then close the Page Properties dialog box. *Hint:* Click the Custom button in the More Colors dialog box to enter the Hue, Sat, and Lum values in the Color dialog box.

5. Select the div containing the company name, Jessica's Jewels, then apply the Heading 1 <h1> style.

6. Change the font color of the <h1> tag for the company name to a teal color (42, 104, 121) by typing the values in the R, G, and B text boxes on the Font Color palette.

7. Center-align the <h1> tag for the company name.

8. Select the div containing the slogan.

9. Change the slogan div's font color to the same teal as the company name.

10. Center-align the slogan div.

11. Change the font size of the slogan div to large.

12. Apply bold and italics to the slogan div.

13. Select the div containing the navigation bar and change the font color to red (120, 0, 0) by typing the values in the R, G, and B text boxes on the Font Color palette, and then bold and center the navigation bar div.

14. Click under the div containing the navigation bar and insert a bulleted list.

15. Type the following list items, pressing ENTER after each line:

    - Hand-beaded jewelry

    - Beginner and advanced classes

    - Monthly artisan workshops

    - Party room available

16. Press ENTER a second time after the last line to end the bulleted list.

17. Select the <ul> tag of the bulleted list and change the font color to the red color used for the navigation text. Press the Increase Indent button eight times to indent the list.

18. Add a div at the bottom of the page for the footer.

19. Press ENTER twice at the beginning of the div to add some space.

20. Type the company address and phone number in the div as follows: 14 Emerson Road, Exeter, NH 03833, (603) 555-1743.

21. Select the footer div, center and bold the div, and then change the font color of the footer div to the previously used teal color, and then bold the div.

22. Select the body tag, then change the font family to Gill Sans, Gill Sans MT, Calibri, Trebuchet MS, sans-serif.

23. Save the default.html Web page.

24. Spell check the Web page.

25. Preview the site in two different browsers or resolutions.

26. Use Print Preview to view the site.

27. Print the site.

28. Change the site properties, as specified by your instructor.

29. Close the default.html Web page and the site.

30. Rename the site using the filename, Apply 1-1 Jewelry Site using Windows Explorer.

31. Submit the revised site in the format specified by your instructor.

Extend Your Knowledge

Extend the skills you learned in this chapter and experiment with new skills. You may need to use Help to complete the assignment.

Formatting a Web Site

Instructions: Start Expression Web. Open the Web site, Extend 1-1 Music Festival, from the Data Files for Students. See the inside back cover of this book for instructions for downloading the Data Files for Students, or see your instructor for information about accessing the required files.

Enhance the Web page to match the one shown in Figure 1–93.

Perform the following tasks:

1. Use Help to learn about changing the default font color and how to insert a horizontal line.

2. Print the default.html page.

3. Make notes on the hard copy as to how you will change the Web page to more closely match Figure 1–93.

4. Use the Page Properties dialog box to change the page background to orange (255, 204, 102) and the default font color to blue (0, 51, 153). (*Hint:* Click Custom in the More Colors dialog box to enter Red, Green, and Blue values.)

5. Change the font family of the masthead div using a font family containing Gill Sans (or another font family of your choice) and the font color to red. Bold and center the masthead text and change the font size to x-large.

Continued >

Extend Your Knowledge *continued*

6. Click at the end of the masthead text and press ENTER. Double-click the Horizontal Line tag in the Toolbox to insert a horizontal line under the masthead.

7. Change the font family of both the bulleted list and the paragraph to one containing Arial.

8. Increase the font size of the bulleted list text to large and apply the bold attribute.

9. Select the text, Incoming Flight, then click the Italic button on the Common toolbar.

10. On a separate piece of paper, draw a mock-up of the final page, identifying each part of the page. Make two suggestions for changes based on your own design preferences.

11. Change the site properties, as specified by your instructor.

12. Save and close the default.html page and the Web site. Using Windows Explorer, rename the Extend 1-1 Music Festival site folder as Extend 1-1 Music Site.

13. Submit the revised site in the format specified by your instructor.

Figure 1–93

Make It Right

Analyze a site and correct all errors and/or improve the design.

Increasing Readability and Correcting Spelling Errors

Instructions: Start Expression Web. Open the Web site, Make It Right 1-1 Swim Club, from the Data Files for Students. See the inside back cover of this book for instructions for downloading the Data Files for Students, or see your instructor for information about accessing the required files.

The site's font colors and sizes do not provide enough contrast to be easily readable from the screen, and the Expression Web dictionary has flagged several words as being erroneous. Using Figure 1–94 to guide you, change the background color of the page, bullet and indent the list, change the text alignment, and then change the font sizes and colors to make the text more readable and to show a hierarchy of information. Apply a font family with Franklin Gothic Medium in it to the entire page. Correct each spelling error by right-clicking the flagged text and clicking the appropriate correction or option on the shortcut menu, then run the spelling checker to make sure there are no other errors. Change the page title in the Page Properties dialog box to Macon Waves Swim Club.

Change the site properties, as specified by your instructor. Save and close the default.html page and close the site. Using Windows Explorer, rename the Make it Right 1-1 Swim Club folder as Make it Right 1-1 Swim Club Site. Submit the revised site in the format specified by your instructor.

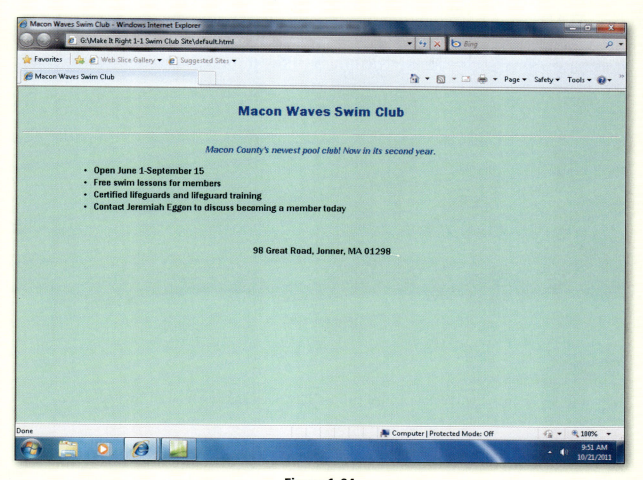

Figure 1–94

In the Lab

Design and/or format a Web site using the guidelines, concepts, and skills presented in this chapter. Labs are listed in order of increasing difficulty.

Lab 1: Creating a New Home Page

Problem: You work part-time at a small bike repair shop. Your boss, Jonas Wolfowitz, has asked you to create a home page for the shop to which he will later add more pages. Create the one-page Web site shown in Figure 1–95 based on Jonas's plan.

Continued >

In the Lab continued

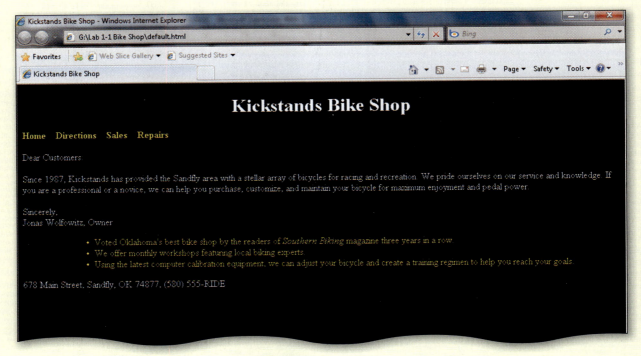

Figure 1–95

Instructions:

1. Start Expression Web.

2. Create a new one-page Web site named Lab 1-1 Bike Shop and save it on a USB flash drive.

3. Open the default.html page.

4. Enter `Kickstands Bike Shop` as the page title, `Bike Sales and Repairs` as the description, and the following keywords: `bike, bicycle, repair, Sandfly, Oklahoma`.

5. Change the page background to black and the default font color to white.

6. Add a masthead that includes the company name, Kickstands Bike Shop. Assign it the Heading 1 <h1> style and center-align the masthead text.

7. Add a div that will include a navigation bar for future pages in the site. Type `Home`, `Directions`, `Sales`, and `Repairs`, pressing TAB between each word.

8. Apply bold to the navigation bar and change the font color to bright yellow.

9. Add a new div, press ENTER, then type the following text. *Hint:* Press ENTER twice before and after the body paragraph to add line spacing.

`Dear Customers:`

`Since 1987, Kickstands has provided the Sandfly area with a stellar array of bicycles for racing and recreation. We pride ourselves on our service and knowledge. If you are a professional or a novice, we can help you purchase, customize, and maintain your bicycle for maximum enjoyment and pedal power.`

`Sincerely,`

`Jonas Wolfowitz, Owner`

10. Click below the owner name and then create a new bulleted list with the bright yellow font color. Indent the list from the left margin. Type the following list:

- `Voted Oklahoma's best bike shop by the readers of` *`Southern Biking`* `magazine three years in a row.`
- `We offer monthly workshops featuring local biking experts.`
- `Using the latest computer calibration equipment, we can adjust your bicycle and create a training regimen to help you reach your goals.`

11. Create a new div for the footer. Type the following text:

`678 Main Street, Sandfly, OK 74877, (580) 555-RIDE`

12. Apply a font family that includes Georgia and Times New Roman to the entire page.

13. Instruct the spell checker to ignore Wolfowitz and Sandfly.

14. View the HTML code using Split view.

15. Practice selecting text in the Code window, but do not make any changes to the HTML code.

16. Switch back to Design view.

17. Save the changes you have made to default.html, then preview the page in a browser.

18. Change the site properties, as specified by your instructor.

19. Submit the site in the format specified by your instructor, then close the site.

In the Lab

Lab 2: Formatting Fonts and Images

Problem: You own a baking business and want to enhance your home page. You finish formatting the site to create the one-page Web site shown in Figure 1–96.

Figure 1–96

Continued >

In the Lab *continued*

Instructions:

1. Start Expression Web.

2. Open the Web site Lab 1-2 Bakery.

3. Open the default.html page.

4. Add `Sweet Tooth Bakery` as the title, `Gourmet confections for all of your events` as the page description, and the following keywords: `cake, bakery, caterer, baking, cookies`.

5. Change the page background to light pink and the default text color to dark brown.

6. Select the <body> tag on the Quick Tag Selector, then change the default font family to one containing Verdana or another font family of your choice.

7. Select the tagline paragraph tag, then apply italics and increase the font size to large.

8. Deselect all text and divs, then right-click the image of the cake to open the shortcut menu for the image.

9. Click Picture Properties on the shortcut menu.

10. Click the Appearance tab in the Picture Properties dialog box, click Right under Wrapping style, then click OK.

11. Run the spell checker and ignore all of the flagged words. Save the changes you have made to default.html, then preview the page in a browser.

12. Change the site properties, as specified by your instructor.

13. Submit the site in the format specified by your instructor, then close the site.

In the Lab

Lab 3: Creating a New Web Site

Problem: Your school's drama club has asked you to prepare a Web page for its upcoming performance. You create the one-page Web site shown in Figure 1–97.

Figure 1–97

Instructions: Perform the following tasks.

1. Start Expression Web.

2. Create a new one-page Web site called Lab 1-3 Drama.

3. Open the default.html page.

4. Add `Ponrolet Drama Club` as the title, `Presenting Brigadoon!` as the page description, and the following keywords: `drama`, `Ponrolet`, `acting`, `Brigadoon`.

5. Change the page background to burgundy and the default text color to yellow (255, 255, 204). *Hint:* Enter values in the Red, Green, and Blue text boxes in the custom Color dialog box.

6. Enter the text and apply the heading, indents, and formatting as shown in Figure 1–97.

7. Change the body font family to one containing Franklin Gothic Medium (or another font family of your choice).

8. Add and position the two horizontal lines using the Toolbox.

9. Save the changes you have made to default.html, then preview the page in a browser. Change the site properties, as specified by your instructor.

10. Submit the site in the format specified by your instructor, then close the site.

Cases and Places

Apply your creative thinking and problem-solving skills to design and implement a solution.

● EASIER   ●●MORE DIFFICULT

● 1: Work with the Expression Web Window

You want to practice working with the Expression Web window. Open any site that you created in Chapter 1, then open that site's default.html page. Use the Page Properties dialog box to add a keyword. Switch to Code view, then split the view. Select text in Code view, but do not make any changes to the HTML code. Switch to Design view. Insert a new paragraph using the Toolbox. In the paragraph, create a numbered list with three items, and include one misspelled word and one name that Expression Web identifies as a misspelling. Check the spelling on the page; correct the misspelled word and ignore the name. Select one item using the Quick Tag Selector, then use the Quick Tag Selector to select the entire list. Close the default.html page without saving any changes, close the Web site, then quit Expression Web.

● 2: Design and Plan a School Web Site

You have just finished a class on Web design. The school administration of Pinkham Academy, a private high school, would like to plan a Web site that will include a home page, and eventually it will add other pages. Sketch a plan on a piece of paper for the home page of the Web site that you can present to the administration and use to gather its feedback. Include a masthead that lists the school name and a navigation bar with links to the library, administration, and calendar. The administration wants to include the school logo on the home page. Include an area for a letter from the principal and a footer for the address. The school's colors are blue and white; indicate on the Web site sketch how you will incorporate the school's colors.

●● 3: Format a One-Page Alumni Web Site

You have recently joined the Connecticut branch of your college alumni association. You have been working on a home page that can tell other local graduates of Gulliver College about upcoming alumni events. You have already entered the text for the home page. Open the site Cases and Places 3 Alumni, then open the page default.html. Use the page properties to add a title, a description, and four appropriate keywords. Use the heading style and other formatting techniques to apply italics, bold, center alignment, and indentations to make the home page easy to read.

●● 4: Create a Job Search Home Page

Make It Personal

When you are looking for a job, it is helpful to have a résumé or list of your skills that you can share with potential employers. What is your dream job? Imagine yourself a decade from now—what amazing skills and job experiences will you have collected? Will you have won any awards, made a scientific discovery, learned a foreign language, or gone to art school? Create a one-page Web site that you can use to show potential employers all of the things that you might have learned and done over the next 10 years that would qualify you for your dream job. Include a masthead, bulleted list, footer, and any other information you think is relevant. Format the Web site attractively, including adding a background color, changing the fonts, and applying effects such as bold and italics. Add a page title, a description, and keywords.

•• 5: Create a Home Page for a Sports Team

Working Together

One of your local sports teams wants to create a multi-page Web site for its fans. The site will include a home page, the calendar for the upcoming season, and biographies of the players and coaches. The home page should include a masthead, a navigation bar, a bulleted list with highlights from the previous season, and a footer with contact information. Working as a team with several of your classmates, design a Web site and create the home page. As a group, decide on the type of sport, the name of the team, and the team colors. Each team member should plan on paper the three pages (home, calendar, biographies) that will eventually be included in the site and present his or her plan to the group. As a group, decide on elements of each plan that you will incorporate into the home page, and start creating the home page using Expression Web. Add a page title, description, and keywords. Format the Web site attractively, including incorporating the team colors into the background and fonts, changing the fonts, and applying effects such as bold and italics. Run the spelling checker, use Print Preview, then print the site. Make notes as a group about any changes you need to make, then preview the site in multiple browsers and resolutions.

2 Working with Images and Links

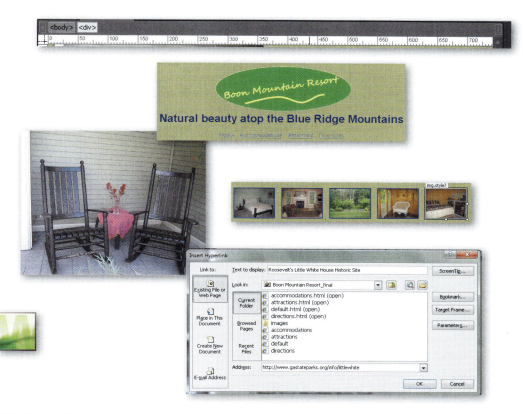

Objectives

You will have mastered the material in this chapter when you can:

- Insert and align an image
- Change the workspace
- Add borders and margins to an image
- Copy page elements to the Clipboard
- Edit an image
- Create an image thumbnail

- Create a folder for images
- Add internal links
- Add external links
- Add a bookmark
- Add an e-mail link
- Add a ScreenTip

2 | Working with Images and Links

Introduction

Text is an important part of Web site content — it describes the purpose of the site and conveys valuable details related to the site's subject matter. No matter how well written the text is, however, a site without images or that is difficult to navigate will not hold a visitor's attention for long. **Graphics** or **images** in Web pages serve a practical purpose by illustrating a product or service described in the text, displaying a company's logo, or serving as links to further information. Images also help make a site more attractive and effective by providing visual interest and continuity. **Hyperlinks**, or simply **links**, are text or graphics used to jump to another location in the same Web page, elsewhere in the site, or to another Web site. A link can also open the visitor's e-mail program that allows the visitor to send an e-mail to the site owner or other recipient. Links, in either text or graphic format, help to organize a site by providing navigation to other areas of the World Wide Web.

Project — Enhancing the Boon Mountain Resort Web Site

A Web site for a business, such as the Boon Mountain Resort, needs to inform and attract current and potential customers. Visitors to a Web site want to get an impression of the product or service very quickly. Sites that feature eye-catching images and that are easy to navigate and informative can help build a customer base, leading to increased success of the business.

A navigation bar that includes links to each of the main pages on a site usually appears on the left side or below the masthead on each page of a site. The navigation bar also might appear in both locations.

The project for this chapter uses Expression Web to add images and links to the home page for the Boon Mountain Resort Web site as shown in Figure 2–1. Additional pages and content have been added to the Web site that you created in Chapter 1, based on the site plan and feedback from site visitors and Boon Mountain Resort staff. Now you will add a logo and images so that visitors to the site can see images of the resort's various accommodations. You will also create a navigational structure, add links to other attractions near the resort, create a bookmark for a long page, and add a link that visitors can use to send an e-mail to the resort.

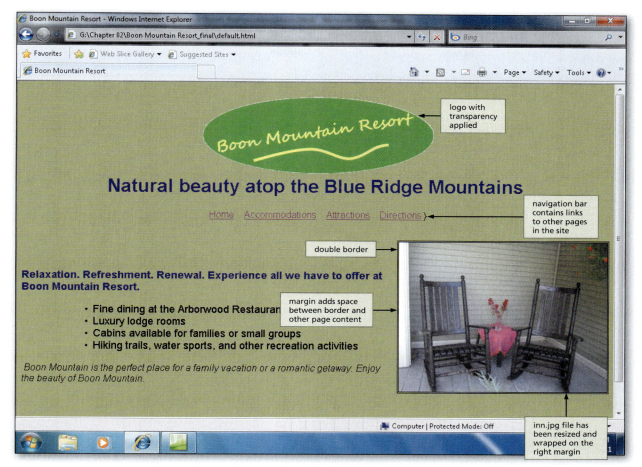

Figure 2–1

Overview

As you read this chapter, you will learn how to add images and links to the Web site shown in Figure 2–1 by performing these general tasks:

- Choose and insert images.
- Adjust the workspace layout.
- Position images in relation to text and page margins.
- Distinguish an image by modifying margins and borders.
- Make changes to the appearance and format of an image.
- Add links to other pages in the site, to other sites, and to an e-mail address.

Plan
Ahead

General Project Guidelines

When adding images and links to a Web site, you should keep in mind the goals of the site. Any images that you add should not only be attractive but should also serve a purpose. Links should assist a reader in finding information quickly. A navigation bar is essential, but additional links to pages, page areas, or external locations can enhance a visitor's experience and allow him or her to find the information needed quickly. As you add text and images to a Web site, such as the project shown in Figure 2–1, you should follow these general guidelines:

1. **Properly use images that enhance the message of your site.** Adding too many images or using poor quality ones will detract from the message you are trying to deliver. Consider having a professional photographer take the pictures to ensure their quality. Always make sure that you have the proper permission to use an image before you add it to your site and that you give credit to your source. You should plan for borders, image placement, and spacing around your image to guide the reader's eye and distinguish your image.

2. **Identify changes to make to the images.** Removing unnecessary background areas by cropping will emphasize the portion of the image that is relevant. Physically resizing an image takes up more or less space on the screen. You can give visitors the option of seeing a larger version of an image by providing them with a thumbnail that, when clicked, enlarges the image. Including thumbnails can make the site quicker to download, increasing the usability of your site. You should also organize the image files into a folder or series of folders.

3. **Determine the necessary internal and external links.** A navigation bar includes links to the main pages in a site. A large site can have thousands of Web pages, but the designers of the site generally organize the pages into categories and subcategories to help visitors quickly find the information they are seeking. Linking to external sites can enhance the information on a site. For example, providing links to area attractions helps visitors learn more about the Boon Mountain Resort vicinity. Providing an e-mail link allows visitors to interact with the site by requesting additional information or by adding their address to a mailing list. Text is often used as a link, but images, such as photos and graphic logos, can also be used as links as well.

   Specific details about these guidelines are presented at appropriate points in the chapter. The chapter will also identify what tasks will be performed and how decisions are made during the creation of the Web site shown in Figure 2–1.

BTW

Sources for Images
You can insert images installed on a disk or network folder to which you have access, use images saved to your Web site folder, or insert images directly from a digital camera or electronic scanner.

BTW

File Sizes
A higher file resolution delivers a better quality image, but larger file sizes take longer to download. You can usually reduce file sizes using compression software without visibly diminishing the quality of the image as displayed on the page.

Choosing Images and File Types

Web page images are digital files that you can acquire as stock photography from a CD or downloaded file, or you can use images that are imported from a device such as a digital camera. Regardless of the origins of your image files, all images included in your site need to be **embedded**, or saved as a part of the Web site so that when you publish your site, all of the files are accessible.

Technical Considerations for Image Files

Adding images to a Web site increases the site's attractiveness but adds complexity in terms of increased page file sizes and variations in graphic resolution. Image files that exceed 100 kilobytes in size can download slowly in a visitor's browser, a situation you should avoid. Image files are composed of dots, or **pixels**, which are the smallest amount of visible data in an image. An image's **resolution** is the concentration of dots that make up the image. High-quality images typically require larger file sizes because higher-quality images are **high resolution** (high res), containing a high concentration of dots per inch (dpi). If an image file has a low resolution (low res), the image can appear jagged, or **pixilated**. A high-resolution file provides a better quality image, so you have to balance the quality of an image with how its size affects the site.

A **file format** is the way the file is encoded and stored electronically. An image's file format differs depending on the type of image, the program that created it, or how it was saved. To appear in a browser, your site's images must be saved in a format supported by most browsers. The most common image file formats used on the Web are .gif (Graphics Interchange Format, pronounced "jiff"), .jpg (Joint Photographic Experts Group, pronounced "jaypeg"), and .png (Portable Network Graphics, pronounced "ping").

The .gif, .jpg, and .png file formats differ in how they **compress**, or reduce the size of, image files by removing extraneous file data. **Lossy** compression means that a certain amount of quality is lost when the image is compressed. For an image that uses broad swatches of uniform colors, this is not usually visible. For photographs, you should use **lossless** compression, where the image retains its quality. Photos that have lost considerable quality appear pixilated and display blocks of color (Figure 2–2).

BTW

Images from External Devices
If you have images stored on a digital camera or captured electronically using a scanner, insert the device or storage media as directed by the device manufacturer, click Insert on the menu bar, point to Picture, then click From Scanner or Camera to insert the image.

squares indicate lossyness

Figure 2–2

Table 2–1 describes common image formats.

Table 2–1 Image File Types			
File Format	**Extension(s)**	**Compression**	**About**
Graphics Interchange Format (GIF)	.gif	Lossless	Introduced by CompuServe in 1987. Best for drawn graphics or logos. Supports animations. Uses data compression for large files. Limited to 256 colors.
Joint Photographic Experts Group (JPEG)	.jpg, .jpeg	Lossy	A compression method and file format used for photographs.
Portable Network Graphics (PNG)	.png	Lossless	Developed as a non-proprietary file format to be used without restrictions. Best for drawn graphics or logos. Does not support animations. Uses data compression for large files.

Accessibility Properties

Because some visitors to your site might have a vision impairment that requires them to use a screen reader program or other adaptive technology, you should complete the information in the Accessibility Properties dialog box that opens when you insert an image. Depending on a visitor's browser and settings, this information, called **alternate text**, appears next to an image while it downloads and provides information to those who use devices to assist with visual impairments.

Write your alternate text to describe the image that it is associated with so that users of visual assistance software will get a complete description of the image and how it differs from other pictures on your site. For instance, on a Web site for a band that features all of the album covers from the past 20 years, the alternate text for each image should have the complete album name, year of publication, and a brief description of the images used on the cover, instead of "album cover."

<table>
<tr>
<td valign="top">**Plan Ahead**</td>
<td>

Properly use images that enhance the message of your site.
When deciding on how to enhance your site with images, consider both the aesthetic value of each image and whether the image conveys the necessary information or message to visitors to your site. Choose only images that are necessary to enhance the site and inform visitors, and make sure to seek permission where necessary.

- **Determine the type of images you will need.** You can enhance your Web page with many types of images:
  - Company logos are graphics created by a designer, usually incorporate the company name, and use color and shapes to create an easily recognizable image that can be used on letterhead, Web pages, and other communications to identify the company. On a Web page, a company logo often appears on the masthead.
  - Photographs taken with a digital camera or scanned into an electronic format are valuable for depicting a location or product.
  - Use a graphic design program to create images that look drawn, such as logos or cartoons, or to decrease the file size or make other enhancements to photographs or other images.
  - **Animated graphics** use a series of motions and sounds to make an image appear to be moving.
- **Store the images in a central folder location, and make sure that you have the proper permissions to use them.**
  - You can create a folder within the Web site to manage your digital assets, such as image files.
  - Acquire permission to use non-original images, give credit to the source, and make sure that you are using the image according to the agreement with the source and any guidelines that may have been set.
  - It is the responsibility of the person using the image to gain permission. Even if an image does not have a copyright notice with it, it is still not free for public use unless express permission has been given.

</td>
</tr>
</table>

The following pages show you how to insert, place, and format images after you have started Expression Web.

Placeholders
A **placeholder** is a container to which you add text or images. The Image icon in the Toolbox is used to insert a placeholder to which you will later add an image. This is helpful if you do not have the image at the time. You can resize the placeholder to determine the spacing and layout of your page until you insert the image.

Inserting an Image

When you insert an image into a Web page, Expression Web automatically creates a paragraph tag to contain the image. To wrap text around an image, insert the image into the tag that contains the text. If you want to align and position the image separately from surrounding text, insert it into its own div.

To Start Expression Web

If you are using a computer to step through the project in this chapter, and you want your screens to match the figures in this book, you should change your computer's resolution to 1024 × 768. For information about how to change a computer's resolution, read Appendix G. If you are using a lab computer or have changed the workspace layout, reset the workspace to the default settings to match the screens in this book.

The following steps, which assume you are running Windows 7, start Expression Web based on a typical installation and reset the workspace layout. You may need to ask your instructor how to start Expression Web for your computer.

Note: If you are using Windows XP, see Appendix E for alternate steps. If you are using Windows Vista, see Appendix F for alternate steps.

1

● Click the Start button on the Windows 7 taskbar to display the Start menu.

● Click All Programs at the bottom of the left pane on the Start menu to display the All Programs menu.

● Click Microsoft Expression on the All Programs menu to display the Microsoft Expression menu.

2

● Click Microsoft Expression Web 3 to start Expression Web.

3

● Click Panels on the menu bar to open the Panels menu, then click Reset Workspace Layout.

To Open a Web Site

An Expression Web site consists of at least one folder and file; most sites include multiple files and folders. When you open a site, all of the files and folders appear in the Folder List and the Site View pane, and can be individually opened and accessed. Always open all of the site's files at once using Expression Web. If you use a Windows Explorer window to open one page or file of a site at a time, you can create errors of inconsistency and broken links. When opening a Web site, there are two Open Site dialog boxes. The first dialog box that opens allows you to browse through recently opened sites, and to type in a file path of a site folder if you know it. To locate a site folder by looking through drives and subfolders, click the Browse button to open the second Open Site dialog box. In this dialog box you can change to a USB flash drive and select a subfolder, for example. The following steps open the Boon Mountain Resort Web site and the default.html page.

1

• With your USB flash drive connected to one of the computer's USB ports, click Site on the menu bar to open the Site menu then point to Open Site (Figure 2–3).

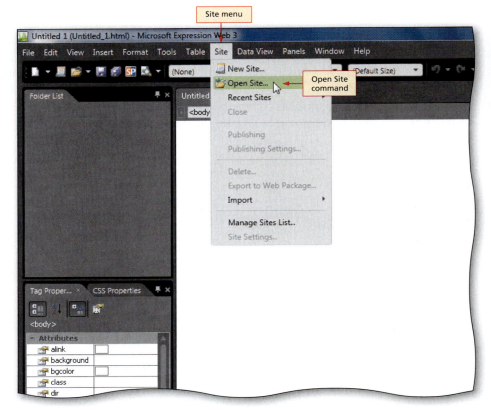

Figure 2–3

2

• Click Open Site on the Site menu to open the Open Site dialog box (Figure 2–4).

• Click the Browse button to open a second Open Site dialog box.

Figure 2–4

● Scroll if necessary
then click Computer
in the left pane
to display a list of
available drives.

● If necessary,
scroll until FLASH
DRIVE or USB (G:)
appears in the list
of available drives
(Figure 2–5).

Figure 2–5

❹

● Scroll down, if
necessary, and then
double-click FLASH
DRIVE or USB (G:) to
display the contents
of the drive.

● Double-click the
Chapter 02 folder to
display its contents.

● Click the
Boon Mountain
Resort_final Web
site folder to select
it (Figure 2–6).

Figure 2–6

5

- Click the Close button to close the second Open Site dialog box.

- Click the Open button to open the site (Figure 2–7).

Figure 2–7

6

- Double-click the default.html page in the Site View pane to open it (Figure 2–8).

Figure 2–8

To Insert an Image

All images that you insert into a page need to be embedded into your site to make them available when your page is viewed in a browser. When you make changes to an image, you will be prompted to resave the embedded file. In the Save Embedded Files dialog box there are options to rename the image, save the image in a folder, assign an action, and change the file type.

All images used in the Boon Mountain Resort site were taken by the owner, so no credits are necessary. The following steps add a picture of the resort's main building to the home page from an external folder, assign accessibility properties, and embed the image into your site.

1

- In the Expression Web editing window, click two lines above the line beginning with the word, Relaxation, to place the insertion point in the div (Figure 2–9).

Figure 2–9

2

- Click Insert on the menu bar to open the Insert menu.

- Point to Picture on the Insert menu, then point to From File (Figure 2–10).

Figure 2–10

3

- Click From File to open the Picture dialog box.

- Navigate to the folder that contains your data files.

- Open the Boon Mountain Resort_images folder to access the images for this site (Figure 2–11).

Q&A Why doesn't my files list look like the list in Figure 2–11?

If your files list looks different, then you are seeing a different files view. To make your screen match the figure, click the More options button arrow on the toolbar and then click Tiles in the menu.

Figure 2–11

4

- Scroll if necessary, then click the inn file to select it (Figure 2–12).

Figure 2–12

5

- Click the Insert button to open the Accessibility Properties dialog box.

- In the Accessibility Properties dialog box, type Front porch of inn in the Alternate text text box (Figure 2–13).

Figure 2–13

• Click the OK button to close the dialog box and see the inserted image on the page (Figure 2–14).

Figure 2–14

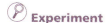

• Press CTRL+S to save the default.html page.

• Click the OK button in the Save Embedded Files dialog box (Figure 2–15).

Experiment

• Click the Change Folder, Set Action, and Picture File Type buttons in the Save Embedded Files dialog box to see the options available in the dialog boxes that open. Click the Cancel button in each dialog box to close it without making any changes.

Figure 2–15

Other Ways

1. Click the Insert Picture from File button on the Common toolbar

Adjusting the Workspace Layout

As you work with Web pages, you may want to adjust the layout of the workspace by opening, moving, maximizing, minimizing, or closing panels. You can open, close, or rearrange panels to best fit your preferences or to access specific tools. You should only open the panels that you need; having too many panels open makes your workspace cluttered and leaves you less room for editing. Expression Web saves the arrangement and uses it as the default the next time you start the program.

As you work with images, it is helpful to display the rulers as a guide for cropping and resizing. Images often are inserted into a Web page at a size that is too large, so you might need to close panels in order to view more of the editing window on the screen and display rulers so that you can accurately size, position, and crop images.

Panels

Expression Web contains 18 panels; the four default panels (Folder List, Tag Properties, Apply Styles, and Toolbox) are docked on the left and right sides of the editing window. Table 2–2 lists different ways you can adjust the workspace using the panels. Examples are shown in Figure 2–16 (a and b).

Table 2–2 Panel Actions

Skill	Method	Effect
Undocking	Click the panel's title bar and then drag the panel to the center of the editing window	Allows you to move it to a new location or have it float anywhere in the Expression Web window (see Figure 2–16 a)
Docking	Click the panel's title bar and then drag the panel to the left or right of the editing window until it docks	Allows you to move it to a fixed location on a side of the Expression Web window (see Figure 2–16 a)
Maximizing	Click the Turn off AutoHide button on the panel title bar	Enlarges a panel so that you can see more of its content (see Figure 2–16 a)
Minimizing	Click the Turn on AutoHide button on the panel title bar	Minimize a panel to view more of another panel in the same column (see Figure 2–16 a)
Opening	Click Panels on the menu bar, then click a panel	Displays a panel in order to access its tools (see Figure 2–16 b)
Closing	Click the Close button on the panel title bar, or to the right of grouped panels, to close the group	Closes a panel or group of panels to see more of another panel or more of the editing window (see Figure 2–16 a)

Figure 2–16 (b) shows the Panels menu, which can be accessed through the Panels command on the menu bar. A check mark next to the panel name in the Panels menu indicates it is visible. To show a panel, click the panel name in the menu to add a check mark. To hide a panel, click the name that contains the check mark to remove the check mark.

(a)

(b)

Figure 2–16

To Close a Panel

The following steps close the panels on the right side of the window, giving you more space in the editing window to format the images.

1

- Point to the Close all button to the right of the Manage Styles panel title bar (Figure 2–17).

Figure 2–17

2

• Click the Close all button to the right of the Manage Styles panel title bar to close the Apply Styles and Manage Styles panels (Figure 2–18).

Figure 2–18

3

- Click the Close button on the Toolbox title bar to close the Toolbox (Figure 2–19).

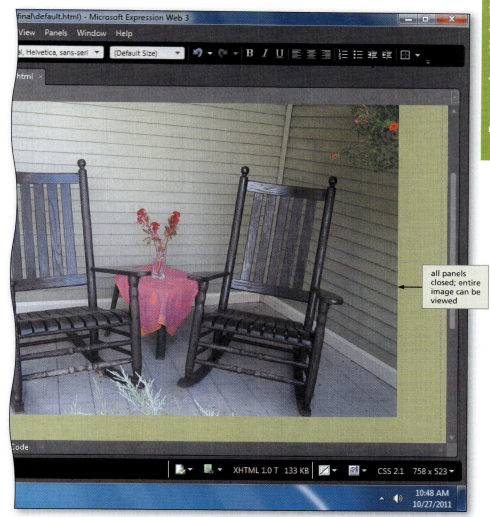

all panels closed; entire image can be viewed

Figure 2–19

To Display the Ruler

The image file you just inserted is too large and you will need to resize it. The Expression Web workspace can include rulers to assist you with adjusting page layout. When you display the rulers, they appear along the left (vertical) and top (horizontal) edges of the window and use pixels as measurement. In the following steps, you will display the rulers so that you can position and size the images and margins.

1

- Click View on the menu bar to open the View menu, then point to Ruler and Grid to display the submenu.

- Point to Show Ruler on the submenu (Figure 2–20).

Q&A Why is the Ruler and Grid command dimmed on my screen?

If the Ruler and Grid command is dimmed, then you have deselected the document window. Click the inn image in the document window and repeat step 1.

Figure 2–20

2

- Click Show Ruler on the submenu to display the rulers (Figure 2–21).

Q&A What should I do if my rulers are already displayed?

Show Ruler is a toggle command, meaning that the same steps are used to turn the rulers on and off. If your rulers were already displayed, either skip these steps or repeat them to display the rulers.

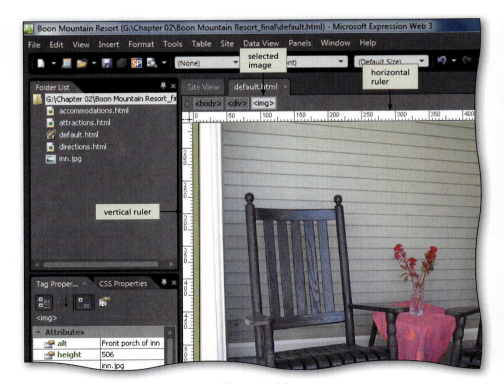

Figure 2–21

Adjusting Proportions

The relationship between an image's height and width is an image's **proportions**, or **aspect ratio**. If an image's proportions are changed, it can distort the image like a carnival funhouse mirror. To maintain the aspect ratio when resizing an image manually, press and hold the SHIFT key and then drag a corner sizing handle to adjust the height and width at the same time. When you change the height of an image in the Picture Properties dialog box, click the 'Keep aspect ratio' check box so that the width automatically adjusts proportionately, and vice versa. After you have resized an image, you should **resample** it to improve the image quality by adjusting the resolution of pixels to the new image size.

Changing Image Size
Resizing an image can make your layout more attractive but does not change the file size of the image. When you make an image larger, you risk decreasing the image quality because as you increase the size on the page, you are stretching the existing pixels in the file. Testing your site in a browser can identify problems with resized images.

To Resize an Image

Expression Web uses the actual pixel width and height of the picture as the size when it inserts the image. You can resize the physical space that the picture takes up by dragging the image using the sizing handles or by specifying the height and width in pixels in the Picture Properties dialog box. In the following steps, you will resize the image, then resample it.

- Verify that the image is selected and then click Format on the menu bar to open the Format menu, then point to Properties (Figure 2–22).

Figure 2–22

2

- Click Properties to open the Picture Properties dialog box.

- Click the Appearance tab (Figure 2–23).

Figure 2–23

3

- If necessary, click the 'Keep aspect ratio' check box to select it.

- Type 400 in the Width box to decrease the figure's size (Figure 2–24).

Figure 2–24

4

- Click the OK button to close the Picture Properties dialog box.

- If necessary, click the picture to select it and make sizing handles appear around the perimeter.

- Position the pointer over the lower-right handle so that it changes to a double-headed arrow.

- Press and hold the SHIFT key and then drag the sizing handle up and to the left so that the width is approximately 350 pixels and the height is approximately 263 pixels, according to the ScreenTip (Figure 2–25).

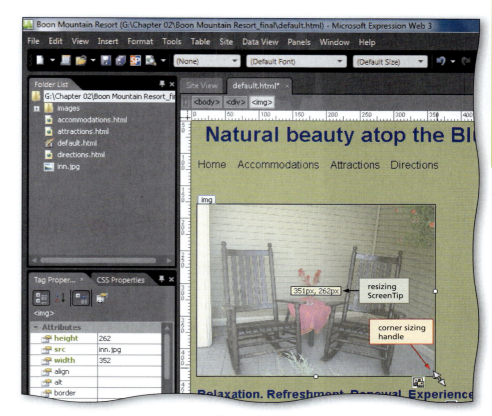

Figure 2–25

5

- Click the Picture Actions button below the resized image to open the menu. Point to Resample Picture To Match Size (Figure 2–26).

Figure 2–26

- Click the Resample Picture To Match Size option button to resample the image, then click outside the picture to deselect it (Figure 2–27).

Figure 2–27

- Press CTRL+S to save the page (Figure 2–28).

- Click the OK button in the Save Embedded Files dialog box to save the embedded file.

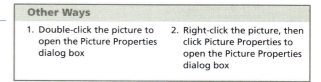

Figure 2–28

Other Ways
1. Double-click the picture to open the Picture Properties dialog box   2. Right-click the picture, then click Picture Properties to open the Picture Properties dialog box

Positioning an Image

Changing the alignment and spacing of text and images allows you to create a flow to your page that is visually interesting and guides the reader's eye down the page. You can choose to align to the left or right margin, or to the center of the page. When you align an image that is surrounded by text, you should position the image in relation to the text. When positioning text around an image, use the **text wrapping** feature to guide how the text flows around the image. This method is preferable to using the alignment buttons on the Common toolbar, which would adjust the image and text alignment at the same time.

To Align an Image

In the following steps, you will align the image to the right margin and wrap the text around it.

1

- Double-click the image to open the Picture Properties dialog box.

- Click the Appearance tab.

- Click the Right button in the Wrapping style section of the Appearance tab (Figure 2–29).

Figure 2–29

2

- Click the OK button to close the dialog box. Click anywhere outside of the image to deselect it.

- Press CTRL+S to save the page (Figure 2–30).

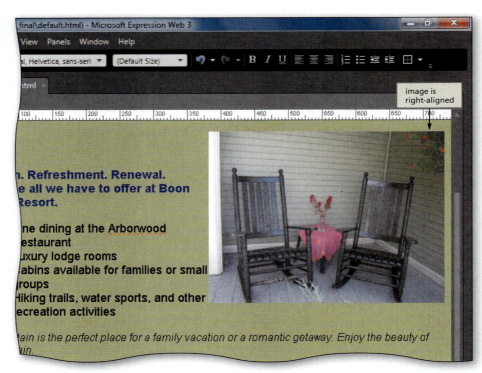

Figure 2–30

Adding Borders and Spacing

There are many different **borders** available from the Borders tab of the Borders and Shading dialog box that you can use to surround your image with lines, graphics, or effects. You can also create a custom border, or use the Borders button on the Common toolbar to add a basic border.

Image **margins** surround the top, bottom, left, and right edges of an image and separate it from adjacent text or images. Adding a margin to an image ensures that the image has sufficient spacing around it. Margins are measured in pixels.

To Add a Border to an Image

A border around an image can give it definition and distinction. As you click an option in the Style list of the Borders and Shading dialog box, the Preview pane of the dialog box changes to show you what the border will look like. The following steps add the double border style to the image.

1

- Click the image to select it.

- Click Format on the menu bar to open the Format menu, then point to Borders and Shading (Figure 2–31).

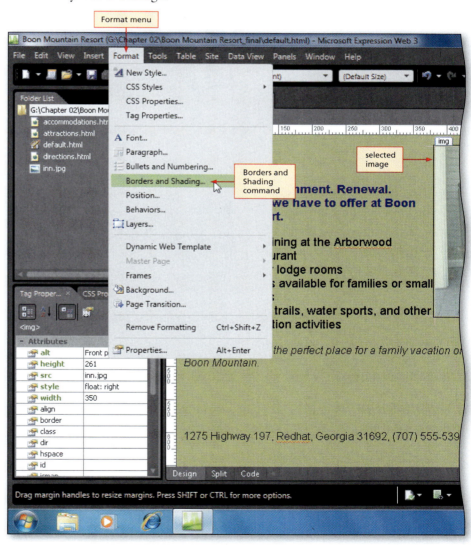

Figure 2–31

2

- Click Borders and Shading on the Format menu to open the Borders and Shading dialog box.

- Click double in the Style list to select it (Figure 2–32).

🔍 **Experiment**

- Click other options in the Style list to view them in the Preview box, then click double to select it.

Figure 2–32

3

- Click the OK button to close the dialog box and apply the border.

Q&A How can I reverse a change to the page?

To undo the last change you have made to a page, press CTRL+Z or click the Undo button on the Common toolbar. Repeat this step to undo multiple changes that have occurred since your last save. After you save a page, you cannot undo the changes.

- Click outside the image to deselect it (Figure 2–33).

- Press CTRL+S to save the page.

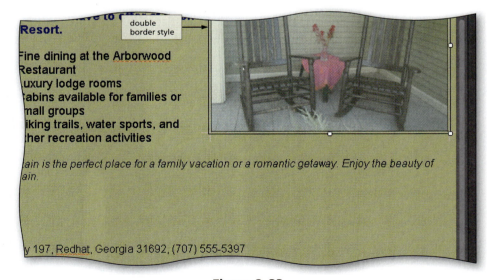

Figure 2–33

Other Ways

1. Select the image, click the Borders button arrow on the Common toolbar, then click an option from the gallery to apply it

To Modify Image Margins

Adding a margin to an image increases the space between the image and the surrounding text and helps the image to stand out. The following steps manually adjust the left and bottom image margins of the image using ScreenTips to determine the size of the margin.

- Click the image to select it.

- Position the pointer over the left margin so that the double-headed arrow appears. The margin ScreenTip will appear, which should be margin-left: (0 px).

- Hold down the left mouse button and drag the left margin border to the left until the ScreenTip shows that it is 25 pixels (Figure 2–34).

Figure 2–34

- Release the mouse button to set the left margin. Using the double-headed arrow pointer, click and drag the bottom margin border down until the ScreenTip shows that it is 20 pixels (Figure 2–35), then release the mouse button.

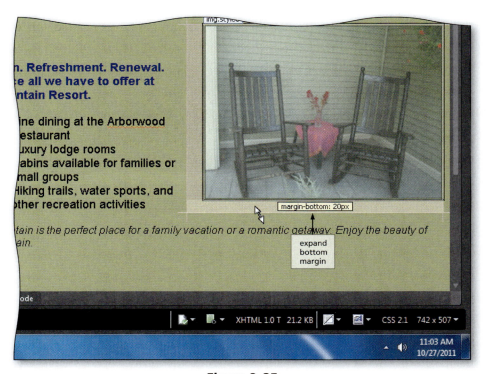

Figure 2–35

3

- Release the mouse button to view the expanded margin.

- Click outside of the image to deselect it (Figure 2–36).

- Press CTRL+S to save the page.

Q&A

Why did my picture resize when I dragged the margin border?

Make sure that you position the pointer over the edge of an image, but not on one of its sizing handles.

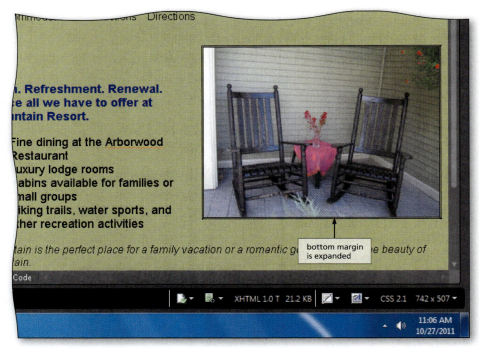

Figure 2–36

BTW

Adjust File Sizes
To adjust the file size or file type of an image, you need to use a graphic design program, such as Expression Design.

Enhancing an Image

Enhancing, or improving, an image can be as simple as removing unnecessary parts by cropping, or it can be more involved, such as subtly changing the brightness of an image. You can use a photo editing program to perform complex image editing and manipulation, but Expression Web provides a comprehensive range of image editing tools on the Pictures toolbar. Table 2–3 lists common image formatting options available, along with other tools, on the Pictures toolbar (Figure 2–37).

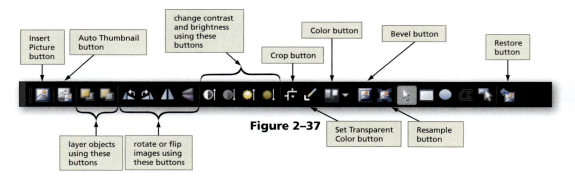

Figure 2–37

Table 2–3 Image Enhancement Options

Enhancement	Effect
Layering	Stacks images on top of each other, specifying the order in which the images appear
Rotating or Flipping	Rotates an image 90 degrees to the left (counterclockwise) or right (clockwise), or flips the image horizontally or vertically
Adjusting Contrast	Changes the contrast between the dark and light colors in your image
Changing Brightness	Increases the brightness of the colors or decreases the brightness to make them duller and more subtle
Cropping	Removes unnecessary or unwanted parts of a picture
Beveling	Adds a bevel, using shadows, so that the edges of an image appear to form a three-dimensional frame, similar to a window pane or mirror
Adjusting Color	Changes an image to grayscale (black and white) or to color washout (fade)
Resampling	Changes the file size by increasing or decreasing the depth of pixel concentration after resizing an image
Creating Transparency	Makes a certain color in an image transparent so that the background can be seen; good for images that have rounded edges and a square background; not possible for JPEG files

Plan Ahead

Identify changes to make to the images.
Making changes to images can increase their relevance, appearance, and usability.

1. **Relevance.** Ensure that the image conveys the correct information. Cropping unnecessary portions helps the visitor focus on the relevant points of the picture and can increase the white space or allow you to increase the image size.

2. **Appearance.** Applying formatting can make the image stand out from the rest of the page.

3. **Usability.** Creating thumbnails that you can use in an image gallery can help compress the image into a format that will download more quickly for the visitor.

To Add Transparency to an Image

An image that has rounded corners, like a logo, may appear with a white background when the image is inserted into a page. To make the logo rounded, you can add transparency to the image background, which removes the image background and makes the page background visible. The following steps replace the resort name in the masthead with a logo. Logos do not typically need very descriptive alternate text. You will add transparency to the logo and resize it.

- At the top of the page, select the words, Boon Mountain Resort.

- Click Insert on the menu bar to open the Insert menu.

- Point to Picture, then point to From File (Figure 2–38).

Figure 2–38

2

- Click From File to open the Picture dialog box. Navigate to the folder that contains your data files then open the folder Boon Mountain Resort_images if necessary.

- Click the innlogo file (Figure 2–39).

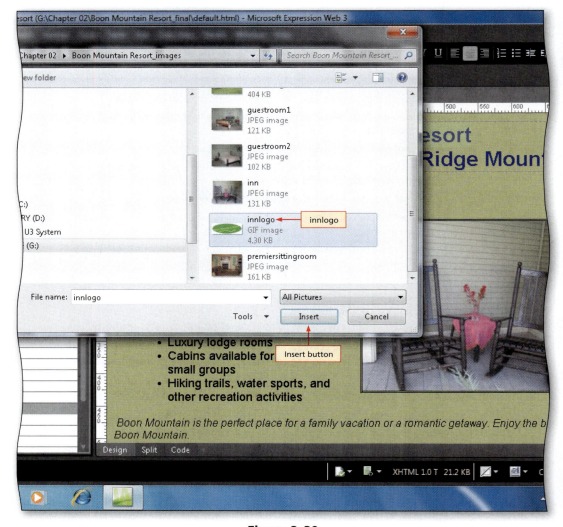

Figure 2–39

3

- Click the Insert button to close the Picture dialog box and open the Accessibility Properties dialog box.

- Type Boon Mountain Resort logo in the Alternate text text box, then click the OK button to close the dialog box (Figure 2–40).

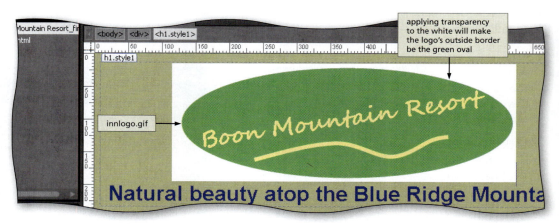

Figure 2–40

4

- Double-click the logo to open the Picture Properties dialog box.
- Click the Appearance tab.
- Change the width to 400 pixels (Figure 2–41).

Figure 2–41

5

- Click the OK button to resize the logo.
- Click the Picture Actions button below the resized image and then point to Resample Picture To Match Size (Figure 2–42).

Figure 2–42

6

- Click the Resample Picture To Match Size option button to resample the logo.

- Right-click a blank area of the Common toolbar to display the Toolbar menu and then point to Pictures (Figure 2–43).

Q&A What if my Pictures toolbar was already displayed?

Opening and closing a toolbar is a toggle command. If your Pictures toolbar was already displayed, either skip the second bullet of Step 6 or repeat it to redisplay the toolbar.

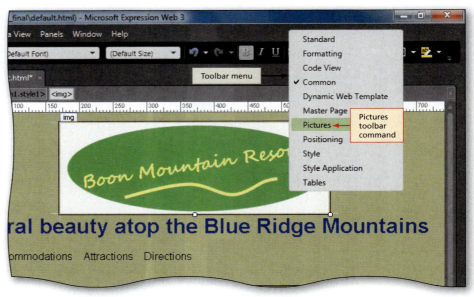

Figure 2–43

7

- Click Pictures to open the Pictures toolbar.

- Click the Set Transparent Color button on the Pictures toolbar (Figure 2–44).

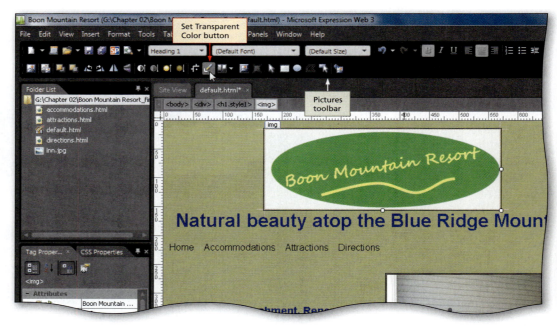

Figure 2–44

8

- Using the transparency pointer, click the white logo background to remove it.

- Click anywhere in the editing window to deselect the image (Figure 2–45).

Q&A

Why is my Pictures toolbar in the middle of the screen?

Dock the toolbar to get it out of the way by dragging it beneath the Common toolbar until it docks.

Figure 2–45

The Clipboard

Instead of recreating an element, such as a navigation bar, on each page, you can copy the element to the Clipboard and paste it in other locations. The **Clipboard** temporarily stores text or page elements so that you can move or copy them to other pages or locations.

To Copy an Image to Other Pages

When creating a Web site, you should repeat certain elements throughout the site to help reinforce the site's message. The following steps copy the modified logo on the default.html page to the Clipboard, and paste it onto the Accommodations, Attractions, and Directions pages in the Boon Mountain Resort site.

1

- Click the logo to select it.

- Click Edit on the menu bar to open the Edit menu and then point to Copy (Figure 2–46).

- Click Copy to copy the logo to the Clipboard.

Figure 2–46

• Double-click the accommodations. html page in the Folder List to open it (Figure 2–47).

Figure 2–47

❸

• Select the words, Boon Mountain Resort, on the Accommodations page.

• Click Edit on the menu bar to open the Edit menu and then point to Paste (Figure 2–48).

• Click Paste to insert the logo on the Accommodations page.

Figure 2–48

- Repeat Steps 2 and 3 to insert the logo on the Attractions and Directions pages (Figure 2–49).

logo is copied and pasted onto directions page

Figure 2–49

❺

- Click File on the menu bar to open the File menu (Figure 2–50).

File menu

Save All command will save changes to all edited pages

Figure 2–50

❻

- Click Save All to save the changes you made to all the pages in the site (Figure 2–51).

- Click the OK button to save the embedded image if necessary.

logo with transparency applied will be embedded into the site

OK button

Figure 2–51

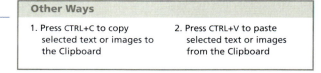

Other Ways

1. Press CTRL+C to copy selected text or images to the Clipboard

2. Press CTRL+V to paste selected text or images from the Clipboard

To Crop an Image

Digital images can be **cropped**, or trimmed, to show only the relevant portions. Cropping an image is done manually to specify exactly what parts of the image you want to crop. When you are cropping an image, a box with sizing handles indicates the area that will remain after you crop. You can adjust the cropped area by dragging the cropping handles until you are satisfied. The following steps insert an image on the Accommodations page and crop it.

- Click the accommodations.html tab to make it the active Web page.
- Click between the masthead and Accommodations to place the insertion point (Figure 2–52).

Figure 2–52

- Click Insert on the menu bar to open the Insert menu, point to HTML to open the HTML submenu, and then point to <div> (Figure 2–53).

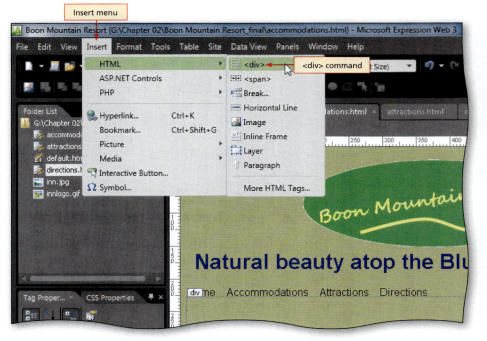

Figure 2–53

3

- Click <div> to insert a new div for the image.

- Click in the new div, if necessary, to place the insertion point (Figure 2–54).

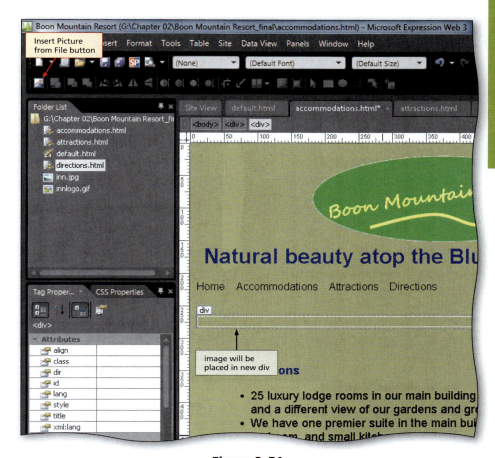

Figure 2–54

4

- Click the Insert Picture from File button on the Pictures toolbar to open the Picture dialog box.

- Click the guestroom1 JPEG image to select it (Figure 2–55).

Figure 2–55

5

- Click the Insert button to open the Accessibility Properties dialog box.

- In the Alternate text text box within the Accessibility Properties dialog box, type Guest room decorated with quilts and artwork (Figure 2–56).

Figure 2–56

6

- Click the OK button to close the Accessibility Properties dialog box and insert the picture (Figure 2–57).

Figure 2–57

7

- Click the image to select it.

- Click the Crop button on the Pictures toolbar to display the cropping area.

- Using the double-headed arrow pointer, drag the cropping handles to adjust the cropping area so that it appears similar to Figure 2–58.

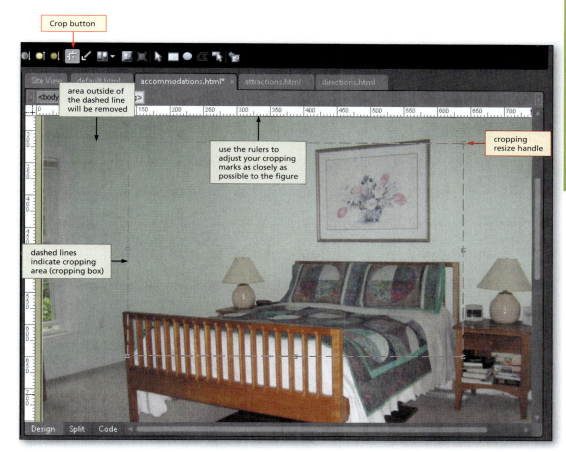

Crop button

area outside of the dashed line will be removed

use the rulers to adjust your cropping marks as closely as possible to the figure

cropping resize handle

dashed lines indicate cropping area (cropping box)

Figure 2–58

8

- Click the Crop button to accept the cropping changes you have made (Figure 2–59).

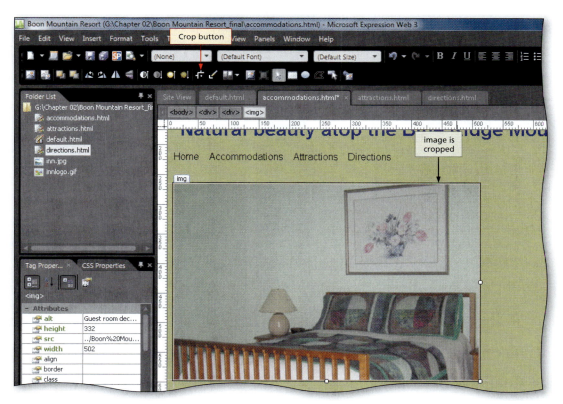

Crop button

image is cropped

Figure 2–59

9

• Click the Center button on the Common toolbar to center the image between the Web page margins (Figure 2–60).

Figure 2–60

10

• Double-click the image to open the Picture Properties dialog box.

• Click the Appearance tab.

• Type 350 in the Width text box (Figure 2–61).

Q&A

Why does the height of my resized image differ?

Depending on the exact cropping you did in Step 6, your image height may differ slightly. This is OK.

Figure 2–61

- Click the OK button to resize the guest room image.

- Click the Picture Actions button below the resized image, and then point to Resample Picture To Match Size (Figure 2–62).

Figure 2–62

⑫

- Click the Resample Picture To Match Size option button to resample the image.

- Press CTRL+S to save the page (Figure 2–63).

- Click the OK button to save the embedded image.

Figure 2–63

Controlling Image Files

Web sites need to be convenient for visitors to use; otherwise, the users will move on to other sites. Including too many large image files in a Web page can make a page slow to download into a visitor's browser, leading to frustration. Recall that the file size in bytes is the determining factor; the visual size of the image on the page does not affect its download speed.

Thumbnail Images

A **thumbnail** version of an image file is a small rendition that serves as a preview of the large version. Thumbnails also have smaller file sizes, which reduces download time. If the visitor clicks the thumbnail image, the larger version opens in its own window.

Thumbnail images are useful when displaying multiple pictures, such as in a product catalog.

BTW

Internet Connection Speed
Depending on a user's Internet connection, the speed at which a site's contents download into his or her browser can vary. You should test your sites using multiple connection types, including high-speed connections such as a digital subscriber line (DSL) or cable, and slower connections such as a dial-up modem.

To Create a Thumbnail

Resizing the image or displaying a thumbnail, a smaller version of an image, frees up room on the Web page. When you use Expression Web to create an automatic thumbnail, Expression Web does three things: changes the image on the page to a smaller version; saves the new version with the filename *imagename*_small.jpg (where *image-name* is the original image's filename); and creates a new window in which the larger version of the thumbnail opens when the user clicks it. The following steps create a gallery of images for different guest rooms and resort areas.

- Click the accommodations.html page tab to make it the active Web page, if necessary.

- Scroll if necessary, then position the insertion point at the end of the last line item in the bulleted list.

- Press ENTER twice to create a new paragraph tag, into which you will insert a gallery of thumbnails (Figure 2–64).

Figure 2–64

- Click the Insert Picture from File button on the Pictures toolbar to open the Picture dialog box.

- Click the guestroom2 image (Figure 2–65).

Figure 2–65

3

- Click the Insert button to open the Accessibility Properties dialog box.

- In the Alternate text text box within the Accessibility Properties dialog box, type Guest room with antique doll collection (Figure 2–66).

Figure 2–66

 4

- Click the OK button to close the dialog box.

- In the editing window, click the image to select it.

- Click the Auto Thumbnail button on the Pictures toolbar to create a thumbnail (Figure 2–67).

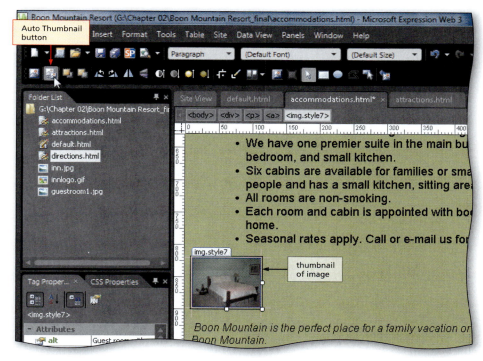

Figure 2–67

5

- Click to the right of the image to deselect it, then press TAB to insert space before the next thumbnail (Figure 2–68).

Figure 2–68

6

- Click the Insert Picture from File button on the Common toolbar to open the Picture dialog box.

- If necessary, drag the scroll box down, then click the premier-sittingroom image (Figure 2–69).

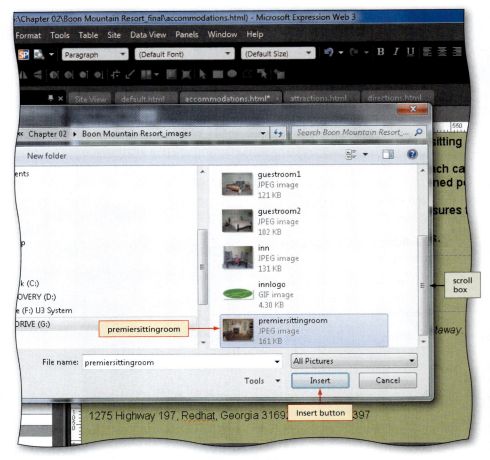

Figure 2–69

7

- Click the Insert button to close the Picture dialog box.

- In the Alternate text text box within the Accessibility Properties dialog box, type Cozy sitting area in premier suite (Figure 2–70).

Figure 2–70

8

- Click the OK button to close the dialog box.

- Click the image in the editing window to select it, then click the Auto Thumbnail button on the Pictures toolbar to create a thumbnail (Figure 2–71).

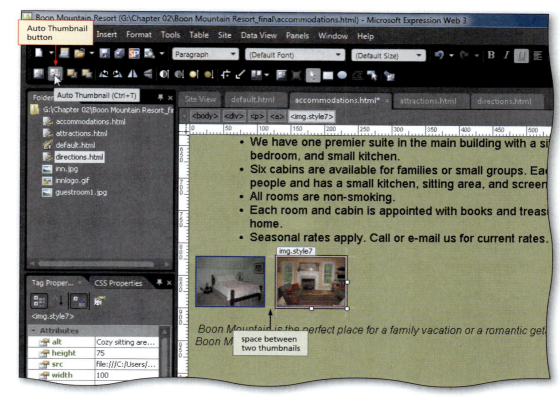

Figure 2–71

9

- Following the instructions in Steps 5–8, create thumbnails for the garden image with the alternate text Lush perennial bed, for the cabinporch image with the alternate text Each cabin has a screened porch, and for the cabinroom image with the alternate text Cabin bedroom with bookshelves (Figure 2–72).

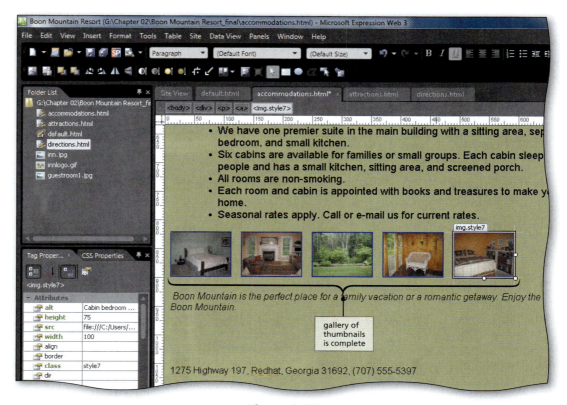

Figure 2–72

10
- Press CTRL+S to save the page (Figure 2–73).

- Click the OK button to save the embedded files.

all inserted and thumbnail images are embedded

Figure 2–73

Other Ways

1. Press CTRL+T to convert a selected image into a thumbnail

To Create a Folder for Images

To keep your site organized and help make updates easier, you should store all media files, including images and video, in a common folder. When you move an image using the Folder List, Expression Web automatically adjusts any coded references to the image file location so that the image can be found and placed appropriately on the page when viewed in a browser. You can create a separate folder for each page that includes the page and any assets, or for a smaller site, you can create one folder for all of the images. The following steps create a folder for storing files and move multiple images into it.

1
- Click anywhere in the Folder List to activate it.

- Click File on the menu bar, point to New, then point to Folder (Figure 2–74).

Figure 2–74

2

• Click Folder to create a new folder in the Folder List (Figure 2–75).

Figure 2–75

3

• Type images, then press ENTER to name the folder (Figure 2–76).

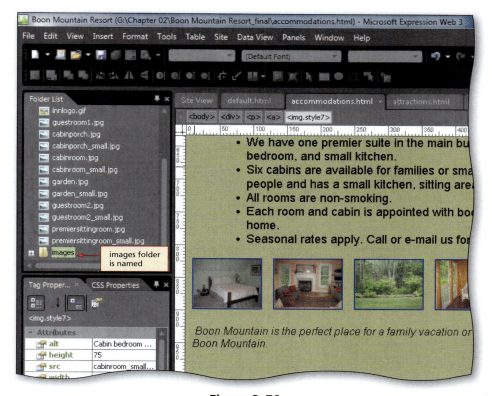

Figure 2–76

4

- Click the Site View tab to display the site contents in the editing window (Figure 2–77).

Q&A Why can't I see the full file names on my screen?

The column needs to be widened to see the full file names. Move the pointer between the Name and Size column headers, and then double-click when the pointer becomes a two-headed arrow.

Figure 2–77

5

- Click the Type column header to sort the files and folders by type (Figure 2–78).

- Click the innlogo.gif image filename to select it.

Figure 2–78

6

- Drag innlogo.gif to the images folder in the Folder List (Figure 2–79).

Figure 2–79

7

- Click the first JPG image, press and hold SHIFT, then click the last JPG image to select all of the image files (Figure 2–80).

Figure 2–80

8

- Drag the selected images to the images folder in the Folder List (Figure 2–81).

Q&A

Why does a dialog box open and close while the images are being moved?

The Rename dialog box opens while the image files are being moved, then closes after. It lets you know that the file path for all of the files you are moving is being automatically renamed and all links to the files are being updated automatically.

Figure 2–81

Adding Navigational Links to a Site

BTW

Browser Bookmarks
Expression Web calls links within a page bookmarks, but you should not confuse them with bookmarks used by browsers, which save a page to a Favorites list.

BTW

Search Boxes
Many large sites include search boxes in addition to navigation bars. Search boxes are forms that allow a visitor to enter keywords and find information within the site that matches the search criteria.

The advantage of looking for information on the Web is that you can easily jump to related information with a simple mouse click. Using hyperlinked text and images, visitors to a site can view the information that is relevant to their experience, interests, and needs. Within your site, you can use internal links called **bookmarks** to let visitors move around within long pages. A bookmark is a page anchor that is attached to a specific portion of the page.

Every page in a site should have a navigation bar that appears in the same location on the page. The navigation bar usually appears vertically on the left side of the page or horizontally under the masthead. The navigation bar for a small site is a group of links to every main page. In a larger site, the navigation bar contains links for each information topic in the site, which take you to a page that gives you more information and allows you to drill down further to reach the information you want.

External links point the visitor's browser to a site that is outside of your own Web site, but that could be useful or interesting for your site's visitors. In addition to browsing related sites of interest, you can use links to open and download files. E-mail links allow users to write and send an e-mail to the site's management or other recipients using the visitor's e-mail editing program. E-mail links are called **mailto links**.

Plan Ahead

Determine the necessary internal and external links.
Web site visitors should easily be able to find the information they seek, whether they are navigating within your site or getting information from other sources.

- Add internal links to create a navigation bar and include the navigation bar in the same place on every page.

- Add external links to sites that might be useful for your visitors.

- When a page is too long to be viewed on the screen without scrolling, consider adding bookmarks so visitors can jump to locations on the same page.

- If appropriate, include e-mail links for your visitors.

To Add an Internal Link

The following steps create the links in the navigation bar to each of the pages in the site.

1

- Click the default.html page tab to make it the active Web page.

- Select the word, Home, in the navigation bar (Figure 2–82).

Figure 2–82

2

- Click Insert on the menu bar to open the Insert menu and then point to Hyperlink (Figure 2–83).

Figure 2–83

- Click Hyperlink to open the Insert Hyperlink dialog box, then click the Existing File or Web Page button if necessary.

- Click the default page in the list to select it as the hyperlink target (Figure 2–84).

Q&A

Why are there two versions of some files, as shown in the Insert Hyperlink dialog box in Figure 2–84?

If a file is open, there may be an option to link to the open or the saved file. Click either to create a link to the page.

Figure 2–84

- Click the OK button to close the Insert Hyperlink dialog box and format the word, Home, as a hyperlink, then click to the right of the new hyperlink to deselect it (Figure 2–85).

Q&A

Why doesn't the link work when I click on it in the editing window?

To test a link in the editing window, press CTRL, then click the link.

Figure 2–85

5

- Select the word, Accommodations, in the navigation bar.

- Press CTRL+K to open the Insert Hyperlink dialog box.

- Click the accommodations.html (open) page in the list to select it as the hyperlink target (Figure 2–86).

Figure 2–86

6

- Click the OK button to close the Insert Hyperlink dialog box and display the new hyperlink, then click to the right of the hyperlink to deselect it (Figure 2–87).

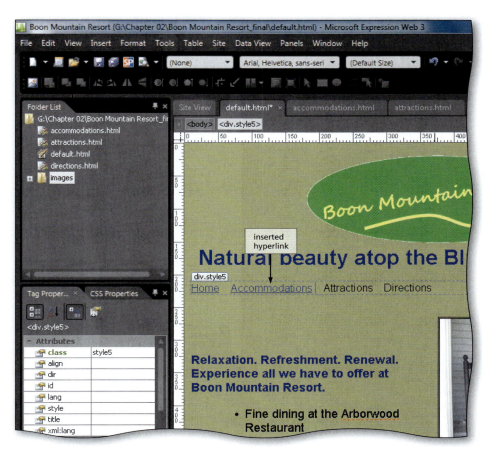

Figure 2–87

7

- Following the instructions in Steps 5 and 6, create a hyperlink from the word, Attractions, in the navigation bar, to the attractions. html page.

- Following the instructions in Steps 5 and 6, create a hyperlink from the word, Directions, in the navigation bar, to the directions.html page, then click to the right of the Directions hyperlink to deselect it (Figure 2–88).

Figure 2–88

8

- On the Quick Tag Selector, click the navigation bar div tag, <div.style5>, to select the div (Figure 2–89).

Q&A

Why does my div name differ?

Div names change based on the actions and order of completion. Your div names might differ slightly.

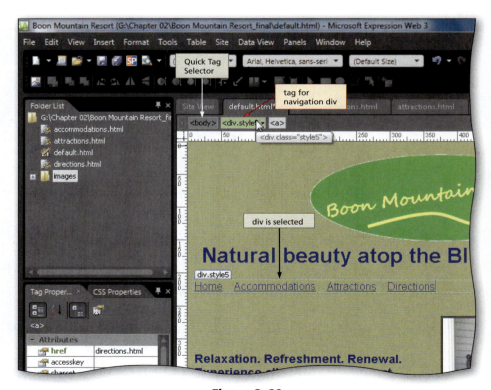

Figure 2–89

9

- Click the Center button on the Common toolbar to center the navigation bar (Figure 2–90).

- Press CTRL+S to save the default.html page.

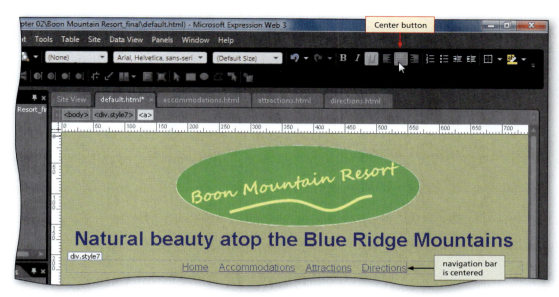

Figure 2–90

To Test Internal Links

The following steps open the page in a browser window and test the links in the navigation bar. Once you have confirmed that the links work, you can copy the navigation bar to the other pages in the site.

1

- Point to the Preview in Windows Internet Explorer 8 button (Figure 2–91).

Q&A

My button has a different name.

Depending on your default browser or past use, your button name may have a different browser name or version. Click the button to open in your default browser, or click the button arrow to see a list of browser choices.

Figure 2–91

- Click the Preview in browser button to display the page in the browser (Figure 2–92).

Figure 2–92

- Click the Accommodations link in the navigation bar to open the Accommodations page (Figure 2–93).

Q&A Why is my browser window not maximized?

Click the Maximize button in the upper-right corner of the browser window to maximize it.

- Click the browser Back button to return to the default page.

Figure 2–93

- Test the remaining two links; click the Attractions link, click the Back button, and then click the Directions link (Figure 2–94).

- Click the Close button to close the browser window to return to Expression Web.

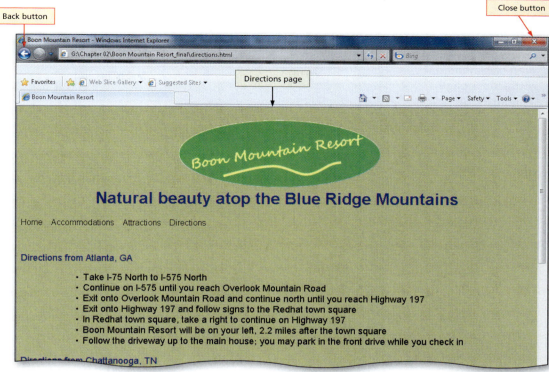

Figure 2–94

To Copy and Paste Internal Links

After you have verified that the navigation bar links work, you will add it to each page in the site in the same location. For layout purposes, a placeholder navigation bar appears on each page, listing the pages but without any links. The following steps replace the placeholder navigation bar on the Accommodations, Attractions, and Directions pages.

- Select the navigation div, if necessary.

- Press CTRL+C to copy the entire navigation div to the Clipboard.

- Click the attractions.html tab to make it the active Web page.

- Click the placeholder navigation bar, and then click the div.style5 tab to select the div (Figure 2–95).

Figure 2–95

2

- Press CTRL+V to insert the navigation bar on the Attractions page (Figure 2–96).

Q&A Why isn't my navigation bar centered?

If the pasted navigation bar isn't centered, select the div, then click the Center button on the Common toolbar.

Figure 2–96

 3

- Follow Steps 1 and 2 to insert the navigation bar below the masthead on the Accommodations and Directions pages (Figure 2–97).

Q&A When I paste the navigation bar onto the accommodations.html page, the formatting does not match the page.

When copying and pasting formatting between pages, errors can occur if the page already includes a style with the same name as the one being pasted. If this occurs, reapply the formatting to the pasted text, for example, change the font family and size.

Figure 2–97

4
- Click File on the menu bar to open the File menu, and then point to Save All (Figure 2–98).
- Click Save All to save all open pages at once.

Figure 2–98

To Add an External Link

Adding external links allows you to include access to resources whose sites and content you do not control. Such links can help visitors to your site gain information that might enhance their experience on your site or with your organization or in a tab within the browser window. The following steps insert links to attractions near the Boon Mountain Resort.

 1
- Click the attractions.html tab to display the Attractions page.
- Select the text in the first bulleted list item.
- Click Insert on the menu bar to open the Insert menu, and then point to Hyperlink (Figure 2–99).

Figure 2–99

2

- Click Hyperlink to open the Insert Hyperlink dialog box.

- In the Address text box, type `http://www.gastateparks.org/info/littlewhite` to create a link to a page in the Georgia State Parks Web site (Figure 2–100).

Figure 2–100

3

- Click the OK button to close the Insert Hyperlink dialog box (Figure 2–101).

Figure 2–101

4

- Select the text in the second bulleted list item (Figure 2–102).

Figure 2–102

5

• Press CTRL+K to open the Insert Hyperlink dialog box.

• In the Address text box, type `http://www.gastateparks.org/info/crookriv` to create a second external link (Figure 2–103).

Figure 2–103

6

• Click the OK button to close the Insert Hyperlink dialog box, then click to the right of the hyperlink to deselect it (Figure 2–104).

Q&A Why can't I add a link to the text I selected?

Make sure that you have not selected a page element, such as a line item or a div. Hyperlinks can only be added to text and images.

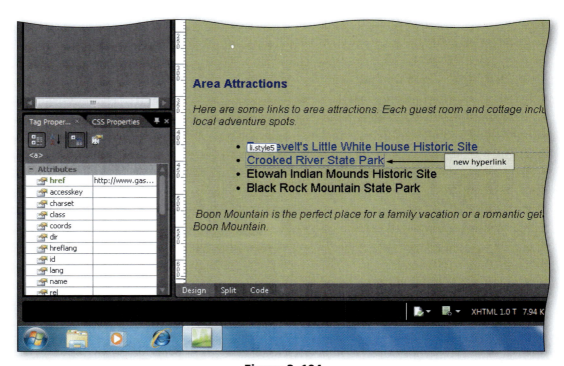

Figure 2–104

7

- Repeat Steps 4–6 to create a link from the third bullet to `http://www.gastateparks.org/info/etowah`.

- Repeat Steps 4–6 to create a link from the fourth bullet to `http://www.gastateparks.org/info/blackrock` (Figure 2–105).

- Press CTRL+S to save the page.

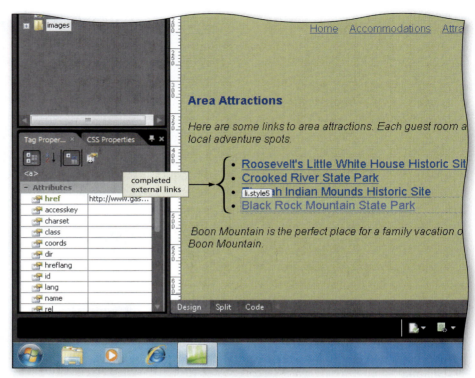

Figure 2–105

To Test External Links

The following steps open the page in a browser window, and test the links in the navigation bar.

1

- Press F12 to display the Attractions page in the browser.

- Click the first bullet link in the list to open the Little White House Web page (Figure 2–106).

Q&A

Why did a new browser window or tab open when I clicked the link?

Depending on your browser and security settings, a new window or tab may open when you click an external link from a Web page saved on your computer.

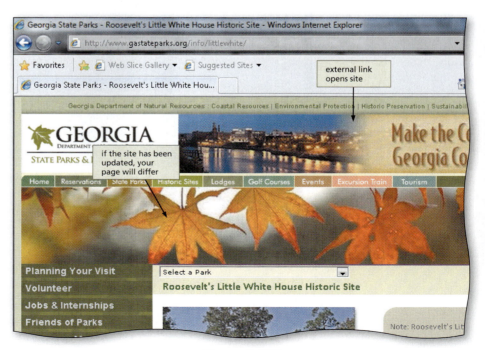

Figure 2–106

2

- Click the Back button or click the Close button if your browser opened the page in a new window. Then click the second bullet link to test it, click the Back button, and repeat for the third and fourth bullet links (Figure 2–107).

Figure 2–107

3

- Click the Close button on the browser window.
- Click the 'Close all tabs' button, if necessary, to close the Internet Explorer dialog box (Figure 2–108).
- Click the Close button on any other open browser windows to return to Expression Web, if necessary.

Figure 2–108

To Add a Bookmark

When creating a bookmark, first you assign the bookmark text or image to which you want to jump (the link's target or destination), then you can insert the bookmark hyperlink in the desired location on the page. The following steps add a bookmark link at the bottom of the Directions page that returns to the top of the page.

1

- Click the directions. html tab to make it the active Web page.

- Select the words, Natural beauty atop the Blue Ridge Mountains, below the logo.

- Click Insert on the menu bar to open the Insert menu, and then point to Bookmark (Figure 2–109).

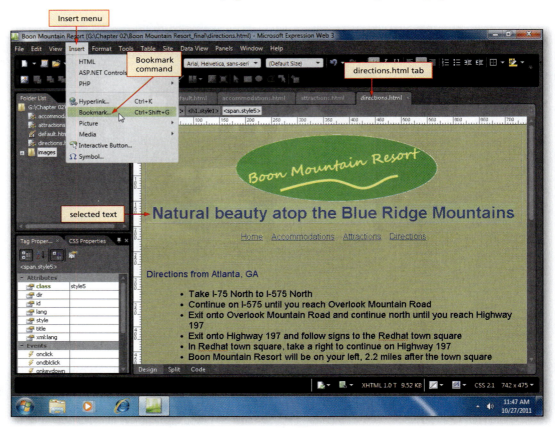

Figure 2–109

Other Ways

1. Press CTRL+G to open the Bookmark dialog box

2

- Click Bookmark to open the Bookmark dialog box.

- Type Top of Page in the Bookmark name text box to specify the wording that will appear as the link (Figure 2–110).

Figure 2–110

3

- Click the OK button to close the Bookmark dialog box (Figure 2–111).

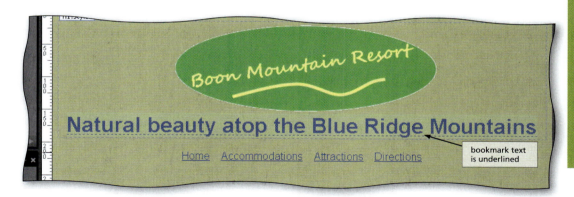

Figure 2–111

4

- Scroll to the bottom of the page and then click at the end of the last bullet list item (below Directions from Redhat County Airport), then press ENTER twice to create a new paragraph tag (Figure 2–112).

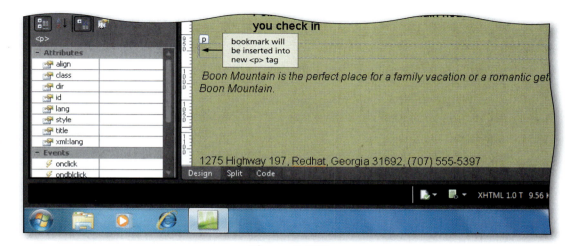

Figure 2–112

5

- Press CTRL+K to open the Insert Hyperlink dialog box.

- Click the Place in This Document button to display the list of bookmarks.

- Click Top of Page to select it as the target bookmark (Figure 2–113).

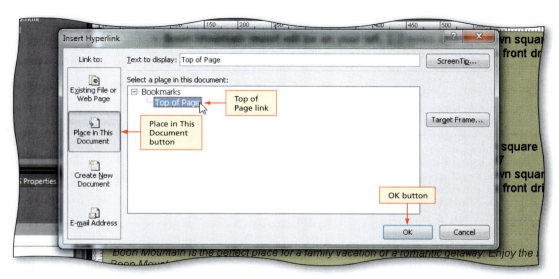

Figure 2–113

6
- Click the OK button to close the dialog box and insert the bookmark link (Figure 2–114).

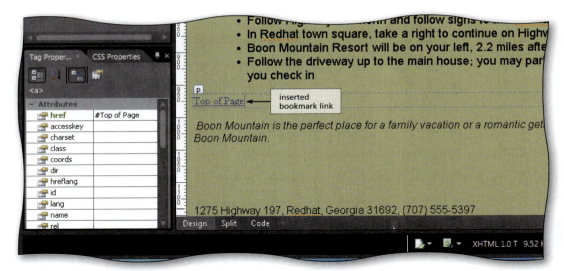

Figure 2–114

7
- Press CTRL, then click the Top of Page link to test the bookmark link (Figure 2–115).

- Click the Save button on the Common toolbar to save the page.

Figure 2–115

BTW

Forms vs. E-Mail Links
There are programs that search the Web collecting e-mail addresses to use in mass e-mailings. Some sites avoid including e-mail links and instead use forms to collect user feedback and requests for this reason.

To Add an E-Mail Link

An e-mail link opens a new, blank e-mail window using the visitor's e-mail program. In the following steps, you will add an e-mail link to your e-mail address for requests for room rates.

1

- Click the accommodations.html page tab so it is the active Web page tab in the editing window.

- In the last bullet item, select the word, e-mail, to make it a hyperlink.

- Press CTRL+K to open the Insert Hyperlink dialog box.

- Click the E-mail Address button.

- In the E-mail address text box, type `mailto:` followed by your e-mail address.

- In the Subject text box, type `Rooms and Rates` (Figure 2–116).

Q&A

Why is there no e-mail address in my 'Recently used e-mail addresses' text box?

The text box is empty because you are using a fresh install of Expression Web 3. Therefore, there have been no previously used e-mail addresses.

Figure 2–116

2

- Click the OK button to close the Insert Hyperlink dialog box and create the mailto link (Figure 2–117).

- Press CTRL+S to save the page.

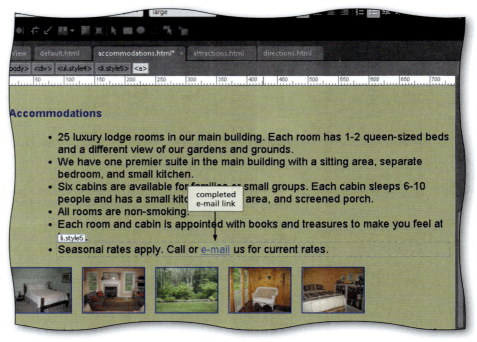

Figure 2–117

❸

- Press F12 to display the page in the browser.

- Scroll down and click the e-mail link to test it.

- If an Internet Explorer Security dialog box appears, click the Allow button.

- The Outlook e-mail window may appear (Figure 2–118).

- Close the e-mail window without saving changes if it opens.

- Close the browser window to return to Expression Web.

<table>
<tr><td>**Q&A**</td><td>Why do I get an error message when I click the e-mail link?</td></tr>
<tr><td></td><td>Your e-mail program or browser might not be configured to process mailto links.</td></tr>
</table>

Figure 2–118

🔍 **Experiment**

- If an e-mail window opens, click the Send button to send the e-mail to yourself.

To Add a ScreenTip

A **ScreenTip** is a window containing descriptive text that appears when you position the pointer over a button or link. Adding a ScreenTip to the e-mail address lets users know that they can contact you with any questions. The following steps add a ScreenTip to the mailto link.

❶

- Select the e-mail link.

- Press CTRL+K to open the Edit Hyperlink dialog box (Figure 2–119).

Figure 2–119

❷

- Click the ScreenTip button to open the Set Hyperlink ScreenTip dialog box.

- In the ScreenTip text text box, type Contact us by e-mail with any questions (Figure 2–120).

Figure 2–120

3

- Click the OK button to close the Set Hyperlink ScreenTip dialog box (Figure 2–121).

- Click the OK button to close the Edit Hyperlink dialog box.

- Press CTRL+S to save the page.

Figure 2–121

To Preview the Site

In the following steps, you will preview the site in your browser to view all of the pages and view and test the ScreenTip.

1

- Click the default. html tab to make it the active Web page.

- Press F12 to open the page in a browser (Figure 2–122).

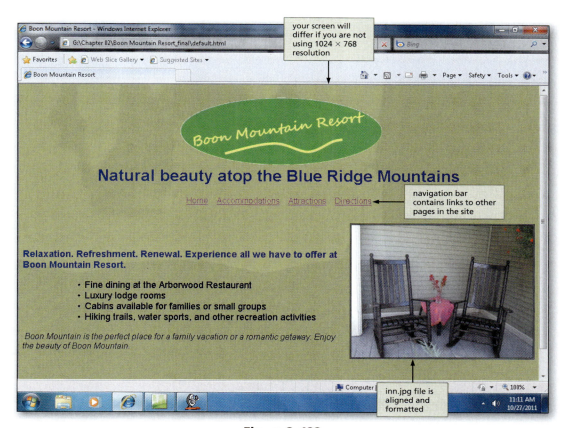

Figure 2–122

2

- Click the Accommodations link on the navigation bar.

- Position the pointer over the e-mail link to view the ScreenTip (Figure 2–123).

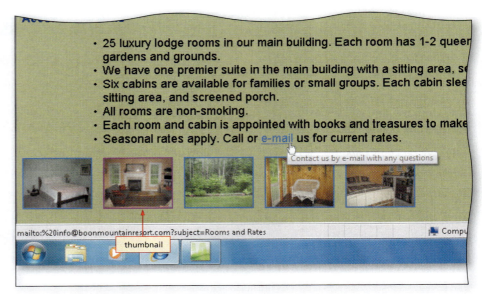

Figure 2–123

3

- Click the second thumbnail image to open the larger image (Figure 2–124).

- Click the Close button to close the browser window and return to Expression Web.

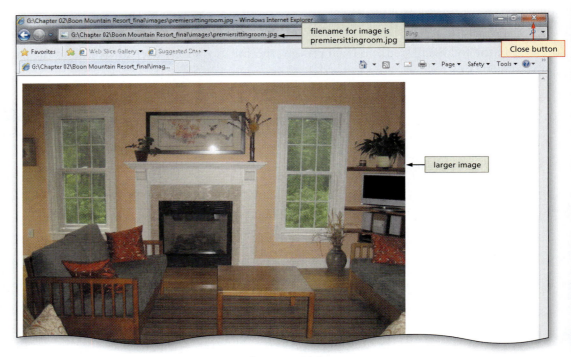

Figure 2–124

To Close a Site and Quit Expression Web

- Click Site on the menu bar, then click Close.

- Click File on the menu bar, then click Exit.

Chapter Summary

In this chapter, you have learned how to use images to enhance and add value to Web pages. You used Expression Web to insert, align, and format images. You learned that controlling image file size and organization is accomplished through the use of thumbnail images and folders. You have also learned to add different types of links, including internal, external, and mail links, to your site. The items listed below include all the new Expression Web skills you have learned in this chapter.

1. Open a Web Site (EW 77)
2. Insert an Image (EW 80)
3. Close a Panel (EW 85)
4. Display the Ruler (EW 87)
5. Resize an Image (EW 89)
6. Align an Image (EW 94)
7. Add a Border to an Image (EW 95)
8. Modify Image Margins (EW 97)
9. Add Transparency to an Image (EW 99)
10. Copy an Image to Other Pages (EW 103)
11. Crop an Image (EW 106)
12. Create a Thumbnail (EW 112)
13. Create a Folder for Images (EW 116)
14. Add an Internal Link (EW 121)
15. Test Internal Links (EW 125)
16. Copy and Paste Internal Links (EW 127)
17. Add an External Link (EW 129)
18. Test External Links (EW 132)
19. Add a Bookmark (EW 134)
20. Add an E-Mail Link (EW 137)
21. Add a ScreenTip (EW 138)
22. Preview the Site (EW 139)

For current SAM information, including versions and content details, visit SAM Central (http://samcentral.course.com). If you have a SAM user profile, you may have access to hands-on instruction, practice, and assessment of the skills covered in this chapter. Since various versions of SAM are supported throughout the life of this text, check with your instructor for the correct instructions and URL/Web site for accessing assignments.

Learn It Online

Test your knowledge of chapter content and key terms.

Instructions: To complete the Learn It Online exercises, start your browser, click the Address bar, and then enter the Web address scsite.com/ew3/learn. When the Expression Web Learn It Online page is displayed, click the link for the exercise you want to complete and then read the instructions.

Chapter Reinforcement TF, MC, and SA
A series of true/false, multiple choice, and short answer questions that test your knowledge of the chapter content.

Flash Cards
An interactive learning environment where you identify chapter key terms associated with displayed definitions.

Practice Test
A series of multiple choice questions that test your knowledge of chapter content and key terms.

Who Wants To Be a Computer Genius?
An interactive game that challenges your knowledge of chapter content in the style of a television quiz show.

Wheel of Terms
An interactive game that challenges your knowledge of chapter key terms in the style of the television show *Wheel of Fortune.*

Crossword Puzzle Challenge
A crossword puzzle that challenges your knowledge of key terms presented in the chapter.

Apply Your Knowledge

Reinforce the skills and apply the concepts you learned in this chapter.

Adding Images and Links

Instructions: Start Expression Web. Open the Web site, Apply 2-1 Photography, from the Data Files for Students. See the inside back cover of this book for instructions for downloading the Data Files for Students, or see your instructor for information about accessing the required files.

The Web site you open contains a home page with formatting and text. Open the default.html file and add and format an image, create thumbnails, and add an e-mail link with a ScreenTip so that the page looks like Figure 2–125.

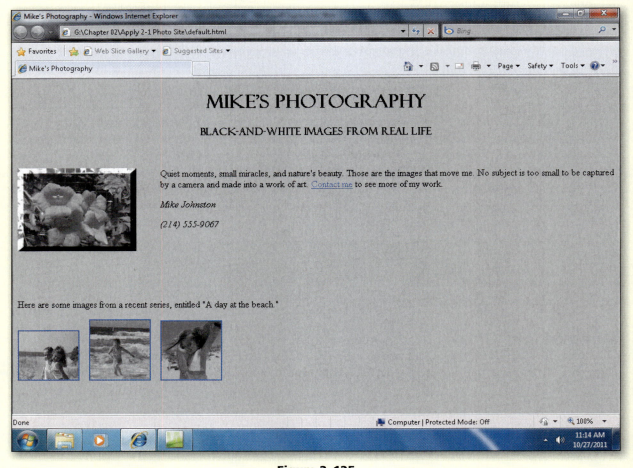

Figure 2–125

Perform the following tasks:

1. Open the default.html Web page.
2. Click before the words, Quiet moments.
3. Click the Insert Picture from File button on the Common toolbar.
4. Select the JPG image flowerphoto from the Apply 2-1 images folder, then click Insert.
5. Type `Lily on bush` in the Alternate text text box, then click OK.
6. Select the image, right-click the image, then click Picture Properties from the shortcut menu.

7. Click the Appearance tab, click the Left Wrapping style button, then click the OK button.

8. Press the SHIFT key and drag the lower-right sizing handle until the picture is resized to approximately 200 × 161 pixels.

9. Drag the right margin to resize the right margin to 40 pixels.

10. Drag the bottom margin to resize the bottom margin to 30 pixels.

11. Click the Bevel button on the Pictures toolbar to add a bevel to the image.

12. Save the default.html page, then click OK to save the embedded picture.

13. Click before the words, Here are some images, then press ENTER three times.

14. Click anywhere below the line that begins, Here are some images, then double-click the div tag in the Toolbox.

15. Insert the JPG image beachphoto1, then type `Two girls on a beach` in the Alternate text text box, and then click OK.

16. Select the image, then click the Auto Thumbnail button on the Pictures toolbar.

17. Click to the right of the image, then press TAB.

18. Insert the JPG image beachphoto2, type `Girl in surf` in the Alternate text text box, create a thumbnail, click next to the image, then press TAB.

19. Insert the JPG image beachphoto3, type `Girl with towel` in the Alternate text text box, then create a thumbnail.

20. Save the default.html page, then click OK to save the embedded pictures.

21. Select the words, Contact me.

22. On the Insert menu, click Hyperlink.

23. Click the E-mail Address button, then type your e-mail address in the E-mail address text box.

24. Click the ScreenTip button, type your e-mail address in the ScreenTip text text box, then click the OK button twice to close the open dialog boxes.

25. Save and then preview the site, and test the thumbnails and links.

26. Change the site properties, as specified by your instructor. Close the site.

27. In Windows Explorer, change the site folder's name to Apply 2-1 Photo Site. Submit the revised site in the format specified by your instructor.

Extend Your Knowledge

Extend the skills you learned in this chapter and experiment with new skills. You may need to use Help to complete the assignment.

Creating Links to Images and Bookmarks

Instructions: Start Expression Web. Open the Web site, Extend 2-1 Music Festival, from the Data Files for Students. See the inside back cover of this book for instructions for downloading the Data Files for Students, or see your instructor for information about accessing the required files.

You will enhance the Web page to match the one shown in Figure 2–126.

Continued >

Extend Your Knowledge *continued*

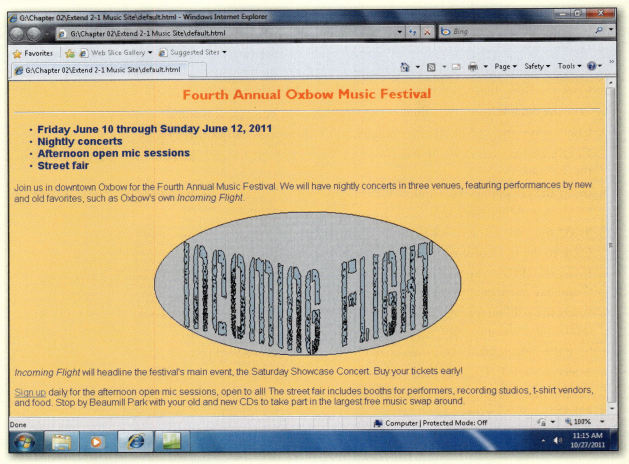

Figure 2–126

Perform the following tasks:

1. Use Help to learn about inserting a link to a file.
2. Open the default.html page, position the insertion point before the words, *Incoming Flight*, at the beginning of the second paragraph, then press ENTER.
3. Click above the words, *Incoming Flight*, to make the empty paragraph tag active. Insert the GIF image bandlogo from the folder Extend 2-1 images, and type `Incoming Flight band logo` as the Alternate text.
4. Center the image on the page.
5. Select the image, then open the Insert Hyperlink dialog box.
6. Click the Existing File or Web page button if necessary, type `http://www.incomingflight band.com` in the Address text box, then click the OK button. (*Note:* This Web page does not exist. You will get an error message when you test it.)
7. Select the words, Sign up, then open the Insert Hyperlink dialog box.
8. Click the Existing File or Web Page button if necessary, click signup_form, then click the OK button.
9. Save the default.html page and the embedded file, preview the page and test all links, then close the browser window.
10. Change the site properties, as specified by your instructor, and then close the site. In Windows Explorer, change the site folder's name to Extend 2-1 Music Site. Submit the revised site in the format specified by your instructor.

Make It Right

Analyze a site and correct all errors and/or improve the design.

Placing and Formatting Images

Instructions: Start Expression Web. Open the Web site, Make It Right 2-1 Swim Club, from the Data Files for Students. See the inside back cover of this book for instructions for downloading the Data Files for Students, or see your instructor for information about accessing the required files.

The site has one image that is large, is not aligned with the text, and has no formatting. In addition, there is no link to the second page of the Web site, which gives more information on swim lessons, and no way to contact the director by sending him an e-mail. Position the image to the right of the bulleted list, resize (approximately 300 pixels wide and maintain aspect ratio) and format it, add a link from the swim lesson text to the swim lesson page, add an e-mail link to the director's name (jeremiah. eggon@maconwaves.com), add a 5-pixel border to the image, and add two empty paragraphs before the footer, as shown in Figure 2–127.

Change the site properties, as specified by your instructor. In Windows Explorer, change the site folder's name to Make It Right 2-1 Swim Club Site. Submit the revised site in the format specified by your instructor.

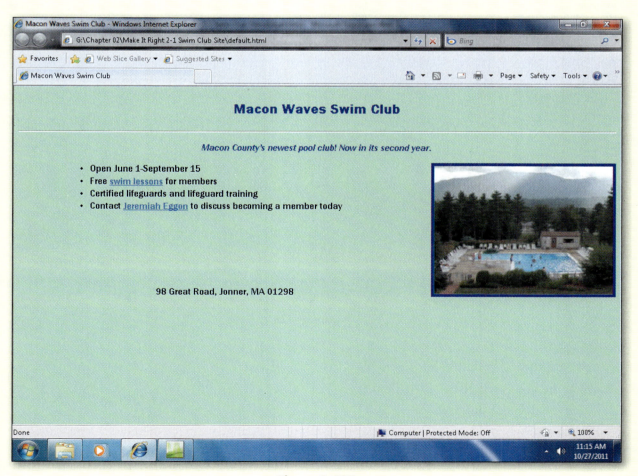

Figure 2–127

In the Lab

Design and/or format a Web site using the guidelines, concepts, and skills presented in this chapter. Labs are listed in order of increasing difficulty.

Lab 1: Creating a Navigation Bar and Inserting an Image

Problem: You work part-time at a small bike repair shop. Your boss has asked you to add images and create a navigation bar for the shop's Web site. Add images and links to the page shown in Figure 2–128.

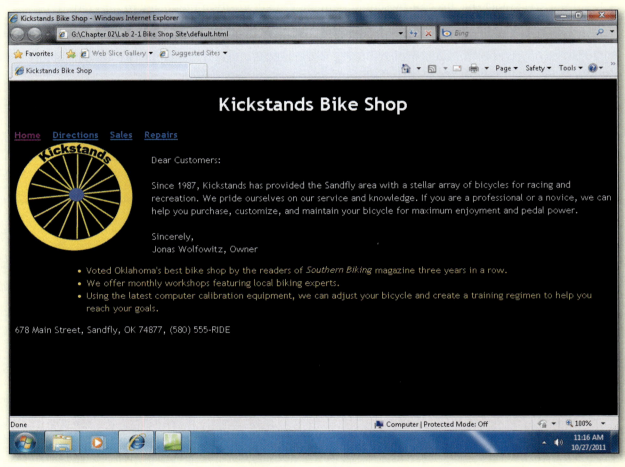

Figure 2–128

Instructions:

1. Start Expression Web.

2. Open the Web site Lab 2-1 Bike Shop.

3. Open the default.html page.

4. Position the insertion point in the line above the words, Dear Customers, then insert a new div.

5. Insert the GIF image kickstands_logo from the Lab 2-1 images folder. Do not assign alternate text.

6. Resize the logo to 200 pixels wide, keeping the image aspect ratio the same so that the height automatically adjusts, and left-align the image around the text. If necessary, drag the image up to align the text as shown in Figure 2–128.

7. Increase the right margin of the logo to 40 pixels.

8. Create a navigation bar using the text below the masthead, then copy it to each page in the site.

9. Save the changes you have made to all pages at once, then preview the site in a browser.

10. Rename the site Lab 2-1 Bike Shop Site. Change the site properties, as specified by your instructor.

11. Close the site, and then submit it in the format specified by your instructor.

In the Lab

Lab 2: Adding a Horizontal Line, Bookmark, and Link to a File

Problem: You own a baking business and want to attract customers by making your site's home page easier to navigate. On the featured recipe section of the home page, add a horizontal line at the top of the recipe and a bookmark link at the bottom to help users navigate back to the top of the page, as shown in Figure 2–129. Also add a link to an order form that users can download.

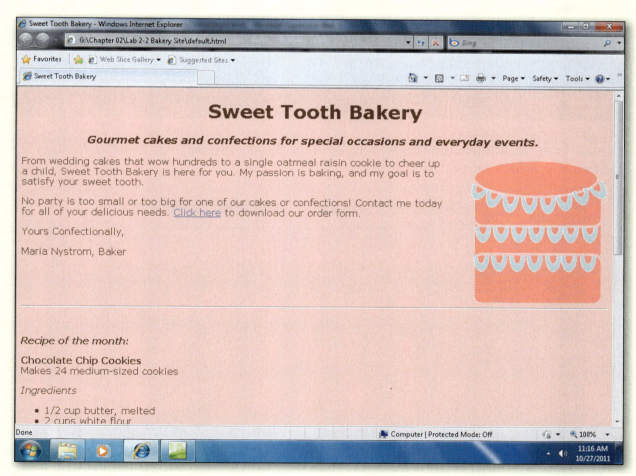

Figure 2–129

Continued >

In the Lab *continued*

Instructions:

1. Start Expression Web.

2. Open the Web site Lab 2-2 Bakery, then open the default.html page.

3. Insert a horizontal line two lines above the text, Recipe of the month. Leave two empty paragraphs before this horizontal rule so that it will not intersect with the cake.

4. Create a bookmark called Top of Page to the words, Sweet Tooth Bakery, in the masthead.

5. At the bottom of the page, between the directions and address, add a new paragraph, type the text `Top of Page`, and create a bookmark link from this text to the bookmark created in Step 4.

6. Add a link from the words, Click here, to the PDF file orderform.

7. Change the left margin of the cake image to 35 pixels.

8. Preview the site in a browser and test the link and bookmark.

9. Rename the site folder Lab 2-2 Bakery Site, then change the site properties, as specified by your instructor.

10. Close the site, and then submit it in the format specified by your instructor.

In the Lab

Lab 3: Formatting an Image

Problem: Your school's travel club has a Web page for its upcoming trip to New York. Insert, align, and format an image as shown in Figure 2–130.

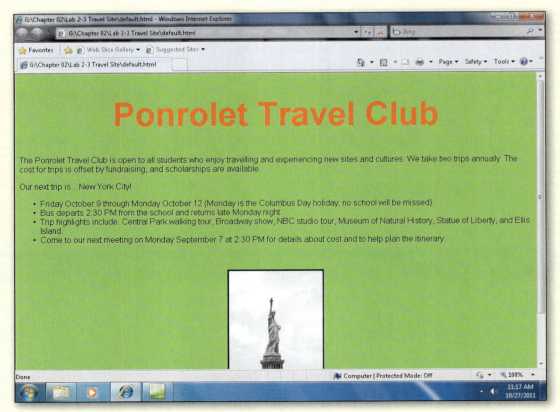

Figure 2–130

Instructions: Perform the following tasks.

1. Start Expression Web.

2. Open the Web site Lab 2-3 Travel.

3. Open the default.html page.

4. Click after the last bulleted list item, press ENTER three times, then insert the image statue.jpg from the Lab 2-3 images folder and add alternate text crediting your name as the photographer.

5. Crop the top, left, and right sides so that the image appears as shown in Figure 2–130.

6. Center-align the image.

7. Use the Borders and Shading dialog box to add a groove border around all sides. (*Hint:* To open the dialog box, click the Borders and Shading command on the Format menu.)

8. Click the More Brightness button twice.

9. Click the Color button arrow, then click Grayscale.

10. Click the More Contrast button twice.

11. Save the changes you have made to default.html and save the embedded image.

12. Preview the page in a browser.

13. Change the site properties, as specified by your instructor.

14. Close the site, rename the site folder Lab 2-3 Travel Site, and submit the site in the format specified by your instructor.

Cases and Places

Apply your creative thinking and problem-solving skills to design and implement a solution.

● EASIER ●●MORE DIFFICULT

● 1: Add Internal and External Links

You want to practice adding links to a Web site. Open any site that you created in Chapter 1, then open that site's default.html page. Add a link to your school's Web page, add a link to your e-mail address, and create and insert a bookmark. Close the default.html page without saving any changes, close the Web site, then quit Expression Web.

● 2: Add Images and Links to a School Web Site

The administration of Pinkham Academy would like to include images and links on a Web site. If you completed the Cases and Places 2 activity in Chapter 1, you can use the sketch of the Web site as a basis for this exercise. Create a one-page Web site that has a masthead, and at least one paragraph and bulleted list describing the school's features. Next to the bulleted list, insert a right-aligned image (use a photo from an exercise in this chapter or use one of your own). Add a margin and a bevel to the image. Add an e-mail link with a ScreenTip to your e-mail address.

●● 3: Add a Gallery of Images to an Alumni Web Site

You have recently joined the Connecticut branch of your college alumni association. You have been working on a home page that can tell other local graduates of Gulliver College about upcoming alumni events. You have already entered the text for the home page. Open the site Cases and Places 2-3 Alumni, then open the page default.html. Add four images and create a gallery of thumbnails for them (use photos from an exercise in this chapter or use your own). Center-align the thumbnails and make sure to add space between each image. Save the changes to the default.html file and embed all image files, then test your thumbnails in your browser.

●● 4: Create a Personal Home Page

Make It Personal

You want to create a personal home page that you can use to link to your favorite sites and allow others to e-mail you. Create a one-page Web site and include a masthead, bulleted list, footer, and any other information you think is relevant. Format the Web site attractively. Add at least one image that you crop, size, and align with text wrapping. Add a border to the image. Insert three links to sites that you like to visit. Add a ScreenTip to each of the links that displays the name of the site or what type of information the visitor will see when he or she clicks it. Insert an e-mail link to your e-mail address.

●● 5: Enhance a Home Page for a Restaurant

Working Together

A local restaurant wants to create a multi-page Web site for its customers. The site will include a home page, a menu page, and a page with directions. All pages should include a masthead, navigation bar with links, at least one image, one or two paragraphs or lists of information, and a footer with contact information. Working as a team with several of your classmates, you are to design and create the Web site. As a group, decide on the name of the restaurant and the menu. Each team member should plan on paper the three pages (home, menu, and directions), and present his or her plan to the group. As a group, decide on elements of each plan that you will incorporate into the home page, and start creating the home page using Expression Web. Format the Web site attractively. Add the text for each page. Add images and use text wrapping, create thumbnails, and apply formatting. Create a navigation bar and copy it to each page.

3 | Working with Templates and Styles

Objectives

You will have mastered the material in this chapter when you can:

- Create an Expression Web site from a template
- Rename a page
- Rename a folder
- Add and delete pages
- Add and delete folders
- Replace content in the template
- Copy and paste text from an external document
- Edit the editable regions
- Make global changes with templates
- Define styles and style sheets
- Modify a style
- Create a style
- Apply a style

3 | Working with Templates and Styles

Introduction

Creating a Web site from scratch allows you the flexibility to choose fonts, layouts, and styles that meet your needs — this is a useful approach when your needs are very specific. But, to save time and ensure consistency, you can use a wide range of pre-established content and layouts to create a Web site.

In its most general form, a template is a model document for creating a new version of an existing document, based on the layout and content of the model. An Expression Web **Web template** is a site that includes sample layouts, pages, styles, fonts, text, and images. You can modify the template-based site's structure, content, and style to suit your needs.

Expression Web uses XHTML-based templates called **dynamic Web templates**. Dynamic Web templates specify a site's layout, formatting, and content, and are saved with the file extension .dwt. When you use a template, a site structure consisting of several folders and an HTML file for each page in the site is created. Each page has common elements, such as a masthead, footer, and navigation bar, which you can modify by editing the master.dwt file.

Project — Personal Portfolio

BTW

Securing Personal Information
When creating a personal Web site, consider your privacy needs before entering personal information, such as your phone number or address. Only provide as much information as is needed for the site's purpose; a business will require additional contact information that a personal blog will not.

A **portfolio** is a collection of documents, images, or projects, compiled to show a variety of examples of someone's work. Portfolios are used by graphic artists, photographers, Web designers, and other creative professionals to show to potential clients the breadth of their experience or range of work. When creating a portfolio, you should include both written information about your experience in the form of a résumé or list of clients and graphic images that illustrate your work.

The project in this chapter uses Expression Web to create the home page and résumé page of an online portfolio, as shown in Figure 3–1. Mary Anderson is working on a degree in Web design and would like to create a Web site to showcase her work. She would also like to have a résumé, some general information about her objectives and experience, and graphics of Web sites she has worked on. Mary chooses an Expression Web site, the Personal 2 template, from the personal category because she likes the colors and graphics in the template. Expression Web's templates provide a quick way to build her site while ensuring consistency and sound design.

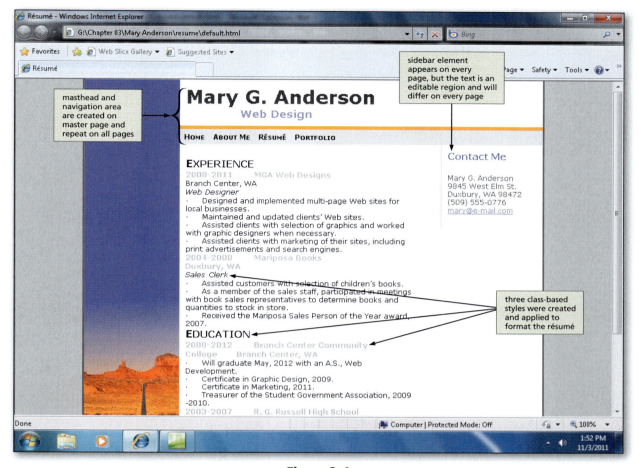

Figure 3–1

Overview

As you read this chapter, you will learn how to create the portfolio Web site shown in Figure 3–1 by performing these general tasks:

- Start a new Web site using a template.
- Specify the page and folder names.
- Insert and remove pages and folders.
- Enter and edit text.
- Paste text from another source.
- Modify the dynamic Web template.
- Modify, create, and apply styles.

Plan Ahead

General Project Guidelines

As you create a portfolio, such as the project shown in Figure 3–1, you should follow these general guidelines:

1. **Consider the purpose of the site.** A Web portfolio is used to display examples of creative work to potential clients, galleries, and customers. You will need to choose a template that meets your needs and reflects your personal design choices.

2. **Determine the structure of the site.** Although you can always add or delete pages, your Web site plan should provide an idea of the general number of pages before starting your site. Pages and folders should be named appropriately in order to keep the site organized.

3. **Determine, accumulate, and organize the content that you will use.** You can enter and edit text directly into the placeholders, which is good for short amounts of text. Pasting content into the site can save you time by using text you have already proofread. Gather all of the images and text files you have already created and collect them in a folder or group of folders. Make a note of any global changes you will need to make to the template to modify it to your specific needs.

4. **Distinguish the sites and CSS using styles.** Use the styles panels and CSS files to assign and modify styles to enhance the content and layout of your site. Changing the formatting using styles ensures consistency among common site elements and increases the professional look of your site.

When necessary, specific details about these guidelines are presented at appropriate points in the chapter. The chapter also will identify the tasks performed and decisions made regarding these guidelines during the creation of the portfolio shown in Figure 3–1.

BTW

Images in Templates
When you use a dynamic Web template, the site you create often has background images that appear on every page. These images are stored in the images folder in the main directory for the site and cannot easily be changed or replaced. Make sure that you like the image in a site template before choosing it.

Starting a New Web Site Using a Template

Many Web sites use similar structures and contain standard elements. A site created with a template provides visitors to your site with familiar page layout and navigation tools, helping new visitors to your site to easily find the content they are looking for. After creating a site with a template, you can customize the page content.

Like the Web site you created in Chapter 1, Web sites created with templates are organized using box-like divs to define areas such as the masthead, navigation area, body content, and footer. You can nest divs within one another to apply formatting, such as centering within the browser window, to a div and any subordinate divs (Figure 3–2).

Figure 3–2

Expression Web includes three types of templates: page, style, and site. Page templates specify the layout of a page, including columns, navigation area, and header and footer. Style templates use CSS to define the formatting of a page or site, including fonts and colors. Site templates include multiple pages and folders in an organized site structure, and a dynamic Web template file that controls the layout and formatting of all pages. In this chapter, you will use a site template that includes multiple HTML pages that share layout and formatting and include content areas, a dynamic Web template page (master.dwt), as well as style sheets that define layout and formatting. Three types of site templates are installed automatically with your software: for personal use, for organizations, and for small businesses.

BTW

Template Types
Templates can be used to create a site with a design theme or that serves a specific purpose, such as for a small business, a charitable organization, or for personal use.

Consider the purpose of the site.
When choosing a template, keep in mind what you would like the completed portfolio to look like and how it will be used. Choose an appropriate type and design, both of which you can modify later.

- **Site categories.** A personal Web site template will contain different content and layout options than one for a small business or organization. Select a category that most closely fits your needs.

- **Template design.** The themes and colors of the template you choose will have an effect on the mood of the site, although you can always modify these. Bright colors used in a site layout can distract from your work samples. Consider your audience. For example, if you are promoting a children's toy store, you will want to choose a very different look for your site than if you are creating a site for an insurance business.

Plan
Ahead

To Start Expression Web and Reset the Workspace Layout

If you are using a computer to step through the project in this chapter, and you want your screens to match the figures in this book, you should change your computer's resolution to 1024 × 768. For information about how to change a computer's resolution, read Appendix G. If you are using a lab computer or have changed the workspace layout, reset the workspace to the default to match the screens in this book.

The following steps, which assume Windows 7 is running, start Expression Web based on a typical installation and reset the panels in the workspace. You may need to ask your instructor how to start Expression Web for your computer.

Note: If you are using Windows XP, see Appendix E for alternate steps. If you are using Window Vista, see Appendix F for alternate steps.

1
- Click the Start button on the Windows 7 taskbar to display the Start menu.
- Click All Programs at the bottom of the left pane on the Start menu to display the All Programs list.
- Click Microsoft Expression on the All Programs list to display the Microsoft Expression list.

2
- Click Microsoft Expression Web 3 to start Expression Web.

3
- Click Panels on the menu bar to open the Panels menu, then click Reset Workspace Layout.
- Point to Ruler and Grid on the View menu, then click Show Ruler to display the rulers, if necessary.

BTW

Naming Files and Folders
The site name, which is the folder that contains the site contents, can include spaces. Within the site, folders and filenames cannot contain uppercase letters, spaces, or certain characters, such as # (the pound sign) or * (an asterisk). You can separate words in a filename by using an underscore (_), such as in the folder name assets_images or the filename web_page2.html.

Placeholders

In a page created using an Expression Web template, a **placeholder** is a div or tag that is used to specify the placement of headers, images, and text on pages. Placeholders, including those for sidebars and a main content area, contain sample text that you replace with your own content. If a placeholder is not needed on your page, delete the placeholder content; when your site is viewed in a browser, the placeholder is not visible.

To Create a New Web Site from a Template

You use the New dialog box to create a new Web site using a template. The New dialog box contains options for creating blank Web pages and Web sites and options for using templates. Select a template type to view a thumbnail of it. After you specify the folder location of your new site, you should also specify the site name.

After selecting a template and closing the New dialog box, the site is open for editing and contains placeholder text, folders, and pages. In the following steps, you create a new Web site from a template.

1

• Click Site on the menu bar to open the Site menu, then point to New Site (Figure 3–3).

Q&A

Why do I have a default site name?

When you create a site in a folder you have used before, or if you are working in a lab setting and your port and file path match that of previous users, Expression Web may assign a default site name, such as personalsite or mysite2, depending on the last site that was created. To select the default site name, select the word(s) that appear after the last backslash (\) in the Location text box.

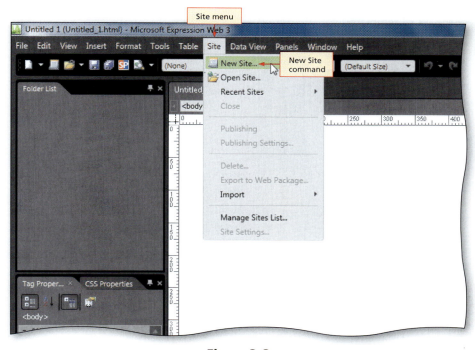

Figure 3–3

2

• Click New Site to open the New dialog box.

• Click Templates in the left pane of the Site tab to display template options (Figure 3–4).

Figure 3–4

3

• Click Personal 2 from the list of templates to view a thumbnail of it (Figure 3–5).

🔍 **Experiment**

• Click other options in the list of templates to view thumbnails in the Preview window.

Figure 3–5

4

• Click the Browse button to open the New Site Location dialog box.

• Navigate to the location where you store your data files in the New Site Location dialog box (Figure 3–6).

Figure 3–6

5
- Click the Open button to select your location.
- Click in the Location text box, then click after the folder name in the Location text box.
- Type Mary Anderson (Figure 3–7).

Figure 3–7

6
- Click the OK button to close the New dialog box and open a new site that contains multiple pages and folders in Design view.
- Double-click the default.html filename in the Folder List to open it (Figure 3–8).

Figure 3–8

BTW

Subfolders
A folder within a folder is called a subfolder.

BTW

Metadata
Metadata is information about styles and structure that is created as part of a Web site. Metadata is stored in hidden files and folders that do not appear in the Folder List, but it will be visible if you view a site's folder contents in Windows Explorer; it should not be deleted, moved, or edited.

Specifying the Structure of the Site

As you learned in previous chapters, a Web site can include folders to organize and store files. A template provides a folder for each page; each page folder includes the HTML file for the page and any embedded placeholder images or files for that page, such as the landscape image included in Mary's portfolio. When you create a new site from a template, you will see the folders for all pages except the main default.html page, which is the home page. Because templates use style sheets to specify the formatting of the site, you will also see a folder for the style sheets. A separate folder exists for the common site images, such as the one on the left side of the page, which appears on all pages. A site created with a template includes many pages, including ones that you might not need or whose names you may want to change. You might also need to add pages to your site. Keeping a site organized includes adding new files and folders, placing newly created files or images that you embed on a page into the correct folder so that you know where to look for them when you need them, and deleting files and folders that are not needed.

Plan Ahead

Determine the folder structure of the site.
In addition to renaming files and folders generated by a template, adding and deleting pages can help you to customize a template-based site to your needs.

- **Change the file and folder names.** File and folder names should be meaningful to you, and should be unique for each folder in your site.

- **Remove extraneous pages.** Including too many pages can make your Web site difficult to navigate. Each page that a user can access should provide relevant information; if a template includes a page for which you have no need, remove it to keep your site streamlined.

- **Remove extraneous folders.** Having extra folders can make managing your Web site unnecessarily complicated. Keep the folder structure as simple as possible. If you add pages and folders to the site, a logical and easy-to-follow folder structure will help you manage the site as it grows.

- **Add necessary pages.** Sometimes templates don't provide all the pages you need. You can add a new blank page or create one based on an existing page or dynamic Web template. Choosing the appropriate method depends on the content of the new page. If you are displaying photographic images of a tree and want a separate page for each season of the year, it would make sense to create four pages that are based on the same page so that the layout for spring, summer, fall, and winter is the same, and your reader can focus on the changes in the images of the tree rather than the changes in the page layout or formatting.

- **Add necessary folders.** Adding a new folder, such as one in which to store a newly created page, can help to keep the HTML file and embedded image files for that page in one location.

To Rename a Folder

You can rename any folder or Web page within the Folder List. Folder and filenames should be lowercase and not contain spaces. Expression Web prompts you to instruct the program to update all links and references to the page or folder you are renaming so that your site contains no broken links. The following steps rename a folder.

1
- Click the about_me folder name in the Folder List, then click the folder name again to select it (Figure 3–9).

Why did the folder's contents display in the Folder List?

Clicking a selected folder or file-name should select the name for editing. However, if you click it again too fast, it is double-clicked and its contents open. Click the folder name again, and it should select the folder name.

Figure 3–9

2
- Type about_mary, being sure to type the underscore between the two words, as the new name (Figure 3–10).

Figure 3–10

● Press ENTER to change the folder name (Figure 3–11).

renamed folder; while the site contents are being updated to reflect the renamed folder, the Rename folder dialog box opens briefly, then closes when the renaming is done

Figure 3–11

Other Ways

1. Right-click the page or folder name in the Folder List, then click Rename on the shortcut menu to select the name

To Rename a Web Page

Renaming a Web page is done using the same steps as renaming a folder. Be sure to add the file extension to the page name. You can use either .htm or .html as the file extension, as they are both used to represent HTML files. Be sure to choose which file extension to use before development and use either .htm or .html for all pages in a Web site. Although the files work the same way, it is usually best to choose .html or .htm and be consistent within your site. The following steps rename the about_mary/default.html Web page.

● Click the about_mary plus button in the Folder List to expand the folder and view its contents (Figure 3–12).

Q&A

Why is there another default.html file?

When Expression Web creates a site from a template, all of the subfolders include a page called default.html. These are different from the main default.html page, and include the subfolder name in the Web page's file path (i.e., contact/ default.html). Make sure when you have several default.html pages open that you are editing the correct one.

+ sign changes to – to indicate that contents are expanded

replaced folder name

contents of about_mary folder

about_mary/ default.html file

Figure 3–12

- Click the default.html filename in the Folder List, then click the filename again to select it.

- Type `about_mary.html`, including the underscore (Figure 3–13).

Figure 3–13

❸

- Press ENTER to open the Rename dialog box (Figure 3–14).

- In the Rename dialog box, click the Yes button to update references to the page.

Figure 3–14

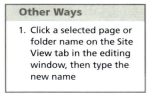

Other Ways

1. Click a selected page or folder name on the Site View tab in the editing window, then type the new name

Modifying the Structure of a Web Site

After determining the site's purpose, objectives, and goals, the next step in planning a site is to determine the number of pages that you will need. In Mary's case, she needs a home page, a résumé page, and a portfolio page. A site created with a template comes with a sample structure, which might not reflect the pages required for your planned site. By deleting, adding, and renaming pages, Mary can organize the structure of her site to reflect her needs, then start customizing or creating the content by adding text and images.

Even though each Web page is stored on your computer as a separate file, you should avoid deleting, renaming, or moving Web site pages or image files using Windows Explorer. When deleting or renaming pages and images with Expression Web, the software prompts you to update all relevant links and make changes within the site that reflect the page deletion. If you use Windows Explorer or another file management program, you risk creating errors, such as broken links, in your site.

BTW

Updating the Navigation Bar
When revising your site structure, you must update the navigation bar to reflect the changes by editing the master.dwt file. You will do so later in this lesson.

To Delete a Web Page

Deleting a page only deletes the HTML file; any folders and embedded files are kept in the site. Removing extra Web pages from your site also helps to reduce the file size of the entire site, increasing its usability. You cannot undo a page or folder deletion, so make sure that you do not need it before you delete it. The following steps delete a Web page, the contact/default.html page, that Mary does not need according to her site plan.

1

- Click the contact folder plus button in the Folder List to expand the folder and view its contents (Figure 3–15).

Figure 3–15

2

- Click the default.html filename in the Folder List to select it (Figure 3–16).

Figure 3–16

3

- Click Edit on the menu bar to open the Edit menu, then click Delete to open the Confirm Delete dialog box (Figure 3–17).

filename appears here

Yes button accepts file deletion

Figure 3–17

4

- In the Confirm Delete dialog box, click the Yes button to delete the file (Figure 3–18).

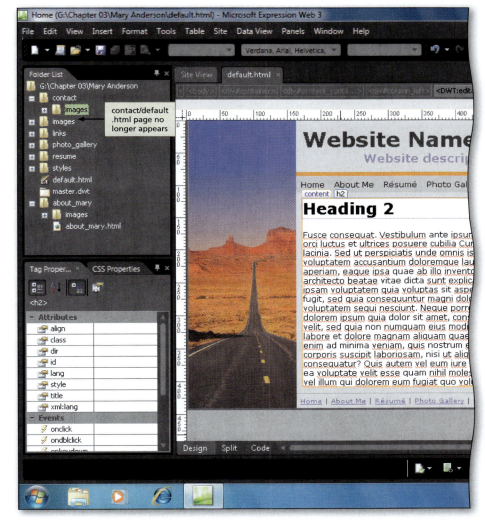

contact/default .html page no longer appears

Figure 3–18

Other Ways

1. Right-click the page name in the Folder List, then click Delete on the shortcut menu to open the Confirm Delete dialog box

2. Click the page name in the Folder List, then press DELETE to open the Confirm Delete dialog box

To Delete a Folder

When you delete a folder, all of its contents are removed. Make sure that any files within the folder are not being used by other pages before you delete a folder and its contents. In the following steps, you will delete folders for contacts, links, and a photo gallery that Mary does not need according to her site plan.

- Right-click the contact folder name in the Folder List to display the shortcut menu, and point to Delete (Figure 3–19).

Figure 3–19

- Click Delete to open the Confirm Delete dialog box.

- In the Confirm Delete dialog box, click the Yes button to delete the contact folder (Figure 3–20).

- Repeat Steps 1 and 2 to delete the links and photo_gallery folders.

Figure 3–20

Other Ways

1. Click the folder name in the Folder List, then press DELETE to open the Confirm Delete dialog box

To Add a Folder

When adding folders to a site, it is important to insert them in the appropriate location. New folders often belong in the site's top-level folder, which stores all of the Web site files. To add a folder in this main folder, select the top folder name in the Folder List. Otherwise, your new folder might be created as a subfolder of another folder, which can be confusing and might not function as intended. The following steps add a new folder to Mary's Web site, to which she will add a newly created Web page in accordance with her site plan.

 1

- Right-click the Mary Anderson folder name, which is the top folder name in the Folder List, point to New to open the New submenu, then point to Folder (Figure 3–21).

Figure 3–21

 2

- Click the Folder command on the New submenu to create a new folder in the Folder List (Figure 3–22).

Figure 3–22

• Type `portfolio` as the new folder name (Figure 3–23).

Figure 3–23

• Press ENTER to rename the folder (Figure 3–24).

Figure 3–24

To Add a Web Page

When you add a page in a site created with a template, you must attach the dynamic Web template to it; otherwise, the page will be blank. You can copy and paste pages in the Folder List to create pages that have similar content and layout and determine whether you need to create a folder in which to store the page, or whether it fits logically into an existing folder. The following steps create the new page Mary needs for a new portfolio, save the page in the portfolio folder, and attach the dynamic Web template to the page so that it matches the other pages in the site.

- Click File on the menu bar to open the File menu, point to New, then point to Create from Dynamic Web Template (Figure 3–25).

Figure 3–25

- Click Create from Dynamic Web Template to open the Attach Dynamic Web Template dialog box.
- Scroll down, if necessary, then click master to attach it to the new page (Figure 3–26).

Figure 3–26

- Click the Open button to create a new, untitled Web page.

- Click the Close button to close the alert box (Figure 3–27).

Figure 3–27

- Press CTRL+S to open the Save As dialog box.

- Double-click the portfolio folder in the right pane of the dialog box to open it.

- Select any text in the File name text box, then type `portfolio.html` to name the page (Figure 3–28).

Figure 3–28

5

- Click the Save button to name the new page and save it in the portfolio folder, then click the portfolio folder plus button to view its contents (Figure 3–29).

Figure 3–29

6

- Right-click the portfolio.html page tab and point to Close (Figure 3–30).

- Click Close to close the page.

Figure 3–30

Entering and Editing Text

All Web pages contain content areas, called **editable regions**, including sidebars, headings, and main content areas. The editable regions are where you include the content and images specific to each page. There are two types of editable regions: headers and body text. Headers are indicated by the header level or description of the content that you should replace it with (such as Heading 1 or About Company). Body text is indicated by Latin text (such as Fusce consequat). Both headers and body text have styles attached to them, but you can modify the formatting to suit your needs.

To enter header or body content, click the area you want to edit, select the div to select all of the placeholder content, then type or paste the new text.

Plan Ahead

Determine, accumulate, and organize the content that you will use.

- Each page should have a header that states its purpose and has appropriate text and graphic content. Make sure to proofread your text before inserting or after typing it into the page. Reusing text from other Web pages or text files will make your work easier and reduces errors.

- Modify the dynamic Web template content on the master.dwt page that is the same for every page: the page title, footer, and navigation area.

To Replace Template Placeholder Text

Mary's portfolio site needs customized headings. The following steps replace heading placeholder text on the home page.

- If necessary, click the default.html page tab.

- If necessary, click in the words, Heading 2, to show the h2 tag's tab (Figure 3–31).

Figure 3–31

2

- Click the <h2> tag on the Quick Tag Selector to select the heading tag and placeholder text (Figure 3–32).

Figure 3–32

3

- Type Who am I? to customize the placeholder (Figure 3–33).

Figure 3–33

4
- If necessary, use the horizontal scroll box to move the page view to the right.
- Click in the words, Heading 4, to show the h4 tab (Figure 3–34).

Figure 3–34

5
- Click the <h4> tag on the Quick Tag Selector to select the placeholder text and heading tag (Figure 3–35).

Figure 3–35

6
- Type `Objective` to customize the placeholder (Figure 3–36).

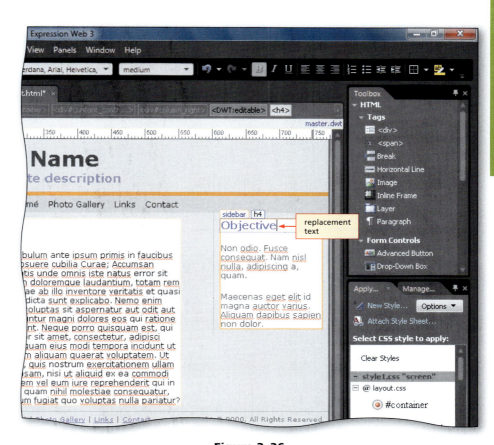

Figure 3–36

7
- Click in the paragraph below the word, Objective.

- Click the <p> tag on the Quick Tag Selector to select the placeholder text and the paragraph tags (Figure 3–37).

Figure 3–37

8

- **Type** To obtain a job as a Web designer in which I can combine my technical background and business knowledge to create Web sites that are attractive, easy-to-use, and meet the needs of my clients. (Figure 3–38).

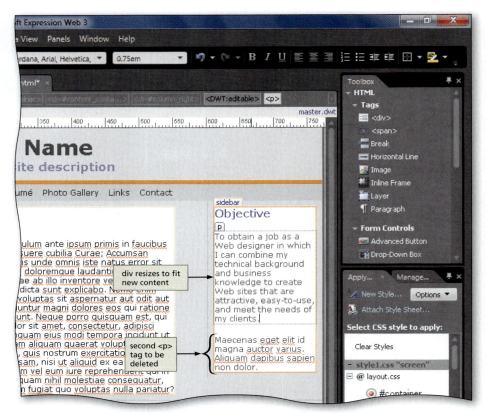

Figure 3–38

9

- Click in the paragraph below the text you just typed, click the <p> tag in the Quick Tag Selector to select the second paragraph in the sidebar, then press DELETE to delete it (Figure 3–39).

- Press CTRL+S to save the page.

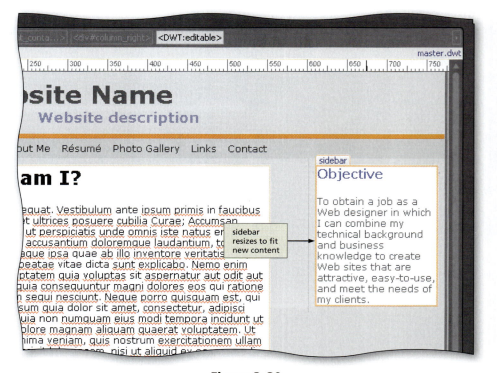

Figure 3–39

Pasting Text

To use content, including text, images, or a table, that is saved in another file or Web page, copy it to the Clipboard, then paste it into the placeholder. The Clipboard, which you used in Chapter 2 to paste text between pages in your site, is shared by other Windows programs and can be used to paste text from other programs, such as Microsoft Word, into Expression Web.

When pasting text into a Web page, it is important to remove any formatting so that it does not clash with the site's formatting. Using the Paste Text command on the Edit menu, you can choose to insert the text with or without line breaks and other paragraph formatting. All character formatting, such as boldface and italics, is removed when using the Paste Text command.

BTW

Removing Formatting
To remove formatting from text, select the text, then click Remove Formatting on the Format menu. Alternatively, you can paste the text and then use the Paste Options button that appears at the bottom of the div containing the pasted text to remove the formatting.

BTW

Extra Line Breaks
Make sure to remove all extra line breaks at the end of a document that you are selecting, or they will appear when pasted into the Web site.

To Paste Text

To insert text from another source, such as a Word document or text file, you first need to open the file in its native program and copy the text to the Clipboard. Mary needs to add her résumé to her Web site. The following steps open Microsoft Word, open a file, copy the text, paste it without formatting into the résumé page, then open another file and do the same.

- Click the Start button on the Windows 7 taskbar to display the Start menu.

- Click All Programs at the bottom of the left pane on the Start menu to display the All Programs list.

- Click the Microsoft Office folder on the All Programs list to display the Microsoft Office list.

- Click Microsoft Office Word 2007 to start Word and open a blank document (Figure 3–40).

Q&A

What if I don't have Word 2007?

If you have another version of Word you can use that, or use any text editor, such as Notepad or WordPad.

Figure 3–40

2

- Click the Office button, then click Close to close the blank document.
- Press CTRL+O to open the Open dialog box.
- If necessary, navigate to your data files, open the mary_documents folder, and then select the hometext file (Figure 3–41).

Figure 3–41

3

- Click the Open button to open the file in Word.
- Press CTRL+A to select all of the text in the document.
- Click the Copy button in the Clipboard group on the Ribbon to copy the selection to the Clipboard (Figure 3–42).

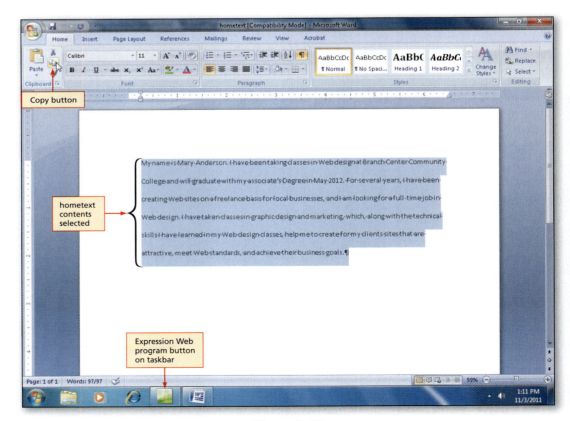

Figure 3–42

4

- Click the Expression Web button on the taskbar to return to Expression Web.

- Scroll if necessary, click in the content div below the text, Who am I?, then click the <p> tag on the Quick Tag Selector to select the paragraph tag and placeholder text (Figure 3–43).

Figure 3–43

5

- Click Edit on the menu bar to open the Edit menu, then point to Paste Text (Figure 3–44).

Figure 3–44

6

- Click Paste Text to open the Paste Text dialog box.

- Click 'Normal paragraphs with line breaks' (Figure 3–45).

Figure 3–45

7

- Click the OK button to close the dialog box and insert the pasted text.

- Press CTRL+S to save the default. html page.

- Click the hometext Word program button on the taskbar to return to Word.

- Repeat Steps 2 and 3 to open the resume file and copy its contents to the Clipboard, and then return to Expression Web.

- Click the resume folder plus button in the Folder List to view its contents (Figure 3–46).

Figure 3–46

8

- Double-click the default.html page in the resume folder in the Folder List to open it.

- Click the content div tab to select the div tag and text (Figure 3–47).

Figure 3–47

9

- Press DELETE to remove the placeholder text from the content div.

- Click Edit on the menu bar to open the Edit menu, then click Paste Text to open the Paste Text dialog box.

- If necessary, click 'Normal paragraphs with line breaks' (Figure 3–48).

- Try pasting text with the other options in the Paste Text dialog box to see the effect.

Figure 3–48

 10

- Click the OK button to paste the text, then scroll up to show the top of the Web page (Figure 3–49).

- Press CTRL+S to save the default. html page.

Figure 3–49

Other Ways

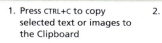

1. Press CTRL+C to copy selected text or images to the Clipboard

2. Press CTRL+V to paste selected text or images from the Clipboard

To Close Microsoft Word

Closing files and quitting programs after you are done working with them frees up computer resources for other tasks and prevents data loss. The following steps close both Microsoft Word windows and the two files, hometext.doc and resume.doc.

• Click the Word program button on the taskbar to return to Word (Figure 3–50).

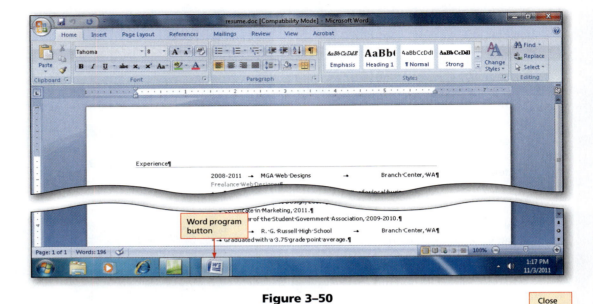

Figure 3–50

2

• Press CTRL+W to close the resume.doc file (Figure 3–51).

• Click the Close button on the title bar to close the hometext.doc file and the program and return to Expression Web.

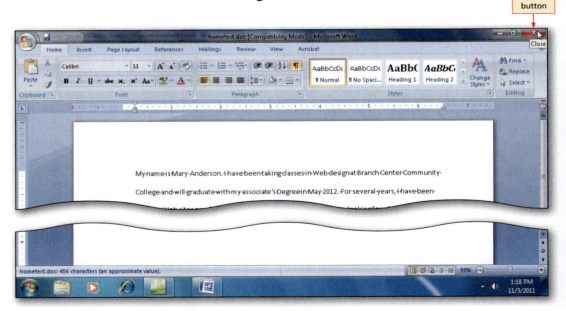

Figure 3–51

Editing Text

When you edit text, you change its content by rewording, removing, adding, or moving words. Sometimes editing requires that you change all occurrences of a word or phrase. Editing can be done directly on the Web page using skills you have likely used in a word-processing program such as Microsoft Word. To edit text by typing additional text or by using keys such as

DELETE or BACKSPACE, you must first position the insertion point (click) where your edits will take place. To delete more than one word or sentence, you must first select the text you want to remove, then delete it by pressing the DELETE or BACKSPACE key, or replace it by typing new text. Table 3–1 outlines different editing commands and shortcuts.

BTW

Quick Reference

For a table that lists how to complete the tasks covered in this book using the mouse, shortcut menu, and keyboard, see the Quick Reference Summary at the back of this book, or visit the Expression Web 3 Quick Reference Web page (scsite.com/ew3/qr).

Table 3–1: Editing Commands and Shortcuts

Action	Effect
Double-click a word	Selects the word and the space after it
Triple-click in a paragraph	Selects the paragraph
Press BACKSPACE	Deletes text one character at a time to the left of the insertion point
Press DELETE	Deletes text one character at a time to the right of the insertion point
Press SHIFT, then the left or right ARROW on the keyboard	Selects text one character at a time to the left or right of the insertion point
Press SHIFT and CTRL, then press the left or right arrow on the keyboard	Selects text one word at a time from the left or right of the insertion point

You can also find and change all instances of a word or phrase using the Find and Replace tools. For instance, to change a person or company's name, you use the Find tool to locate each instance of the name, then replace or ignore each instance individually, or replace all at once.

To Edit Text

The heading of the sidebar is, by default, the page name, Résumé. The sidebar text and heading on the resume page need to be revised to reflect Mary's contact information. When entering lines of text into a paragraph <p> tag, pressing ENTER automatically inserts a new <p> tag for the next line and adds space between the tags. To create multiple lines of text within one paragraph tag, press SHIFT+ENTER instead of ENTER to insert a line break that moves the insertion point to the next line but keeps it in the tag. The following steps edit text using the keyboard to delete and type text and using the mouse to select text.

- Use the vertical and horizontal scroll bars, if necessary, to view the sidebar.

- Drag to select the sidebar heading, Résumé, then type Contact Me to replace the placeholder text (Figure 3–52).

Figure 3–52

2

• Drag to select the sidebar text (Figure 3–53).

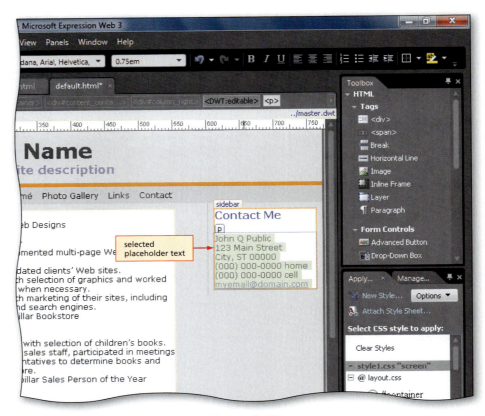

Figure 3–53

3

• Press DELETE to delete the placeholder text.

• Type Mary G. Anderson, then press SHIFT+ENTER to start a new line in the <p> tag (Figure 3–54).

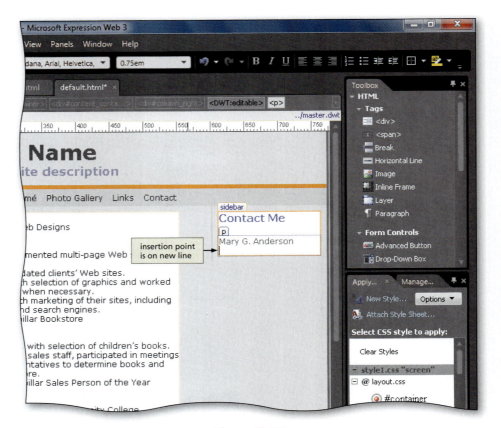

Figure 3–54

4
- Type 9845 West Elm St., then press SHIFT+ENTER.
- Type Duxbury, WA 98472, then press SHIFT+ENTER.
- Type (509)555-0776, then press SHIFT+ENTER.
- Type mary@e-mail.com, then press the SPACEBAR to create the e-mail hyperlink (Figure 3–55).

Figure 3–55

5
- Scroll if necessary, click after the word, Bookstore, in the content div (about one-third of the way down the document).
- Press BACKSPACE four times to change the word to Books (Figure 3–56).

Figure 3–56

6
- Double-click the word, Freelance, which is the first word on the fourth line of the content div, to select it.

- Press BACKSPACE to delete the word (Figure 3–57).

- Press CTRL+S to save the page.

the word, Freelance, is removed

Figure 3–57

To Find and Replace Text

You can use the Find and Replace commands to locate and change single instances or all occurrences of a word or phrase, or use the Replace command on its own to replace words or phrases without first using the Find command. The bookstore where Mary has been working has recently changed its name from Caterpillar to Mariposa. Mary is not sure whether the name change occurred before or after she last saved her résumé, so she will first use the Find command, then the Replace command. The following steps find all instances of the word, Caterpillar, and replace them with Mariposa.

- Click Edit on the menu bar to open the Edit menu, then point to Find (Figure 3–58).

Edit menu

Find command

Figure 3–58

2

- Click Find to open the Find and Replace dialog box.

- If necessary, select any text in the Find what text box and type Caterpillar (Figure 3–59).

Figure 3–59

3

- Click the Find All button to display the search results in the Find 1 panel at the bottom of the editing window (Figure 3–60).

Figure 3–60

4

- Click Edit on the menu bar to open the Edit menu, and then click Replace to open the Find and Replace dialog box.

- If necessary, select any text in the Find what text box and type `Caterpillar`, click in the Replace with text box, and then type `Mariposa` (Figure 3–61).

Figure 3–61

5

- Click the Replace All button to replace the text and open an alert box (Figure 3–62).

Figure 3–62

6

- Click the OK button in the alert box to confirm the replacement (Figure 3–63).

Experiment

- Open the Find and Replace dialog box, click the HTML Tags tab, and try searching for tags such as <div> and <p>.

Figure 3–63

7

- Click the Close button on the Find 1 panel to complete the find and replace operation.

- Press CTRL+S to save the résumé page (Figure 3–64).

- Click the Close button on the resume/default.html page tab to close the page.

Q&A

What if I get an alert box?

If you get an alert box telling you that you will not be able to undo the Replace command, click Yes or OK, depending on the type of alert you receive. You are still able to undo the replace if necessary.

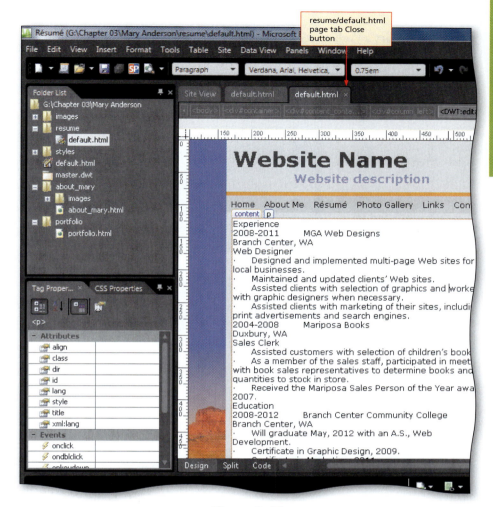

Figure 3–64

Dynamic Web Page Template Pages

Each page in a site contains common text or image elements that relate general information about the site. This information can include a masthead with a company name or logo, a footer with copyright information or the company's address, and a navigation bar with links to the main pages of the site. The dynamic Web template uses placeholders for this information; these placeholders can only be edited from the master.dwt page. Placeholders on the master.dwt page describe the type of information that you need to add, such as Website name or Website description.

To edit master page information, such as the Web site title or description, you must edit the dynamic Web page master file, master.dwt. You should save and close all open pages prior to opening the master.dwt page. When you make edits to the master page, you must save the master page before the changes are applied to the affected pages. You will be prompted to accept the changes for all pages, or you can accept them individually.

BTW

Creating Templates

You can also create a dynamic Web template from an existing page to create additional pages that share the same formatting and layout. To do so, you need to remove all text and define the editable regions.

To Make Global Changes to a Template

All of Mary's Web pages should include a name for her Web site (in this case, her name), a description, and copyright information. The following steps edit the master.dwt page to add text to the masthead and footer. You will also edit the navigation bar on the master.dwt page to reflect the pages you have added and deleted by deleting, renaming, and reassigning the hyperlinks. These changes will be made to all pages that are attached to the template.

1

- Right-click the default.html page tab, then click Close to close the page.

- Double-click the master.dwt page in the Folder List to open it in the editing window.

- Select the text in the Website Name heading (Figure 3–65).

Figure 3–65

2

- Type `Mary G. Anderson` to customize the site name.

- Select the text in the Website description heading, then type `Web Design` to reflect the site's purpose.

- Scroll right if necessary, click in the Copyright paragraph, select 0000, then type `2011` to update the year (Figure 3–66).

Figure 3–66

- In the footer, double-click the word, Contact, to select it.
- Press DELETE to remove the link.
- Select the word, Links, and the vertical lines before and after it, then press DELETE to remove the link and the pipe characters.
- Select the words, Photo Gallery, then type `Portfolio` to change the link name (Figure 3–67).

Figure 3–67

- In the navigation bar below the Web Design header, click in the word, Contact.
- Click the <a> tag on the Quick Tag Selector bar to select the tag (Figure 3–68).

Figure 3–68

- Press DELETE to remove the Contact link.
- Select the Links tag, then press DELETE to remove the link.
- Select the words, Photo Gallery, then type `Portfolio` to change the link name (Figure 3–69).

Figure 3–69

• Drag to select the word, Portfolio.

• Click Insert on the menu bar to open the Insert menu, then click Hyperlink to open the Edit Hyperlink dialog box (Figure 3–70).

Figure 3–70

• Double-click the portfolio folder to open it.

• Click the portfolio file to select it (Figure 3–71).

• Click the OK button to update the hyperlink.

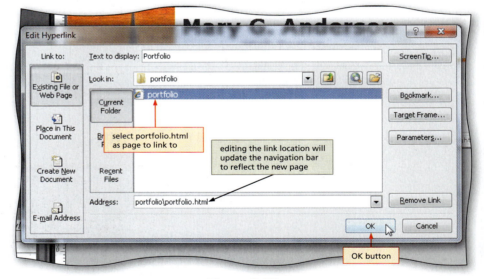

Figure 3–71

8

• Repeat Steps 6 and 7 to update the portfolio link in the bottom navigation bar.

• Press CTRL+S to save the master.dwt page and open an alert box confirming that the changes will be made to all site pages (Figure 3–72).

Figure 3–72

9

- Click the Yes button in the alert box to update the four attached files (Figure 3–73).

Figure 3–73

10

- Click the Close button to close the alert box.

- Click the Close button on the master .dwt page tab to close the master template.

- Double-click the main default.html file in the Folder List to open the default. html page and see the changes you made on the master.dwt page (Figure 3–74).

- Click the Close button on the default.html page tab to close the page.

Figure 3–74

Defining Styles and Style Sheets

In a Web page created using an Expression Web template, the layout and formatting are saved to cascading style sheet (CSS) files. You can customize the look of your site by creating, modifying, and applying styles that use a combination of formatting attributes, and that can be used to create consistency across all pages.

A style is a formatting attribute or group of attributes applied to a single character, a word, a section, or an entire Web site. A **style sheet** is a collection of style rules that are applied to specific elements. CSS is a type of style sheet. The style rules list the properties, such as formatting and layout, that apply to an element. Using style sheets ensures consistency of styles among elements. For instance, to change all bulleted lists from round to square bullets, you can simply change the style in the style sheet, and the change is applied to all bulleted lists in your site. Style sheets separate the content of a page (written in HTML) from the formatting. **Cascading** refers to the weighting, or prioritizing, of potential style conflicts. Priority is determined by **specificity**, which generally means that the rule that is higher in the priority is used if there is a conflict. A site can have several style sheets, each of which controls different aspects of formatting and layout. Expression Web templates come with embedded styles saved to style sheets, which are stored in the styles folder.

BTW

Expression Web Help
The best way to become familiar with Expression Web Help is to use it. Appendix A includes detailed information about Expression Web Help and exercises that will help you gain confidence in using it.

BTW

Web Standards
For more information on Web standards, see Appendix B.

Style Sheet Types

Style sheets can be internal, which means they are associated with a page or site, or external, which means they are saved as a separate file that can be applied to multiple pages or sites. By storing styles in a separate file, called an **external style sheet**, you can control the formatting of a site and also apply that style sheet to other pages or sites. Styles can also be saved as an **internal style sheet** by embedding them into the header of an XHTML page; an internal style sheet can only be used on the page in which it is embedded, however. An **inline style** is used to format a section of text and is defined by including a tag in the body of the document. An inline style only applies to the exact section of text or element to which you apply it and cannot be reused for other elements or pages. When style conflicts arise, inline styles have first priority and are applied first, followed by internal styles, then external styles.

BTW

CSS Versions
All browsers support slightly different features of CSS. It is important to test your site using various browsers before publishing it to make sure that the formatting appears the same on all browsers.

Style Rule Syntax

In general, syntax refers to a set of rules; for instance, to specify wording and punctuation in HTML or CSS code. A style rule's syntax has three parts: a **selector** (the element to which the rule applies, such as h1), a **property** (how the element will be changed, such as font style or font size), and a **value** (the specific change or degree of change, such as bold or large). Selectors can refer to a specific element, a class of element, or a single instance of an element.

As with HTML, you do not need to know how to code a style when creating it, but it is important to understand the **syntax**, or the order of the rules. The first part of a style is the selector, followed by the property and value, which together make up the **declaration** (Figure 3–75). Proper use of punctuation, such as braces, semicolons, and colons, ensures that your styles are interpreted correctly by a browser. Make sure to enter a semicolon to separate each style rule, and do not move or delete braces or other punctuation marks, unless you are sure that they are unnecessary.

Figure 3–75

> **Distinguish the site using styles.**
> When deciding on the styles to use in your site, note that you can modify an existing style, create element-based styles that can apply to all instances of an element, or format a specific element or text area by creating a class-based style rule.

Plan Ahead

To Modify a Style

To apply, create, and modify styles and style sheets, you can use the Apply Styles and Manage Styles panels, located below the Toolbox. When you add or edit a style, the style sheet file opens and needs to be saved along with the page that you are modifying.

Mary would like to modify the look of her site by revising the appearance of the links. The following steps change the style of the navigation bar.

- Double-click the master.dwt page in the Folder List to open it.

- In the Apply Styles panel, point to the #navigation style, click the arrow to open the menu, and then point to Modify Style (Figure 3–76).

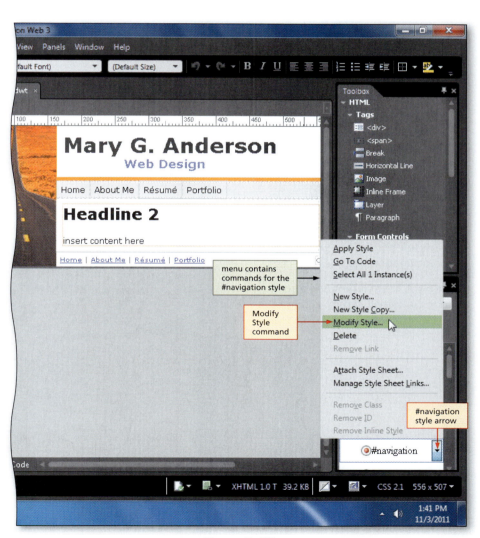

Figure 3–76

2

- Click Modify Style on the menu to open the Modify Style dialog box (Figure 3–77).

Figure 3–77

3

- Click the font-weight box arrow, then click bold to apply bold to the navigation bar.

- Click the font-variant box arrow, then click small-caps to change the lettering style (Figure 3–78).

Figure 3–78

4

- Click the OK button to close the Modify Style dialog box.

- Close the master .dwt file.

- Press CTRL+S to save the layout.css file (Figure 3–79).

- Click the Close button on the layout.css page tab to close the page.

Q&A

What is the layout.css file and why did it open?

When you edit a style, the style sheet where it is stored opens and must be saved in order to save the updated styles.

Figure 3–79

5

- Open the main default.html page to view the modified navigation bar (Figure 3–80).

- Close the default.html page.

Figure 3–80

To Create a Style

You create styles in the New Style dialog box and save them to the current page, a new style sheet, or an existing style sheet. When you create multiple styles, you only have to specify the saved location once; subsequent styles are by default saved to the location you choose when defining the first style. When naming a class-based style, you must include a period before the name, such as .category. Within the New Style dialog box, Expression Web inserts a period before the default style name. Do not delete this period. The following steps create three styles for Mary's résumé to an existing style sheet, which you will apply to sections of the résumé, formatting it to be readable.

- In the Folder list, click the resume folder plus button to open it, if necessary.

- Double-click the default.html page in the resume folder in the Folder List to open it (Figure 3–81).

Figure 3–81

2

- Click the New Style link on the Apply Styles panel to open the New Style dialog box.

- In the Selector text box, type category to name the new style for the general headings in Mary's résumé.

- Click the Define in box arrow, then click Existing style sheet to add the new style to a pre-existing style sheet.

- Click the URL box arrow, then point to ../styles/style1.css (Figure 3–82).

- Click ../styles/style1.css to specify style1.css as the style sheet to which the new .category style will be added.

Q&A

Why does the style sheet URL include "styles/"?

Styles is the folder name where the style sheet is stored.

Figure 3–82

- Click the font-size box arrow, then click large to make the new style large.

- Click the font-weight box arrow, then click bold to make the new style bold.

- Click the font-variant box arrow, then click small-caps to change the new style to small caps (Figure 3–83).

Figure 3–83

4

- Click the OK button in the New Style dialog box to save the new style rules.

- Click the New Style link on the Apply Styles panel to open the New Style dialog box and create another new style.

- In the Selector text box, type dates to name the new style for the dates that appear in Mary's résumé.

- Click the font-size box arrow, then click small.

- Click the font-weight box arrow, then click bold.

- Click the color box arrow to display the color palette, and then point to the Silver swatch (Figure 3–84).

Figure 3–84

5
- Click Silver on the color palette.
- Click the OK button in the New Style dialog box to save the new .dates style.
- Click the New Style link on the Apply Styles panel to open the New Style dialog box and create another new style.
- In the Selector text box, type jobtitle to name the new style for the job titles in Mary's résumé.
- Click the font-size box arrow, then click small.
- Click the font-style box arrow, then click italic (Figure 3–85).

Figure 3–85

6
- Click the OK button to close the New Style dialog box.
- Scroll in the Apply Styles panel to see the new styles in the panel (Figure 3–86).

Figure 3–86

7
- Click the style1.css page tab to activate the page, if necessary, then press CTRL+S to save the style1.css file (Figure 3–87).

- Click the style1.css page tab Close button to close the style sheet.

Figure 3–87

To Apply a Style

The following steps apply the styles you created to format the résumé attractively.

- Select the word, Experience, at the top of the résumé.

- Click .CATEGORY in the Apply Styles panel to apply the .category style.

- Apply the .category style to the words, Education and Technical Background (Figure 3–88).

Figure 3–88

2

- Select the text, 2008-2011 MGA Web Designs Branch Center, WA.

- Click .dates in the Apply Styles panel to apply the dates style.

- Apply the .dates style to the text, 2004-2008 Mariposa Books Duxbury, WA.

- Apply the .dates style to the text, 2008-2012 Branch Center Community College Branch Center, WA.

- Apply the .dates style to the text, 2003-2007 R. G. Russell High School Branch Center, WA (Figure 3–89).

Figure 3–89

3

- Select the words, Web Designer.

- Click .jobtitle in the Apply Styles panel to apply the job title style.

- Select the words, Sales Clerk.

- Click .jobtitle in the Apply Styles panel to apply the job title style (Figure 3–90).

- Press CTRL+S to save the default.html page.

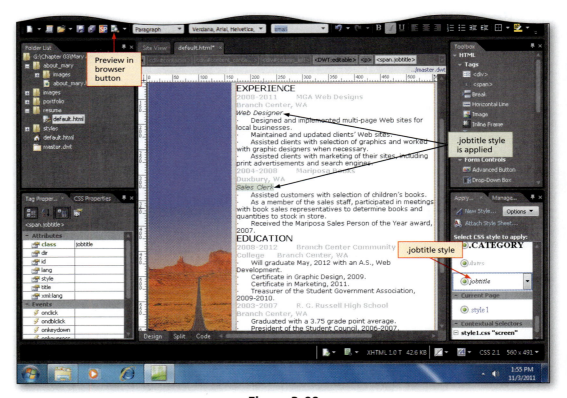

Figure 3–90

To Preview the Site

The following steps preview the site in a browser window and test a link.

 1
- Click the Preview in browser button on the Common toolbar to open the Résumé page in Internet Explorer (Figure 3–91).

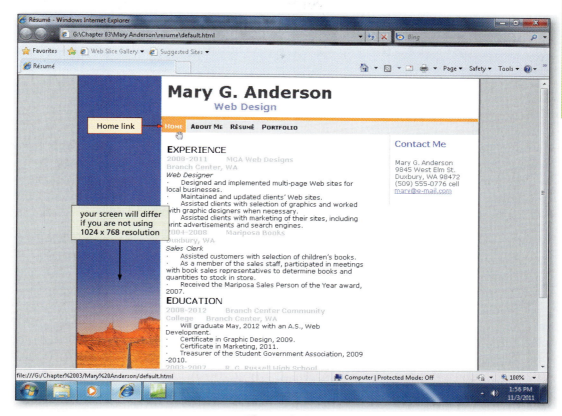

Figure 3–91

2
- Click the Home link on the navigation bar to test the link and open the Home page (Figure 3–92).
- Click the Close button on the browser window title bar to close Internet Explorer.

Figure 3–92

To Close a Site and Quit Expression Web

- • Click Site on the menu bar to open the Site menu, then click Close.

- • Click File on the menu bar to open the File menu, then click Exit.

Chapter Summary

In this chapter, you learned how to create a new site from a template and modify the structure of the template by adding, deleting, and renaming files and folders and attaching the template to a new Web page. You learned how to replace template text by typing or pasting text, and you edited the text. By making changes in the master.dwt page, you learned how to make changes to all pages in the Web site at once. You created, modified, and applied styles using CSS. The items listed below include all the new Expression Web skills you have learned in this chapter.

1. Create a New Web Site from a Template (EW 157)
2. Rename a Folder (EW 161)
3. Rename a Web Page (EW 162)
4. Delete a Web Page (EW 164)
5. Delete a Folder (EW 166)
6. Add a Folder (EW 167)
7. Add a Web Page (EW 169)
8. Replace Template Placeholder Text (EW 172)
9. Paste Text (EW 177)
10. Close Microsoft Word (EW 182)
11. Edit Text (EW 183)
12. Find and Replace Text (EW 186)
13. Make Global Changes to a Template (EW 190)
14. Modify a Style (EW 195)
15. Create a Style (EW 198)
16. Apply a Style (EW 201)
17. Preview the Site (EW 203)

For current SAM information, including versions and content details, visit SAM Central (http://samcentral.course.com). If you have a SAM user profile, you may have access to hands-on instruction, practice, and assessment of the skills covered in this chapter. Since various versions of SAM are supported throughout the life of this text, check with your instructor for the correct instructions and URL/Web site for accessing assignments.

Learn It Online

Test your knowledge of chapter content and key terms.

Instructions: To complete the Learn It Online exercises, start your browser, click the Address bar, and then enter the Web address `scsite.com/ew3/learn`. When the Expression Web Learn It Online page is displayed, click the link for the exercise you want to complete and then read the instructions.

Chapter Reinforcement TF, MC, and SA
A series of true/false, multiple choice, and short answer questions that test your knowledge of the chapter content.

Flash Cards
An interactive learning environment where you identify chapter key terms associated with displayed definitions.

Practice Test
A series of multiple choice questions that test your knowledge of chapter content and key terms.

Who Wants To Be a Computer Genius?
An interactive game that challenges your knowledge of chapter content in the style of a television quiz show.

Wheel of Terms
An interactive game that challenges your knowledge of chapter key terms in the style of the television show *Wheel of Fortune*.

Crossword Puzzle Challenge
A crossword puzzle that challenges your knowledge of key terms presented in the chapter.

Apply Your Knowledge

Reinforce the skills and apply the concepts you learned in this chapter.

Creating a Site from a Template
Instructions: Start Expression Web. Create a new Web site from a template, replace template text, delete and add folders and files, paste text from a Word document, and apply and modify styles so that the page looks like Figure 3–93.

Continued >

Apply Your Knowledge *continued*

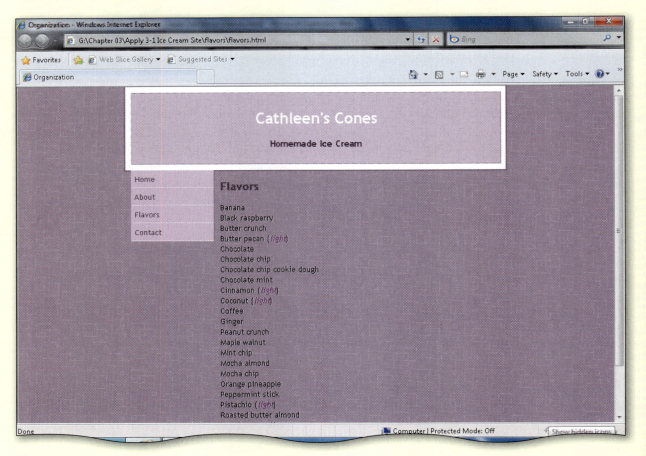

Figure 3–93

Perform the following tasks:

1. Create a new site called Apply 3-1 Ice Cream Site using the Organization 4 site template.

2. Open the faq folder.

3. Delete the faq/default.html file.

4. Delete the faq, information_links, news, photo_gallery, and calendar folders.

5. Add a new folder named menu to the top folder in the site (the one that lists the drive and folder name).

6. Insert a new page into the menu folder and attach the master.dwt file to it.

7. Save the new page as flavors.html in the menu folder.

8. Change the name of the menu folder to flavors.

9. If necessary, open the flavors.html page.

10. Open Microsoft Word 2007.

11. Open the document flavors.doc from the Apply 3-1 documents folder in your data files folder.

12. Select the list and copy the text to the Clipboard, then close Word.

13. Return to Expression Web.

14. Select the text in the paragraph tag below Heading 2.

15. Click Edit on the menu bar, then click Paste Text.

16. Click the 'Normal paragraphs with line breaks' option, then click OK.

17. Replace all instances of lowfat with light.

18. Select the Heading 2 tag, then type `Flavors`.

19. Save the flavors page, then close it.

20. Open the master.dwt page.

21. Change the left navigation bar to have four links: `Home`, `About`, `Flavors`, and `Contact`.

22. Change the hyperlink of the Flavors link to link to `flavors.html`.

23. Select the paragraph tag containing the bottom navigation bar and delete it. Then, delete the footer div.

24. Change the main heading (Organization) to `Cathleen's Cones` and the subheading (Organization Description) to `Homemade Ice Cream`, then save and close the master.dwt page, updating attached pages.

25. Create a new class-based style called `.light` in the style1.css file.

26. Assign the Purple font color and the italic font style to the .light style.

27. Open the flavors.html page, then apply the .light style to the four instances of the word, light.

28. Save the style1.css style sheet and the flavors.html page.

29. Preview the site and test the links, then close the browser.

30. Change the site properties, as specified by your instructor, then close the site. Submit the revised site in the format specified by your instructor.

Extend Your Knowledge

Extend the skills you learned in this chapter and experiment with new skills. You may need to use Help to complete the assignment.

Modifying a Template

Instructions: Start Expression Web. Create a new site based on a template, and then modify the text and styles in the master.dwt file to make the default.html page match the one shown in Figure 3–94.

Continued >

STUDENT ASSIGNMENTS

Extend Your Knowledge *continued*

Figure 3–94

Perform the following tasks:

1. Use Help to learn about adding an editable region to a dynamic Web template.

2. Use the Organization 2 template to create a Web site named Extend 3-1 Softball Site, then open the master.dwt page.

3. Click before the Home link in the footer, press ENTER, then click the blank paragraph above the footer.

4. Point to Dynamic Web Template on the Format menu, then click Manage Editable Regions.

5. In the Editable Regions dialog box, type `fact` in the Region name text box.

6. Click the Add button, then click the Close button.

7. Create a new style named `.fact`.

8. Choose the medium font size, the italic font style, and the Maroon color, then click the OK button.

9. Drag to select the fact paragraph placeholder text, then apply the .fact style.

10. Replace ORGANIZATION with `THE LASALLE SHARKS`, then replace Organization Description with `Girls'Softball`.

11. Save the master.dwt page, update all attached pages, close the master.dwt page, then open the main default.html page.

12. Replace the contents of the Heading 2 tag with `The 2011 Season is here!`.

13. Replace the contents of the paragraph tag under the heading with `Players, parents, and fans... Get ready for another great year of Sharks softball.`

14. Change the sidebar heading to 2010 League Champions.

15. Change the sidebar caption to Congratulations to the 2010 Sharks, who won the Tri-County League Champion game 10-8.

16. Delete the sidebar photo.

17. Replace the contents of the fact paragraph with Shortstop Katie Yang has a 3.9 GPA and plays the viola.

18. Save the default.html page, preview the page, then close the browser window.

19. Change the site properties, as specified by your instructor. Submit the revised site in the format specified by your instructor.

Make It Right

Analyze a site and correct all errors and/or improve the design.

Placing and Formatting Images

Instructions: Start Expression Web. Open the Web site, Make It Right 3-1 Tools, from the Data Files for Students. Additional files needed for this activity are located in the Make It Right 3-1 Files folder. See the inside back cover of this book for instructions for downloading the Data Files for Students, or contact your instructor for information about accessing the required files.

The site needs to be revised to match Figure 3–95. In the master.dwt page, change the contact information, remove the Calendar link from the two navigation bars, and change the copyright information in the footer. Update the links in the bottom navigation bar by deleting those not on the side navigation bar, making sure the order matches the side navigation bar, and that the links in the bottom navigation bar all appear on one line. One of the unneeded links should be changed to the Contact link which links to the contact/contact.html page. Also insert and apply the tool_logo.gif to the master. dwt page, change the size of the logo, and apply transparency to the logo's background color (*Hint:* to change the logo image, right-click the Logo placeholder, then click Picture Properties on the shortcut menu, then click Browse and open tool_logo from the Make It Right 3-1 Files folder in your Chapter 03 data files). After the image is inserted, use the Appearance tab on the Picture Properties dialog box to change the width to 150. Use the Pictures toolbar to make the background color of the logo transparent. Delete the msfp_smbus2_01.jpg image. On the main default.html page, delete the msfp_smbus2_01.jpg image, change the headline, description, and subheading as shown in Figure 3–95. Insert the New Sales Opportunity subheading and then copy and paste the contents of the tool_sales .doc file from the Make It Right 3-1 Files folder into the paragraph placeholder. Delete the remaining placeholder text and tags. Create a new style on the style1.css style sheet called .highlight that uses bold, italics, Navy font color, and small font size, and apply it as shown in Figure 3–95. Delete the extra content folders (*Hint:* keep the images and styles folders).

Change the site properties, as specified by your instructor. Rename the site folder, Make It Right 3-1 Tools Site. Submit the revised site in the format specified by your instructor.

Continued >

Make It Right *continued*

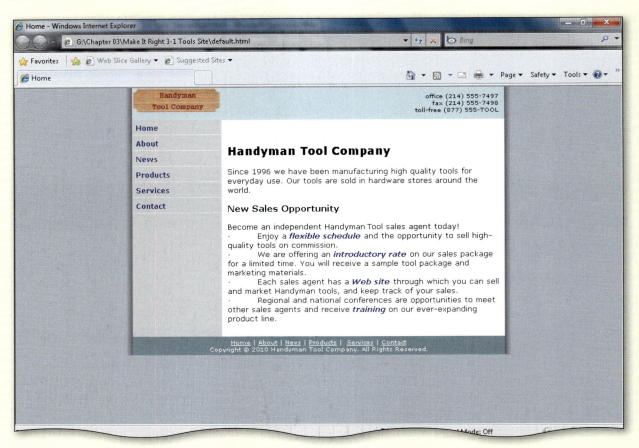

Figure 3–95

In the Lab

Design and/or format a Web site using the guidelines, concepts, and skills presented in this chapter. Labs are listed in order of increasing difficulty.

Lab 1: Creating a New Site from a Template

Problem: You have been hired to create a Web site for a local park. As part of creating the site, you are to add and edit page content. Use a template to create the new site, and insert and edit text to create the site shown in Figure 3–96.

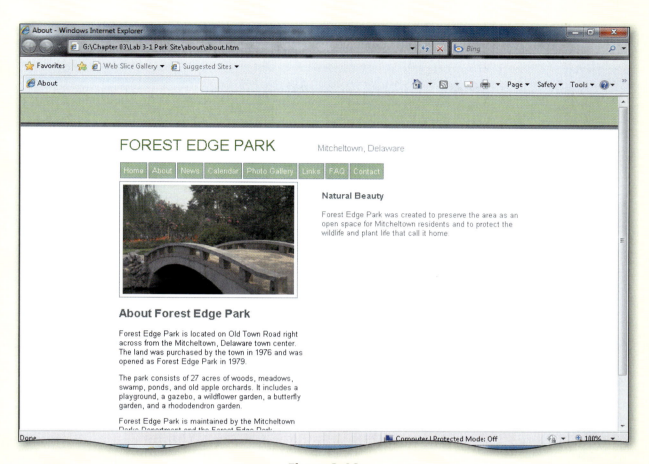

Figure 3–96

Instructions:

1. Start Expression Web.

2. Create a new Web site called Lab 3-1 Park Site using the Organization 1 template.

3. Open the master.dwt page. Replace the word, ORGANIZATION, with FOREST EDGE PARK. Replace the words, Organization Description, with Mitcheltown, Delaware.

4. Save and close the master.dwt page, and update all associated pages.

5. In the Folder List, click the about plus button. Change the about/default.html filename to about .html and update links.

6. Open the about.html page. Change the Heading 2 About placeholder to About Forest Ridge Park.

7. Start Word and open the about_park.doc file from the Lab 3-1 documents folder. Select and copy the text, then close the file and Word.

8. Paste the text as normal paragraphs without line breaks into the paragraph under About Forest Ridge Park. If necessary, delete any empty paragraphs that follow the pasted text.

9. Use the Replace command to replace all instances of the word, Ridge, with Edge. Close the Find and Replace dialog box.

10. In the right sidebar, replace the words, Additional Resources, with Natural Beauty. In the paragraph below Natural Beauty, replace the placeholder text by typing Forest Edge Park was created to preserve the area as an open space for Mitcheltown residents and to protect the wildlife and plant life that call it home.

11. Save the changes to the about.html page, preview the site in a browser, then close the browser and the page.

12. Close the site, then submit the site in the format specified by your instructor.

In the Lab

Lab 2: Replacing Template Text and Modifying the Dynamic Web Template

Problem: You are the owner of an interior design company. You want to create a Web site you can use to attract new clients. Use a template to create a new site, modify the site contents, and modify styles to create the site shown in Figure 3–97.

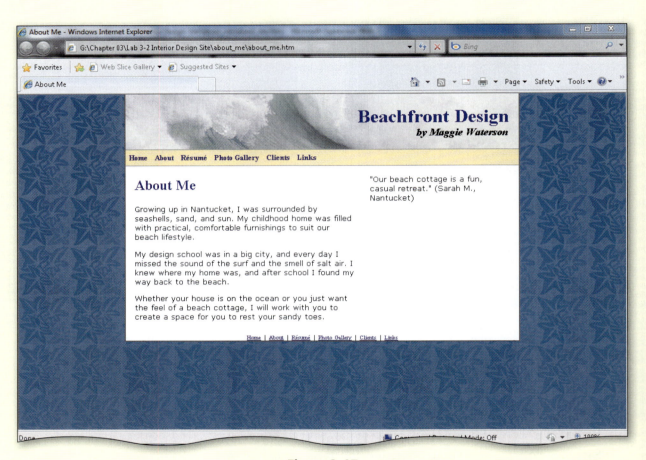

Figure 3–97

Instructions:

1. Start Expression Web.

2. Create a new Web site called Lab 3-2 Interior Design Site using the Personal 7 template.

3. Change the contact folder name to `clients`, and change the contact/default.html filename to `clients.html`, updating links.

4. Open the master.dwt page. In both navigation bars, change the Contact link name to `Clients`. Verify that the hyperlinks for both link to the clients.html page and edit if necessary.

5. Replace the words, My Website, with `Beachfront Design`. Replace the words, Website description, with `by Maggie Waterson`.

6. Add the styles as noted in Table 3–2 below. The styles should be defined in the current page. The #masthead h3 style already exists and therefore can be modified.

Table 3–2

Style Name	Affects	Values
#masthead h1	Beachfront Design	Navy; bold; Times New Roman, Times, serif; xx-large
#masthead h3	by Maggie Waterson	Black; italic; Times New Roman, Times, serif; large
#navigation	Top navigation bar	Navy; bold; Times New Roman, Times, serif
h2	Headline 2	Navy; bold; Times New Roman, Times, serif; x-large
a	Bottom navigation bar	Navy; Times New Roman, Times, serif

7. Save and close the master.dwt page, and update all attached pages. Save and close the style3.css file.

8. In the Folder List, click the about_me plus button. Change the about_me/default.html filename to about_me.html.

9. Open the about_me.html page. Change Heading 2 to About Me.

10. Start Word, and open the aboutme.doc file from the Lab 3-2 documents folder. Select and copy the text, then close the file and Word.

11. Select the placeholder text in the paragraph under About Me, then paste the copied text as normal paragraphs without line breaks. If an empty paragraph appears below these new paragraphs, delete it.

12. Delete the bottom sidebar div. In the right sidebar, type "Our beach cottage is a fun, casual retreat." (Sarah M., Nantucket).

13. Save the changes to the about_me.html page, then preview the site in a browser.

14. Change the site properties, as specified by your instructor.

15. Close the site and then submit the site in the format specified by your instructor.

In the Lab

Lab 3: Creating and Applying Styles

Problem: Your client owns a coffee shop and has asked you to add a page with a menu to a site he has created using a template. Create a new page, add links to it, and create and apply styles to format the page as shown in Figure 3–98.

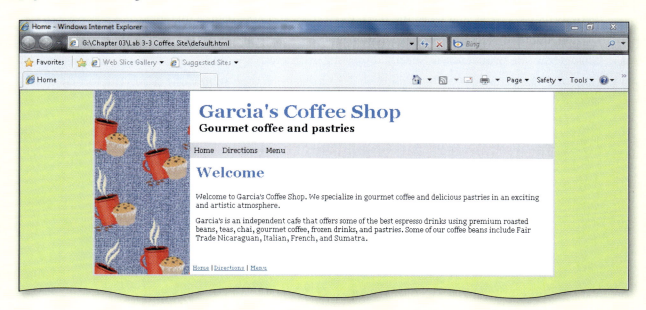

Figure 3–98

Continued >

In the Lab *continued*

Instructions: Start Expression Web. Open the Web site, Lab 3-3 Coffee, from the Data Files for Students. An additional file needed for this activity is located in the Lab 3-3 documents folder of the Data Files for Students. See the inside back cover of this book for instructions for downloading the Data Files for Students, or see your instructor for information about accessing the required files.

Perform the following tasks.

1. Create a new folder in the main site folder called `menu`.

2. Create a new page from a dynamic Web template, using the master.dwt page from the site. Save the page as `menu.html` in the menu folder.

3. Select the text, Headline 2, then type `Menu`.

4. Open Word. Open the file menu.doc from the Lab 3-3 documents folder. Select all of the text, then copy it to the Clipboard. Close the document and quit Word.

5. Use the Paste Text command to insert the copied text into the paragraph under the Menu heading using normal paragraphs without line breaks.

6. Create a new style called `.category` and define it in the existing style0.css style sheet. Format the style with the large font size, bold font weight, and small-caps font variant. Click the underline and overline check boxes in the text-decoration section, then click OK to complete the new style.

7. Create a new style called `.item` and define it in the style0.css style sheet. Format the style with the medium font size, italic font style, and Silver color. Click OK to complete the new style. Attach the style0.css style sheet to the menu.html page. (*Hint:* Open the menu.html page. Click the Attach Style Sheet link in the Apply Styles task pane. Click the Browse button, navigate to and click style0.css, click the OK button, then click the OK button to attach the style sheet.)

8. Apply the .category style to the following lines: JUST FOR BREAKFAST, MUFFINS, SCONES/BISCUITS/CROISSANTS, FOR THE YOUNG AT HEART, and DRINKS.

9. Apply the .item style to the following lines: Sandwich, Parfait, Morning Glory, Blueberry Bran, Corn, Lowfat Raspberry, White Chocolate Ginger, Cheddar Chive Biscuit, Croissant, Strawberry Tart, Blueberry Turnover, and Cinnamon Twist.

10. Save and close the menu.html page and the style sheet, if necessary.

11. Open the master.dwt page and create a link in both navigation areas from the word, Menu, to the menu.html page. Save and close the master.dwt page and update attached files.

12. Preview the main default.html page in a browser.

13. Change the site properties, as specified by your instructor.

14. Close the site, rename the site folder Lab 3-3 Coffee Site, then submit the site in the format specified by your instructor.

Cases and Places

Apply your creative thinking and problem-solving skills to design and implement a solution.

• EASIER • • MORE DIFFICULT

• 1: Changing a Site Structure

Practice adding and removing pages and folders to and from a Web site by first creating a site using any template. Delete a folder and its contents. Open a folder that contains a page and delete the page, then delete the folder. Rename a file and folder. Add a new folder to the main directory, then add a new page based on the master.dwt page to the new folder. Close the site without saving any changes, then quit Expression Web.

• 2: Make Global Changes to a Web Site

Create a new site for your book club using a template. Delete at least one page and its folder. Open the master.dwt page, and add a title and description for your site. Update the navigation area by deleting references to the pages you deleted. Change other information, such as copyright or logo, as necessary. Save and close the master.dwt page. Open the default.html page and view the changes you made.

• • 3: Paste and Edit Text

Using one of the Small Business templates, create a site for a travel agency. Use Word to create an itinerary for a trip you have taken or would like to take. Include a word that you will later replace with another after you have pasted the text into your Web site. Copy and paste the text into a page in your Web site. Use the Replace command to find and replace at least one word in the text. Practice selecting words and characters and deleting text. Enter text into the other editable regions on the page, then save and close the page. Open the master.dwt page, then edit the placeholder text. Save and close the master.dwt page, then close the site.

• • 4: Create a Personal Home Page

Make It Personal

You want to create a site that includes your résumé and information about you. Create a new site using one of the Personal templates. Enter information on the master.dwt page and the default.html page, then save and close the pages. Use Word to create a résumé, open a previously created résumé, or open the résumé file from the project in this chapter. Copy the résumé to the Clipboard. Open the résumé page, then paste the résumé from the Clipboard. Create at least two styles and apply them to the résumé page to format it. Save the pages and style sheets, then close the site.

• • 5: Enhance Text Using Styles

Working Together

Your local pizzeria wants to create a site for its business with three pages: home, menu, and directions. Working as a team with several of your classmates, plan and create the Web site. As a group, decide on the name of the restaurant and the menu. Each team member should create the text for the three pages in Word. As a group, decide on an Expression Web template for the pizzeria site. Add, delete, and rename pages as necessary so that your site contains the appropriate pages. Edit the text and navigation area(s) on the master.dwt page as necessary. Modify two of the existing styles in the style sheet. On each of the three pages, edit the placeholder text and insert the Word files you have created. On the menu and directions pages, create and apply at least two styles. Preview the site, test the navigation bar, and make sure that your site is readable and attractive. Save and close the pages and style sheet, then close the site.

Expression Web Design Feature

Web Design Basics

Objectives

You will have mastered the material in this special feature when you can describe how to:

- Identify a Web site's purpose, target audience, and structure

- Plan a site's navigation system

- Use color and page layout to unify the look and feel of a Web site

- Write and format effective Web page text

- Select and format appropriate Web page images, animation, and multimedia elements

- Perform pre- and post-publishing testing

Introduction

A successful Web site is one that winningly communicates its overriding message — learn something new, have fun, share ideas, make a purchase, and so forth — while, at the same time, satisfies site visitors' expectations. Creating a successful Web site begins with developing a solid design plan that provides answers to a variety of Why?, What?, How?, and Who? questions:

- Why will the site exist?
- Who is likely to visit the site and why will they do so?
- What types of Web pages will be included?
- How will the site's structure, color scheme, and page layout support its overall message?
- How will visitors navigate among the site's pages?
- What content will appear on the site's individual pages?
- How can I make certain that the site's features continue to work correctly and its content remains up to date and accurate?

Incorporating the answers to these and similar questions into a formal design plan enables you to apply the elements of good basic Web design to your site: a consistent color scheme; effective content positioning; easy-to-understand linking relationships; easy-to-read, accurate, and up-to-date text; and attractive, useful images.

To learn more about Web site planning, visit **scsite.com/ew3/websources** and click a link under Special Feature 1, Planning a Web Site.

Web Site Purpose, Target Audience, and Structure

Your first step in developing a Web site should be to establish the site's goals and objectives in order to clarify the site's overall purpose. Next, you should identify its potential visitors. Once the site's purpose is established and its potential visitors are identified, you are ready to identify the types of Web pages to be included at the site and the site's overall structure.

Establishing Your Site's Purpose

The planning process for successful Web sites of all types — from personal sites to small business sites to large commercial enterprise sites — begins with establishing one or more goals for the site. A **Web site goal** is a time-bounded and measurable result of a Web-based activity. The individuals and organizations that own Web sites often identify a single **primary goal** for their sites, augmented by several **secondary goals**. For example, the primary goal for an e-commerce Web site might be to increase the sales of products or services by 10 percent over 12 months; the secondary goals might include improving customer support by cutting support response time by 8 percent over 24 months and providing daily updated information about the company's stock price and other relevant information for investors.

A **Web site objective** is the method you choose to accomplish your Web site's goals. In our previous example, the Web site's sales goal might be accomplished by a variety of design objectives, such as creating an attractive product catalog that includes images, adding a site search feature to help visitors quickly find a specific product or service, or adding an easy-to-use shopping cart system. Summarizing a Web site's goals and the objectives necessary to accomplish those goals into a formal statement of purpose (Figure SF 1–1) for the site can help set the stage for its development.

**Web Site Design Plan
Statement of Purpose**

The Web site's primary goal is to increase sales of products and services by 10 percent over the first 12 months after the site is published. The site's secondary goals are to improve customer support by cutting support response time by 8 percent over 24 months and provide up-to-date stock prices and other relevant information for investors on a daily basis.

To accomplish these goals, the company will develop an attractive, easy-to-use Web site that includes a(n):
- product catalog with images,
- site search feature,
- easy-to-use shopping cart system,
- live chat customer support feature, and
- 'From the President' page with current information about the company.

Figure SF 1–1

Identifying Your Site's Target Audience

Potential visitors to a site are called its **target audience**. A site might have more than one target audience. Identifying the target audience requires developing a general profile for audience members. While the target audience for a small personal site might be well known to the site's owner, a small business owner or the management of a large commercial enterprise will likely find it necessary to research the demographic characteristics (age, gender, educational level, income, and so forth) and psychographic characteristics (social group affiliations, purchasing preferences, political affiliations, and so forth) that define their sites' target audience in order to build a satisfactory profile.

Good sources of material for developing a target audience profile include the U.S. Department of Labor, the Census Bureau, and the Small Business Administration Web sites and publications. After creating a target audience profile to identify who will likely visit your site, you should determine the types of pages to be featured at your site and each page's general content.

Types of Web Pages

Your site will have a starting page, called its home page. Because the home page is generally the primary page at a site — and often a visitor's entry point to the site — it is important that the home page content answers three important questions:

- *Who* owns and publishes the site?
- *What* information is available at the site?
- *Where* is specific information located at the site?

Figure SF 1–2, the Harry & David site home page, illustrates content that adequately answers visitors' Who?, What?, and Where? questions. The owner's name, graphic logo, and similar identifying content elements on the home page identify the site's owner. Text and images on the home page tell visitors what information or features can be found at the site, while links tell visitors where the information or features are located at the site.

Figure SF 1–2

The type and number of additional pages, called **subsidiary pages**, vary depending on a site's purpose. While a personal Web site might include only a home page and one or two subsidiary pages, a commercial Web site is likely to have a much more complex set of subsidiary pages. For example, Figure SF 1–3 illustrates just three subsidiary pages of the many pages at the Harry & David site: a product catalog page, a shopping cart page, and an About Us page. Each of these subsidiary pages can be quickly viewed by clicking a link on the Harry & David home page.

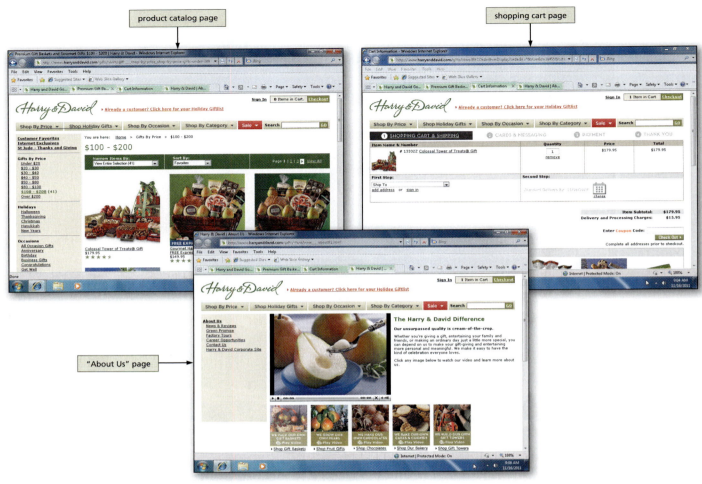

Figure SF 1–3

A **splash** or **entry page** is generally used to introduce a site and, where used, appears before the home page appears. The use of entry or splash pages is not universally supported by Web designers. Many designers think that splash or entry pages are a distraction that unnecessarily comes between the site visitor and the information he or she wants to find at a Web site. Additionally, many Web visitors do not like dealing with splash or entry pages.

Organizing your site's pages in a logical way will determine how well visitors can move from page to page at the site and how quickly they can find what they need.

Site Structure

The way in which you organize the pages at your site creates their linking relationships and is called the site's **structure**. Common Web site structures include the:

- **linear structure**, in which pages are organized and linked in sequential order; for example, in a step-by-step presentation of information

- **hierarchical structure**, in which pages are organized by level of detail; links flow from the home page, which provides summary information, to the first level of detail pages, then from first level detail pages to a second level of detail pages, and so forth; each subsequent level provides pages with an increasing amount of detailed information

- **webbed structure**, in which pages are not organized or linked in any specific order; visitors can jump from page to page, depending on their interests

More complex Web sites are typically organized using some effective combination of these basic structures, as shown in Figure SF 1–4. The goal of any site's structure is to create logical linking relationships that enable visitors to find what they are looking for by clicking a minimum number of links; the structure you choose for your site should help you best achieve this goal. You can manually draw a flowchart of your site's structure or use a variety of software tools, such as the Microsoft Office drawing tools, to draw your site's structure.

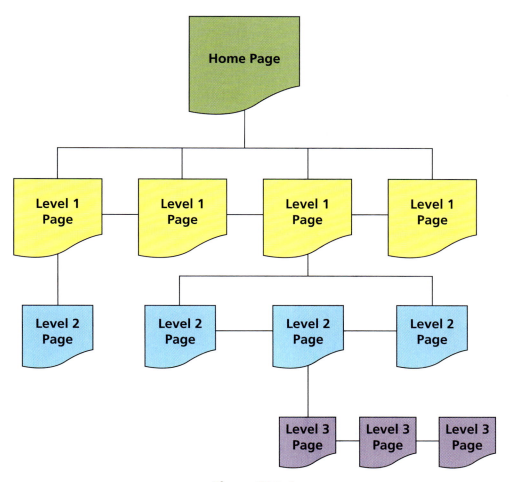

Figure SF 1–4

Now that you have planned your site's pages and structure, you are ready to design its navigation system.

Site Navigation System

Your site's **navigation system** should combine different types of links from the home page to subsidiary pages and from subsidiary page to subsidiary page, as necessary. When designing your site's navigation system, your first consideration should be your target audience's needs and expectations for moving from page to page at your site. Site visitors should be able to easily identify your site's navigational elements, quickly determine the logic behind the linking relationships at your site, and comfortably move from page to page based on their interests.

Depending on the complexity of your site, you will likely use a combination of different navigational elements, including text links, navigation menus, bars, tabs, image links, a site map, a breadcrumb trail, and, for a large complex site, a site search feature.

- **Text link** — a commonly used navigational element generally presented as underlined, often colored, text
- **Navigation menu** — a list of related text links
- **Navigation bar** — related links presented as a series of graphic buttons
- **Navigation tabs** — a series of tabs, similar to folder tabs, that often present alternate views of similar content
- **Image links** — an image to which a link has been added
- **Site map** — a summary list of all major links at a site
- **Breadcrumb trail** — a horizontal list of followed links
- **Site search feature** — keyword search capability for the site's pages

Figures SF 1–5 and SF 1–6 illustrate these various types of navigational elements at the Dell Web site.

Figure SF 1–5

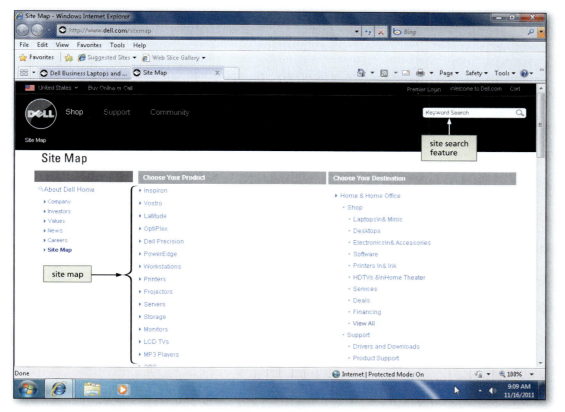

Figure SF 1–6

To help ensure a positive visitor experience at your site, follow these basic Web design guidelines when creating and positioning your site's links:

- Be consistent in the style and placement of navigational elements on all pages at your site. Using the same formatting for text links and the same style for navigation bars and menus and then positioning the navigational elements in the same location on every page helps visitors quickly identify links as they move from page to page.

- Place the most important navigational elements at the top and/or down the left side of your pages. Studies indicate a typical visitor first looks at the top of a page and then down the page's left side before focusing on the content at the center of the page.

- Clearly identify a link's target (destination) page. For example, use Contact Us or similar short, clearly worded text for a link to a subsidiary page containing contact information.

- Never use color alone to identify a link, and provide a text equivalent for a graphic link, such as a clickable hot spot on an image map.

- Place a Home Page link on all subsidiary pages to help visitors quickly jump back to your site's home page. If using a linear structure with pages to be visited in sequential order, add Next Page or Previous Page links.

- Provide a site map and a site search feature for a complex site with many subsidiary pages.

- Add a breadcrumb trail, if desired, to provide visitors with a visual guide of the links they have followed; however, a breadcrumb trail should only be used *in addition to* other navigational elements, such as navigation menus and bars.

Avoid rollover links — a link that appears only when the mouse pointer hovers over it — or other hidden navigational elements that might hinder your visitors' ability to quickly and easily find what they want and need at your site. Remember that your site's design, including its navigational elements and other content, should focus on communicating your site's message and satisfying your visitors' expectations, not on displaying your technical skills.

A good way to ensure that your site's navigation system will be easy to use is to perform **usability testing** of the system during its development and design phase. Participants in a usability testing team should include representative members of your site's target audience in addition to other interested parties, such as development team members, friends, family, and so forth.

The color scheme you choose and the way you position content elements on your site's pages directly affect the pages' attractiveness and usability.

Color Schemes and Page Layout

An important part of designing your Web site is to unify its look and feel through the consistent application of color and by repeating content elements, such as logos and navigational elements, across all the pages at your site. Figure SF 1–7 illustrates the unified look and feel of the Rackspace Web site's pages achieved by applying a distinct white/black/red color scheme and by repeating content elements, such as the logo and critical links, on all pages at the site.

logo, navigation elements, color scheme repeated across pages

Figure SF 1–7

BTW

Web Templates
A template is a model document. Web templates are models that contain consistent formatting, element placement, and color scheme used to give Web pages a unified look and feel. For more information about Expression Web templates, see Chapter 3.

Adding Contrast
Choose font colors that contrast strongly with the page background. Only use light-colored fonts on very dark backgrounds. When selecting a background color, keep in mind that it should be either very dark or very light to allow for enough font contrast to be readable.

Color Schemes

Color is an important design tool that you can use to ensure the unity and overall look and feel of your Web site's pages. To create an attractive and appropriate color scheme, you can choose three or four colors; for example, from the primary or secondary colors on the traditional color wheel (Figure SF 1–8). Choose colors that both set the mood — energetic and fun, competent and trustworthy, or crisp and businesslike — for your site and also help communicate its message. Figures SF 1–9 and SF 1–10 illustrate the different color schemes that support the very different Web site messages at the TD Waterhouse home page and Ben & Jerry's Fun page for kids.

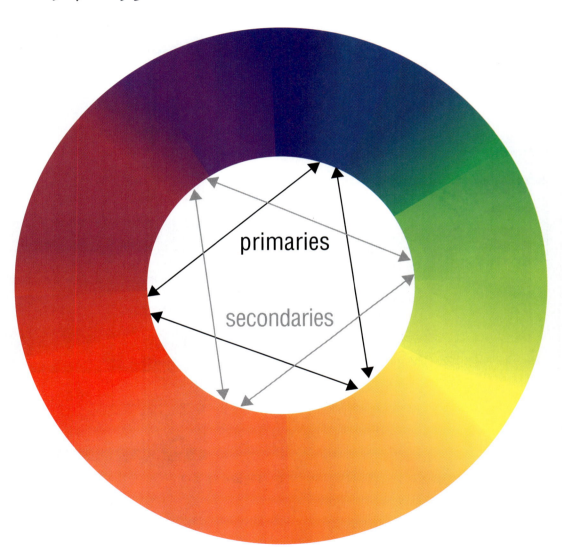

Figure SF 1–8

calm,
business-like
color scheme
invokes
feelings of
confidence
and trust

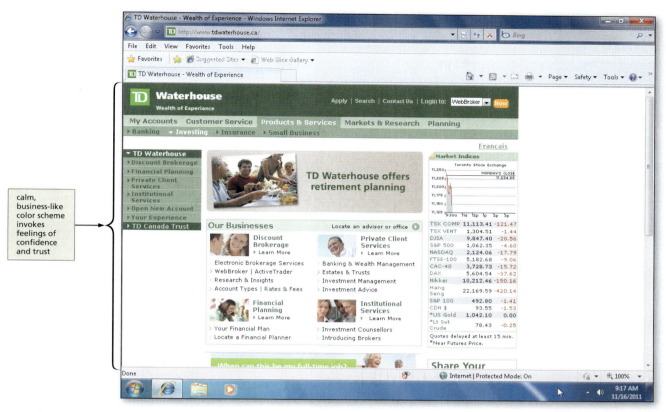

Figure SF 1–9

lively color
scheme sets
the mood
for fun and
play

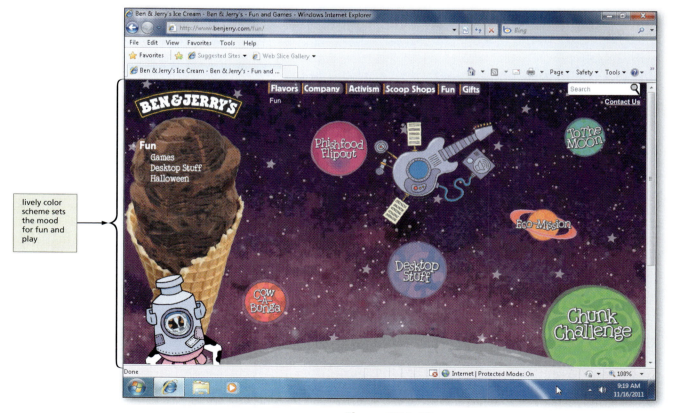

Figure SF 1–10

BTW

Web-Safe Palette
The Web-safe palette
consists of 216 of the
256 colors that can
be displayed by an
8-bit computer screen.
Because most Web site
visitors today use com-
puter screens that can
display millions of colors,
many Web designers no
longer adhere to the
Web-safe palette.

Additionally, you should choose background and foreground colors that provide adequate contrast. For example, the light-colored background, dark text, and comple-mentary accent colors in the TD Waterhouse site's color scheme provide an appropriate background and foreground contrast, as do the more vibrant colors in the Ben & Jerry's Fun page color scheme.

Colors have significant psychological and cultural traits that you must consider when choosing your Web site's color scheme. To learn more about color traits and design-ing with color, visit **scsite.com/ew3/websources** and click a link under Special Feature 1, Designing with Color.

Page Length and Content Positioning

Web site visitors characteristically dislike scrolling Web pages either vertically or horizontally, so you should create a logical layout for each of your site's pages that keeps page length as close to a single screen's viewing area as possible while also positioning the most important content elements so that visitors can easily see and access them. For exam-ple, consider positioning identifying information, such as a logo or name, in the upper-left corner of each page, major navigational elements near the top and/or on the left side of each page, and important text and image content in one or two columns in the center of the page below and to the right of the identifying and navigational elements — all within a single viewing screen, if possible.

The Our Food: Food Facts page at the Taco Bell Web site (Figure SF 1–11) success-fully limits page length to a single screen (when viewed at the common 1024 $\times$ 768 screen resolution). Additionally, critical navigational and identification content are effectively positioned at the top of each page.

Figure SF 1–11

The screen resolution at which visitors view your Web pages will vary and can affect their need to scroll pages either vertically or horizontally (or both) to view the pages' content. To learn more about designing Web sites to accommodate different screen resolutions, visit **scsite.com/ew3/websources** and click a link under Special Feature 1, Screen Resolution.

Arranging individual elements on a page so that the page conveys the correct message and evokes the desired mood requires that you combine the basic design concepts of balance, proximity, alignment, and focus in positioning page content elements.

BTW

Legal and Privacy Issues
Certain types of content related to legal and privacy issues, such as a copyright statement or links to pages that contain the site owner's privacy policy statement or its disclaimer of liability statement, are generally positioned at the bottom of a site's pages.

Balance, Proximity, Alignment, and Focus

Balance refers to the symmetric (in balance) or asymmetric (out of balance) arrangement of elements in relationship to each other. Like color, balance can set the mood of a Web site. For example, the U.S. House of Representatives site's home page (Figure SF 1–12) uses a symmetric arrangement of content elements to evoke a professional, conservative mood. On the other hand, an educational site directed at children, such as the Discovery Kids site (Figure SF 1–13), can effectively use an asymmetric arrangement of elements to create a mood of excitement, enthusiasm, and fun.

Figure SF 1–12

an exciting asymmetric arrangement of content

Figure SF 1–13

Placing related content elements near each other — for example, an image and its caption — uses **proximity** to visually link the related elements. **Alignment** of page elements horizontally and/or vertically gives a page a well-organized, professional look. The most dominant element, or **focal point**, on a page is the element upon which visitors concentrate their attention when they view a page. Photographs or other striking images, such as those in the center column in Figure SF 1–12, are commonly used as a page's focal point. The U.S. House of Representatives home page illustrates the effective use of balance, proximity, alignment, and focus to grab visitors' attention and reinforce the site's message: Check out the Congressional resources available here!

One of the most important content elements at your site is the text you use to convey accurate and current information. How you write and organize your site's textual content plays an important role in enhancing your site's usability.

BTW

Layout Tables and Frames
Although Web standards support using CSS to control element positioning and page layout, most modern WYSIWYG editors, including Expression Web, also provide tools for using layout tables to control element positioning. Using frames to display multiple Web pages on the same screen is, like layout tables, considered to be an outdated layout approach.

Writing Web Page Text

When composing the text for your Web pages, remember that visitors typically scan Web page text for useful information instead of reading the text word for word. Unless a page's textual content is intended to be printed and read offline, your pages' text should be easily scannable.

You can write scannable text by:

- using simple, modern language
- avoiding slang or industry jargon
- structuring your topic paragraphs in a chunked text style composed of a short sentence or two followed by a bulleted or numbered list that summarizes the paragraph's essential information
- organizing your text so that the main point or masthead appears on the home or major level page in the site's structure and relevant details appear on subsidiary pages
- avoiding text formatting that implies a link, such as the traditional colors of blue or purple or underlining the text, and using bold or italic formatting sparingly
- avoiding excessive use of uppercase characters that are more difficult to scan

Figure SF 1–14 compares a densely worded topic paragraph written for the printed page and then a portion of the paragraph summarized as scannable text for a Web page.

Identifying the potential visitors to a site, called its **target audience**, requires developing a general profile for audience members. While the target audience(s) for a small personal site might be well known to the owner, a small business owner or the management of a large commercial enterprise will likely find it necessary to research the demographic characteristics (age, gender, educational level, income, and so forth) and psychographic characteristics (social group affiliations, purchasing preferences, political affiliations, and so forth) that define their sites' targeted audiences in order to build a satisfactory profile.

densely worded paragraph for printed page

Target Audience Profile
- Demographic Characteristics
  - age
  - gender
  - educational level
  - income
- Psychographic Characteristics
  - social group affiliation
  - purchasing preferences
  - political affiliations

scannable text for Web page

Figure SF 1–14

A **font** is a combination of typeface, size, and style used to create text characters. You are likely familiar with selecting a font, such as Times New Roman or Arial, when creating a word-processing document. A **serif** is a small line added to the top and bottom edges of a character. Readability studies conducted in the early days of the Web suggested that certain fonts designed specifically to enhance readability of printed characters, called serif fonts, decreased the scannability of online text and should be avoided. Modern studies suggest that the readability of online text is more likely to be affected by other issues, such as character size and spacing, the length of the text line, and the amount of surrounding white space.

Today, both serif and sans serif fonts are widely used on Web pages. Web designers are more likely to make their font selection based on the availability of fonts on the typical visitor's computer system and the way in which the site's fonts help establish the look and feel of the site to convey the site's message.

Selecting the right serif or sans serif font for your Web page text can enhance the pages' readability. For more information about selecting fonts and Web page readability, visit **scsite.com/ew3/websources** and click a link under Special Feature 1, Fonts and Readability.

Web page images, animation, and multimedia elements, like text, are also used to communicate with visitors and enhance their experiences at your site.

Web-Ready Images and Multimedia

Web page images — drawings, photographs, animated characters — and multimedia elements that combine images with audio and video, such as Flash movies or interactive games, are powerful tools for attracting visitors to your site, communicating with those visitors, and then encouraging them to take some type of action at your site.

For example, the Dell e-commerce site, illustrated previously in Figures SF 1–5 and SF 1–6, emphasizes unity by identifying pages with a graphic logo while converting shoppers into buyers by including attractive product photographs. The Taco Bell site, illustrated previously in Figure SF 1–11, successfully uses multimedia elements to help keep page content to a single viewing screen and interest visitors in menu items. Cable news sites use multimedia to tell today's interesting stories and encourage visitors to upload their own newsworthy audio and video for sharing with other site visitors. At social networking sites, member networking is enhanced by the inclusion of members' photographs in their profiles.

While Web page images can add impact to your site, poorly chosen or sloppily edited images can detract from your site's message and discourage return visitors. Consider the following guidelines when choosing images and multimedia elements for your site:

- Include only those images and multimedia elements that are in context with and support the other content at your site; never include images or multimedia elements just because they look great or to show off your technical skills.
- Use animated images and multimedia — including animated GIFs, gadgets, avatars, audio, video, and Flash movies — sparingly, and then only in context.
- Select images whose colors harmonize with your site's color scheme.
- Prepare Web-ready images by using image creation and editing software, such as Expression Design, to crop and clean up photographs, convert drawings into bitmap images, and optimize saved bitmap files for size and quality.
- Add alternate text to each image that appears when browser images are turned off.
- Never use images alone to convey information; include a text equivalent for every image so that visitors using assistive technologies, such as screen readers, can access your site's content.

For more information about selecting, editing, and optimizing images for the Web, visit **scsite.com/ew3/websources** and click a link under Special Feature 1, Web-Ready Images. To learn about current design standards and guidelines for Web page images, visit **scsite.com/ew3/websources** and click a link under Special Feature 1, Design Standards and Guidelines.

Testing your site's features and content during development, before you publish it, and on an ongoing basis after it is published is a critical part of your Web site planning and design.

Pre- and Post-Publishing Testing

Earlier in this feature, you learned about the importance of performing usability testing of your site's navigational system during the site's developmental phase. After your site is completely developed, but before you publish it to a live server, you should personally test all of the site's features and content by:

- reviewing the site's pages in various browsers and browser versions running under different operating systems
- verifying that all link text clearly indicates the link's target and that navigational elements work as designed
- ensuring that all images appear in the correct position on each page, that text equivalents are available for each image, and that alternate text is provided if browser images are turned off
- establishing that all textual content is accurate and current

Additionally, you should gather a team of testers, including representative members of your target audience and other interested parties, to test and critique your site's usability. Testing team members should review the site's structure, navigation system, color and page layout, and content, including the use of text and images.

After making revisions and corrections to your site based on the results of the pre-publishing testing, you are ready to publish your site to a live Web server. Once your site goes live, you should schedule periodic testing of the site's features and content to make certain content is up to date and features continue to work properly.

For a closer look at the Web site examples used in this feature, visit **scsite.com/ ew3/websources** and click a link under Special Feature 1, Web Design Examples.

Feature Summary

In this feature, you have learned how important it is to first identify a Web site's purpose, target audience, and structure before you begin creating its pages. You should also carefully plan the site's navigation system, color scheme, and individual page layout to give the site a unified look and feel. You also learned how to use the design concepts of balance, proximity, alignment, and focus to lay out attractive Web pages.

You learned how to write scannable text for your pages and the importance of including only those Web-ready images, animations, and multimedia elements that support a site's message. Finally, you learned about the significance of pre- and post-publishing testing of the site and all its features.

In the Lab

Use the Web design concepts discussed in this special feature to evaluate the design of existing Web sites, create your own Web sites with a unified look and feel, and edit existing text to be scannable Web page text.

Lab 1: Evaluating Web Site Design

Problem: You are the administrative assistant to the manager of a Web design firm. Your manager is putting together a seminar for new employees that will review Web design basics. She asks you to find three examples of existing sites she can use during the seminar to illustrate Web design issues.

Instructions: Use the search tool of your choice to locate three Web sites: a personal site, an educational site, and a site that sells products or services directly to consumers.

1. Evaluate each of the three sites based on the following questions:
   a. What is the site's overall purpose or message?
   b. Who is the site's target audience?
   c. How well do the site's design elements (structure and navigational system, fonts, color scheme, and page layout) and content elements (text, images, and other content) support the site's message, satisfy target audience expectations, and contribute to the overall look and feel of the site? Be specific by discussing the effectiveness of each design or content element.
   d. Are the design concepts of balance, proximity, alignment, and focus evident in the site's design? If yes, where? If no, what changes would you suggest to incorporate these design concepts?
   e. Does the home page adequately provide answers to visitors' Who?, What?, and Where? questions? If yes, how? If no, what suggestions can you make for design or content that will adequately answer these basic home page questions?

2. Summarize your evaluation in a word-processing document.
3. Save the document using the filename, `Lab SF1-1 Evaluation`.
4. Print the document at the direction of your instructor.

In the Lab

Lab 2: Designing for a Unified Look and Feel

Problem: Two family friends, who know about your experience using Expression Web, ask for your help in designing a unified look and feel for their proposed Web sites. The sites have very different messages and target audiences. Create two sample multipage Web sites that illustrate the use of color, fonts, and navigational elements to create a unified look and feel appropriate for each site.

Instructions:
1. Start Expression Web.
2. Create a multipage Web site named `Lab SF1-2 Design Consulting`. The site should include, at minimum, a home page and two subsidiary pages. *Do not use a Web site template.*
3. Apply a unifying color scheme of your choice to the pages. The color scheme should be appropriate for a small business that will sell consulting services to other businesses through its new Web site.
4. Add sample content of your choice, including text, images, and navigational elements, to each page. Make certain that your choices, such as font selection or images, are consistent with the color scheme and are appropriate for the consulting business site.

5. Change the site properties, as specified by your instructor.

6. Save the site and submit it in the format specified by your instructor and then close the site.

7. Create a multipage Web site named `Lab SF1-2 Design Sports`. The site should include, at minimum, a home page and two subsidiary pages. *Do not use a Web site template.*

8. Apply a unifying color scheme of your choice to the pages. The color scheme should be appropriate for a Web site that promotes extreme sports and provides information on extreme sports events.

9. Add sample content of your choice, including text, images, and navigational elements, to each page. Make certain that your choices, such as font selection or images, are consistent with the color scheme and are appropriate for the extreme sports site.

10. Change the site properties, as specified by your instructor.

11. Save the site and submit it in the format specified by your instructor, and then close the site.

In the Lab

Lab 3: Writing Scannable Text

Problem: You need to convert text written for a document to be printed and read offline into scannable text for a Web page.

Instructions:

1. Open the data file Lab SF1-3 Text in Microsoft Word and save it as `Lab SF1-3 Web Text`.

2. Revise the dense paragraph text into scannable text using short introductory paragraphs and bulleted lists.

3. Resave the edited document.

4. Print the edited document at the direction of your instructor.

4 | Creating Styles and Layouts with CSS

Objectives

You will have mastered the material in this chapter when you can:

- Create ID-based styles
- Position content with CSS
- Format text with CSS
- Identify CSS syntax
- Use the CSS Properties panel
- Create a font family
- Create an external style sheet

- Modify a style sheet using code
- Attach a style sheet
- Add a Web page using CSS layouts
- Copy and paste elements among pages
- Organize style sheets
- Create a CSS report

4 | Creating Styles and Layouts with CSS

Introduction

Styles are rules used to control the formatting and layout of pages as well as individual elements and text in a Web page. The goal of using styles is to create consistently formatted pages that can be easily updated. You can apply styles directly to text or an element to format it individually, or you can save groupings of styles to a file called a **style sheet**. When a style sheet is **attached** to a Web page or pages, or to all pages in a Web site, it formats all like elements the same way. You can apply multiple style sheets to a single Web page: one for layout and one for text formatting, for instance.

Expression Web uses **Cascading Style Sheets (CSS)**, a style sheet language, to store style rules. CSS is the W3C preferred method for page layout and font. Expression Web is a great tool for using CSS to define formatting and layout. Expression Web will even create styles for you based on changes that you make to your page content, and uses panels and dialog boxes to create, modify, and apply styles. The actual styles are saved to style sheets as CSS files, which can be viewed and edited by using the style language to enter and modify the style code.

Project — Gallery Web Site

Galisteo Art Gallery in Goldstream, California, has a Web site that is in need of enhancing. The site currently consists of a few pages of simple text and images. The owner would like the site to look more professional and have the page elements consistent within the site. She also wants to add a new page that has a different layout and use CSS to make the new page's formatting consistent with the other site pages.

The project in this chapter uses Expression Web to create, modify, and apply formatting and layout guidelines using CSS to enhance the content and images of the unformatted Web site. The consistently formatted elements will appear on each page. You will create a new style sheet and define style rules while viewing the style sheet code. You will also add a page that uses CSS to define its layout and run a report to check for unused or incorrect CSS codes. The enhanced site is shown in Figure 4–1.

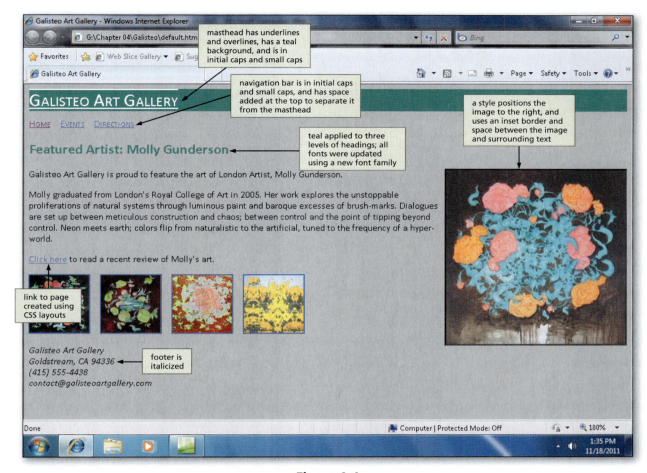

masthead has underlines and overlines, has a teal background, and is in initial caps and small caps

navigation bar is in initial caps and small caps, and has space added at the top to separate it from the masthead

a style positions the image to the right, and uses an inset border and space between the image and surrounding text

teal applied to three levels of headings; all fonts were updated using a new font family

link to page created using CSS layouts

footer is italicized

Figure 4–1

Overview

As you read this chapter, you will learn how to create the Web site shown in Figure 4–1 by performing these general tasks:

- Use CSS to format and lay out Web pages
- Create and modify styles
- Create a new font family
- Create an external style sheet
- Modify style sheet codes
- Attach a style sheet to pages in a Web site
- Add a Web page using CSS layouts
- Create a CSS report

**Plan
Ahead**

BTW

Web Accessibility
See Appendix B for more information about Web standards and accessibility and assistive technology.

General Project Guidelines
When formatting a Web site with CSS, you should keep in mind the purpose of using styles: to create consistent, accessible Web sites that are easy to maintain.

As you plan to enhance a Web site using styles, such as the one shown in Figure 4–1, you should follow these general guidelines:

1. **Define formatting and layout using styles.** Formatting and layout are two ways to enhance and organize your site. With CSS, you can use and create style rules that define the appearance (formatting) and position (layout) for each element on your Web site.

2. **Create your own styles and style sheets.** Saving the styles you create in Expression Web to a style sheet allows you to edit the style sheet(s) to make modifications to your site by rewriting the code or using panels and dialog boxes. When saving styles, you must specify whether the styles are part of an inline style that is used for only one instance of one element, as an embedded or internal style sheet that is applied only to the current page, or as an external style sheet that you can apply to other Web pages. Viewing the CSS style rules in Expression Web's Code view allows you to see text-based code that you can modify, copy, and reprioritize. Attaching the same style sheet to multiple pages ensures style consistency.

3. **Evaluate style sheets.** You can test the compatibility of your site with its associated style sheet(s) by running a CSS report. A CSS report alerts you to areas that you may need to fix, such as unused or conflicting style rules.

BTW

Removing Formatting
You can remove all associated styles from selected text or an element by clicking Remove Formatting from the Format menu.

Using CSS to Control Formatting and Layout

A style sheet is a file that stores style rules using a coded stylesheet language. CSS is the type of stylesheet language used with Expression Web. There are three ways to save styles using CSS: external, internal, and inline. Table 4–1 defines and distinguishes the three ways to save styles.

Table 4–1 CSS Style Saving Options		
Storage option	**Stored in**	**Used for**
External style sheet	A file that contains only the CSS code and that is saved with the extension .css	Applying styles to a page, a site, or multiple site pages
Internal style sheet	The Head section of the XHTML file for the page	Formatting the document in which it is created
Inline style	The Body section of the XHTML file for the page	Applying formatting to a single instance of an element or selection

BTW

Extensible Stylesheet Language (XSL)
XSL is another stylesheet language supported by the W3C. Unlike CSS, it has the capability to transform already-created documents into HTML files with supporting CSS. CSS is considered easier to use.

CSS Syntax

A CSS rule has three parts: a selector (the "what," such as h1), a property (the "how," such as font-size), and a value (the "how much," such as xx-large). There are three main types of selectors: a specific element, a class of element, or an ID selector, which affects a single instance of an element. You can even assign a style rule to multiple selectors. There are also three selectors that are used when creating internal and external CSS styles: element, class, and ID. A selector defines the target to which a style rule is applied; an inline style only applies to one instance, which is the selector. When viewing the style rules in a CSS file, the selector appears before the bracketed information.

Figure 4–2 shows a style sheet from the Galisteo Web site. Expression Web uses color coding to distinguish the different parts of the style rules. Gray is used to show comments or headings that give information about the styles or style sheets, but that do not contain code. Line breaks and indentations help differentiate rules and parts of rules. Braces are used to show beginnings and endings of rules.

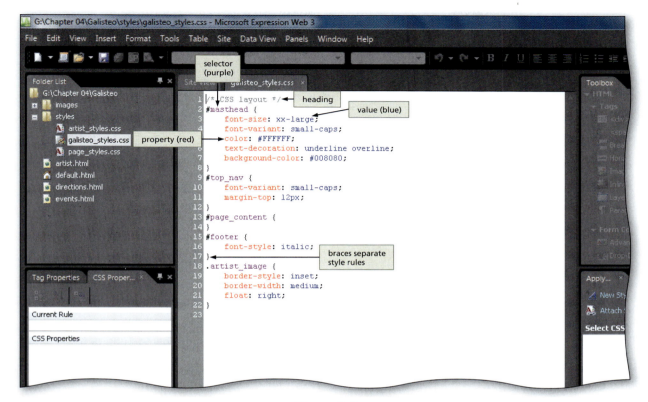

Figure 4–2

An **element-based style rule** affects an HTML page element, such as paragraphs, lists, or body text, and applies that rule to all instances of that element. When you create an element-based style rule, it uses **inheritance**, which means that it affects not only the element to which you apply the rule but also any elements contained within that element — for instance, the body element, which can contain paragraphs, lists, and so on. A **class-based style rule** is used to format a specific instance of an element or a part of an element. When you create a class-based style rule, you must manually apply it to page content, as opposed to an element-based style rule, which automatically is applied to all instances of that element. An **ID-based style rule** is used to format a specific element that only appears once per page, such as in the footer. An ID-based style rule must be applied directly to the element for it to take effect. Table 4–2 defines and distinguishes the three CSS types.

Table 4–2 CSS Style Types		
Style type	**Used for**	**Example**
Element	A rule that you want applied for every instance of an HTML element, such as defining the margins that surround every p tag	h1 {font-size: xx-large}
Class	A rule that you want to repeat several times in a page or site, such as to format headings within a block of text that contains a résumé	.jobtitle {color: red; font-size: large}
ID	A rule that you want applied to a single instance that will appear only once per page, such as a footer or masthead	#footer {color: blue; font-variant: italic}

Using CSS to Prioritize Rules

Because a single page might have multiple CSS rules and style sheets associated with it, CSS applies styles in a specific order of priority. Style rules are prioritized by their specificity or locality. Inline styles take precedence over internal styles, and internal styles take precedence over external styles. ID style rules are applied over conflicting class or element style rules.

If a portion of a rule is overruled, such as font size, by the precedence of a higher priority rule, any other non-conflicting portions of the rule, such as font color, will still be applied. For example, an inline style that formats header fonts as extra-large will take precedence over an internal style sheet that formats header fonts as large and navy blue. The navy blue font color is still applied. Within a style sheet, conflicts are resolved by giving precedence over whichever rule is furthest down in the list of rules.

Plan Ahead

Define formatting and layout using styles.
When enhancing a Web page, you should consider the types of elements you need to format and the type of CSS rule that best fits each element. Keep in mind the goal of achieving consistency within the site.

- Use direct formatting sparingly, doing so only to emphasize certain words or phrases that are not repeated.

- Create ID-based style rules to easily update like page elements, such as the masthead or footer on all pages at once.

- Create class-based style rules to change the style of headings or paragraphs, or to reposition or add a border to an image.

- Use a combination of panels, dialog boxes, and Code view to create and modify styles.

Storing Color Information
Although Expression Web prompts you to select colors by their names, the specification for colors can also be coded using the # sign followed by numbers and/or letters (a hex value) that indicate the exact color to the browser.

To Start Expression Web and Reset the Workspace Layout

If you are using a computer to step through the project in this chapter, and you want your screens to match the figures in this book, you should change your computer's resolution to 1024 × 768. For information about how to change a computer's resolution, read Appendix G.

You may need to ask your instructor how to start Expression Web for your computer. The following steps, which assume Windows 7 is running, start Expression Web based on a typical installation and reset the panels in the workspace to the default.

Note: If you are using Windows XP, see Appendix E for alternate steps. If you are using Windows Vista, see Appendix F for alternate steps.

1 Click the Start button on the Windows 7 taskbar to display the Start menu.

2 Click All Programs at the bottom of the left pane on the Start menu to display the All Programs list.

3 Click Microsoft Expression on the All Programs list to display the Microsoft Expression list.

4 Click Microsoft Expression Web 3 to start Expression Web.

5 Open the Panels menu, and then click Reset Workspace Layout.

6 Click View on the menu bar, point to Ruler and Grid, then click Show Ruler to turn on the rulers, if necessary.

To Open a Web Site and Web Page

The following steps open the Galisteo Web site and the default.html page.

1

- Click Site on the menu bar to open the Site menu, then point to Open Site (Figure 4–3).

Figure 4–3

2

- Click Open Site to open the first Open Site dialog box, then click Browse to open the second Open Site dialog box.

- Navigate to and open the folder where you keep your data files (Figure 4–4).

Q&A

Why is the left column in my window narrower?

You can widen the left column in Windows Explorer by pointing to the right side of the column's border, then when the pointer with the left and right pointing arrows appears, drag the column border to the right.

Figure 4–4

3

- Click the Galisteo folder, click the Open button to close the second Open Site dialog box, then click the Open button to open the site in Expression Web (Figure 4–5).

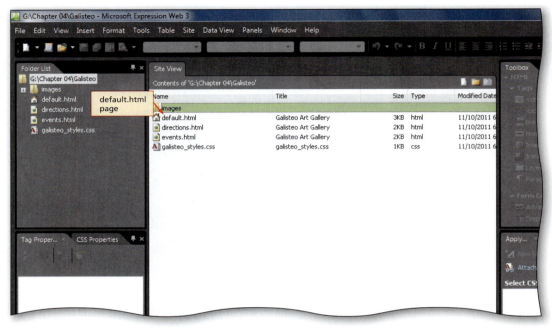

Figure 4–5

4

- Double-click the default.html page in the Site View panel to open it (Figure 4–6).

- Scroll through the page to view the current layout and formatting.

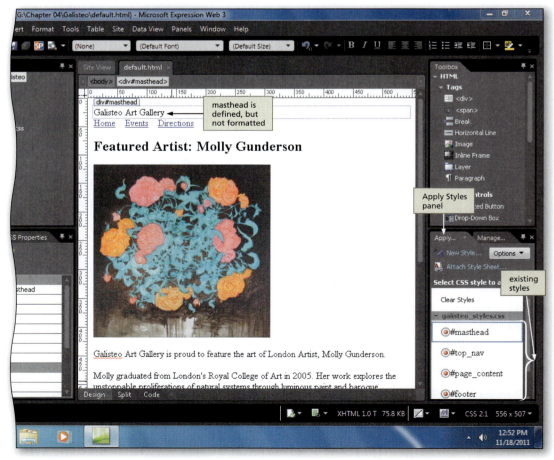

Figure 4–6

To Define an ID-Based Style

When creating an ID-based style, you must define the element to which it will apply, such as the masthead or the footer. The Galisteo Web pages were created using a CSS layout, which means that ID-based styles for the four page elements were created when the page was created. These styles appear in the Apply Styles panel, but no formatting has been assigned, so the elements look very plain. Using the Modify Style dialog box, the following steps modify the ID-based styles to format the masthead and footer elements for all pages.

1

- Place the pointer over the #masthead style in the Apply Styles panel so that the style arrow appears, click the arrow to view the menu, then point to Modify Style (Figure 4–7).

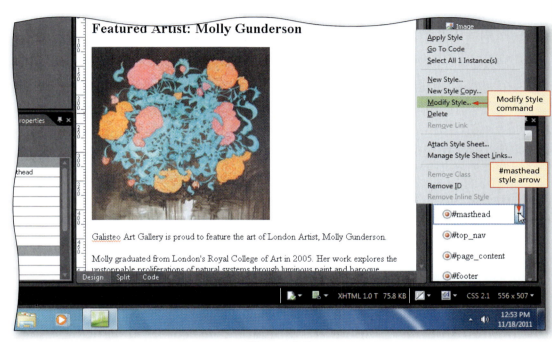

Figure 4–7

2

- Click Modify Style to open the Modify Style dialog box.

- Click the font-size box arrow to display the font size options (Figure 4–8).

Figure 4–8

3

- Click xx-large to change the masthead text size.

- Click the font-variant box arrow, then click small-caps to change the masthead text style.

- Click the color box arrow, then click White to change the masthead text color.

- Click the underline and overline check boxes in the text-decoration section to further customize the masthead (Figure 4–9).

Experiment

- Select other font-color, font-size, and font-variant options to view their effects in the Preview box. Change your dialog box selections back to match Figure 4–9.

Q&A Why is the Preview box blank?

The white font color cannot be seen on a white background. Steps 4 and 5 change the background color of the masthead to contrast with the white font color.

Figure 4–9

4

- Click Background in the Category list to display background formatting options.

- Click the background-color box arrow to display the color palette (Figure 4–10).

Figure 4–10

5

- Click Teal to make the masthead background teal (Figure 4–11).

Figure 4–11

- Click the OK button to close the Modify Style dialog box (Figure 4–12).

Figure 4–12

• Click the #footer style arrow in the Apply Styles panel to view the menu, then point to Modify Style (Figure 4–13).

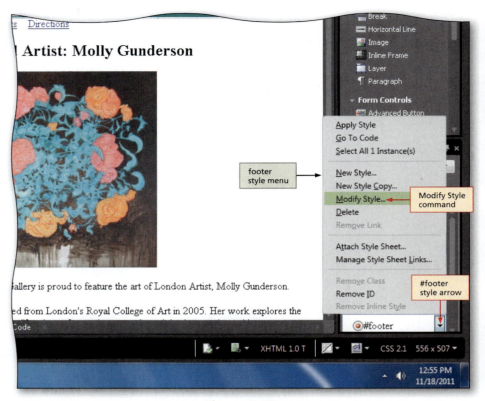

Figure 4–13

7

• Click Modify Style to open the Modify Style dialog box.

• Click the font-style box arrow, then point to italic (Figure 4–14).

• Click italic to change the footer font style.

Figure 4–14

8
- Click the OK button to close the Modify Style dialog box.

- If necessary, drag the vertical scroll box to scroll down the page and view the changes in the footer (Figure 4–15).

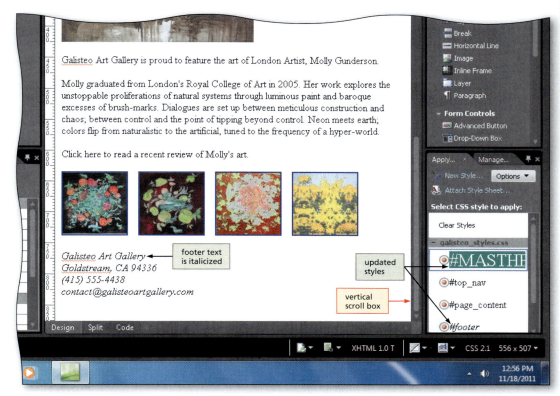

Figure 4–15

9
- Click File on the menu bar, then point to Save All (Figure 4–16).

- Click Save All to save changes to all open pages.

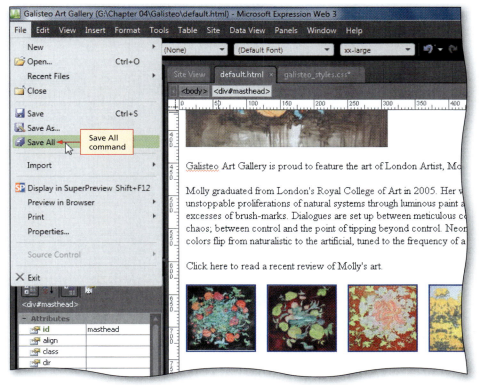

Figure 4–16

To Position Content Using a Class-Based Style

Using CSS, you can specify the position of elements such as images. The following steps create a class-based style for the main image on the home page by specifying its position and defining a margin.

- Click the New Style link on the Apply Styles panel to open the New Style dialog box (Figure 4–17).

Figure 4–17

2

- In the Selector box, type artist_image to name the new style. Be sure the initial period remains in the text box.

- Click the Define in box arrow, then click Existing style sheet to activate the URL box.

- Click the URL box arrow to display a list of existing style sheets.

- Click galisteo_styles. css to select the location where the new style will be saved (Figure 4–18).

Figure 4–18

3

- Click Layout in the Category list to display layout formatting options.

- Click the float box arrow, then point to right (Figure 4–19).

- Click right to align the element to which the style will be applied with the right page margin.

Figure 4–19

4

- Click Border in the Category list to display border formatting options.

- Click the top border-style box arrow to display the menu, then click inset from the menu.

- Click the top border-width box arrow, then point to medium (Figure 4–20).

- Click medium to add a medium-width border to the element to which the style will be applied.

Figure 4–20

5

- Click the OK button to close the New Style dialog box.

- If necessary, drag the vertical scroll box up to view the image at the top of the page.

- Click the image at the top of the page to select it.

- If necessary, scroll down in the Apply Styles panel and click .artist_image to apply the new style to the image (Figure 4–21).

- Save all open files and click the OK button to save the embedded file, if necessary.

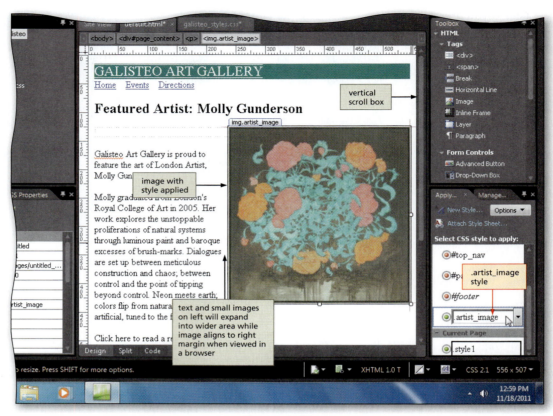

Figure 4–21

To Use the CSS Properties Panel

You can also modify styles directly in the CSS Properties panel instead of opening the Modify Style dialog box. Changes you make in the CSS Properties panel are applied automatically. The following steps use the CSS Properties panel to apply small caps to the navigation bar and to add a space at the top of the navigation bar to separate it from the masthead.

1

- Click the CSS Properties tab in the Tag Properties panel to display the CSS Properties panel (Figure 4–22).

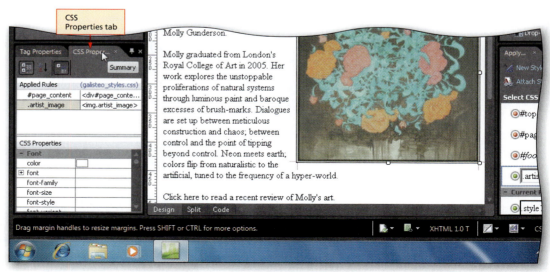

Figure 4–22

2

- Scroll up in the editing window, if necessary, and click in the navigation bar to display the style properties in the CSS Properties panel (Figure 4–23).

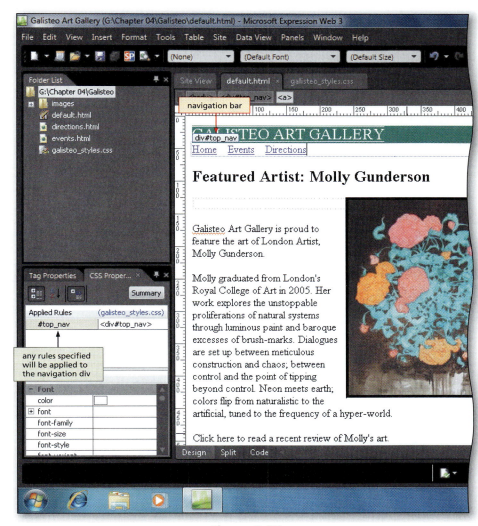

Figure 4–23

3

- If necessary, scroll down in the CSS Properties panel and click in the font-variant box to display the arrow.

- Click the font-variant box arrow, then point to small-caps (Figure 4–24).

- Click small-caps to apply small caps to the navigation bar.

Figure 4–24

4

- In the CSS Properties list, scroll down to the Box section, then click in the margin-top box to display the arrow.

- Click the margin-top box arrow to display the margin-top list (Figure 4–25).

Figure 4–25

5

- Click Pick Length to open the Length dialog box, where you will specify how much space to add between the masthead and the navigation bar.

- Type 12 in the Length value box to specify 12 pixels of space between the top of the navigation bar and the masthead (Figure 4–26).

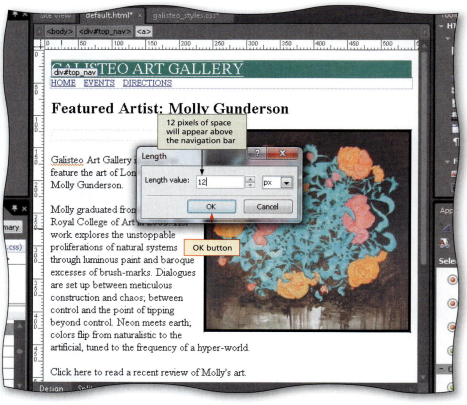

Figure 4–26

6

- Click the OK button to close the Length dialog box (Figure 4–27).

- Save changes to all open and embedded files.

Figure 4–27

Creating and Attaching Style Sheets

Before CSS, formatting was specified within the individual HTML pages of a site, requiring that the formatting and layout for each element be specified at each occurrence. CSS allows you to store the style rules for an element in a CSS file and the content in the HTML files. This separation allows for greater flexibility when making changes.

You can create style sheets that separate styles for a certain purpose, such as all of the layout guidelines, or all of the general page guidelines. Style rules for a new style sheet can be defined either by using the New Style dialog box to name, define, and save a style, or by entering style code directly in the style sheet. A style sheet can be attached to the active Web page, to all open pages, or to all pages in the site.

BTW

Speed
Pages styled using CSS are usually faster to download because the HTML page is smaller as it doesn't contain formatting. The first visited page may take longer as the browser has to download both the CSS and the HTML file; for subsequent site pages, the CSS will already be in the browser's cache, so only the HTML file will need to be downloaded.

Plan Ahead

Create your own styles and style sheets.
A style sheet can be used to group certain styles so that they can be applied to Web sites as a collection of specific formats. For example, you can apply styles for the font family and page background by creating a style sheet that specifies just those elements. You can then apply the style sheet to pages that may use different layouts.

When creating style sheets, plan for the following:

- **The number of style sheets for your site.** Do you need one for layout and one for formatting? Are there pages that require their own style sheets?

- **The priority of styles.** Are there styles that may be conflicting? How will you ensure the priority of rules?

- **The organization of style sheets.** How will you name the sheets to ensure that you know what each includes? Will you store your style sheets in a folder or series of folders?

BTW

User-Defined Style Sheets
Another accessibility feature of CSS is that a user can instruct his or her browser to override a site's CSS styles and apply a local CSS file, which will present the Web site in a format that fits the user's needs.

To Create an External Style Sheet

A style sheet that you create in Expression Web is a blank file with the extension .css. To specify styles, you must enter code by typing it in the file or assign styles to the CSS file in the New Style dialog box. The following steps create a new, blank style sheet in the Galisteo Web site. You will later enter code into the style sheet for all of the general page specifications, then attach it to all site pages.

- Open the File menu, then point to New to open the New submenu (Figure 4–28).

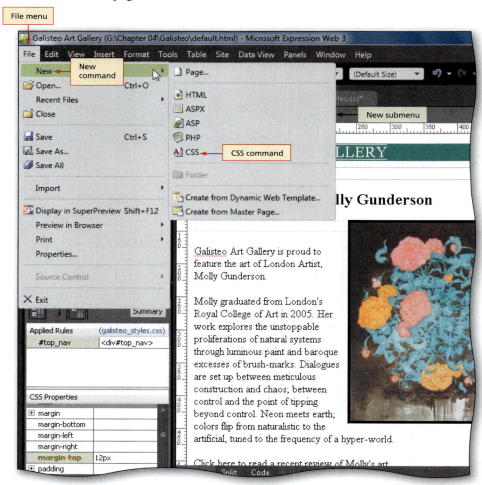

Figure 4–28

2

- Click CSS to open a new, untitled CSS file (Figure 4–29).

Figure 4–29

3

- Press CTRL+S to open the Save As dialog box.

- Type page_styles.css in the File name box (Figure 4–30).

Q&A

Do I have to type .css at the end of the filename?

Yes. The default file type for new Expression Web files is HTML, so you must specify that the file is a style sheet by including the file extension .css.

Figure 4–30

- Click the Save button to name the new CSS file (Figure 4–31).

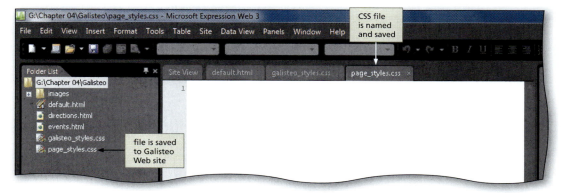

Figure 4–31

Font Families

Using a consistent font family in your site provides visitors with a common experience, regardless of the fonts they have installed on their computer. A **font family**, or font set, is a collection of similar font styles that a browser applies to text on a Web page. Expression Web includes three default font families, and you can also create your own. Specifying font families increases the usability of your site by providing a default font, then providing alternative fonts and font styles in case the font you specify isn't available on the Web page visitor's system. Font families, like other formatting characteristics, can be applied as a style. You can specify the default font or font family for a Web page by including it in the body section of a style sheet.

There are three types of fonts that are preferred according to CSS specifications, due to availability on users' systems and also readability on the screen: serif, sans-serif, and mono-space. Serifs refer to the strokes at the ends of a letter's lines; **serif** fonts have strokes, and **sans-serif** fonts do not. **Monospace** fonts resemble old-style computer fonts, and are not as commonly used as serif and sans-serif fonts. Two other types of fonts, cursive (or script) and fantasy fonts, should be avoided because they are not considered Web-safe as they are difficult to read online and not available on all users' systems.

When creating a font family, first decide whether to use all serif or all sans-serif fonts, then choose two or three fonts of that type that are generally available in most browsers. Lastly, include a generic font type, such as serif, sans-serif, or monospace, in your font family. Including a generic font type as part of your font family ensures that a browser can display a substitute font type in the event that your site's specific fonts are not available on the site visitor's system.

To Create a Font Family

The following steps create a font family using two sans-serif fonts and the generic sans-serif font type. You will later use this font family to define the body font in a style sheet, then apply the style sheet to all of the pages in the Galisteo site.

- Click Tools on the menu bar to open the Tools menu (Figure 4–32).

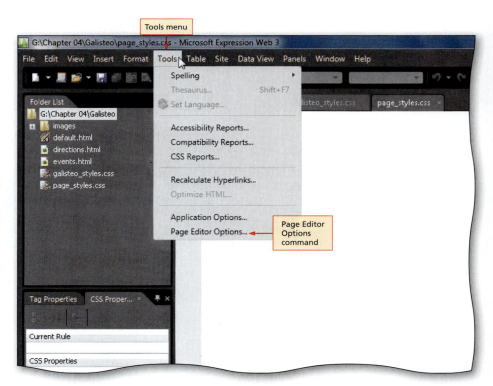

Figure 4–32

2

- Click Page Editor Options to open the Page Editor Options dialog box (Figure 4–33).

Figure 4–33

3

- Click the Font Families tab to display font family options.

- If necessary, click (New Font Family) in the Select font family list to start creating a new font (Figure 4–34).

Q&A

How do I know what fonts look like and what type they are?

If you don't have a specific font in mind or are not sure what font type a font is, click the Font list arrow in the Expression Web window to view fonts available on your system and see a preview of each font. Make a list of the fonts you would like to use, then do an Internet search for Web-safe fonts and see if yours comply.

Figure 4–34

EW 264 Expression Web Chapter 4 Creating Styles and Layouts with CSS

4

• Scroll to and click Calibri in the Add font list.

Q&A What if Calibri isn't available?

Fonts can vary based on the software installed on your computer. If Calibri is not available, then find another sans-serif font to include, such as Verdana.

• Click the Add button to create a new font family with Calibri as the main font (Figure 4–35).

🔍 **Experiment**

• Scroll through the list of available fonts to view all of the possible options.

Figure 4–35

5

• Scroll to and click Gill Sans MT in the Add font list, then click the Add button to add Gill Sans MT as the second font in the new font family (Figure 4–36).

Figure 4–36

6

- Scroll to and click sans-serif in the Add font list, then click the Add button to include a generic sans-serif font to the font family (Figure 4–37).

- Click the OK button to close the Page Editor Options dialog box.

Q&A Will the font family I create be available for me when I am working with other Web sites?

Yes. Font families that you create are stored on your computer and are available when you are using your version of Expression Web.

Figure 4–37

Entering CSS Code

When entering code into a style sheet, it is good design practice to include headings and comments that explain the background of the sheet and its rules. As you enter CSS code in a style sheet, Expression Web uses a feature called **IntelliSense** to prompt you by displaying shortcut menus of suggested selectors and options based on what you type. When a shortcut menu appears, double-click an option, press ENTER to accept the highlighted option, or continue typing to narrow your choices.

BTW

Comments in a CSS File
Comments are added to a document using the /*comment text*/ syntax. Adding comments to a CSS file can help you and others understand the CSS code by pointing out the effects the styles will have on a Web page, or by noting changes that you have made to the CSS code.

To Modify a Page in Code View

When creating an element-based style rule, you can use multiple selectors, such as different heading levels, to apply the same rule, such as font-color, to each of them by separating them with commas.

Remember to enter code very carefully, as your styles will not be properly applied if the code contains typing errors. Using the IntelliSense shortcut menus can help eliminate errors. The following steps use Code view to enter a heading and define style rules for the Galisteo Web site body font and page background color, then enter code to change three levels of headings to teal.

- Click in the new CSS file, type /*External Style Sheet to define page content by Your Name*/ (type your own name) to add a title to the page_styles.css page, then press ENTER twice (Figure 4–38).

Figure 4–38

- Type bo to display the shortcut menu (Figure 4–39).

Figure 4–39

- Double-click body on the shortcut menu to start defining the styles for the body of the page.

- Press the SPACEBAR, then type { to start a declaration block for the body content.

- Type f to display the shortcut menu, then point to the font-family option (Figure 4–40).

Figure 4–40

4

- Double-click font-family to select it and open the font-family shortcut menu (Figure 4–41).

Figure 4–41

5

- Scroll down if necessary, then double-click Calibri, Gill Sans MT, sans-serif to specify this font family (Figure 4–42).

Figure 4–42

6

- Type ; then press ENTER to start a new line of code.

- Double-click background-color on the shortcut menu to select it.

- Scroll down and double-click silver on the shortcut menu to select silver as the color for the page background, then type ;.

- Press ESC, press DOWN ARROW, then press ENTER to start a new line of code (Figure 4–43).

Figure 4–43

7

- Type `h1,h2,h3 {` to start a new rule that will be applied to three heading levels, then press ENTER.

- Scroll down and double-click color on the shortcut menu to select color as the property.

- Scroll down and double-click teal on the shortcut menu to select teal as the value, then type;.

- Press the ESC key to close the shortcut menu (Figure 4–44).

- Press CTRL+S to save the style sheet.

Figure 4–44

Other Ways

1. When the shortcut menu appears and the word you want to insert is selected, press ENTER to insert it

To Attach a Style Sheet

When attaching a style sheet, you can attach it to a single page or to all pages in the site. The following steps open the events.html page, attach the page_styles.css style sheet to all pages in the Galisteo Web site at once, and view the changes.

1

- Double-click events.html in the Folder List to open the page (Figure 4–45).

Figure 4–45

2

- Click the Attach Style Sheet link in the Apply Styles panel to open the Attach Style Sheet dialog box.

- Click the All HTML pages option button to select it (Figure 4–46).

- Verify that the Link option button is selected.

Figure 4–46

3

- Click the Browse button to open the Select Style Sheet dialog box.

- Click page_styles to select it (Figure 4–47).

Q&A Why do the icons next to my style sheets appear different?

Depending on the default program your system recognizes for CSS files, these icons may be different. This is OK.

Figure 4–47

- Click the Open button to close the Select Style Sheet dialog box (Figure 4–48).

Figure 4–48

4

• Click the OK button to close the Attach Style Sheet dialog box (Figure 4–49).

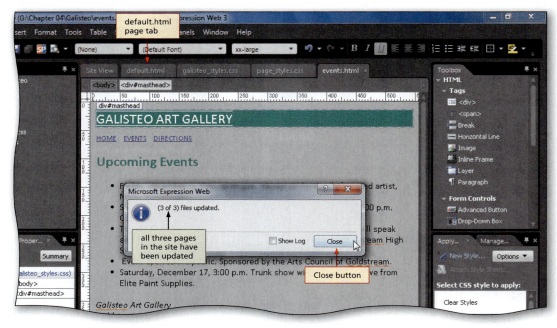

Figure 4–49

5

• Click the Close button to close the alert box.

• Double-click the default.html page in the Folder List to view the changes (Figure 4–50).

• Save changes to all open and embedded files.

Figure 4–50

Pre-Built CSS Layouts

Expression Web provides blank pages that use a CSS layout that includes divs for all of the page elements (masthead, content area, footer, columns, and so on) that are defined by using ID-based styles. When you use a CSS layout to create a new page, two files will open: an HTML page and a style sheet that includes the ID-based styles, which are blank. You can attach additional style sheets to the new Web page to apply formatting consistent with other pages in your site.

To Use Pre-Built CSS Layouts

The owner of the Galisteo Web site needs a new page added with a different layout. The following steps create and save the new page and the style sheet.

1
- Open the File menu, point to New, then click Page to open the New dialog box (Figure 4–51).

Figure 4–51

- Click CSS Layouts in the left pane to display CSS layout options.

- Click 'Header, nav, 2 columns, footer' in the middle pane to select it as the new page layout and view the page preview thumbnail (Figure 4–52).

Experiment

- Click the other CSS layout options to view them in the Preview box, then click 'Header, nav, 2 columns, footer.'

Figure 4–52

- Click the OK button to close the New dialog box and open the blank page and style sheet (Figure 4–53).

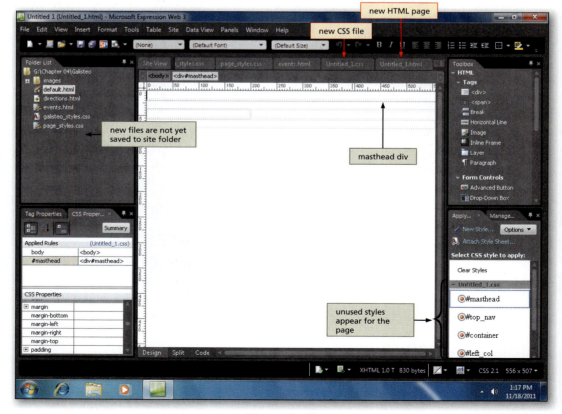

Figure 4–53

4

- Press CTRL+S to open the Save As dialog box.

- Type `artist.html` in the File name text box (Figure 4–54).

Figure 4–54

5

- Click the Save button to open the Save As dialog box for the CSS file.

- Type `artist_styles.css` in the File name text box (Figure 4–55).

Figure 4–55

6

- Click the Save button to save the CSS file to the site folder (Figure 4–56).

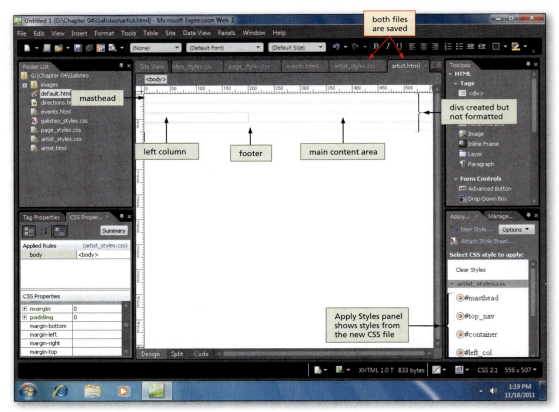

Figure 4–56

To Copy and Paste Elements

The following steps add content to the new artist page by copying and pasting text from other pages. Later in this chapter you will attach style sheets to the artist.html page to make the formatting consistent with the other site pages.

1

- Click in the masthead, then type Galisteo Art Gallery as the masthead text (Figure 4–57).

Figure 4–57

- If necessary, click the left scroll arrow so the default.html page is in view, then click the default. html page tab to display the default.html page.

- Click in the navigation bar, then click div#top_nav on the Quick Tag Selector to select the entire div (Figure 4–58).

Figure 4–58

- Press CTRL+C to copy the navigation div to the Clipboard.

- If necessary, click the right scroll arrow until the artist.html tab is in view, click the artist.html page tab to display the artist.html page.

- Click in the navigation div, then click <div#top_nav> on the Quick Tag Selector to select the div (Figure 4–59).

Figure 4–59

- Press CTRL+V to replace the existing div with the copied navigation bar (Figure 4–60).

Figure 4–60

- Repeat Steps 2 through 4 to copy and paste the footer from the default.html page to the artist.html page (Figure 4–61).

- Press CTRL+S to save the artist.html page.

Figure 4–61

To Complete Page Content

The following steps add content and a link to the new artist page by copying and pasting text from a Word file, and typing directly into divs.

1

- Click the Start button on the task bar, point to All Programs, click Microsoft Office, then click Microsoft Office Word 2007 to start Microsoft Word (Figure 4–62).

Q&A

What if I don't have Word 2007?

If you have another version of Word you can use that, or use any text editor, such as Notepad or WordPad.

Figure 4–62

2

- Press CTRL+O to open the Open dialog box.

- Navigate to the location where your data files are stored.

- Double-click the galisteo_documents folder to open it.

- Click the about_artist file (Figure 4–63).

Figure 4–63

3

- Click the Open button to open the file in Word (Figure 4–64).

Figure 4–64

4

- Press CTRL+A to select all of the content.

- Press CTRL+C to copy the content to the Clipboard (Figure 4–65).

Figure 4–65

5

- Click the Close button on the title bar to close the file and quit Microsoft Word.

- Click in the #page_content div to position the insertion point (Figure 4–66).

Figure 4–66

6

- Click Edit on the menu bar and then point to Paste Text (Figure 4–67).

Figure 4–67

7

- Click Paste Text to open the Paste Text dialog box.

- Click 'Normal paragraphs without line breaks' (Figure 4–68).

Figure 4–68

8

- Click the OK button to insert the text.

- Click in the #left_col div to position the insertion point.

- Type by Xi Lu, then press ENTER.

- Type London Art Weekly, then press ENTER.

- Type July, 2011 (Figure 4–69).

Figure 4–69

- Select the words, London Art Weekly, then click the Italic button on the Common toolbar to italicize the text (Figure 4–70).

- Press CTRL+S to save the artist.html page.

Other Ways

1. Click the Copy button on the Common toolbar (Expression Web) or the Ribbon (Word) to copy selected text or images to the Clipboard

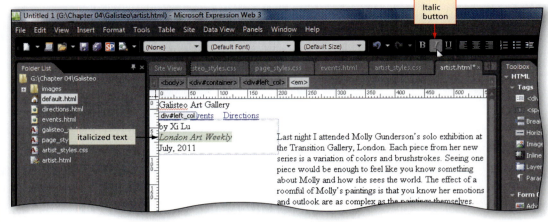

Figure 4–70

To Attach Multiple Style Sheets

To format the artist.html page so that it is consistent with the other site pages, you will attach two style sheets to the page. The galisteo_styles.css file was created when the default.html page was created, and it contains the styles for the masthead and other page elements, which you updated earlier. You created a new style sheet, page_styles.css, to define styles for the page background and headers. The artist_styles.css file was created when the artist.html page was created. It defines the page objects, such as the masthead, navigation bar, and footer, but there are no formatting style rules associated with that style sheet. When you attach the galisteo_styles.css file, the style rules for the masthead, footer, and navigation bar will be applied to those objects on the artist.html page. Because no formatting is defined in the artist_styles.css file, no conflicts will occur. The following steps attach the page_styles.css and the galisteo_styles.css style sheets to the new page.

- Click the Attach Style Sheet link in the Apply Styles panel to open the Attach Style Sheet dialog box (Figure 4–71).

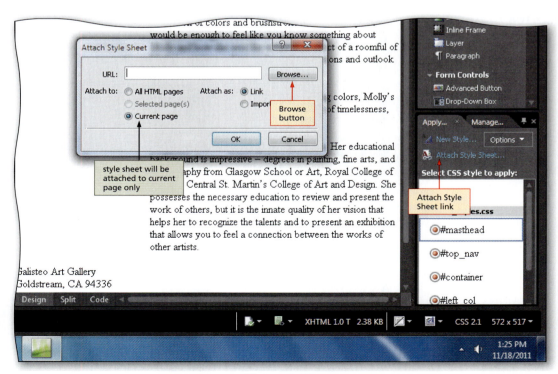

Figure 4–71

2

- Click the Browse button to open the Select Style Sheet dialog box.

- Click the page_styles file to select it (Figure 4–72).

Figure 4–72

3

- Click the Open button to close the Select Style Sheet dialog box (Figure 4–73).

Figure 4–73

4

- Click the OK button to close the Attach Style Sheet dialog box and attach the page_styles.css style sheet to the new Web page (Figure 4–74).

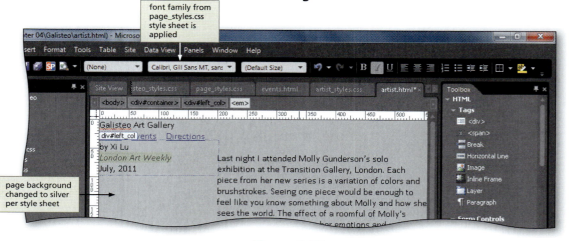

Figure 4–74

5

- Repeat Steps 1 through 4 to attach the galisteo_styles.css style sheet from the Galisteo site folder to the artist.html page (Figure 4–75).

- Press CTRL+S to save the page.

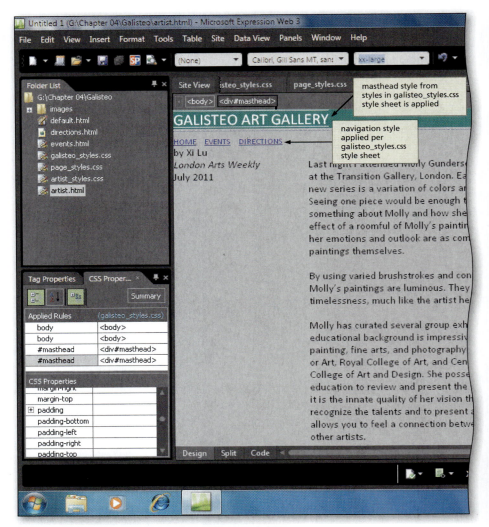

Figure 4–75

To Add a Hyperlink

The following steps create a link from the default.html page to the artist.html page.

1

- Double-click the default.html page in the Folder List to return to the default.html page.

- If necessary, scroll down and select the words, Click here (Figure 4–76).

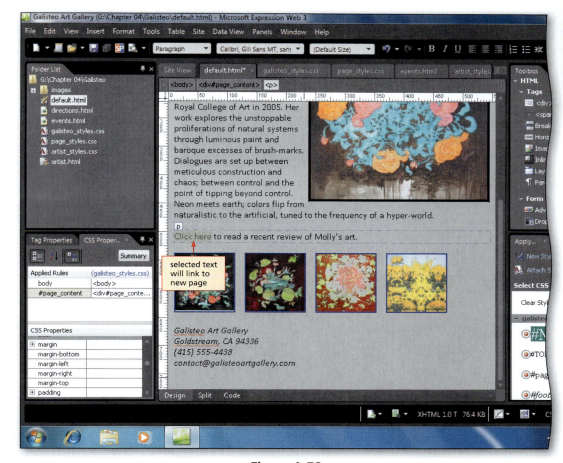

Figure 4–76

2

- Press CTRL+K to open the Insert Hyperlink dialog box, then click the Existing File or Web Page button, if necessary.

- Scroll if necessary, then click artist to select it as the link target (Figure 4–77).

Figure 4–77

• Click the OK button to close the Insert Hyperlink dialog box and create the link, then save the page (Figure 4–78).

Figure 4–78

To Organize Style Sheets

It is important to keep your site organized by adding folders to store related files. Keeping all of the style sheets in one folder makes them easy to locate. The following steps add a new folder and move the three style sheets into it.

• Click the Site View tab to display the Web site contents (Figure 4–79).

Q&A

Why are my files in a different order?

Depending on past usage, your files may be sorted in a different order (by name, title, size, etc.).

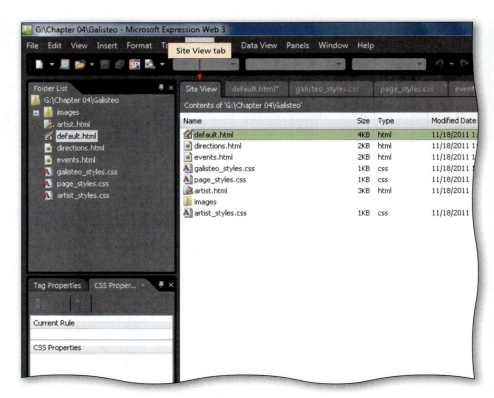

Figure 4–79

2

- Right-click a blank area of the Site View window to open the shortcut menu.

- Point to New, then point to Folder (Figure 4–80).

Figure 4–80

3

- Click Folder to add a new unnamed folder to the Web site.

- Type styles as the new folder name, then press ENTER. If the Confirm Rename alert box appears, click Yes to continue (Figure 4–81).

Figure 4–81

4

- Save all files, then click a blank area of the Site View window to deselect the styles folder.

- Press and hold CTRL, then click each of the three style sheets (the .css files) to select them (Figure 4–82).

Figure 4–82

• Drag the selected files over the styles folder in the Site View window to move them into the new styles folder (Figure 4–83).

Other Ways

1. Click File on the menu bar, point to New, then click Folder
2. Press and hold CTRL, then click each filename individually to select non-adjacent files

Figure 4–83

Plan Ahead

Evaluate style sheets.
A CSS report is a panel that lists any possible errors, including style conflicts or unused styles. You can run a report for the entire site, for a particular page, or for a specific style. The panel can be used to scroll through the results, open the style sheet that contains an error, or sort or filter the results.

To Create a CSS Report

The following steps run a CSS report. You do not need to fix either of the errors because you want to keep the unused styles for future site pages and content.

• Open the Tools menu, then point to CSS Reports (Figure 4–84).

Figure 4–84

- Click CSS Reports to open the CSS Reports dialog box.

- Click the All pages option button to include all the Galisteo Web site pages in the report.

- Click any unselected check boxes in the Check for section to specify the report options (Figure 4–85).

Figure 4–85

3

- Click the Check button to start the check and open the CSS Reports panel (Figure 4–86).

- Examine the report results, then click the Close button on the CSS Reports panel to close it.

- Save all open and embedded files.

Figure 4–86

To Preview the Site

The following steps preview the site and check the links.

1

- Click the default.html tab to make it active.

- Click the Preview in browser button arrow on the Common toolbar to open the menu, then point to Windows Internet Explorer 8.0 (Figure 4–87).

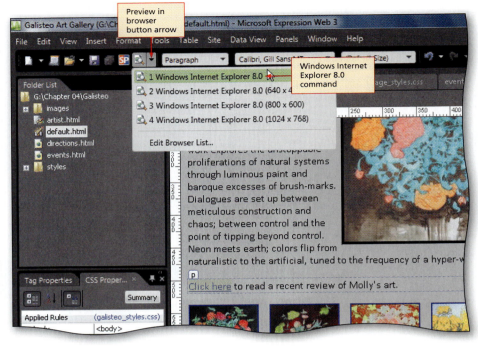

Figure 4–87

2

- Click Windows Internet Explorer 8.0 to open the page in a browser window (Figure 4–88).

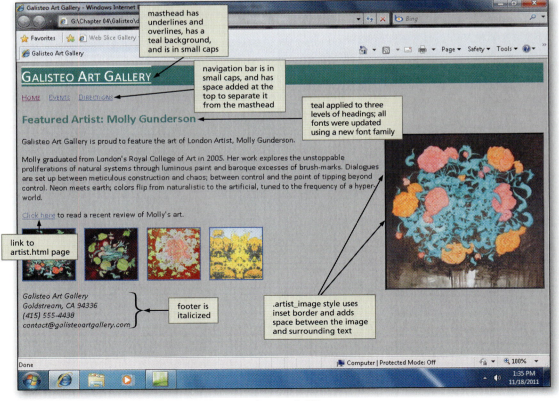

Figure 4–88

3
- Click the Click here link to display the artist.html page in the browser (Figure 4–89).

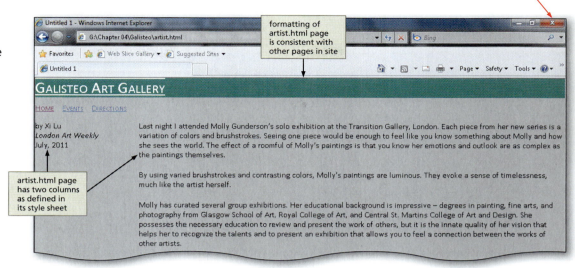

Figure 4–89

To Close a Site and Quit Expression Web

1 Click the Close button on the browser title bar to close the browser window.

2 On the Site menu, click Close.

3 On the File menu, click Exit.

Chapter Summary

In this chapter, you have learned to work with style sheets to create and modify styles that formatted and positioned text and elements. You created a style sheet using code based on Expression Web prompts. You created a new font family and a new page that included CSS layouts. You practiced attaching style sheets to individual pages and all pages in a site. The items listed below include all the new Expression Web skills you have learned in this chapter.

1. Open a Web Site and Web Page (EW 247)
2. Define an ID-Based Style (EW 249)
3. Position Content Using a Class-Based Style (EW 254)
4. Use the CSS Properties Panel (EW 256)
5. Create an External Style Sheet (EW 260)
6. Create a Font Family (EW 262)
7. Modify a Page in Code View (EW 266)
8. Attach a Style Sheet (EW 268)
9. Use Pre-Built CSS Layouts (EW 271)
10. Copy and Paste Elements (EW 274)
11. Complete Page Content (EW 276)
12. Attach Multiple Style Sheets (EW 280)
13. Add a Hyperlink (EW 283)
14. Organize Style Sheets (EW 284)
15. Create a CSS Report (EW 286)
16. Preview the Site (EW 288)

For current SAM information, including versions and content details, visit SAM Central (http://samcentral.course.com). If you have a SAM user profile, you may have access to hands-on instruction, practice, and assessment of the skills covered in this chapter. Since various versions of SAM are supported throughout the life of this text, check with your instructor for the correct instructions and URL/Web site for accessing assignments.

Learn It Online

Test your knowledge of chapter content and key terms.

Instructions: To complete the Learn It Online exercises, start your browser, click the Address bar, and then enter the Web address scsite.com/ew3/learn. When the Expression Web Learn It Online page is displayed, click the link for the exercise you want to complete and then read the instructions.

Chapter Reinforcement TF, MC, and SA
A series of true/false, multiple choice, and short answer questions that test your knowledge of the chapter content.

Flash Cards
An interactive learning environment where you identify chapter key terms associated with displayed definitions.

Practice Test
A series of multiple choice questions that test your knowledge of chapter content and key terms.

Who Wants To Be a Computer Genius?
An interactive game that challenges your knowledge of chapter content in the style of a television quiz show.

Wheel of Terms
An interactive game that challenges your knowledge of chapter key terms in the style of the television show *Wheel of Fortune*.

Crossword Puzzle Challenge
A crossword puzzle that challenges your knowledge of key terms presented in the chapter.

Apply Your Knowledge

Reinforce the skills and apply the concepts you learned in this chapter.

Creating a Site from a Template
Instructions: Start Expression Web. Create a new Web site with a CSS layout, enter text and images, and create and attach a style sheet so that the page looks like Figure 4–90.

Figure 4–90

Perform the following tasks:
1. Point to New on the File menu, click Page, then click CSS Layouts.
2. Click the second instance of 'Header, nav, 2 columns, footer' from the list, make sure that the preview shows the narrower column on the right side, then click the OK button.

3. Open the Save As dialog box, navigate to the drive and folder where you save your data files, click the New Folder button, then name the new folder Apply 4-1 Bakery Site.

4. Save the page as default.html and the style sheet as bakery_styles.css in the Apply 4-1 Bakery Site folder.

5. Click in the masthead div, then type `Sweet Tooth Bakery`.

6. Click in the navigation div, then type `Home`, press **TAB**, type `Orders`, press **TAB**, then type `About`.

7. Click in the footer, then type `17 Cherry Road, Delman, TX 79006 (214) 555-3210`.

8. Click in the right column, then type `"Emma's Hollywood-themed birthday cake was the hit of her birthday party!"`, press **ENTER**, then type `Jerri C.`.

9. Click in the page content area, then type the following:

   `From wedding cakes that wow hundreds to a single oatmeal raisin cookie to cheer up a child, Sweet Tooth Bakery is here for you. My passion is baking, and my goal is to satisfy your sweet tooth. No party is too small or too big for one of our cakes or confections! Contact me today for all of your delicious needs.`

10. Click the masthead arrow on the Apply Styles panel, then click Modify Style.

11. Modify the style so that the font is xx-large, bold, small-caps, and has an underline, and that the text is center-aligned. (*Hint:* text-align is in the Block category.)

12. Use the Modify Style dialog box to center-align the navigation bar. Use the Modify Style dialog box to modify the page content area so that the right margin is 200 pixels.

13. Display the CSS Properties panel, then click in the footer.

14. Scroll to the Block heading in the CSS Properties panel, click the text-align box arrow, then click center.

15. Display the bakery_styles.css file. Click at the end of the line, float: right; to edit the styles for the right column of the page.

16. Press **ENTER**, type `background-color:white;`, press **ENTER**, type `border:medium;`, press **ENTER**, then type `border-style:double;`, press **ENTER**, then type `margin-bottom:10px.` Add 10 pixels of margin to the bottom of the right column.

17. In the #page_content tag, add a new style after the line margin-right. The new style should be margin-left:25px;.

18. Click Page Editor Options on the Tools menu, then click the Font Families tab.

19. Create a new font family using Georgia, Book Antiqua, and serif.

20. Point to New on the File menu, then click CSS. Save the new CSS file as site_styles.

21. Type the following in the new style sheet:

    ```
    /*Style Sheet to define page content by Your Name*/
    body {
    font-family:Georgia, "Book Antiqua", serif;
    background-color:#FFCCFF;
    }
    }
    ```

22. Attach the new style sheet to the default.html page.

23. Save all pages at once.

24. Preview the site.

25. Change the site properties as specified by your instructor. Save all pages, then close the site. Submit the revised site in the format specified by your instructor.

Extend Your Knowledge

Extend the skills you learned in this chapter and experiment with new skills. You may need to use Help to complete the assignment.

Modifying a Template

Instructions: Start Expression Web. Create a new Web site with one page that uses a CSS layout and styles to make the default.html page match the one shown in Figure 4–91.

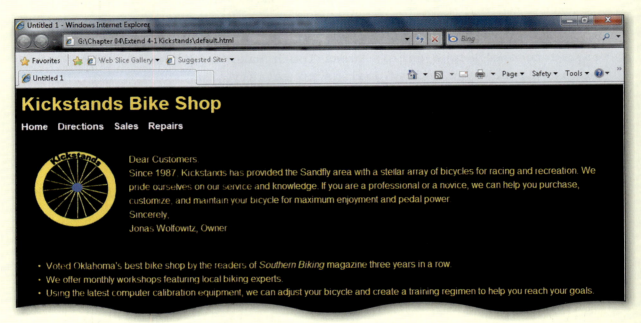

Figure 4–91

Perform the following tasks:

1. Click Site on the menu bar, then click New Site.
2. Click Empty Site in the General category.
3. Click the Browse button and navigate to the folder where you save your data files and open the folder. Type `Extend 4-1 Kickstands` after the path in the Location box, then click the OK button.
4. Click File on the menu bar, point to New, then click Page.
5. Click the CSS Layouts category, click 'Header, nav, 1 column, footer,' then click the OK button.
6. Save the HTML page as default.html and the CSS as kickstand_styles.css.
7. Type `Kickstands Bike Shop` in the masthead div.
8. Type `Home`, `Directions`, `Sales`, and `Repairs` in the navigation div, pressing TAB between each word.
9. Click in the page_content div, then type:

   `Dear Customers:`

   `Since 1987, Kickstands has provided the Sandfly area with a stellar array of bicycles for racing and recreation. We pride ourselves on our service and knowledge. If you are a professional or a novice, we can help you purchase, customize, and maintain your bicycle for maximum enjoyment and pedal power.`

   `Sincerely,`

   `Jonas Wolfowitz, Owner`

10. Press ENTER twice. Insert a paragraph tag.

11. Click the Bullets button on the Common toolbar.

12. Type the following list:

    · Voted Oklahoma's best bike shop by the readers of *Southern Biking* magazine three years in a row.

    · We offer monthly workshops featuring local biking experts.

    · Using the latest computer calibration equipment, we can adjust your bicycle and create a training regimen to help you reach your goals.

13. Delete any empty paragraph tags after the bulleted list, if necessary. Click in the footer div, then type 678 Main Street, Sandfly, Oklahoma, 74877, (580) 555-RIDE.

14. Save the default.html page, then display the kickstand_styles.css file.

15. Click after the first line of code (/* CSS layout */), then press ENTER.

16. Type the following, using the shortcut menu as necessary:

    ```
    body {
    background:black;
    font-family:Arial, Helvetica, sans-serif;
    color:yellow
    }
    ```

17. Save the kickstand_styles.css file, then display the default.html page.

18. In the Apply Styles panel, click the arrow next to #masthead, then click Modify Style.

19. Apply the following rules: font-size: xx-large; font-weight: bold; text-transform: capitalize. Then click the OK button.

20. Click in the top_nav div, click <div#top_nav> on the Quick Tag Selector, then display the CSS Properties panel.

21. Use the CSS Properties panel to apply the following styles to the navigation bar: color: white; font-weight: bold; margin-top: 12 px; margin-bottom: 12 px.

22. In the Apply Styles panel, click the arrow next to #page_content, then click Modify Style.

23. Click the Block category, click the line-height box arrow, click (value), type 24, then click the OK button.

24. Click in the footer, click the footer div on the Quick Tag Selector, then use the CSS Properties panel to apply the following rules: color: white; font-style: italic; text-align: center; margin-top: 24.

25. Click in the page_content div before Dear Customers, press ENTER, then press the UP ARROW.

26. Click Insert on the menu bar, point to Picture, then click From File.

27. Insert the image kickstands_logo.gif from the Extend 4-1 Image folder. Do not enter text in the Accessibility Properties dialog box.

28. Open the Picture Properties dialog box, click the Appearance tab, verify that the 'Keep aspect ratio' check box is checked, enter 140 for the width, then click OK.

29. Click the New Style link on the Apply Styles panel.

30. Create a new style called .image and define it in kickstand_styles.css. Apply the following rules: float: left; margin: 20px. Then click the OK button. (*Hint:* The float property is in the Layout category of the New Style dialog box.)

31. Select the image, then apply the .image style to it. Attach the kickstand_styles.css style sheet to the default.html page. Save all files.

32. Preview the page, then close the browser window.

33. Change the site properties as specified by your instructor. In Windows Explorer, rename the Web site folder Extend 4-1 Kickstands Site. Submit the revised site in the format specified by your instructor.

Make It Right

Analyze a site and correct all errors and/or improve the design.

Placing and Formatting Images

Instructions: Start Expression Web. Open the Web site, Make It Right 4-1 Drama, from the Data Files for Students. See the inside back cover of this book for instructions for downloading the Data Files for Students, or see your instructor for information about accessing the required files.

Create and apply an external style sheet using panels, dialog boxes, and Code view to format the Web page while keeping in mind the guidelines for this chapter to create the home page shown in Figure 4–92.

Figure 4–92

1. Create and save a new CSS file called drama_styles.css.

2. Add a comment to the CSS page by typing /*Page Styles created by Your Name*/.

3. Define the body styles by typing:

```
body {
    background-color:maroon;
    font-family:Arial, Helvetica, sans-serif;
    color:#FFFF99
}
```

4. Save the drama_styles.css file, then attach it to the default.html page.

5. Create a new style called .cast_list and save it to the drama_styles.css page. The style should have font-style: italic and list-style-type: square.

6. Apply the .cast_list style to the bulleted list of cast members.

7. Change the site properties as specified by your instructor. Save all pages, preview the default.html page in the browser, then close the site.

8. Using Windows Explorer, rename the site folder as Make It Right 4-1 Drama Site. Submit the revised site in the format specified by your instructor.

In the Lab

Design and/or format a Web site using the guidelines, concepts, and skills presented in this chapter. Labs are listed in order of increasing difficulty.

Lab 1: Creating a New Style Sheet

Problem: You are a photographer, and you want to update your business's home page by creating a style sheet that you can apply to future pages. Create styles and a style sheet to create the page shown in Figure 4–93.

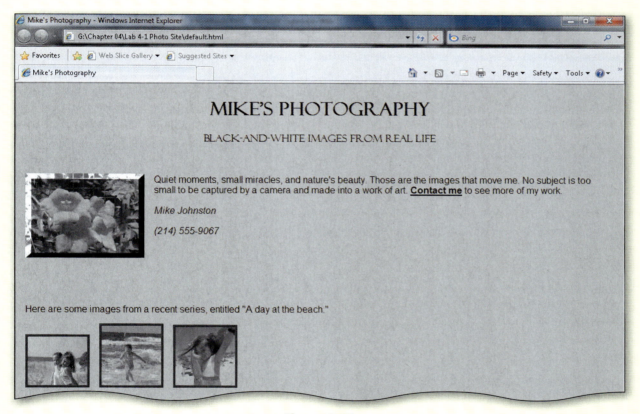

Figure 4–93

Instructions:

1. Start Expression Web.

2. Open the Web site, Lab 4-1 Photo, from the location in which you store your data files.

3. Create a new CSS file and save it as photo_styles.css.

4. Type the following comment at the top of the CSS file: /*External Style Sheet to define page content by Your Name*/.

5. Use the shortcut menu to apply the Arial, Helvetica, sans-serif font-family and the silver background color to the body tag.

6. Save the changes to the style sheet, then attach it to the default.html page.

Continued >

In the Lab continued

7. Select the flower image, then use the CSS Properties panel to add a 16-pixel margin to the right of the image.

8. Create a new style called .thumbnail in the photo_styles.css style sheet. Click the Border category. Specify that the border is the same for all sides, and use the ridge style, medium width, and black color.

9. Apply the .thumbnail style to each of the three thumbnails at the bottom of the page.

10. Create a new style called .e-mail in the photo_styles.css style sheet. Specify that the font weight is bold and the color is black, and apply underline. Save the changes to the style sheet.

11. Select the e-mail link, Contact me, and apply the .e-mail style.

12. Save the changes to the default.html page, preview the page in a browser, then close the site. Using Windows Explorer, rename the site folder Lab 4-1 Photo Site.

13. Submit the site in the format specified by your instructor.

In the Lab

Lab 2: Creating and Applying Styles

Problem: You have volunteered to update the Web site for the Connecticut branch of the Gulliver College Alumni Society. Modify the styles to format the site as shown in Figure 4–94.

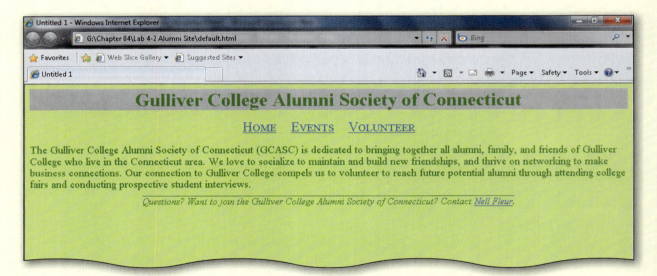

Figure 4–94

Instructions: Start Expression Web. Open the Web site, Lab 4-2 Alumni, from the Data Files for Students. See the inside back cover of this book for instructions for downloading the Data Files for Students, or see your instructor for information about accessing the required files.

Perform the following tasks:

1. Open the style sheet. Click after the comment, press ENTER to start a new line, then type and use the shortcut menu to specify the following style rules for the body: font-family: Times New Roman, Times, serif; color: green; background-color: #CCFF66; font-size: large. (*Hint:* The hex color value must be typed including the semicolon that follows.)

2. Save the style sheet, then open the default.html page and attach the alumni_styles.css style sheet.

3. Modify the style rules for the masthead using the Modify Style dialog box. Specify the following formatting: background-color: silver; font-size: xx-large; font-weight: bold; text-align: center.

4. Modify the style rules for the top_nav div using the CSS Properties panel. Specify the following formatting: margin-top: 16px; margin-bottom: 16px; text-align: center; font-size: x-large; font-variant: small-caps.

5. Use whatever method you prefer to modify the style rules for the footer. Specify the following formatting: margin-top: 10px; text-decoration: overline; font-size: medium; font-style: italic; text-align: center.

6. Save all pages at once.

7. Preview the default.html page in a browser and use the navigation bar to view all pages.

8. Change the site properties as specified by your instructor, then close the site.

9. Using Windows Explorer, rename the site folder Lab 4-2 Alumni Site, then submit the site in the format specified by your instructor.

In the Lab

Lab 3: Creating a Site Using a CSS Layout

Problem: Your client, a preschool, wants to create a home page that it can use to attract clients, and to which it will later add other pages. Create a Web site and use CSS to lay out and format the default.html page shown in Figure 4–95.

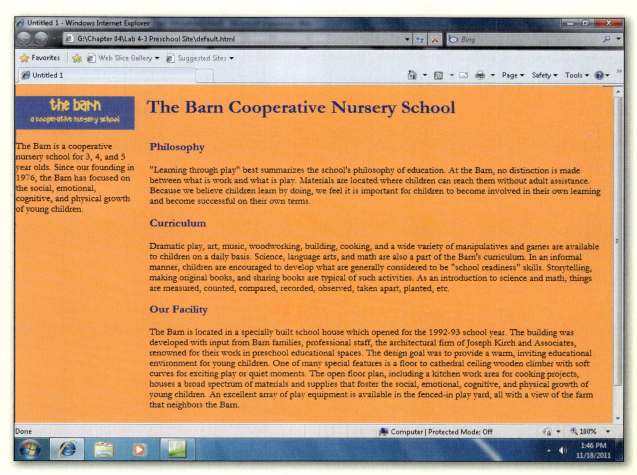

Figure 4–95

Continued >

In the Lab *continued*

Instructions:

1. Start Expression Web.

2. Create a new empty Web site called Lab 4-3 Preschool Site.

3. Add a new page based on the Header, logo, 2 columns, footer CSS layout.

4. Save the page as default.html and the associated style sheet as preschool_styles.css.

5. In the logo div, insert the image preschool_logo.gif from the Lab 4-3 Preschool Files folder in your data files. Resize the logo to 200 pixels wide, then resample it. (*Hint:* Right-click the image, click Picture Properties, click the Appearance tab, enter 200 in the Width box, verify that the 'Keep aspect ratio' check box is checked, click OK, right-click the image, then click Resample.)

6. Create a new style named .image in the preschool_styles.css style sheet. Add a 20px bottom margin to the style and apply it to the preschool_logo.gif image.

7. In the header div, type `The Barn Cooperative Nursery School`, then apply Heading 1 `<h1>` to the div.

8. In the left_col div, type `The Barn is a cooperative nursery school for 3, 4, and 5 year olds. Since our founding in 1976, the Barn has focused on the social, emotional, cognitive, and physical growth of young children.`

9. Start Microsoft Word, navigate to the Lab 4-3 Preschool Files folder in your data files, then open the file preschool_text.doc. Select all text in the file, copy it to the Clipboard, then close the file and Word.

10. In the page_content div (the right column), paste the text without line breaks.

11. Apply Heading 3 `<h3>` to the lines Philosophy, Curriculum, and Our Facility.

12. In the footer div, type `43 Maple Street, Snow Hill, IL 61998`, press ENTER, then type `(224) 555-4098`.

13. Create a new font family with the fonts Garamond, Century Schoolbook, and serif.

14. In the body section of the style sheet, add a rule that uses the new font family. Specify the background color #FF9933. (*Hint:* Type the hex value after picking background-color on the shortcut menu.)

15. In the #page_content section of the style sheet, change the margin-left value to 225px.

16. Add two new styles for h1 and h3 that use the blue font color. Add a 20px left margin to the h1 style.

17. Use the CSS Properties panel to specify that the footer text is italicized and center-aligned.

18. Save both files and the edited image, then preview the site in a browser.

19. Change the site properties as specified by your instructor, then save and close the site.

20. Submit the site in the format specified by your instructor.

Cases and Places

Apply your creative thinking and problem-solving skills to design and implement a solution.

• Easier ••More Difficult

• 1: Creating a New Page Using CSS Layouts

Create a new blank Web site about a favorite vacation and add a page using the CSS layout of your choice. Enter content in all of the divs. Modify the style sheet to specify formatting for the page. Add rules for the page background, font family, and text color. Use panels and dialog boxes to modify the styles for two content areas, such as the footer or masthead. Close the site without saving any changes, then quit Expression Web.

• 2: Updating a Site Using CSS

Create a new site using a dynamic Web template. Use a small business such as a video store or fitness center as the site's focus. Preview the site in your browser and choose at least four style rules that you would like to modify. Open the CSS (if there is more than one style sheet, choose one) in Code view and change two style rules. Save the style sheet as Cases and Places 4-2.css, close the style sheet, and view the changes. Use the CSS Properties panel to change one style rule and use the Modify Style dialog box to change another. Keep modifying styles until you are satisfied with your changes. Save the modified style sheet.

•• 3: Removing Conflicting CSS Rules

Open any multi-page Web site you created in Chapter 2. Create a new style sheet and add three style rules to it. Attach it to all files in the site at once. Make note of areas where inline styles are taking priority over the style sheet. See if you can remove any conflicting inline styles by deleting them in the Apply Styles panel. Rename and save the pages and style sheets, then close the site.

•• 4: Creating a Personal Home Page

Make It Personal

You want to create a one-page site that includes information about your favorite hobby. Create a new blank site and add a page using one of the two-column CSS layouts. Enter information on the default.html page, and include at least one photo and two heading styles (h1, h2, etc.). Assign style rules using the style sheet that came with the CSS layout. Create a new style sheet and add a title, specifications for the page background, and font-family. Create one rule that changes the font color of all of the heading styles you have used on your default page, and another that defines borders and margins for the image. Apply the new image style and attach the new style sheet to the default.html page. Save the pages and style sheets, then close the site.

•• 5: Enhancing Text Using Styles

Working Together

A tutor wants to create a site for his business with three pages: home, references, and résumé. Working as a team with several of your classmates, plan and create the Web site. Each team member should contribute to creating text for the three pages in Word. As a group, decide on a CSS layout for each page in your site (they can all be the same or all be different) and create the site folder and the pages. Create the navigation bar by inserting hyperlinks in the pages. On each of the three pages, edit the placeholder text and insert the Word files you have created. Use the style sheets to define the page elements. If your site has multiple style sheets, practice copying style rules between the pages, attaching a style sheet to another page, and using other methods to ensure consistency among page elements in the site. Preview the site, test the navigation bar, and make sure that your site is readable and attractive. Save and close the pages and style sheet, then close the site.

5 Working with Data Tables and Inline Frames

Objectives

You will have mastered the material in this chapter when you can:

- Use a preformatted style sheet
- Insert a data table
- Change table and cell properties
- Add text and images
- Add rows and columns
- Merge and split table cells

- Format a table using CSS
- Convert text to a table
- Use table AutoFormat
- Distribute rows and columns
- Create an inline frame
- Target links in an inline frame

5 | Working with Data Tables and Inline Frames

Introduction

A **data table** is used to display data in a combination of horizontal **rows** and vertical **columns**. The intersection of a row and a column is called a **cell**. Cells organize the table data, such as text, values, or images. By aligning information in rows and columns and using row and column headers to identify categories of information, information can be presented in an orderly, organized way.

Table properties can be defined by specifying the width of the table as a fixed pixel width or as a percentage of a page, or by allowing the width to be manually adjusted or fit to the text. You can modify the table structure by changing the number of columns or rows. You can format data tables using styles or Expression Web tools such as AutoFormat to add borders or background colors.

An **inline frame**, or **I-frame**, is a fixed-size window that displays another HTML page. When the embedded page contains more information than can be shown in the I-frame, scroll boxes appear to allow the visitor to view more of the embedded page.

Project — Hair Salon

Marcus and Elisa Goldman are the owners of The Upper Cut Salon. They want to create a home page for their company that includes a list of their services and prices. They have asked you to create the home page with whatever Web design tools you recommend. Based on the needs of the site, your plan is to create the home page and attach a preformatted style sheet to it. You will create a table on a separate HTML page, enter data and images, format the table, then add the table as an inline frame to their home page. You will also create a table from text on the home page and update it using AutoFormat.

The project in this chapter shows you how to use a preformatted style sheet, insert a table, add data, modify table structure, and format tables to create the pages shown in Figure 5–1. You will also learn how to convert text to a table, use AutoFormat to apply table formatting, and embed an HTML page that contains the table as an inline frame in the home page.

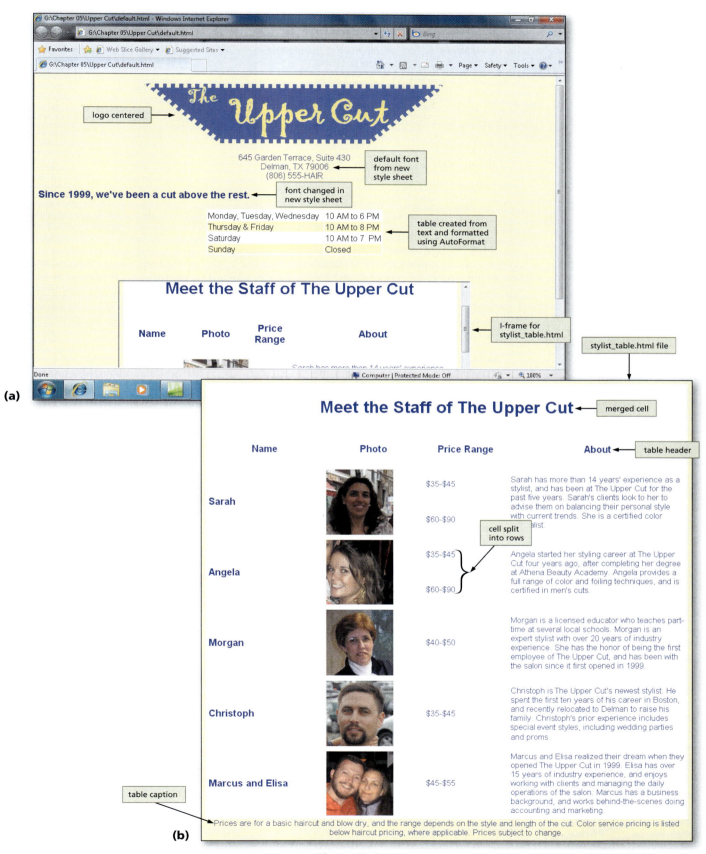

Figure 5–1

Overview

As you read this chapter, you will learn how to create the Web page shown in Figure 5–1 by performing these general tasks:

- Use a preformatted style sheet
- Insert a data table
- Modify table structure
- Add text and images
- Format table text
- Format table backgrounds
- Create a table from text
- Use inline frames

Plan Ahead

General Project Guidelines

When adding a table to a Web page, you will need to create a basic table, then adapt the table structure, content, and formatting as needed by performing actions such as adding and deleting rows and columns, splitting and merging cells, and applying text and table formatting.

As you plan to enhance a Web page by adding a table, such as the one shown in Figure 5–1, you should follow these general guidelines:

1. **Plan the basic table structure.** Use a style sheet to provide formatting consistency between the table content and the rest of the page. When creating a new data table, you should have some idea of the number of rows and columns that you will need before you start, by planning the content that will be displayed in the table. If necessary, sketch a plan for the table on paper, or make a list of the rows and columns you might need.

2. **Add and arrange table content.** Once your table is created, add headings as needed to help you identify where to enter data. Table cells usually contain text (words or numbers), but including images in a table can provide visual data, or make your table more attractive. Once the table's content has been entered, delete rows and columns that you do not need, or add cells for more data. Arranging the table data by combining cells that contain like data, or separating one cell into two to provide additional information within a row or column, helps organize the table.

3. **Design the table.** Determine the degree to which your table should stand out from the rest of the page. Depending on the data in your table and the information on the rest of the page, you may want your table to be a subtle tool to organize data, or it could be a bold page element that will catch a visitor's eye. Choosing the appropriate table background and border options or using AutoFormat will help your table meet the design needs. Using styles to format your table helps maintain consistency with other site pages and makes the table format easier to update.

4. **Organize existing content into the table.** Text that exists in your site can be converted from regular text into a table. The benefit of organizing data into a table is that you can align rows and columns so that the text is easier to read.

5. **Add an inline frame to display a page.** Any HTML page can be embedded into an inline frame on a Web page to provide visitors with a view of the embedded page while controlling the viewing size and not requiring an additional link. For a site that is only one page, you can keep more of the main page visible within the browser window by providing a small, scrollable window that displays additional information.

To Start Expression Web and Reset Workspace Layout

If you are using a computer to step through the project in this chapter, and you want your screens to match the figures in this book, you should change your computer's resolution to 1024 × 768. For information about how to change a computer's resolution, read Appendix G.

The following steps, which assume Windows 7 is running, start Expression Web based on a typical installation, and reset the panels in the workspace to the default layout. You may need to ask your instructor how to start Expression Web for your computer.

> **Note:** If you are using Windows XP, see Appendix E for alternate steps. If you are using Windows Vista, see Appendix F for alternate steps.

1 Click the Start button on the Windows 7 taskbar to display the Start menu.

2 Click All Programs at the bottom of the left pane on the Start menu to display the All Programs list.

3 Click Microsoft Expression on the All Programs list to display the Microsoft Expression list.

4 Click Microsoft Expression Web 3 to start Expression Web.

5 Click Panels on the menu bar, then click Reset Workspace Layout.

6 Click View on the menu bar, point to Ruler and Grid, then click Show Ruler to turn on the rulers if necessary.

To Create a New Web Site and Web Page

The following steps create the Upper Cut Web site folder and the default.html page.

1
- Click New Site on the Site menu to open the New dialog box (Figure 5–2).

Figure 5–2

2
- Click One Page Site, then click the Browse button to open the New Site Location dialog box.

- Navigate to and open the folder in which you keep your data files, then click Open.

- Type Upper Cut at the end of the folder path in the Location text box, then click the OK button to open the site in Expression Web (Figure 5–3).

Figure 5–3

3
- Double-click the default.html page in the Folder List to open it.

- Point to Picture on the Insert menu, then click From File to open the Picture dialog box.

- Navigate to the location of your data files, and double-click the uppercut_images folder to open it.

- Click uppercut_logo to select it (Figure 5–4).

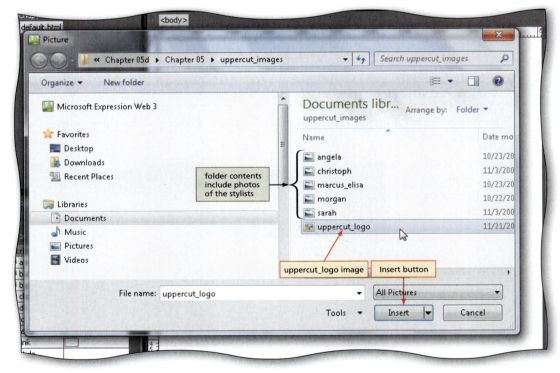

Figure 5–4

4
- Click the Insert button to open the Accessibility Properties dialog box.

- Type The Upper Cut logo in the Alternate text text box (Figure 5–5).

Figure 5–5

5

- Click the OK button to insert the logo at the top of the home page.

- Click the <p> tag on the Quick Tag Selector to select the paragraph containing the image, then click the Center button on the Common toolbar to center the image (Figure 5–6).

Figure 5–6

 6

- Click below the logo to deselect it.

- Double-click Paragraph in the Toolbox to insert a new paragraph.

- Type 645 Garden Terrace, Suite 430 as the first line of the address, then press SHIFT+ENTER to start a new line in the paragraph.

- Type Delman, TX 79006, then press SHIFT+ENTER to start a new line in the paragraph.

- Type (806) 555-HAIR.

- Click the <p> tag on the Quick Tag Selector to select the paragraph, then click the Center button on the Common toolbar to center the paragraph (Figure 5–7).

Figure 5–7

7

- Click below the paragraph to position the insertion point.

- Double-click Paragraph in the Toolbox to insert a new paragraph.

- Type Since 1999, we've been a cut above the rest..

- Click the <p> tag on the Quick Tag Selector to select the paragraph.

- Click the Style box arrow on the Common toolbar to display the Style menu, then point to Heading 3 <h3> (Figure 5–8).

Figure 5–8

8

- Click Heading 3 <h3> to apply it to the text (Figure 5–9).

Figure 5–9

9

- Press CTRL+S to save the default.html page, and click the OK button in the Save Embedded Files dialog box to save the logo to the site (Figure 5–10).

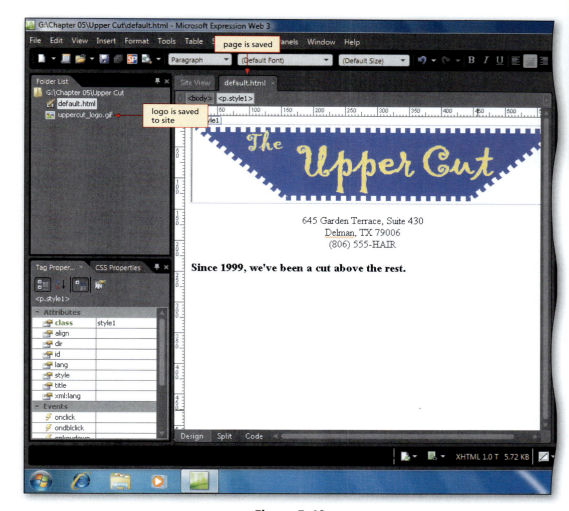

Figure 5–10

Other Ways

1. Point to HTML on the Insert menu, then click Paragraph to insert a new tag

Using a Preformatted Style Sheet

Just as you can create a new Web page using a CSS layout or a new Web site using a dynamic Web template, you can create a new style sheet using a preformatted option provided by Expression Web. Using a preformatted style sheet saves you time and ensures that the code is entered correctly. Like any completed style sheet, a preformatted style sheet contains code that you can edit and modify to suit your needs.

Plan the basic table structure.

Plan the formatting for all pages in the site, including the page that you will embed as an I-frame. Use a preformatted style sheet as a basis, then modify it as necessary. Determine the approximate number of columns and rows that you will need to display the data, including any necessary row and column headers. If your table includes a title, consider whether to add it as a line of text above the table, or as a merged cell that spans the width of the table. A caption above or below your table describes the table contents or its purpose. You should specify table and cell properties, such as text alignment, alignment of the table relative to the page margins, and spacing between cells.

Plan Ahead

BTW **Nested Table**
A nested table is a table inside another table.

To Create a New Style Sheet

The following steps create the uppercut_styles.css file using a preformatted style sheet. You want all of the fonts to be the same throughout the page, so you will delete the code that specifies a different font type and color for the heading styles. Then you will attach the style sheet to the default.html page.

- Point to New on the File menu, then click Page to open the New dialog box.
- Click Style Sheets in the left pane to display the style sheet options.
- Click the Sweets style sheet option to select it (Figure 5–11).

Experiment

- Click different options in the Style Sheets list to view descriptions. Select the Sweets style sheet.

Figure 5–11

- Click the OK button to create the new style sheet (Figure 5–12).

Figure 5–12

3

- Select the code and brackets in lines 19 through 46 that formats the headings in a different font and also in different colors (Figure 5–13).

- Press DELETE to delete the code.

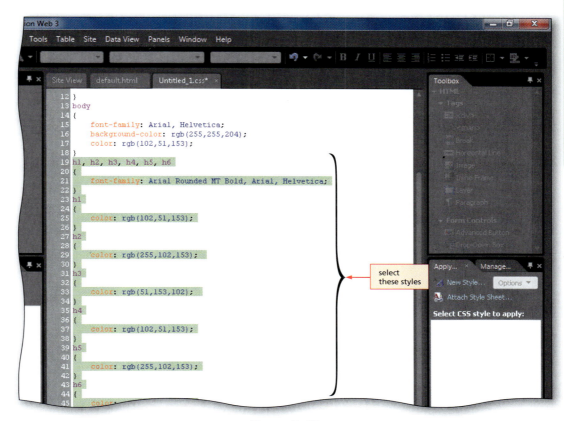

Figure 5–13

4

- On line 17, select rgb(102,51,153).

- Press BACKSPACE twice, press the SPACEBAR to activate the shortcut menu, then point to blue (Figure 5–14).

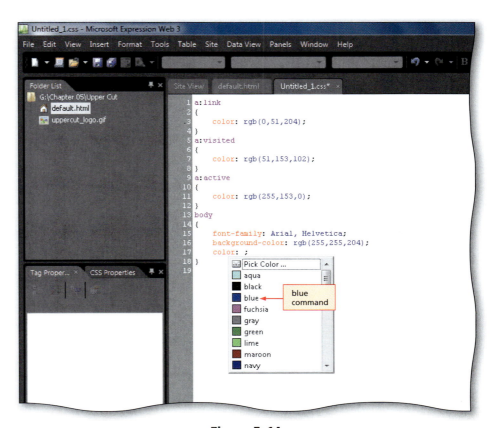

Figure 5–14

5

• Double-click blue to change the body font to blue (Figure 5–15).

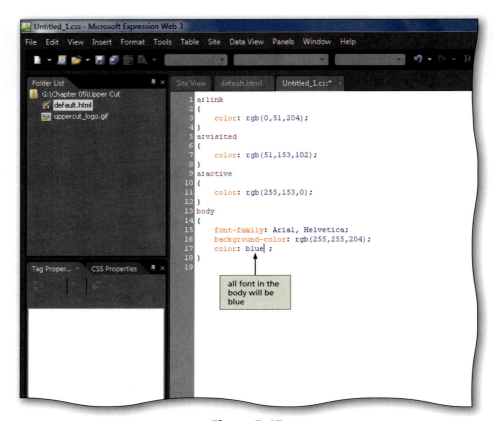

Figure 5–15

6

• Press CTRL+S to open the Save As dialog box.

• Type uppercut_ styles.css in the File name text box (Figure 5–16).

Figure 5–16

7

- Click the Save button to save the style sheet.

- Close the style sheet.

- Click the Attach Style Sheet link in the Apply Styles panel to open the Attach Style Sheet dialog box (Figure 5–17).

Figure 5–17

8

- Click the Browse button to open the Select Style Sheet dialog box.

- Click uppercut_styles to select it (Figure 5–18).

Figure 5–18

- Click the Open button to close the Select Style Sheet dialog box.

- Click the OK button to close the Attach Style Sheet dialog box and attach the style sheet to the page (Figure 5–19).

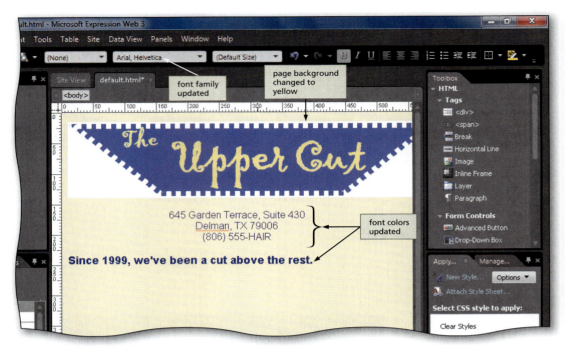

Figure 5–19

10

- Right-click the toolbar to display the shortcut menu, then click Pictures to display the Pictures toolbar.

- Click the logo to select it.

- Click the Set Transparent Color button on the Pictures toolbar to change the pointer to the transparency pointer.

- Click an area of the white color around the logo to make it transparent (Figure 5–20).

Figure 5–20

- Save the default.html page and click OK to save embedded files.

Other Ways
1. Click the New Document button arrow on the Common toolbar, then click Page to open the New dialog box   2. Point to CSS Styles on the Format menu, then click Attach Style Sheet to open the Attach Style Sheet dialog box

To Create a New Page and Attach a Style Sheet

You must create a new page for the table so that you can embed it as an inline frame on the home page. The page background, font family, and other styles for the page containing the table should be consistent with other pages in the site, so you will attach the style sheet from the default.html page to the new page. The following steps create a new blank page and attach the uppercut_styles CSS.

1

- Click the New Document button on the Common toolbar to insert a new blank page.

- Click the Attach Style Sheet link in the Apply Styles panel to open the Attach Style Sheet dialog box (Figure 5–21).

Figure 5–21

2

- Click the Browse button to open the Select Style Sheet dialog box.

- Click uppercut_styles to select it.

- Click the Open button to close the Select Style Sheet dialog box (Figure 5–22).

Figure 5–22

3
- Click the OK button to close the Attach Style Sheet dialog box.
- Press CTRL+S to open the Save As dialog box.
- Type stylist_table.html in the File name text box, then click the Save button to save the new page (Figure 5–23).

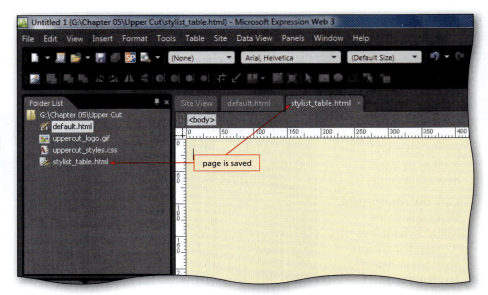

Figure 5–23

Other Ways

1. Press CTRL+N to open a new blank page

Creating Data Tables

BTW

Table Background Image
Another way to make your table stand out is to add a background image that appears behind the table. Only use this option when necessary because it increases the file size (causing slower download time in a browser), and can distract from the table data.

A table used to present data is called a **data table**, or just a table. Data is entered into cells, and cells are arranged in horizontal rows and vertical columns. When creating a table, you begin by specifying numbers of rows and columns, and then you modify the table properties to customize its appearance.

Tables are often used on Web pages and other documents to list items and characteristics. For example, a list of products offered at a store can show each product on its own new row, with columns of characteristics, such as description, price, item number, and so on. Column headers for each characteristic enable the visitor to scan through the list of items and determine the relevant information about each.

BTW

Saving Default Table Settings
In the Table Properties dialog box, click the 'Set as default for new tables' check box to save your settings for future tables in your site to ensure consistency and save you time.

You could attempt to present information in columns and rows by using the TAB key to insert space between words to simulate columns and the ENTER key to start new lines to simulate rows, but this method will cause your text to misalign when presented at different screen resolutions and is not a good practice. Creating a table enables you to use CSS to ensure that your data will be accessible, consistently presented, and easy to format and reorganize. Tables use HTML tags to define captions (<tc>), rows (<tr>), headers (<th>), cell data (<td>), and the entire table (<table>).

A **caption** is a line of text used to describe the table to visitors using screen readers or other adaptive devices, or to provide additional information about the table. A caption typically appears above or below the table. Although CSS has the option to create a caption on the side of the table, this is not widely supported by browsers, so Expression Web does not offer this capability.

Working with Data Tables

Cell divisions in a table are shown as dotted lines, which are a type of visual aid called **tracer lines**. By default, there are no gridlines that separate table row and column borders, so it is important to have Visual Aids turned on when working with a table so that you can see where cells are divided.

To Insert a Data Table

All of the information on the new page will be included as part of the table. The salon has three stylists, each of whom will have his or her own row; you will need one row for owners Marcus and Elisa; and you will need to include a row that contains column headers — so you will include a total of five rows. Each stylist will have a column for his or her name, a picture, and a description of the stylist's background and services, so you will need three columns — a total of 15 cells. You will also add a table caption to appear at the bottom of the table. The following steps insert a new blank table using the Insert Table dialog box and add a table caption.

- Right-click the toolbar to display the shortcut menu, then click Pictures to close the Pictures toolbar.

- Click Insert Table on the Table menu to open the Insert Table dialog box.

- Type 5 in the Rows box to specify a five-row table, then press TAB to move to the Columns box.

- Type 3 in the Columns box to specify a three-column table (Figure 5–24).

Figure 5–24

2

- Click the OK button to close the Insert Table dialog box and insert the new table (Figure 5–25).

Q&A Why can't I see the borders of the table on my screen?

Visual Aids must be turned on to see the table borders. Point to Visual Aids on the View menu and click Show to turn on Visual Aids.

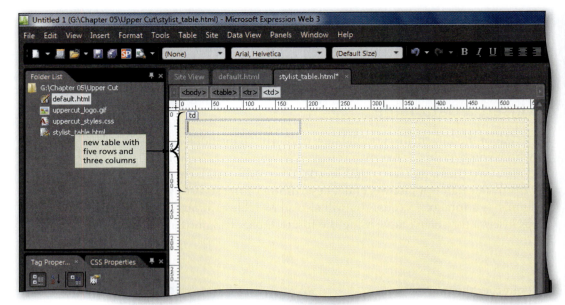

Figure 5–25

3

- Point to Insert on the Table menu, then click Caption to insert a tag for the table caption above the table (Figure 5–26).

Figure 5–26

4

• Right-click the caption row to open the shortcut menu, then click Caption Properties to open the Caption Properties dialog box (Figure 5–27).

Figure 5–27

5

• Click the 'Bottom of table' option button to select it.

• Click the OK button to close the Caption Properties dialog box and position the caption at the bottom of the table (Figure 5–28).

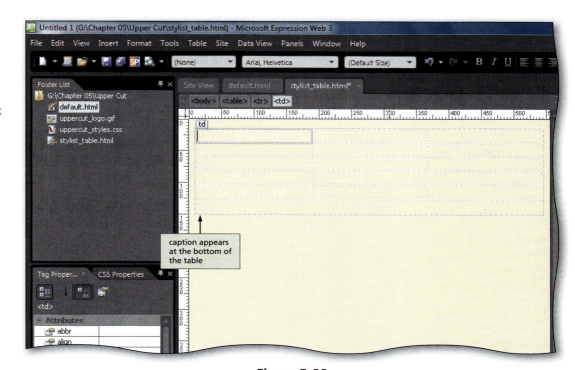

Figure 5–28

Other Ways

1. Point to Table Properties on the Table menu, then click Caption to open the Caption Properties dialog box

Table and Cell Properties

Table properties define the alignment, borders, and background of the table, and also define default cell settings, such as padding and text alignment. Table properties apply to all cells in a table. You can change the same settings (alignment, background, and so on) for a certain amount of cells by changing their cell properties. Changing the cell properties modifies the settings for the cell containing the insertion point, or for any selected cells, rows, or columns.

To select an entire row or column, position the I-beam pointer to the left of the row or the top of the column to select; then when the pointer changes to the row selector, a small black arrow, click to select the row or column.

Defining a **header** row assigns the <th> HTML tag for that row and applies bold formatting to the text in that row. Headers are often distinguished from the body of the table with different text formatting, such as a heading style or bold, or by applying a dif- ferent background color. When a table is being read by a screen reader for a visitor with visual impairment, the screen reader will read the header categories when reading the data for each row. For example, in a table that lists the members of John's basketball team and includes the name, number, and position of each player, the screen reader would read Name: John; Number: 33; Position: Center.

By default, the table will span 100% of the page width. You can create a data table that does not span the entire width of the page by reducing the width percentage to less than 100% or by specifying the data table's width in pixels instead of a percentage. A data table that does not span the entire width of the page can be aligned at the left or right margin of the page or centered between the margins. By default, the height of a table is not specified when you create the table. Because the height for each row might need to expand to fit the cell contents, it is best to leave the height of the table unspecified in order to avoid truncating table data.

To Change Table and Cell Properties

The following steps use the Table Properties dialog box to add padding to increase the white space between the cell contents and cell margins. You will also add a table background color, format the cell properties of the top row to change the text alignment to center, and specify the table header.

1

- Point to Table Properties on the Table menu, then click Table to open the Table Properties dialog box.

- Click the Cell padding up arrow three times to change the padding to 4 pixels.

- Click the Color box arrow in the Background section to display the color palette (Figure 5–29).

Figure 5–29

- Click White on the color palette to change the table background to white.
- Click the OK button to close the Table Properties dialog box (Figure 5–30).

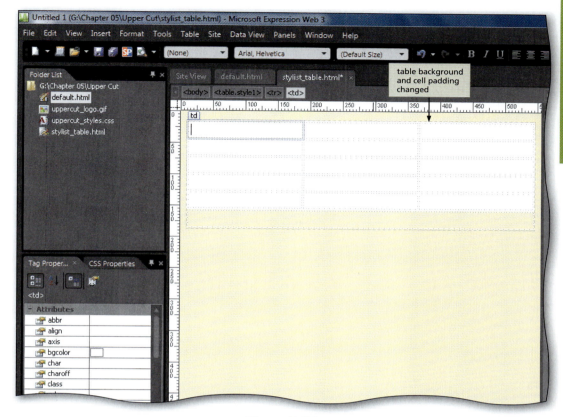

Figure 5–30

3

- Position the pointer over the left side of the top row until the pointer becomes the row selector, a black, right-pointing arrow.
- Click to select the top row of the table (Figure 5–31).

Figure 5–31

4
- Point to Table Properties on the Table menu, then click Cell to open the Cell Properties dialog box.

- Click the Horizontal alignment box arrow, then click Center to center-align the text in the top row of the table.

- If necessary, click the Header cell check box to select it and define the top row of the table as the header (Figure 5–32).

Figure 5–32

5
- Click the OK button to close the Cell Properties dialog box (Figure 5–33).

🔎 **Experiment**

- Open the Table Properties dialog box again and select different options, such as changing the table width or background. Close the dialog box, view your changes, then press CTRL+Z to undo them.

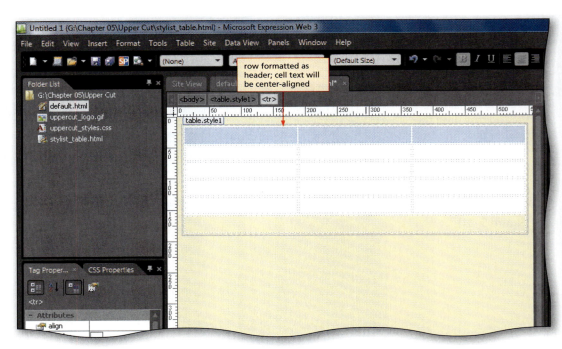

Figure 5–33

Other Ways

1. Right-click an area of the table, then click Table Properties or Cell Properties to open the Table or Cell Properties dialog box

Add and arrange table content.
Including a table header simplifies data entry by clearly indicating where information should appear. Once the content has been added to the table, you should evaluate the table to see whether additional rows or columns are needed, and whether any cells should be combined or divided. Consulting with a colleague or your client is a good way to ensure that your table reads well to others and that no additional content is needed. Splitting and merging cells gives you flexibility when presenting data — you can combine cells to show relationships between data or to create a table header, or you can separate cells to add additional information.

Plan Ahead

BTW

Controlling Column Width
To control a column's width when typing the header data, position cell content onto two lines by pressing SHIFT+ENTER to insert a line break. Do not insert line breaks in non-header cells, as this will cause your table data to flow awkwardly when viewed at different screen resolutions.

Entering Text into Cells

In a blank data table, all columns are the same width and all rows are the same height. As you enter data, the width of the current column expands and the other columns adjust.

Click the cell in which you want to enter content, then start typing. To navigate in a table, you can use the pointer to click a cell or use the keyboard shortcuts outlined in Table 5–1 to move the insertion point around the table.

Table 5–1 Table Navigation Keyboard Shortcuts

Press	To go to
TAB	The next cell in the row, or when at the end of a row, to the first cell in the next row.
SHIFT+TAB	The previous cell in the row, or when at the beginning of a row, to the last cell in the previous row.
DOWN ARROW	The cell in the row below.
UP ARROW	The cell in the row above.
RIGHT ARROW	The next empty cell in the table, if there is no content in the cell. If there is content in the cell, the insertion point moves forward through the content one character at a time.
LEFT ARROW	The previous empty cell in the table, if there is no content in the cell. If there is content in the cell, the insertion point moves backward through the content one character at a time.

To Add Text to a Table

The following steps enter data in the header row, caption, and other cells in the table. You will leave the Photo column blank for now.

- Click the upper-left cell in the table to position the insertion point in the header row.

- Type Name, then press TAB to move to the next cell (Figure 5–34).

Figure 5–34

2

- Type Photo, then press TAB to move to the next cell.

- Type About, then press TAB to move to the first cell in the next row (Figure 5–35).

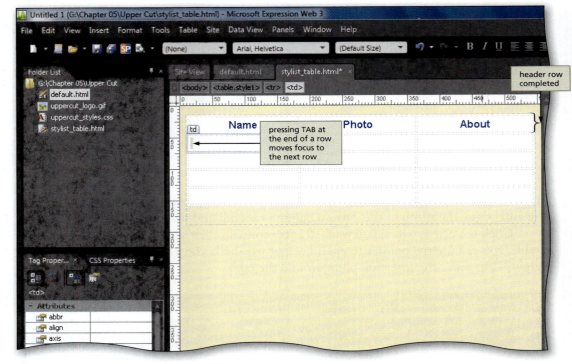

Figure 5–35

3

- Type Sarah, then press TAB twice to move to the About column.

- Type Sarah has more than 14 years' experience as a stylist, and has been at The Upper Cut for the past five years. Sarah's clients look to her to advise them on balancing their personal style with current trends. She is a certified color specialist., then press TAB to move to the first cell in the next row (Figure 5–36).

Figure 5–36

- Click the Close button on the Folder List and click the Close all button on the Tag Properties panel to provide more space in the editing window.

- If necessary, click in the first cell of the third row, type Angela, then press TAB twice to move to the About column.

- Type Angela started her styling career at The Upper Cut four years ago, after completing her degree at Athena Beauty Academy. Angela provides a full range of color and foiling techniques, and is certified in men's cuts., then press TAB to move to the first cell in the next row.

Figure 5–37

- Type Morgan, then press TAB twice to move to the About column.

- Type Morgan is a licensed educator who teaches part-time at several local schools. Morgan is an expert stylist with over 20 years of industry experience. She has the honor of being the first employee of The Upper Cut, and has been with the salon since it opened in 1999., then press TAB to move to the first cell in the next row.

- Type Marcus and Elisa, then press TAB twice to move to the About column.

- Type Marcus and Elisa realized their dream when they opened The Upper Cut in 1999. Elisa has over 15 years of industry experience, and enjoys working with clients and managing the daily operations of the salon. Marcus has a business background, and works behind-the-scenes doing accounting and marketing.

- Click in the caption cell to position the insertion point (Figure 5–37).

5

- Type `Prices are for a basic haircut and blow dry, and the range depends on the style and length of cut. Color service pricing is listed below haircut prices, where applicable. Prices subject to change.` **as the caption text (Figure 5–38).**

- Press CTRL+S to save the page.

caption text is center-aligned

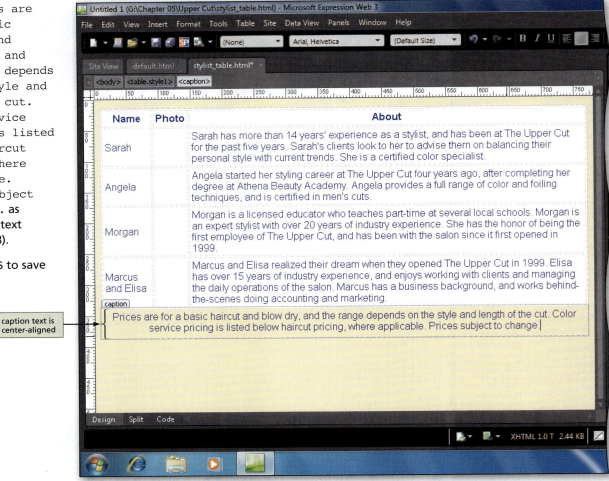

Figure 5–38

Adding Images into Cells

Images will increase the file size of the page containing the table, so you should take into consideration some of the decisions and actions discussed in Chapter 2. Use images that display with the correct quality, but with a file size that does not considerably slow down the page when downloading in a browser. Only include images to enhance and illustrate table data, and make sure that the image is resized to fit the desired space.

To Add Images to a Table

The following steps add images to the Photo column for Sarah, Angela, Morgan, and Marcus and Elisa.

1
- Click the cell to the right of the word, Sarah, to position the insertion point.

- Point to Picture on the Insert menu, then click From File to open the Picture dialog box.

- Click the sarah file to select it (Figure 5–39).

Figure 5–39

2
- Click the Insert button to open the Accessibility Properties dialog box.

- Type `Sarah's photo` in the Alternate text text box, then click the OK button to insert the image (Figure 5–40).

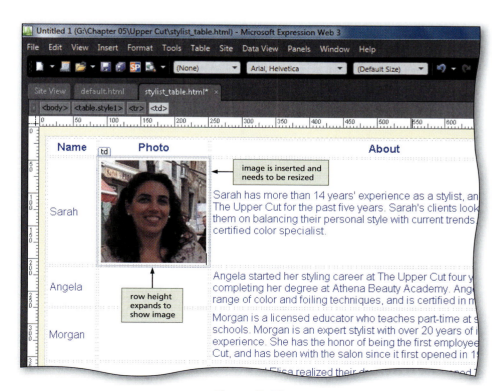

Figure 5–40

3

- Right-click the image to open the shortcut menu, then click Picture Properties to open the Picture Properties dialog box.

- Click the Appearance tab to display the sizing options.

- Verify that the 'Keep aspect ratio' check box is checked, then type 125 in the width box to change the height and width to 125 pixels (Figure 5–41).

Figure 5–41

4

- Click the OK button to close the Picture Properties dialog box and insert the image.

- Click the Picture Actions button to display the menu (Figure 5–42).

- Click the Resample Picture To Match Size option button to resample the image.

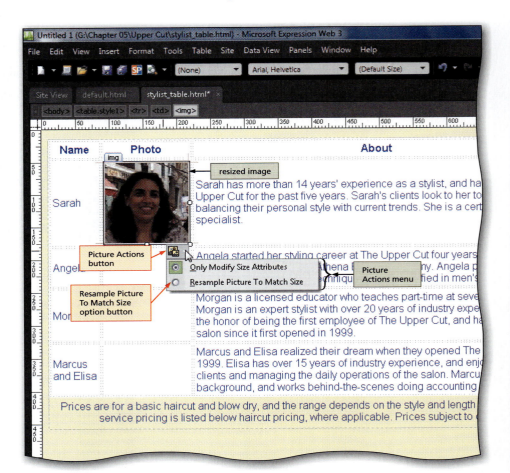

Figure 5–42

5

- Repeat Steps 1 through 4 to insert and resample the angela.jpg, morgan.jpg, and marcus_elisa.jpg images (Figure 5–43).

- Save the page and all embedded images.

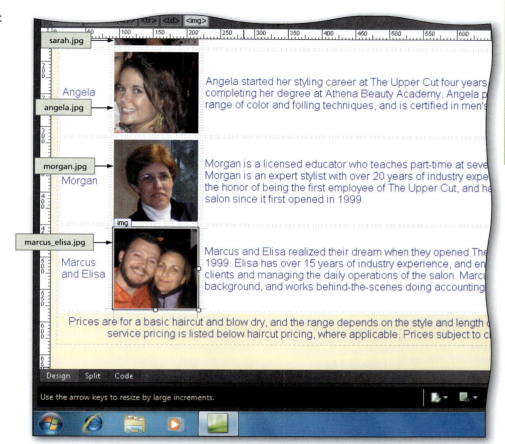

Figure 5–43

Adding Rows and Columns

After creating a table, you might need to add rows and columns to it. To add a row when entering content, you can simply press TAB after entering data in the last cell in the table, and a new row is automatically added to the end of a table. You can also insert rows above or below any row in the table, or insert columns to the left or right of any column in the table.

The Tables Toolbar

The commands for adding rows and columns are available on the Table menu, as well as on a task-specific Tables toolbar. Like the Pictures toolbar that you used in previous chapters to modify images, the Tables toolbar provides access to the necessary tools to make modifications to your table. Using buttons on the Tables toolbar, you can insert and delete rows and columns, merge and split cells, and specify table and cell properties, such as text alignment and background color.

To Add Rows and Columns

The following steps display the Tables toolbar, add a column for the price range for each stylist, add a new row for a stylist who has just joined The Upper Cut staff, and then enter his data.

1

● Right-click a blank area above the Common toolbar to open a shortcut menu, then click Tables to display the Tables toolbar (Figure 5–44).

Q&A

My Tables toolbar is not docked.

Position the insertion point over the toolbar's title bar, click, then drag the toolbar up below the Common toolbar until it docks.

Figure 5–44

2

● Click any cell in the About column to position the insertion point.

● Click the Column to the Left button on the Tables toolbar to add a new column (Figure 5–45).

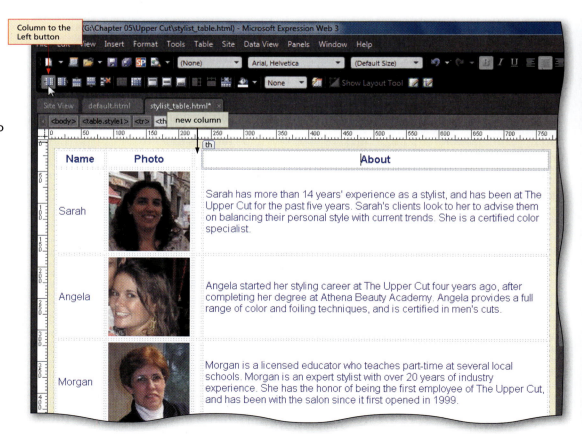

Figure 5–45

3

- Click the top cell in the new column to position the insertion point in the column header.

- Type `Price Range` to add a header to the new column (Figure 5–46).

Figure 5–46

4

- Click any cell in the Morgan row to position the insertion point.

- Click the Row Below button on the Tables toolbar to add a new row (Figure 5–47).

 Experiment

- Add another row or column, select it, then click the Delete Cells button on the Tables toolbar to practice deleting rows or columns.

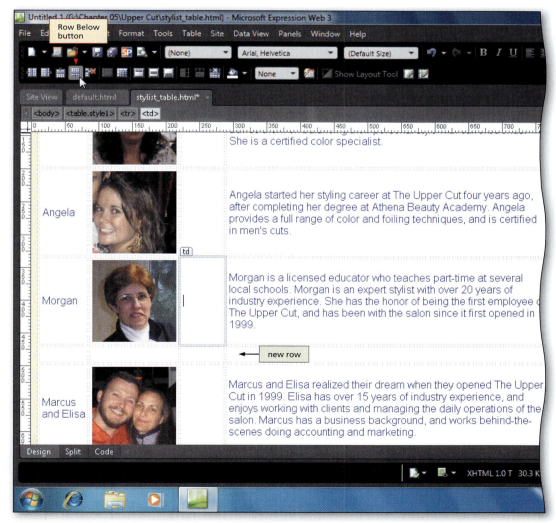

Figure 5–47

5

- Click the first cell in the new row to position the insertion point.

- Type Christoph, then press TAB to move to the next cell.

- Point to Picture on the Insert menu, then click From File to open the Picture dialog box.

- Click the christoph image to select it.

- Click the Insert button to open the Accessibility Properties dialog box.

- Type Christoph's photo, then click the OK button to close the Accessibility Properties dialog box and insert the image.

- Right-click the image to open the shortcut menu, then click Picture Properties to open the Picture Properties dialog box.

- Click the Appearance tab, then type 125 in the Width box to change the height and width to 125 pixels (Figure 5–48).

Figure 5–48

6

- Click the OK button to close the dialog box and insert the image.

- Click the Picture Actions button to display the menu.

- Click the Resample Picture To Match Size option button to resample the image (Figure 5–49).

Figure 5–49

7

- If necessary, press RIGHT ARROW to deselect the image but keep the insertion point in the cell.

- Press TAB twice to position the inser- tion point in the About column.

- Type `Christoph is The Upper Cut's newest stylist. He spent the first ten years of his career in Boston, and recently relo- cated to Delman to raise his fam- ily. Christoph's prior experience includes special event styles, including wed- ding parties and proms.` to complete the new row content (Figure 5–50).

- Save the stylist_ table.html page and embedded files.

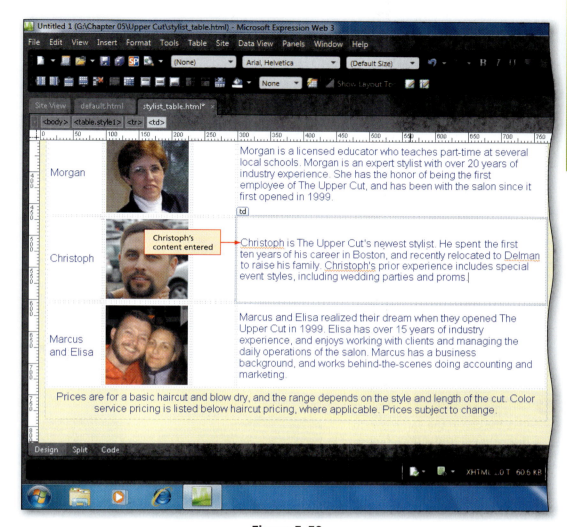

Figure 5–50

Other Ways

1. Point to Insert on the Table menu, then click an option to add or delete rows or columns

Table Fill

Using the **Table Fill** command, you can complete a column or row of data with the same data content to save time when entering table data. Table Fill is a useful feature when most or all of the data in a row or column is the same. For example, at the salon, many of the stylists have the same rates for services. For the cells with content that differs from the filled data, select the cells and replace the data with the correct data.

To Use Table Fill

The following steps use Table Fill to fill the price range column. You will then edit two entries in the column.

- Click the third cell in the Sarah row to position the insertion point in the new Price Range column.

- Type $35–$45 to enter the data that will be used to fill the column (Figure 5–51).

Figure 5–51

- Select the cell in the Sarah row in which you entered a price range and drag down to select the rows below it to specify the fill value and range (Figure 5–52).

Q&A

I can't see the cell in the last row. How will I know if it is selected?

When selecting the column, drag down below the document window over the status bar. The last cell in the column should be selected even though it isn't visible.

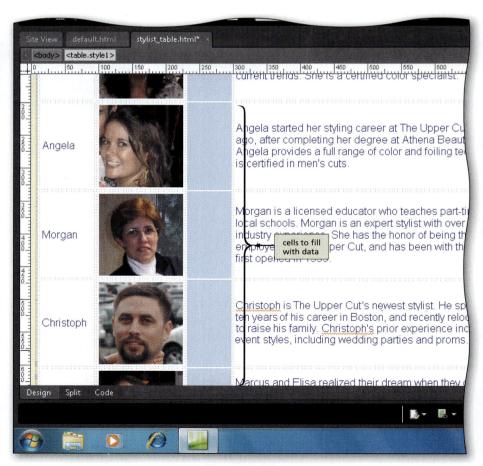

Figure 5–52

3

- Point to Fill on the Table menu (Figure 5–53).

Figure 5–53

4

- Click Down to fill the value in the column (Figure 5–54).

 Experiment

- Add a new row, type text into the first cell, then select the row. Point to Fill on the Table menu, then click Right to practice filling a row. Delete the row.

Figure 5–54

5

- Click in the cell containing Morgan's price range.

- Select the current text, then type $40–$50.

- Click in the cell containing Marcus and Elisa's price range.

- If necessary, select the current text, then type $45–$55 (Figure 5–55).

- Save the stylist_table.html page.

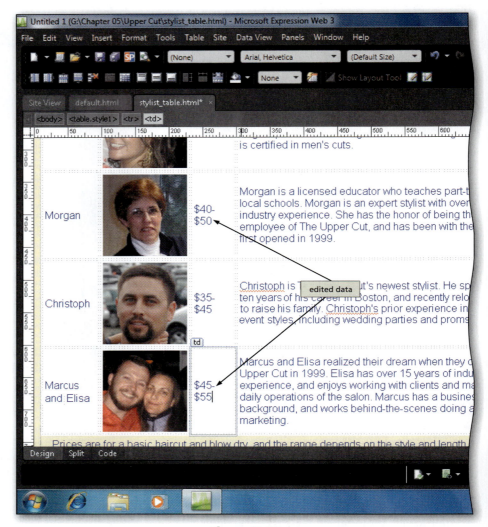

Figure 5–55

Merging and Splitting Cells

Combining two or more adjacent cells is called **merging**. **Splitting** a cell creates two or more rows or columns within a cell. Merging and splitting cells is done to combine or separate content in order to clarify table data.

Merging a row at the top of the table is often done to create a **title row** for the table; the title row has the same properties as the rest of the table. A title row differs from a caption. A caption is a description of the table contents or purpose, whereas a title row is used to name the rows in the table.

To Merge Table Cells

The following steps add a new row for the table title, then merge the cells in the new row.

- Click anywhere in the table header row to position the insertion point.

- Click the Row Above button on the Tables toolbar to insert a new row (Figure 5–56).

Figure 5–56

- Position the pointer over the left side of the new row to change the pointer to the row selector.

- Click to select the top row of the table.

- Click the Merge Cells button on the Tables toolbar to merge all the header cells into one cell (Figure 5–57).

Figure 5–57

❸

- Click in the merged cell to position the insertion point.

- Type `Meet the Staff of The Upper Cut` to enter the table title (Figure 5–58).

- Save the page.

Q&A

Why is the text centered in the cell?

Because the merged cells were inserted above the table header row, they are formatted as a header; in this case, with centered text.

Figure 5–58

To Split Table Cells

As noted in the text you typed in the table caption, some stylists have a separate price range for their haircut and coloring services. The following steps split the price range cells for Sarah and Angela into rows and enter price ranges for coloring services.

- Click in the Price Range cell in Sarah's row to position the insertion point.

- Click the Split Cells button on the Tables toolbar to open the Split Cells dialog box.

- Click the 'Split into rows' option button to select it (Figure 5–59).

Figure 5–59

- Click the OK button to split the cells (Figure 5–60).

Figure 5–60

• Click the second row of the split cell to position the insertion point.

• Type $60–$90 to enter the cell content (Figure 5–61).

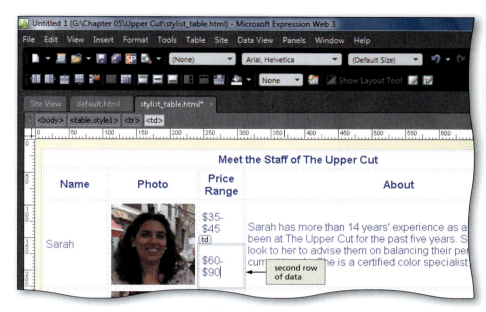

Figure 5–61

• Repeat Steps 1 through 3 to split Angela's price range cell into two rows and enter $60–$90 as the content for the second row of the split cell (Figure 5–62).

• Save the page.

Experiment

• Select any cell in the table, then click the Split Cells button. Click the 'Split into columns' option button, type 3 in the 'Number of columns' box, then click the OK button to close the dialog box and see the cell split into three columns. Press CTRL+Z to undo the split.

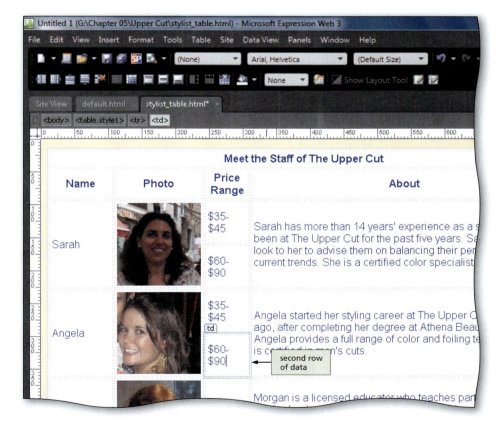

Figure 5–62

Other Ways

1. Point to Modify on the Table menu, then click an option to merge or split cells

Formatting Table Text

CSS text styles, such as headings, can be used to format table text so that it uses the styles defined in the attached style sheet. Using an AutoFormat allows you to apply several formatting choices at once, including font color and contrasting background colors for rows and columns (called **striping**).

Plan Ahead	**Design the table.** Determine the style of the table and how much emphasis it should have on the page: a strong emphasis, as in a different background color or with bold font color choices, or more subtle, to blend in with the existing page content. Using styles to format the table ensures consistency and enables you to update your table as changes are made to styles that affect the rest of the page or pages in your site. When choosing an AutoFormat, make sure that the look of the table matches your design plan.

To Apply Styles to Table Text

The following steps assign text styles to distinguish the row and column headers.

1

• Click anywhere in the merged cell at the top of the table to position the insertion point.

• Click the <th> tag on the Quick Tag Selector to select the tag.

• Click the Style box arrow on the Common toolbar, then point to Heading 1 <h1> (Figure 5–63).

Figure 5–63

- Click Heading 1 <h1> to apply the style to the title row.

- Position the pointer to the left of row 2 to change the pointer to the row selector.

- Click to select row 2.

- Click the Style box arrow on the Common tool-bar, then point to Heading 3 <h3> (Figure 5–64).

Figure 5–64

- Click Heading 3 <h3> to apply the style to the header row.

- Select the five cells containing the styl-ists' names.

- Click the Style box arrow on the Common toolbar, then click Heading 3 <h3> to apply the style to the selected cells (Figure 5–65).

- Save and close the stylist_table.html page.

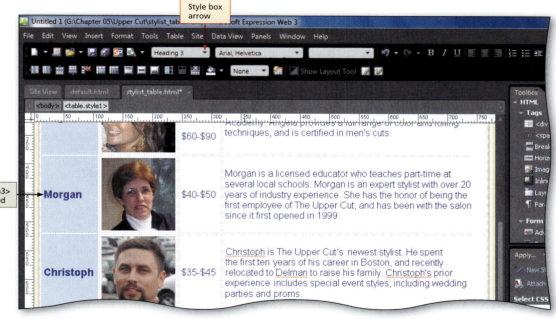

Figure 5–65

Converting Text to a Table

You may encounter a situation when you realize that text you entered on a page would be better formatted as a table. When entering large amounts of text in a document, you should consider this before you start typing; but for small amounts of text, it is fine to convert text to a table after it is typed. In order to convert text into a table, it needs to be properly **delineated**, or separated into groupings using commas, spaces, or tabs. When entering text, do not attempt to align it by adding extra spaces or tabs. Doing so will create cells for each extra delineation, causing your table to be misaligned.

Plan Ahead

Organize existing content into the table.
Converting text to a table allows text to be aligned in columns and rows and formatted consistently. Text in tables appears in rows and columns, and you can add headers to describe the table data.

To Convert Text to a Table

The following steps return to the default.html page, enter text in a new paragraph tag, and convert it to a table.

1

- Verify that default .html is open in Expression Web, then click below the line with the words, Since 1999, to position the insertion point.

- Double-click Paragraph in the Toolbox to insert a new paragraph.

- Type Monday, Tuesday, Wednesday, then press TAB to insert space as the column delineator.

- Type 10 AM to 6 PM, then press ENTER to complete the first line of the table text (Figure 5–66).

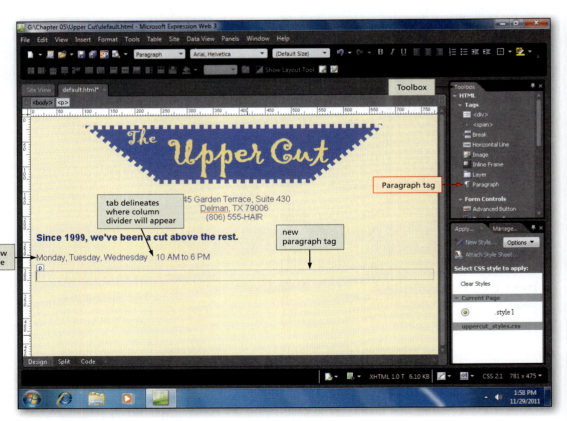

Figure 5–66

2

- Type `Thursday & Friday`, then press TAB to insert space.

- Type `10 AM to 8 PM`, then press ENTER to complete the second line of the table text.

- Type `Saturday`, then press TAB to insert space.

- Type `10 AM to 7 PM`, then press ENTER to complete the third line of the table text.

- Type `Sunday`, then press TAB to insert space.

- Type `Closed`, then press ENTER to complete the table text (Figure 5–67).

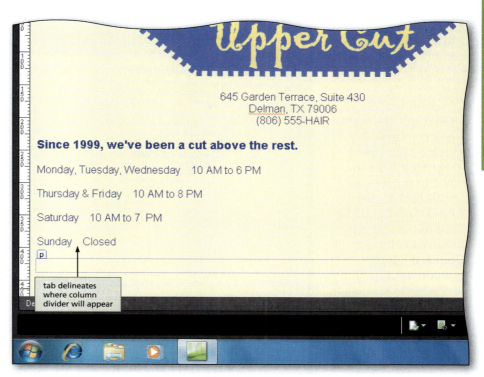

Figure 5–67

3

- Select the four new lines of text.

- Point to Convert on the Table menu, then click Text To Table to open the Convert Text To Table dialog box.

- Click the Tabs option button to select it (Figure 5–68).

Figure 5–68

- Click the OK button to create a table from the text (Figure 5–69).

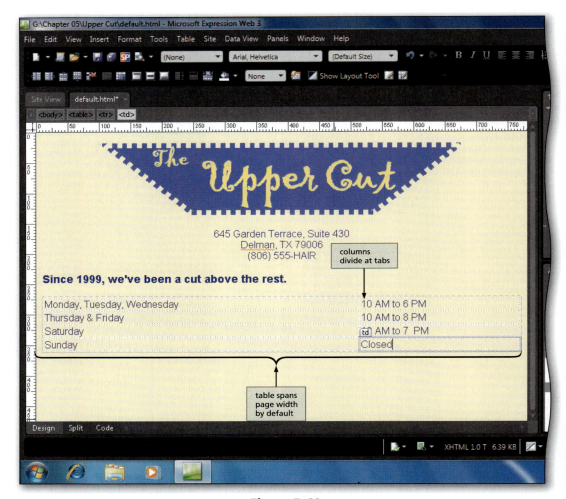

Experiment

- Select the new table, point to Convert on the Table menu, then click Table To Text to convert the table back to text. Press CTRL+Z to undo the conversion, and then click the last cell in the table.

Figure 5–69

To Distribute Rows and Columns

The following steps deselect the Specify width table property; doing so automatically **distributes** the columns, or resizes the width of each column to fit to the width of its content. You will then center the table on the page.

1

- Right-click the table to open the shortcut menu, then click Table Properties to open the Table Properties dialog box.

- Click the Specify width check box to deselect it (Figure 5–70).

Figure 5–70

2

- Click the OK button to close the Table Properties dialog box and change the column width (Figure 5–71).

 Experiment

- Position the pointer between two columns until the pointer turns into a two-sided arrow, then drag left or right to manually adjust the column width. Press CTRL+Z to undo the change.

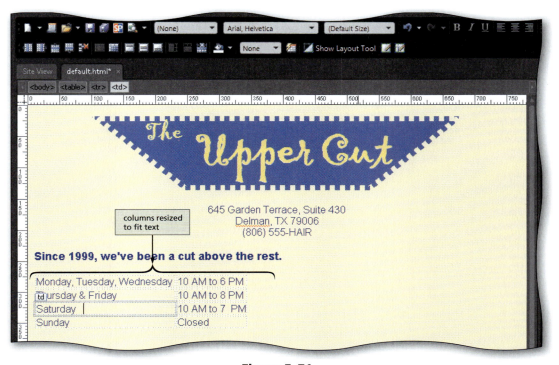

Figure 5–71

3
- Click the <table> tag on the Quick Tag Selector to select the table.

- Click the Center button on the Common toolbar to center the table (Figure 5–72).

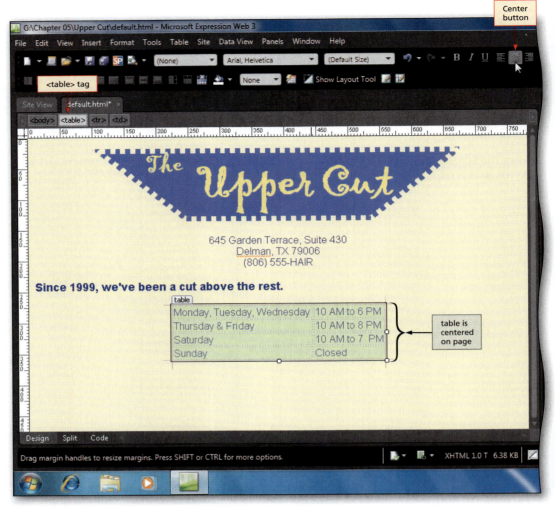

Figure 5–72

Table AutoFormat

Table AutoFormat is an Expression Web feature that offers predetermined formatting options for tables. AutoFormat lets you specify rows or columns to differentiate as headers, and specify whether to modify features such as the border, shading, or font. AutoFormat is a formatting feature unique to Microsoft applications such as Microsoft Word. In Expression Web AutoFormat is used to format Web pages. As an AutoFormat is applied, Expression Web creates and saves styles as inline styles, not to a style sheet.

To Use Table AutoFormat

To add visual appeal, Marcus and Elisa want to add formatting to the table on the default.html page. The following steps apply an AutoFormat to the new table. Your table does not have header or column row text, so you will not have special formatting applied to the first row or column in the table.

1

- Click the Table AutoFormat button on the Tables toolbar to open the Table AutoFormat dialog box (Figure 5–73).

Experiment

- Click options in the Formats list to view them in the Preview window.

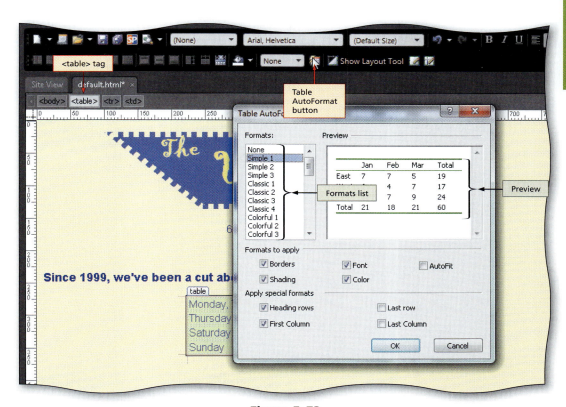

Figure 5–73

2

- Click the Heading rows check box to deselect it.

- Click the First Column check box to deselect it.

- Click the Borders check box to deselect it.

- Scroll down the Formats list, then click the Subtle 1 option to select it (Figure 5–74).

Figure 5–74

3

- Click the OK button to close the Table AutoFormat dialog box and apply the formatting to the table.

- Click outside of the table to deselect it (Figure 5–75).

- Save the page.

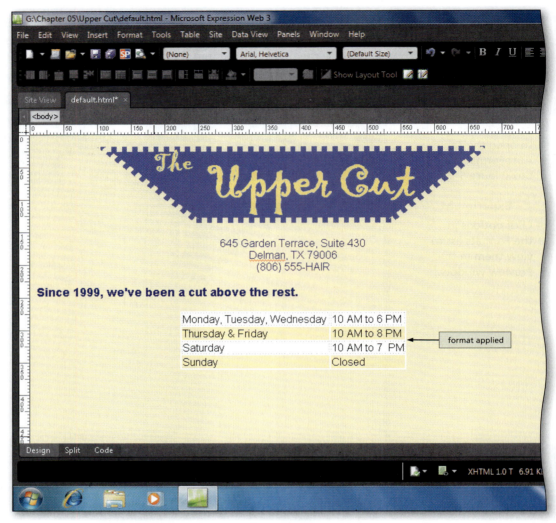

Figure 5–75

Other Ways

1. Point to Modify on the Table menu, then click Table AutoFormat to open the Table AutoFormat dialog box

BTW

I-Frame Security
I-frames have been used by hackers to implant malicious code onto legitimate Web sites, causing security issues for the site visitors.

About Inline Frames

An inline frame, or an I-frame, is a way to embed one HTML file into another. Specifying the size of the frame that contains the embedded HTML page helps control the page size of the original HTML file when it is viewed in the browser. Recall that every element on a Web page contributes to the page's overall file size. Scroll boxes make it possible to view the content of the embedded HTML file if the frame in which it is embedded is not large enough to view the entire HTML file.

I-frames are helpful to display a table or other pages with large amounts of data that may not be of interest to all visitors. Embedding an advertisement or including information that may be in a sidebar of a printed publication are other uses for I-frames.

One advantage of using an I-frame is that the main page and the embedded file load in a browser separately. The site visitor can perform various actions within the embedded file without affecting the main page. For instance, clicking an item on a navigation bar can cause a new embedded HTML page to load without the browser having to reload the original page.

Add an I-frame to display a page.

An important consideration when adding an I-frame to a Web page is the display size of the main HTML page. Adding a frame for a table allows the visitor to see all or most of the page content without scrolling. For a table that provides additional reference information but is not the main focus of the page, having a small, scrollable window allows visitors to peruse the information in the table if they wish, while keeping their browser window on the original page. Changes to the table do not affect the main page, and vice versa.

Plan Ahead

To Create an I-Frame

The following steps insert and resize the I-frame that will contain the stylist table.

- Click below the table, then press ENTER to position the insertion point where the I-frame will appear (Figure 5–76).

Figure 5–76

2
- If necessary, double-click Paragraph in the Toolbox to insert a new paragraph tag.

- Point to HTML on the Insert menu, then click Inline Frame to insert a new I-frame (Figure 5–77).

Q&A

Why is my I-frame in a different location?

If there are extra <p> tags between the table and the I-frame, delete them so that your I-frame placement matches Figure 5–79.

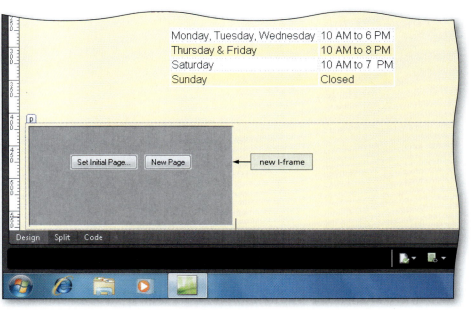

Figure 5–77

3

- Click the right edge of the frame, then click the sizing handle and drag to the right until the right edge is at 700 on the horizontal ruler and the status bar reads, width: 680px (Figure 5–78).

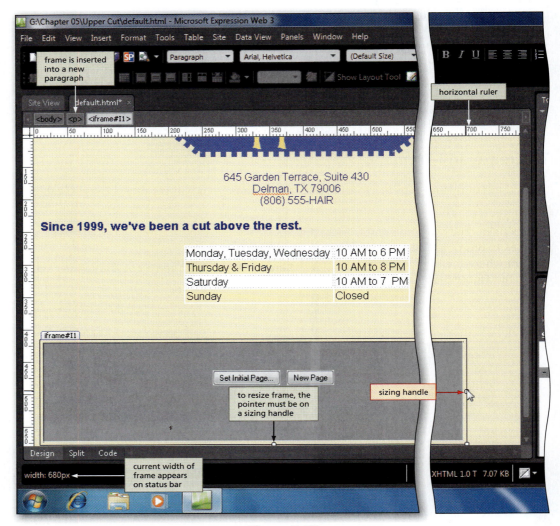

Figure 5–78

4

- Click the Center button on the Common toolbar to center the frame between the page margins.

- Click the bottom sizing handle on the frame, then drag down until the bottom edge is at 750 pixels on the vertical ruler and the status bar reads, height: 325px (Figure 5–79).

- Save the page.

Q&A Can I increase the height of the I-frame if 750 is not visible on the vertical ruler?

Yes, drag the bottom sizing handle down and the window will scroll as you drag until 750 comes into view on the vertical ruler.

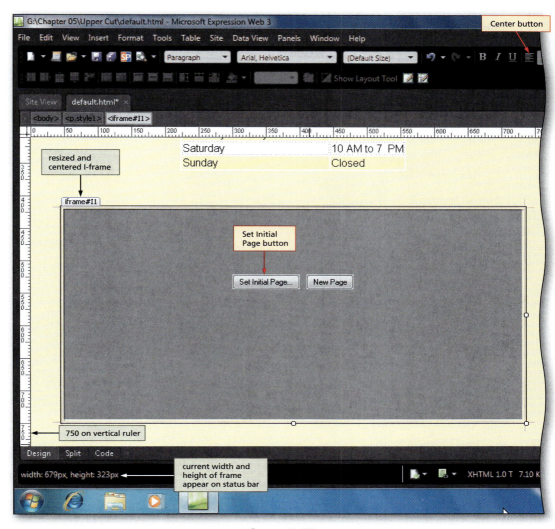

Figure 5–79

Other Ways

1. Double-click the Inline Frame tag in the Toolbox to insert an I-frame

To Target Links in an I-Frame

The following steps embed the stylist_table.html file into the I-frame.

- Click the Set Initial Page button in the Frame to open the Insert Hyperlink dialog box.

- Verify that the Existing File or Web Page button is selected, then click stylist_table to select it as the frame link (Figure 5–80).

Figure 5–80

- Click the OK button to close the Insert Hyperlink dialog box and insert a link to the table (Figure 5–81).

- Save the page.

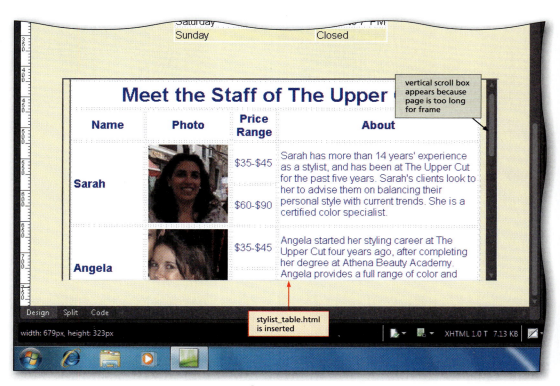

Figure 5–81

3

- Click the 'Preview in browser' button arrow on the Common toolbar, then click Windows Internet Explorer 8.0 to open the page in the browser (Figure 5–82).

Why does my table caption appear at the top of the table?

Expression Web uses the valign attribute with the caption tag to align a table caption. This attribute is incompatible with some browsers. To align the caption correctly, open the stylist_table.html page in Code view, change valign on line 105 to align, save the page, then refresh your browser.

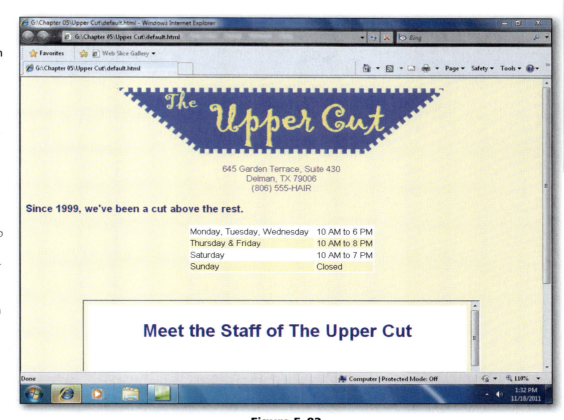

Figure 5–82

4

- Scroll through the embedded page to view the table contents (Figure 5–83).

- Click the Close button on the browser title bar to close the browser window.

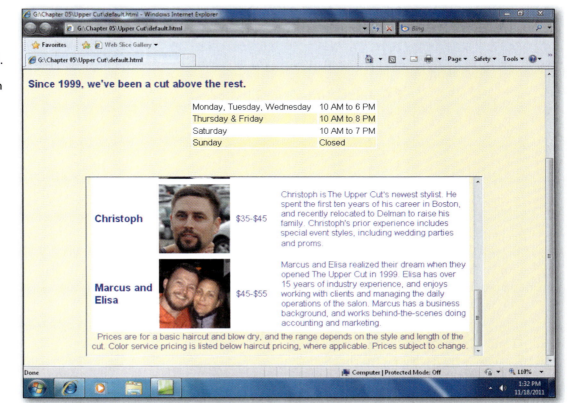

Figure 5–83

Using Frames and Tables to Lay Out a Web Page

Framesets and HTML tables are two methods that have historically been used to lay out Web pages. A **frameset** is a single Web page constructed from multiple HTML files (the "frames"), while an HTML **layout table** controls the positioning of elements within a page by the table properties. With the development of CSS and other style sheet languages that position page elements using styles, however, frames and tables are now considered outdated, non-standards-compliant techniques. Layout frames and layout tables can cause issues with browsers, bookmarks, search engines, and printing. You may encounter existing Web pages designed using layout frames or tables, which is why these approaches are mentioned here.

Framesets define page areas by including each area (footer, content, navigation, and so on) as a separate HTML file. Frames allow certain page elements, such as the masthead and navigation area, to remain consistent and only load once in the browser, while the main page content changes from page to page. Frames also can be used to separate page content to make a page easier to update. If you only wanted to change the navigation bar, you would simply replace that HTML file, and the rest of the page would be unchanged.

To create a frames page in Expression Web, choose one of the Frames Pages options in the New dialog box. For each frame, click the Set Initial Page button, then select the page to display within that frame. You can customize the frames page by resizing, splitting, and deleting frames, or changing the page that displays.

Layout tables are another method that can be used to lay out Web pages. Unlike framesets, which treat each page element as a separate file, tables include each page component within a row, column, or cell. Layout tables must be copied from page to page to maintain consistency of common elements such as navigation, which makes updating these items problematic.

To create a page using a layout table in Expression Web, click Layout Tables from the Table menu to display the Layout Tables panel. Click an option in the Table layout section of the panel to get started, then add, delete, resize, split, and merge cells to create the page layout you want, then enter the page content.

To Close a Site and Quit Expression Web

1 On the Site menu, click Close.

2 On the File menu, click Exit.

Chapter Summary

In this chapter, you have learned to create and modify a new style sheet using a preformatted style sheet provided by Expression Web. You created a data table, entered text and added images, defined cell and table properties, added styles, and split and merged cells. You created a table from delineated text, then applied an AutoFormat. Lastly, you created an I-frame, resized it, and added a link to an HTML page.

The items listed below include all the new Expression Web skills you have learned in this chapter.

1. Create a New Web Site and Web Page (EW 305)
2. Create a New Style Sheet (EW 310)
3. Create a New Page and Attach a Style Sheet (EW 315)
4. Insert a Data Table (EW 317)
5. Change Table and Cell Properties (EW 320)
6. Add Text to a Table (EW 323)
7. Add Images to a Table (EW 327)
8. Add Rows and Columns (EW 330)
9. Use Table Fill (EW 334)
10. Merge Table Cells (EW 337)
11. Split Table Cells (EW 338)

12. Apply Styles to Table Text (EW 340)
13. Convert Text to a Table (EW 342)
14. Distribute Rows and Columns (EW 345)

15. Use Table AutoFormat (EW 347)
16. Create an I-Frame (EW 349)
17. Target Links in an I-Frame (EW 352)

 For current SAM information, including versions and content details, visit SAM Central (http://samcentral.course.com). If you have a SAM user profile, you may have access to hands-on instruction, practice, and assessment of the skills covered in this chapter. Since various versions of SAM are supported throughout the life of this text, check with your instructor for the correct instructions and URL/Web site for accessing assignments.

Learn It Online

Test your knowledge of chapter content and key terms.

Instructions: To complete the Learn It Online exercises, start your browser, click the Address bar, and then enter the Web address `scsite.com/ew3/learn`. When the Expression Web Learn It Online page is displayed, click the link for the exercise you want to complete and then read the instructions.

Chapter Reinforcement TF, MC, and SA
A series of true/false, multiple choice, and short answer questions that test your knowledge of the chapter content.

Flash Cards
An interactive learning environment where you identify chapter key terms associated with displayed definitions.

Practice Test
A series of multiple choice questions that test your knowledge of chapter content and key terms.

Who Wants To Be a Computer Genius?
An interactive game that challenges your knowledge of chapter content in the style of a television quiz show.

Wheel of Terms
An interactive game that challenges your knowledge of chapter key terms in the style of the television show *Wheel of Fortune*.

Crossword Puzzle Challenge
A crossword puzzle that challenges your knowledge of key terms presented in the chapter.

Apply Your Knowledge

Reinforce the skills and apply the concepts you learned in this chapter.

Creating a Data Table
Instructions: Start Expression Web. Create a new Web site, add a new page, and create and attach a new style sheet to each page. Create a data table and enter data and change the properties, then insert a new page into an I-frame so that the page looks like Figure 5–84.

Continued >

Apply Your Knowledge *continued*

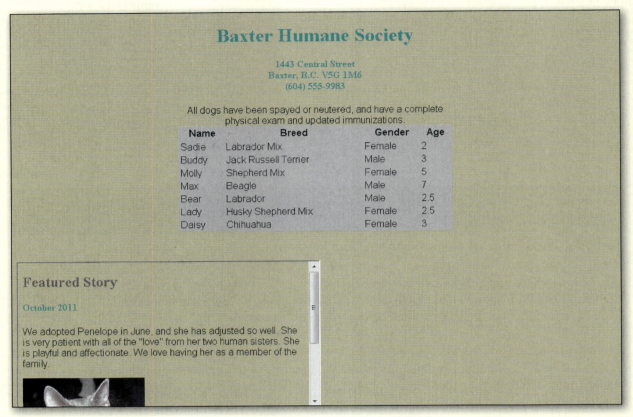

Figure 5–84

Perform the following tasks:

1. Click New Site on the Site menu, then click One Page Web Site in the General category.

2. Click Browse, then navigate to the drive and folder where you save your data files, type `Apply 5-1 Baxter` at the end of the file path in the Location text box, then click OK.

3. Point to New on the File menu, then click Page. Click Style Sheets, click the Bars style sheet type, then click the OK button.

4. Save the new style sheet as `baxter_styles.css`.

5. Open the default.html page, then attach baxter_styles.css.

6. Insert a paragraph tag for the page header, type `Baxter Humane Society`, then format the paragraph with the Heading 1 <h1> style and center it.

7. Click below the header, select the Heading 4 <h4> style and center the heading, then type the following, pressing SHIFT+ENTER at the end of lines one and two:

   ```
   1443 Central Street
   Baxter, B.C. V5G 1M6
   (604) 555-9983
   ```

8. Click below the phone number, then insert a new table with seven rows and four columns. Type the following headers and data into the table:

Name	Breed	Gender	Age
Sadie	Labrador Mix	Female	2
Buddy	Jack Russell Terrier	Male	3
Molly	Shepherd Mix	Female	5
Max	Beagle	Male	7
Lady	Husky Shepherd Mix	Female	2.5
Daisy	Chihuahua	Female	3

9. Right-click the table, then click Table Properties to open the Table Properties dialog box.

10. Verify that the Specify width check box is checked, type 450 in the Specify width box, click the In pixels option button if necessary, center-align the table, apply a silver table background, then click the OK button to close the dialog box.

11. Select the top table row, right-click the row, then click Cell Properties to open the Cell Properties dialog box.

12. Click the Header cell check box, then click the OK button to close the dialog box.

13. Insert a new row above the row with Lady's data. (*Hint:* Use the Tables toolbar.)

14. Type the following in the new row:

Bear	Labrador	Male	2.5

15. Right-click the table, point to Insert, then click Caption. Right-click the caption, then click Caption Properties to open the Caption Properties dialog box.

16. Click the 'Bottom of table' option button, then click the OK button. Type the caption, All dogs have been spayed or neutered, and have a complete physical exam and updated immunizations.

17. Press CTRL+N to create a new blank page, then save it as october_feature.html.

18. Attach the baxter_styles.css style sheet to the new page.

19. Insert a paragraph tag for the page header, type Featured Story, then format the paragraph with Heading 2 <h2>.

20. Click below the Featured Story header, insert a paragraph tag for the page subheading, type October 2011, then format the paragraph with Heading 4 <h4>.

21. Insert a new paragraph tag and type the following: We adopted Penelope in June, and she has adjusted so well. She is very patient with all of the "love" from her two human sisters. She is playful and affectionate. We love having her as a member of the family.

22. Press ENTER, click the Insert Picture from File button on the Common toolbar, navigate to your data files folder, double-click the humane_image folder to open it, click the penelope image, then click the Insert button to open the Accessibility Properties dialog box.

23. Type Gray cat in the Alternate text text box, then click the OK button.

24. Double-click the image to open the Picture Properties dialog box, click the Appearance tab, type 200 in the Width text box, then click the OK button.

25. Click the Picture Actions button, then click the Resample Picture To Match Size option button.

26. Save the page and the embedded image, then close the page.

27. Return to the default.html page, click below the table, press SHIFT+ENTER twice, then double-click Inline Frame in the Toolbox to insert a new I-frame.

Continued >

Apply Your Knowledge *continued*

28. Select the I-frame, then drag the right and bottom sizing handles to resize the frame to 500 pixels wide and 250 pixels high.

29. Click the Set Initial Page button, click the october_feature file, then click the OK button.

30. Save the default.html page.

31. Preview the site and test the I-frame and image.

32. Change the site properties, as specified by your instructor. Save all pages, then close the site.

33. Submit the revised site in the format specified by your instructor.

Extend Your Knowledge

Extend the skills you learned in this chapter and experiment with new skills. You may need to use Help to complete the assignment.

Converting Text to a Table

Instructions: Start Expression Web. You will open a Web site and insert a text file with delineated data, then convert the data to a table. Change the table properties to add a background image, and manually adjust the column width. Add a new I-frame to make the default.html page match the one shown in Figure 5–85.

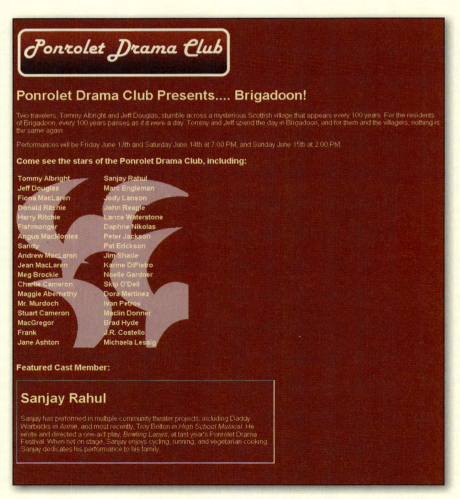

Figure 5–85

Perform the following tasks:

1. Click Site on the menu bar, then click Open Site.

2. Click the Browse button and navigate to your data files folder, click the Extend 5-1 Drama folder to select it, click the Open button, then click the second Open button.

3. Open the default.html page, then position the insertion point in the paragraph tag below the line, Come see the stars…

4. Open Microsoft Word and open the file brigadoon_cast.doc from the drama_files folder in your data files folder.

5. Select the text, copy it to the Clipboard, then quit Microsoft Word.

6. Click Paste Text on the Edit menu, click the 'Normal paragraphs with line breaks' option, then click the OK button.

7. Select the pasted text.

8. Point to Convert on the Table menu, then click Text to Table.

9. Click the Commas option button, then click the OK button.

10. Open the Table Properties dialog box, then specify that the table width is 400 pixels.

11. Add a background image, using the file background_image.gif from the drama_files folder, then close the Table Properties dialog box. (*Hint:* Click the 'Use background picture' check box, then browse to the background image.)

12. Drag the divider between the two columns until the first column is 196 pixels wide. (*Hint:* View the ScreenTip to note the width as you drag.)

13. Select the table, then click the Bold button.

14. Select the right column, then click the AutoFit to Contents button on the Tables toolbar.

15. Click in the last cell in the table, after the name, then press TAB to insert a new row.

16. Type Jane Ashton, press TAB, then type Michaela Lessig. Apply bold to these two new cells, if necessary.

17. If necessary, insert a new paragraph tag below the table, type Featured Cast Member:, then format the paragraph as Heading 3 <h3>.

18. Click below the heading, then insert a new I-frame. Resize the frame to 600 pixels wide and 200 pixels high.

19. Set the initial page to the sanjay_feature.html page from the Extend 5-1 Drama folder.

20. Save the default.html page and the embedded image. Preview the page, scroll to view the entire page contents, then close the browser window.

21. Change the site properties as specified by your instructor. In Windows Explorer, rename the site folder Extend 5-1 Drama Site. Submit the revised site in the format specified by your instructor.

Make It Right

Analyze a site and correct all errors and/or improve the design.

Creating and Fixing a Data Table

Instructions: Start Expression Web. Open the Web site, Make It Right 5-1 Fitness, from the Data Files for Students. See the inside back cover of this book for instructions for downloading the Data Files for Students, or see your instructor for information about accessing the required files.

Continued >

Make It Right *continued*

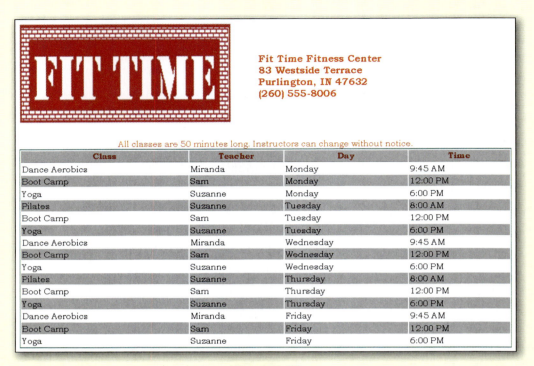

Figure 5–86

Open the default.html page. Find the five issues in the text that will cause problems when the text is converted into rows and columns. Make the necessary changes to the file. (*Hint:* The issues will lead to an extra row and column being added to the table. If the table doesn't look right when you create it, undo then try again.) Select the lines of delineated text (from Class to Friday 6:00 pm). Create a new data table on the default.html page by converting the lines of delineated text into a table, separating text at commas. Add a new row between the second and third rows, and enter the following data: Boot Camp, press tab, Sam, press tab, Monday, press tab, 12:00 PM. Define the top row as a table header and center-align the text. Add a caption to the top of the table, and type All classes are 50 minutes long. Instructors can change without notice. Apply the List 1 Table AutoFormat to the table and set the first column so it is the same as the others. (*Hint:* Deselect the First Column check box in the Table AutoFormat dialog box) to create the page shown in Figure 5–86. Change the site properties as specified by your instructor. Save and close the site. In Windows Explorer, rename the site using the folder name Make It Right 5-1 Fitness Site. Submit the revised site in the format specified by your instructor.

In the Lab

Design and/or format a Web site using the guidelines, concepts, and skills presented in this chapter. Labs are listed in order of increasing difficulty.

Lab 1: Creating a New Table

Problem: You are a photographer and want to update your home page by creating a list of prices for printed photos. Insert a table, specify the table and cell properties, and enter table data to create the page shown in Figure 5–87.

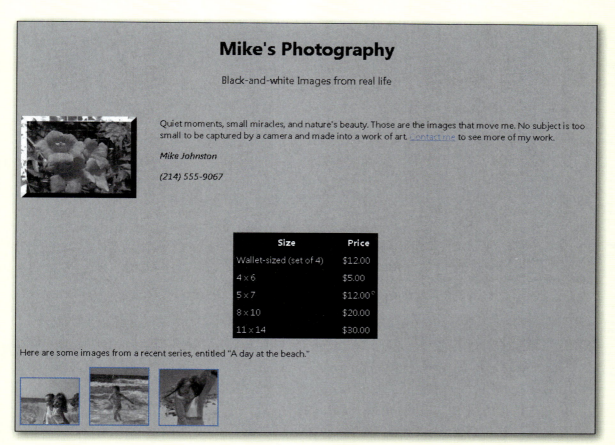

Figure 5–87

Instructions:

1. Start Expression Web.

2. Open the Web site, Lab 5-1 Photo, from your data files folder, and open the default.html page.

3. Scroll down and create a new table with five rows and two columns in the empty paragraph just above the line, Here are some images...

4. Enter the following headers and data into the table, pressing TAB at the end of the last row in the table in order to create a new row for the last row of data:

Size	Price
Wallet-sized (set of 4)	$12.00
4 x 6	$5.00
5 x 7	$12.00
8 x 10	$20.00
11 x 14	$30.00

5. Define the top row as the header.

6. Specify the following table properties: black background, 250 pixels wide, and 4 pixels of cell padding.

7. Change the font color of the table text to white and center the table on the page.

8. Save the changes to the default.html page, preview the site in a browser, then scroll to view the entire page content.

9. Close the site, then submit the site in the format specified by your instructor.

In the Lab

Lab 2: Creating an I-Frame

Problem: You have volunteered to update the Web site for the Connecticut branch of the Gulliver College Alumni Society. Create a new page with a table and insert it as an I-frame onto the default.html page, as shown in Figure 5–88.

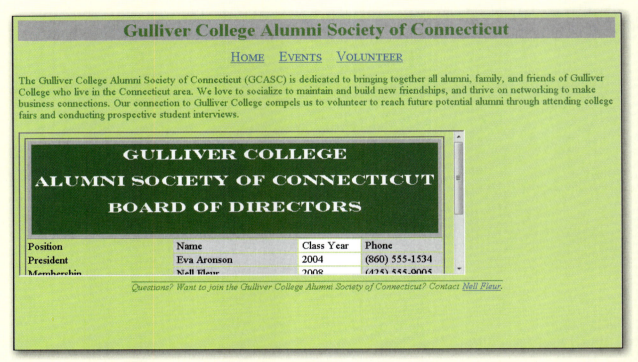

Figure 5–88

Instructions: Start Expression Web. Open the Web site, Lab 5-2 Alumni, from the Data Files for Students. See the inside back cover of this book for instructions for downloading the Data Files for Students, or see your instructor for information about accessing the required files.

Perform the following tasks:

1. Create a new, blank page. Save it as alumni_board.html and attach the alumni_styles.css style sheet.

2. Open Microsoft Word and open the board.doc file from the Lab 5-2 Documents folder. Copy and paste the contents of the Word document into Expression Web as normal paragraphs with line breaks. Close the Word document and quit Microsoft Word.

3. Convert the pasted text into a table.

4. Use the Table Properties dialog box to set the table at a fixed width of 700 pixels.

5. Create a new row above the table and merge the cells into one.

6. Insert the board_logo.gif file from the Lab 5-2 Documents folder into the merged cell. Enter `Gulliver College Alumni Society of Connecticut Board of Directors logo` as the alternate text.

7. Apply the Column 5 Table AutoFormat, keeping the Heading rows and First Column check boxes selected.

8. Modify the .ms-column5-left style that is created from the AutoFormat using the Modify Style dialog box to have normal font-weight instead of bold.

9. Save and close the alumni_board.html page and the embedded file, then open the default.html page.

10. Click after the words, student interviews (be sure to click after the period), then press ENTER twice.

11. Insert a new I-frame using the Toolbox.

12. Drag to resize the I-frame so that it is 750 pixels wide and 250 pixels high.

13. Set the initial page to the alumni_board.html page.

14. Save the default.html page.

15. Preview the page in a browser and scroll through the table.

16. Close the site, in Windows Explorer rename the site folder Lab 5-2 Alumni Site, and submit the site in the format specified by your instructor.

In the Lab

Lab 3: Creating a New Web Page as an I-Frame

Problem: Your client, a tutor, wants to create a home page that he can use to attract clients. Create a one-page Web site and a new style sheet using a preformatted style sheet, and add another page in an I-frame to the home page shown in Figure 5–89.

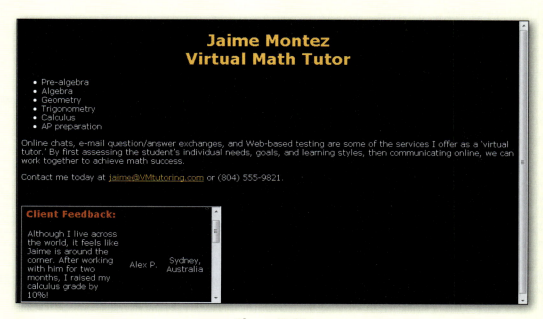

Figure 5–89

Continued >

In the Lab *continued*

Instructions:

1. Start Expression Web.

2. Create a one-page Web site called Lab 5-3 Tutor Site, then open the default.html page.

3. Create a new style sheet based on the Highway style sheet, save it as tutor_styles.css, then attach it to the default.html page.

4. Insert a new blank paragraph.

5. Type `Jaime Montez`, press SHIFT+ENTER, then type `Virtual Math Tutor`.

6. Format the paragraph tag as h1, then center it.

7. Click below the heading, then insert a new bulleted list.

8. Type the following as the bulleted list text, pressing ENTER after each line and pressing ENTER twice at the end of the last line:

   - `Pre-algebra`
   - `Algebra`
   - `Geometry`
   - `Trigonometry`
   - `Calculus`
   - `AP preparation`

9. In the new paragraph tag, type the following: `Online chats, e-mail question/answer exchanges, and Web-based testing are some of the services I offer as a 'virtual tutor.' By first assessing the student's individual needs, goals, and learning styles, then communicating online, we can work together to achieve math success.`

10. Press ENTER to start a new paragraph, then type `Contact me today at jaime@VMtutoring.com or (804) 555-9821.`.

11. Press ENTER twice, then insert a new I-frame.

12. Resize the I-frame to 400 pixels wide and 200 pixels high.

13. Click the New Page button in the I-frame to create a new blank HTML page within the frame.

14. Save the page as client_feedback.html. (*Hint:* If necessary, press CTRL+S to open the Save As dialog box for the new page.)

15. Open the client_feedback.html file, then attach the tutor_styles.css style sheet.

16. Insert a new paragraph tag, type `Client Feedback:`, then format the text as Heading 3 <h3>.

17. Create a new table with four rows and three columns, then type the following data into the table:

Although I live across the world, it feels like Jaime is around the corner. After working with him for two months, I raised my calculus grade by 10%!	Alex P.	Sydney, Australia
The extra online exams I took helped increase my confidence in test taking, and allowed me to see my progress.	Sarah J.	Ithaca, NY
Our weekly online chats gave me the personal, real-time instruction that I needed to fully understand the concepts being taught in my geometry class.	Wilhelm C.	Enid, OK
I recommend Jaime to all of my AP math students. He will work with them individually to offer extra one-on-one assistance as well as test-taking skills.	Bailey W.	Strayer, WI

18. Save both files, then preview the default.html page in a browser.

19. Change the site properties as specified by your instructor, then close the site.

20. Submit the site in the format specified by your instructor.

Cases and Places

Apply your creative thinking and problem-solving skills to design and implement a solution.

• Easier •• More Difficult

• 1: Creating a New Table

Create a new blank Web site that contains information about your favorite musician or musical group, and add a page using the CSS layout of your choice. Enter content in all of the divs. Create a new style sheet based on a preformatted style sheet and attach it to the page. Modify at least one of the styles, such as the page background or font family. Create a table listing the musician's albums and songs and format it using headings. Merge the top row of the table to create a table title. Enter a caption at the bottom of the table. Define and enter content for a header row. Delete a row from the middle of the table, and add a row at the end of the table by pressing TAB. Save and close all pages, then quit Expression Web.

• 2: Creating an I-Frame

Create a new one-page Web site dedicated to your favorite professional athlete. Add a new blank HTML page to the site. Create a style sheet using a preformatted option, and attach it to both pages. Enter data into both pages, featuring career highlights on the default.html page. On the second page, include at least one table of statistics to which you add an image, apply an AutoFormat, and merge and split cells. Create an I-frame Create an I-frame on the home page and set the second page as the initial page. Resize the frame so that when the home page is previewed in the browser, the entire home page is visible.

•• 3: Troubleshooting Tables

Create a new blank HTML page for your current class schedule. Enter information that you will convert to a table and delineate the data using commas or tabs. In at least one row, add an extra delineator, and add a blank line in the middle of the table. Convert the text to a table, then move data, and delete rows and columns. Select the table, then convert it back to text. Select the data and convert it back to a table and fix any table errors. Change the table properties and formatting of the table. Save the page, then close it.

•• 4: Creating a Research Home Page

Make It Personal

You want to create a one-page site that includes information from a paper or research project you have done for another class. Create a new one-page site and a style sheet from a preformatted style sheet and attach the style sheet. Enter information on the default.html page, including a table with a caption and header row. Create an I-frame and a page to link to it that includes information relevant to the topic. Save the pages and style sheets, then close the site.

•• 5: Creating a Web Page with an I-Frame

Working Together

A video store wants to display a list of new releases in an I-frame on its home page. Working as a team with several of your classmates, you are to plan and create the home page and table page. Each team member should contribute to supplying titles, ratings, descriptions, or other information for the list. As a group, decide on the information you need for the table, including the number of columns of information and the number of rows you need to list all of the titles you have come up with. Create a site folder with a blank page and attach a style sheet that you create using a preformatted style sheet.

Continued >

Cases and Places *continued*

Make at least one modification to the styles in the style sheet. Enter information on the page, such as a logo or masthead, address, and other relevant information. Create a new blank page and attach the style sheet to it. Create a table using the planned data, and make sure to merge and split some cells. Format the site using table and cell properties, headings, and other formatting techniques. Insert and resize an I-frame on the home page, and link the table page to it. Preview the site, test the navigation bar, and make sure that your site is readable and attractive. Save and close the pages and style sheet, then close the site.

6 | Adding Interactivity

Objectives

You will have mastered the material in this chapter when you can:

- Create an interactive button
- Duplicate an interactive button
- Edit an interactive button
- Test an interactive button
- Define how behaviors work
- Use the Behaviors panel

- Add a jump menu behavior
- Add a status message behavior
- Add a swap image behavior
- Modify a behavior
- Test a behavior
- Create an image map

6 | Adding Interactivity

Introduction

Interactivity is the term used to describe the connection that occurs between a Web site and a site visitor through actions such as clicking a button, list item, or part of an image. Interactivity goes beyond simple site navigation through hyperlinks; users can trigger an event, such as opening a new Web page or e-mail, zooming in on an image, or launching a chat window by performing actions such as clicking or hovering the mouse pointer over an element. Interactive tools are commonly used in site navigation, but can also provide additional information to site visitors by changing an image or displaying a message in a new window or in the status bar.

Elements that are interactive have behaviors attached to them. **Behaviors** are the embedded functions that occur as a result of site events, such as a page opening in a browser window, or user interaction, such as clicking or hovering the mouse. Expression Web tools create behaviors using code from a scripting language called **JavaScript**. As with HTML and CSS, you do not need to know JavaScript to create and modify behaviors in Expression Web.

There are many ways to add interactivity to your Web page, including **interactive buttons**, also called **rollover buttons**, that look different when they are inactive, have a mouse pointer hovering over them, and are clicked. **Jump menus** are lists that contain links. **Image maps** are graphics that have links, called **hotspots**, associated with different areas of the graphic.

Project — Farm Stand Web Site

Wisteria Farms, a farm stand and grocery store in Dilton, New Hampshire, currently has a Web site that needs more interactivity. The site has four main pages for the home page, store, events, and directions, but no method for navigating between them. You will create a navigation bar for the main site pages by adding interactive buttons to each page. The owners want it to be easy to view descriptions of the store's main areas. You will create a jump menu on the home page as well as an image map on the store page that allows users to view pages about the different store departments.

The project in this chapter shows you how to use Expression Web to add interactivity to create the site shown in Figure 6–1. You will create a navigation bar using interactive buttons that you will copy to each main page of the site. You will create a jump menu and an image map and place them appropriately to link to each of the store pages. You will create behaviors for an image swap and a status bar message. Although Expression Web provides tools for creating many types of interactivity, you will add only these four types of behaviors so that your site is not overwhelmed by interactivity.

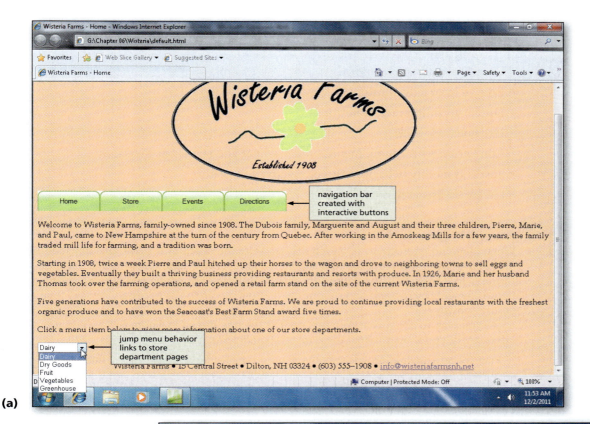

Figure 6–1

Overview

As you read this chapter, you will learn how to create the Web page shown in Figure 6–1 by performing these general tasks:

- Create an interactive button
- Edit an interactive button
- Duplicate an interactive button
- Use behavior tools
- Add behaviors for jump menus, image swaps, and status bar messages
- Test and modify behaviors and interactive buttons
- Create an image map

BTW

Adding Interactivity
See Special Feature 1 for alternatives and concerns regarding adding interactive elements.

Plan Ahead

General Project Guidelines

When planning interactivity in a Web site, consider the needs of the site. Like any feature, only add what makes sense for your site plan and what will help site visitors to navigate through your site easily. Use Expression Web tools instead of typing complicated code. Reuse elements by copying and pasting them, then modifying as necessary, to save time and ensure consistency.

As you plan to enhance a Web site, such as the one shown in Figure 6–1, by adding interactivity, you should follow these general guidelines:

1. **Plan the site navigation.** Identify the main site pages for which links will need to be added to all pages of your site. The navigation bar should be located on the same place on each page to make your site easier to use. What will the site navigation look like? Interactive buttons are often stacked vertically or horizontally (or both) to make an attractive and user-friendly navigation bar.

2. **Determine which elements you can reuse and copy to save time and ensure consistency.** After creating one interactive button, you can copy it to create the others. Interactive buttons are editable, so once you have created one, you will only need to change the text on the button and the page to which it is linked. After you have created the navigation bar, you can copy and paste it to each site page.

3. **Identify behaviors that will improve site visitors' experiences.** Avoid adding behaviors such as sound and pop-up messages that visitors could find annoying or distracting. Consider adding behaviors that assist a user by providing necessary access to other site elements. Take into account the file size of the page when adding behaviors; the code used to program interactivity adds to your page's file size, which will increase the download time in a visitor's browser. Balance the value of the interactivity against the increase in file size. Test all behaviors and buttons to confirm that they work as intended.

4. **Assess how you will provide access to site pages that do not have links in the primary navigation bar.** Sometimes you want to create an HTML page to provide additional information that is not appropriate to add to the primary navigation bar, which should contain the most important page names or categories of pages. A **secondary navigation element** can link to more specific information about a topic. For example, in a site for an elementary school, there could be a link in the primary navigation bar for the school's curriculum; then on the curriculum page, a secondary navigation element could provide links to grade-specific curriculum information. A jump menu is an example of a secondary navigation element that allows visitors to use a list to link to pages for specific additional information. An image map is an excellent way to present information visually, while providing a way to navigate by clicking hotspots.

To Start Expression Web and Reset Workspace Layout

If you are using a computer to step through the project in this chapter, and you want your screens to match the figures in this book, you should change your computer's resolution to 1024 × 768. For information about how to change a computer's resolution, read Appendix G.

The following steps, which assume Windows 7 is running, start Expression Web based on a typical installation, and reset the panels in the workspace to the default layout. You may need to ask your instructor how to start Expression Web for your computer.

Note: If you are using Windows XP, see Appendix E for alternate steps. If you are using Windows Vista, see Appendix F for alternate steps.

1 Click the Start button on the Windows 7 taskbar to display the Start menu.

2 Click All Programs at the bottom of the left pane on the Start menu to display the All Programs list.

3 Click Microsoft Expression on the All Programs list to display the Microsoft Expression list.

4 Click Microsoft Expression Web 3 to start Expression Web.

5 Click Panels on the menu bar, then click Reset Workspace Layout.

6 Click View on the menu bar, point to Ruler and Grid, then click Show Ruler to turn on the rulers if necessary.

To Open a Web Site and Web Page

The following steps open the Wisteria Farms Web site and the default.html page:

1 Click Site on the menu bar to open the Site menu, then click Open Site to display the Open Site dialog box.

2 Click the Browse button to open the next Open Site dialog box.

3 Navigate to the data files folder.

4 Click the Wisteria folder, click the Open button, then click the Open button to open the site in Expression Web.

5 Double-click the default.html page in the Folder List to open it (Figure 6–2).

Other Ways
1. Double-click the default.html page in the Site View pane to open it

Figure 6–2

Creating an Interactive Navigation Bar

BTW

Dynamic Web Templates
Interactive buttons were a part of the dynamic Web templates you used in Chapter 3.

As you have seen in previous chapters, a navigation bar, at minimum, contains text-based hyperlinks for each of the main site pages. To make your navigation bar more attractive and professional looking, add interactive buttons. Several of the button options are to be used for columns or rows of buttons, and are identified as such in the Interactive Buttons dialog box.

When you create an interactive button using Expression Web, you are actually creating image files for each state of the button. At any given time, a button is in one of three states:

- Being pressed
- Hover, where the visitor's pointer is hovering over the button
- Inactive, where the visitor's pointer is elsewhere on the page

BTW

Fonts on Interactive Buttons
Because interactive buttons are saved as image files, you can use any font for the text, not just those that are considered Web-safe.

You can use interactivity to visually depict these three different states. To add interactivity to a button, Expression Web creates three interchangeable images that replace each other depending on the state of the button. Setting your page to download all three images into the visitor's browser when the page downloads is called **preloading** and increases the speed of interactivity.

Interactivity and Web Browsers

Expression Web embeds the interactive functions you add to your page as **ActiveX controls**, which are Microsoft-developed small programs used to enhance functionality in a program or Web page.

For security purposes, many Web browsers automatically block interactive site features to protect you from potentially harmful scripts that could infect your computer with a virus or that look for personal information on your computer.

When a browser loads a page, it looks for ActiveX controls and other scripted code, and displays a message letting you know that content has been blocked. These messages may differ depending on your browser or the type of script detected, but they most often appear as dialog boxes or alert messages at the top of the page.

Because the site you are viewing in this chapter is one that you have created yourself, you know that the scripts and controls on the pages you view are safe, and therefore you can temporarily allow them. You will most likely have to enable them each time you load a new page in your browser. Although you could change your browser security settings to allow these types of controls to display automatically, that is not a recommended setting. If you cannot enable the interactive content because of your security settings (for instance, if you are on a shared or lab computer), ask your instructor or technical support person for assistance.

BTW

The Expression Web User Guide
The best way to become familiar with the Expression Web User Guide is to use it. Appendix B includes detailed information about the Expression Web User Guide and exercises that will help you gain confidence in using it.

Plan the site navigation.
As with any feature you add to your site pages, consider the desired look of the button, including colors, shape, font, and size. These attributes are set in the Interactive Buttons dialog box. Keep the button text simple, preferably one word, and make sure that the button's label clearly indicates where the button will take the site visitor. A navigation bar should be located on the same place on each page of the site, and should include a button to return to the site's home page.

Plan Ahead

To Create an Interactive Button

The following steps create and test an interactive button for the home page and set a different text color for the hovered state. It is important to test a button before duplicating it; otherwise, you will have to change each copied instance. By default, when you create one interactive button, three images will be created: for inactive, hovering, and pressing states. You can create fewer button images by changing the settings on the Image tab.

- Click in the top navigation div (div#top_nav) below the logo to position the insertion point (Figure 6–3).

Figure 6–3

2

- Click Interactive Button on the Insert menu to open the Interactive Buttons dialog box (Figure 6–4).

 Experiment

- Click options in the Buttons list to view a description and available preview of various button types.

Figure 6–4

3

- Drag the scroll box in the Buttons list down, then click the Metal Tab 2 option.

- Select the words, Button Text, in the Text text box, then type Home (Figure 6–5).

Figure 6–5

4

- Click the Browse button to open the Edit Hyperlink dialog box, then click the Existing File or Web Page button if necessary to view pages that you can link to in the Wisteria site folder (Figure 6–6).

Figure 6–6

5

- Click the default page, then click the OK button to close the Edit Hyperlink dialog box (Figure 6–7).

Figure 6–7

6
- Click the Font tab to display Font choices.

- Click the down arrow, then click the Times New Roman option in the Font box to change the font for the buttons.

- Click the Hovered Font Color box arrow to display the color palette, then point to Purple under Standard Colors (Figure 6–8).

Figure 6–8

7
- Click Purple in the color palette to change the font color for the button when the mouse pointer is positioned over it, then click the Image tab to display the image options (Figure 6–9).

Figure 6–9

8

- Type 120 in the Width text box, then click the OK button to close the Interactive Buttons dialog box and insert the button (Figure 6–10).

Figure 6–10

9

- Press CTRL+S to save the page, then click OK in the Save Embedded Files dialog box.

- Click the 'Preview in browser' button to open the default. html page in a browser window (Figure 6–11).

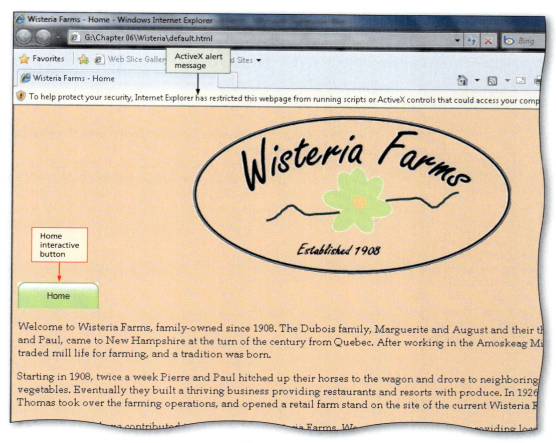

Figure 6–11

10

- Position the pointer over the Home button to view the change in button text color in hovered state (Figure 6–12).

- Click the Close button to close the browser and return to Expression Web.

Q&A

Why is there is a message at the top of my browser window saying that ActiveX content is restricted?

Depending on your security settings, interactive features may be blocked automatically. Click the message at the top of the browser window, click Allow Blocked Content, then click the Yes button in the alert box to allow ActiveX controls for this site, or ask your instructor or technical support person for permission and assistance. You will have to perform this step every time you view a new page in a browser.

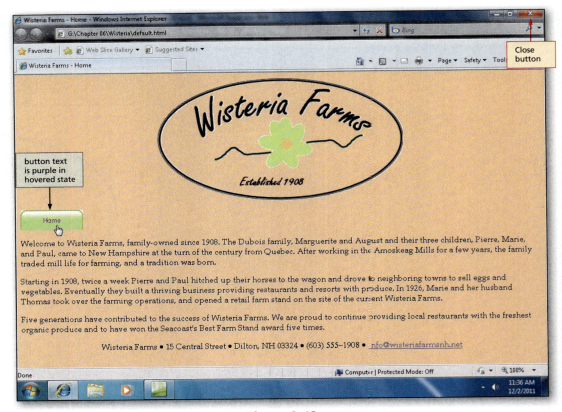

Figure 6–12

Plan Ahead

Determine which elements you can reuse and copy to save time and ensure consistency.
Efficient Web page creators reuse elements by copying, pasting, and modifying them as needed. Creating each button from scratch can introduce errors if you forget to include a certain feature or formatting, or enter text or a link incorrectly. After you copy and paste the buttons, you should move the image files into folders to keep your site organized.

BTW

Other Uses for Interactive Buttons
You can place an interactive button anywhere on a page. For example, at the end of a form page for user input, include a button to submit the form data.

To Duplicate an Interactive Button

The following steps copy the button image from the home page to the Clipboard and paste the button three times to create a total of four links — one for each of the main pages.

- Right-click the Home button to display the shortcut menu, then click Copy to copy the button and its properties to the Clipboard.

- Click to the right of the button to position the insertion point next to it.

- Press CTRL+V to paste a copy of the Home button.

- Press CTRL+V to paste another copy of the Home button.

- Press CTRL+V to paste the final copy of the Home button (Figure 6–13).

Q&A

Why are my button file names different?

Your button file names might differ depending on past usage. This is fine.

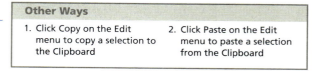

Figure 6–13

Other Ways
1. Click Copy on the Edit menu to copy a selection to the Clipboard
2. Click Paste on the Edit menu to paste a selection from the Clipboard

Editing and Organizing Interactive Buttons

When you edit a copied interactive button, you should only change the specifications that are necessary to distinguish each button: the target link and the button text. Unless your site design can support other changes, such as different colors for each button or a pattern of button colors, keep everything else the same.

Once your navigation bar is complete, you should test it before copying it and pasting it to other site pages. That way, if you choose the wrong target or mistype the button text, you will only have to correct it once, instead of in each pasted location.

To Edit an Interactive Button

The following steps edit each interactive button by changing the text and link.

 1
- Right-click the second button from the left to display the shortcut menu (Figure 6–14).

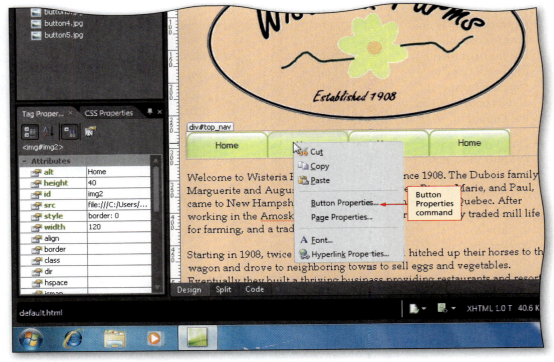

Figure 6–14

2
- Click Button Properties to open the Interactive Buttons dialog box.

- Select the word, Home, in the Text text box, then type Store (Figure 6–15).

Figure 6–15

3

- Press TAB to move the insertion point to the Link text box and select the text box contents, then click the Browse button to open the Edit Hyperlink dialog box.

- Double-click the store folder to open it.

- Click the store page to select it (Figure 6–16).

Figure 6–16

4

- Click the OK button to close the Edit Hyperlink dialog box.

- Click the OK button to close the Interactive Buttons dialog box and accept the edits to the button text and link (Figure 6–17).

Figure 6–17

• Follow Steps 1
through 4 to edit the
third button from the
left to read Events
and link to the events
page in the main site
folder. When in the
Edit Hyperlink dialog
box, use the 'Up
One Folder' button
to return to the
main folder.

• Follow Steps 1
through 4 to edit
the fourth button
from the left to read
Directions and
link to the directions
page in the main site
folder (Figure 6–18).

• Save the page and
all embedded files.

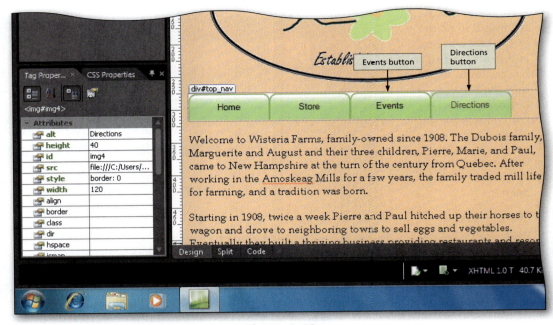

Figure 6–18

Other Ways

1. Double-click a button
   to open the Interactive
   Buttons dialog box

To Test Interactive Buttons

The following steps test the completed navigation bar in the browser.

• Press F12 to open the
default.html
page in a browser window
(Figure 6–19).

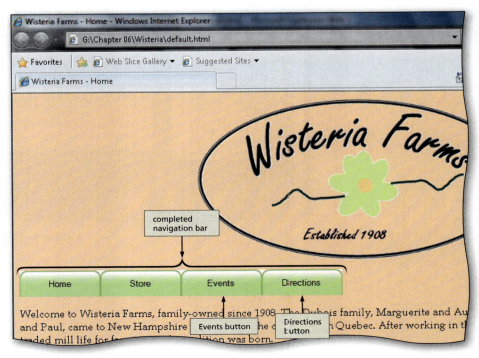

Figure 6–19

2

- Position the mouse pointer over the Store button to view the hover image (Figure 6–20).

Q&A Why isn't the purple hover color showing on my screen?

If interactive content is blocked then the purple hover color will not show. Therefore, remember to allow blocked content if the alert message appears in your browser.

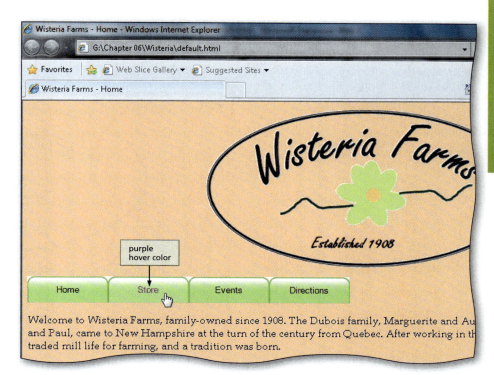

Figure 6–20

3

- Click the Store button to display the store.html page (Figure 6–21).

Figure 6–21

4

- Click the Back button to return to the default.html page.

- Click the Events button to display the events.html page (Figure 6–22).

Figure 6–22

5

- Click the Back button to return to the default.html page.

- Click the Directions button to display the directions.html page (Figure 6–23).

- Click the Close button to close the browser and return to Expression Web.

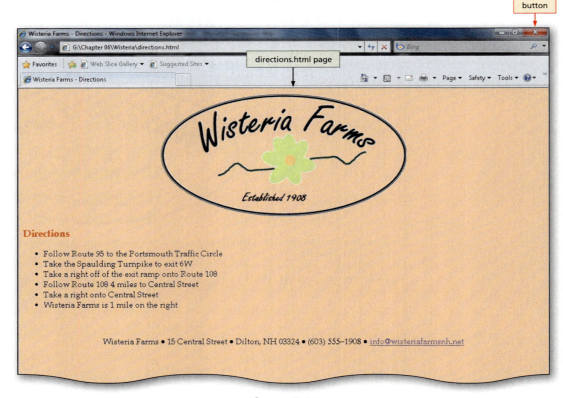

Figure 6–23

To Copy and Paste the Navigation Bar

The following steps open the three other main site pages: store.html, events.html, and directions.html; and copy the navigation bar from the default.html page and paste it into the navigation div for each page to create a consistent and functional navigation bar.

1
- Click the div#top_nav visual aid to select the navigation bar (Figure 6–24).

- Press CTRL+C to copy the navigation bar to the Clipboard.

Q&A | Can I just select the buttons?

Make sure to select the entire navigation div when both copying and pasting the navigation bar.

Figure 6–24

2
- Click the store folder plus sign in the Folder List to display the contents of the folder.

- Double-click the store.html page in the Folder List to open it (Figure 6–25).

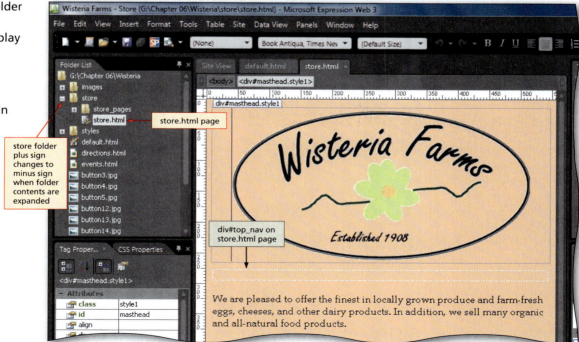

Figure 6–25

3

• Click in the div#top_nav div, then click the div#top_nav visual aid to select the empty navigation div.

• Press CTRL+V to paste the navigation bar from the Clipboard to the store.html page (Figure 6–26).

Figure 6–26

4

• Repeat Steps 2 through 3 to open the events.html and directions.html pages from the Folder List and paste the navigation bar onto both pages (Figure 6–27).

• Save all pages at once, and click OK three times to save the embedded images you added to the store, events, and directions pages.

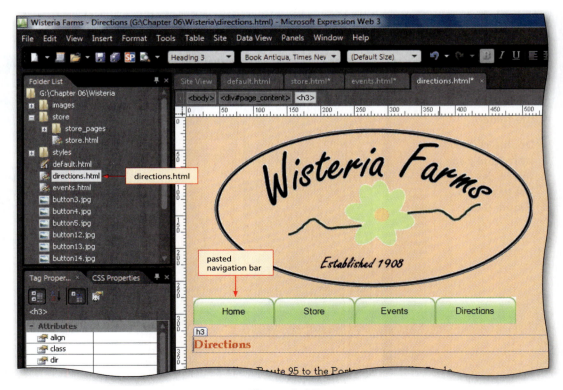

Figure 6–27

To Organize the Button Images into Folders

Every interactive button on every page has three image files associated with it. This creates a lot of image files in the site folder (which contains all of the button images for the default, events, and directions pages) and the store page's subfolder (which only contains the images for the store page). When you move the buttons to a folder, Expression Web updates the links. The following steps create folders for the button images, and move the button images into the folders.

- Click the Site View tab to display the contents of the site folder (Figure 6–28).

Figure 6–28

- Point to New on the File menu, then click Folder to insert a new folder (Figure 6–29).

Figure 6–29

3

- Type navigation_ buttons, then press ENTER to name the folder. If the Confirm Rename dialog box appears, click Yes (Figure 6–30).

Figure 6–30

4

- Click the JPEG image file above the navigation_buttons folder, press and hold SHIFT, scroll up using the vertical scroll box, then click the top JPEG image file in the site folder to select all of the navigation button image files.

- Scroll back down so the navigation_buttons folder is in view, then drag the selected files to the navigation_buttons folder to move them (Figure 6–31).

Figure 6–31

5

- Double-click the store folder to open it.

- Point to New on the File menu, then click Folder to insert a new folder.

- Type navigation_buttons, then press ENTER to name the folder. Click Yes if the Confirm Rename dialog box appears (Figure 6–32).

Figure 6–32

 6

- Click the JPEG image file above the store page, press and hold SHIFT, then click the top JPEG image file in the store folder to select all of the navigation button image files.

- Drag the selected files to the navigation_buttons folder to move them (Figure 6–33).

Figure 6–33

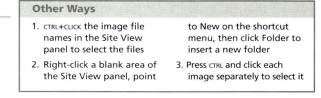

Other Ways

1. CTRL+CLICK the image file names in the Site View panel to select the files

2. Right-click a blank area of the Site View panel, point

to New on the shortcut menu, then click Folder to insert a new folder

3. Press CTRL and click each image separately to select it

Defining Behaviors

Behaviors are actions triggered by events. They include changes in page appearance, such as the replacement of one image with another or a change in font size. Behaviors can also include functions such as an alert message displaying or a new browser window opening. They occur as a result of activity by the site visitor or are automated occurrences when the page loads. For example, moving a pointer over a specific area of the page (a visitor-triggered event) can result in a behavior such as a change in button appearance. Behaviors are generally used to increase the interactivity and utility of a given page without requiring much additional code.

Some behaviors are one-step occurrences, such as when a site checks the visitor's computer for a browser version or plug-in, or displays text in the status bar. Others, such as swapping one image for another upon mousing over or clicking an image, or changing the properties of an element, can require an additional step to restore an element to its original state using the Restore command. The Restore command is available after the original behavior is established.

Table 6–1 lists behaviors that you can add using Expression Web.

Table 6–1: Interactive Behaviors in Expression Web	
Behavior	**Used To**
Call Script	Insert JavaScript without switching to Code View. Used to add JavaScript code to create a behavior that does not exist in Expression Web. You must know JavaScript to use this behavior.
Change Property/Restore	Change the font, position, borders and shading, and visibility of an element. Change Property/Restore returns the element to its original state.
Check Browser	Determine whether the visitor's browser is the correct type and version necessary to view all of the site features.
Check Plug-in	Determine whether the visitor's browser has a browser plug-in, such as a video player, necessary to view a site feature.
Go To URL	Open a Web page in a browser upon an event, such as mousing over or double-clicking.
Jump Menu/Go	Create a list box with a menu that contains hyperlinks.
Open Browser Window	Open a new browser window as a pop-up window, such as to display an advertisement.
Play Sound	Play sound files, such as MP3 files.
Popup Message	Open an alert window that the user has to close.
Preload Images	Load the images on a Web page before the rest of the page's content. This is a default option when creating interactive buttons, as they require three image files per button.
Set Text	Add a message to a frame or layer, or more commonly, to the status bar.
Swap Image/Restore	Change from one image to another upon clicking or hovering. Swap Image/Restore returns the image to its original state.

Plan Ahead

Identify behaviors that will improve site visitors' experiences.
The goal of a behavior is to enhance visitors' experiences with your site by providing them with additional information. Add behaviors that allow for additional navigation or that provide an attractive or interesting way to interact with your site, but avoid including behaviors that visitors might find annoying, such as background sound and pop-up messages. Behaviors add to the file size of your page. Incorporate testing of behaviors into your page creation process and consider file size implications of interactive behaviors to ensure visitors have good experiences and do not encounter any problems on your site.

Creating a Jump Menu

A jump menu is a secondary navigation device. Unlike button-based navigation bars, a jump menu most likely only appears in one location on the site.

When creating a jump menu, you must create text for each link. Like adding text for an interactive button, the text for each menu item should describe the page to which it links in as few words as possible. You can reorder the items in the list by moving them up and down in the order to show the most commonly used ones at the top, or group like items together. Each menu item is assigned a target page to which the browser will navigate when the menu item is clicked.

To Add a Jump Menu Behavior

The following steps add a jump menu to the store departments on the home page.

1

- Click the default.html tab to display the default.html page.

- Scroll down, if necessary, and click at the end of the third paragraph of text, then press ENTER to insert a new paragraph.

- Type Click a menu item below to view more information about one of our store departments., then press ENTER (Figure 6–34).

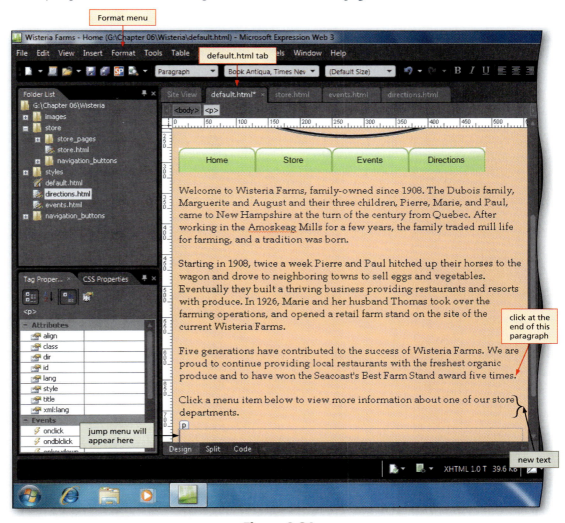

Figure 6–34

2

• Click Behaviors on the Format menu to open the Behaviors panel (Figure 6–35).

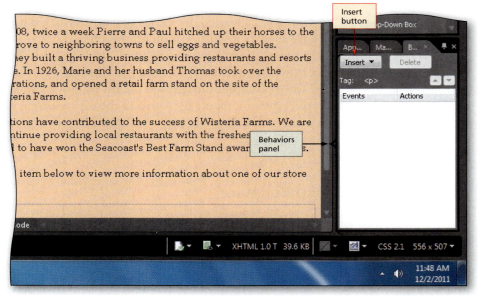

Figure 6–35

3

• Click the Insert button on the Behaviors panel to display the Insert menu, then point to Jump Menu (Figure 6–36).

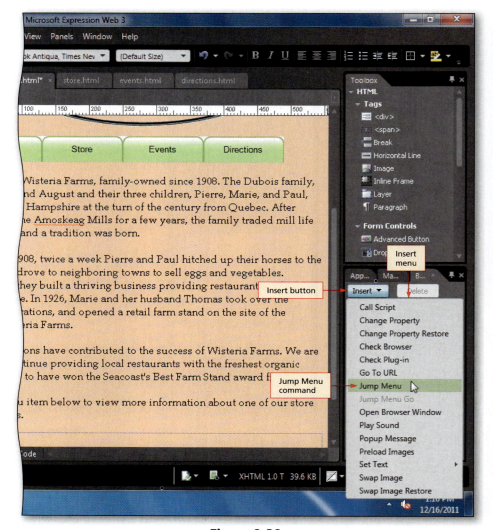

Figure 6–36

4
- Click Jump Menu on the menu to open the Jump Menu dialog box (Figure 6–37).

Figure 6–37

5
- Click the Add button to open the Add Choice dialog box (Figure 6–38).

Figure 6–38

6
- Type Dairy in the Choice text box, then click the Browse button to open the Edit Hyperlink dialog box.

- Double-click the store folder to open it, if necessary.

- Double-click the store_pages folder to open it, then click dairy to select it as the link target (Figure 6–39).

Figure 6–39

- Click the OK button to close the Edit Hyperlink dialog box.

- Click the OK button to close the Add Choice dialog box (Figure 6–40).

Figure 6–40

- Repeat Steps 5 through 7 to insert choices for Dry Goods, Fruit, Greenhouse, and Vegetables, and link them to the appropriate HTML files (Figure 6–41).

Figure 6–41

- Click Vegetables to select it, then click the Move Up button to move it up in the list so that it is below the Fruit menu item (Figure 6–42).

Figure 6–42

- Click the OK button to close the Jump Menu dialog box and insert the jump menu (Figure 6–43).

- Press CTRL+S to save the page.

Figure 6–43

- Press F12 to open the page in a browser window. Allow blocked content, if necessary.

- Scroll down, if necessary, then click the jump menu box arrow to display the menu (Figure 6–44).

Figure 6–44

12

- Click Vegetables from the jump menu to view the vegetables.html page (Figure 6–45).

- Click the Back button to return to the default.html page.

- Test the other links in the jump menu box, then click the Close button to close the browser and return to Expression Web.

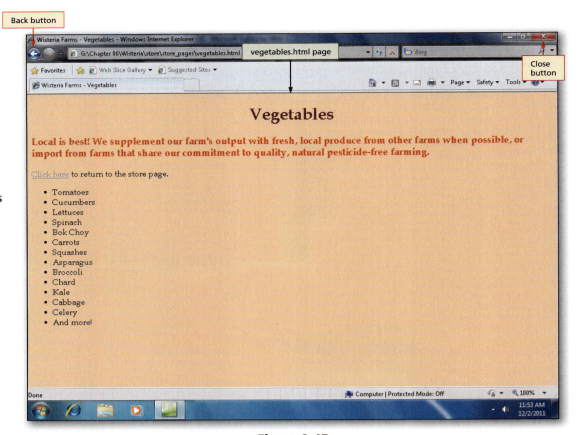

Figure 6–45

Creating a Status Bar Behavior

Adding text that appears in the status bar lets you deliver a message to your site visitors. A **status bar behavior** can be assigned to a particular element on the page or to the page itself. If you want to have the message associated with the page itself, you need to click a blank area of the page before creating the behavior. When a status bar behavior is associated with the page (as opposed to an element on the page), by default it appears when the page loads. Do not include status bar behaviors for information that is important for all site visitors, such as your store hours or announcing a sale, as not all browsers will display a status bar by default, so your message might not reach all visitors.

To Add a Status Bar Behavior

The following steps add a message on the status bar for the home page, welcoming users to the site.

- Scroll to the bottom of the default.html page if necessary, click below the e-mail address, and make sure only the body tag appears on the Quick Tag Selector.

- Click the Insert button on the Behaviors panel to display the Insert menu, point to Set Text, then click Set Text of Status Bar to open the Set Text of Status Bar dialog box.

- Type Welcome to Wisteria Farms in the Message text box (Figure 6–46).

Figure 6–46

2

- Click the OK button to close the Set Text of Status Bar dialog box (Figure 6–47).

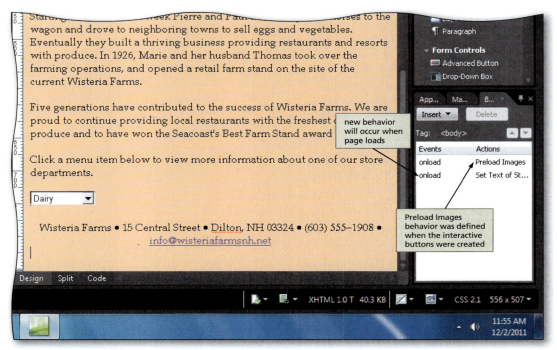

Figure 6–47

3

- Press CTRL+S to save the default. html page, then press F12 to open the page in a browser window. Allow blocked content, if necessary (Figure 6–48).

- View the message in the status bar.

- Click the Close button on the title bar to close the browser window and return to Expression Web.

Q&A Why can I not see the status bar on my browser window?

Press the ALT key to show the Internet Explorer menu, click View on the menu bar, point to Toolbars, then click Status Bar to display the status bar, if necessary.

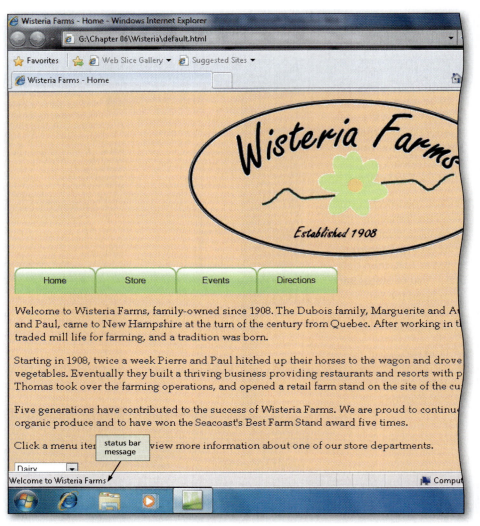

Figure 6–48

Creating a Swap Image Behavior

BTW **Web Accessibility** See Appendix B for more information about accessibility and assistive technology.

A **swap image** behavior is used to display two images — one that displays by default, and one that replaces the default image upon an event such as hovering the mouse or clicking. Swap images can be used to display an answer to a question, show a transformation (before and after), or to add visual interest to your site. When adding a swap image, it is important to make sure that the images are of the same dimensional size (or close to it) to prevent issues with the page layout when the images are swapped.

You may want to include a restore behavior that displays the original image upon another event, such as moving the mouse away (onmouseout) or clicking the image again (onclick). To add a swap image restore behavior, you must have first created a swap image. In the Swap Image Restore dialog box, the only option is to click OK; Expression Web will use the information about the original image from the swap image behavior to create the restore behavior.

To Add a Swap Image Behavior

The following steps insert an image on the store page and add a swap image behavior that displays a coupon when the mouse pointer is hovering over the image (called mouseover; this is the default event for the swap image behavior).

- Click the store.html tab to display the store.html page.

- Click at the end of the paragraph of text that starts, We are pleased, then press ENTER to insert a new paragraph (Figure 6–49).

Figure 6–49

- Point to Picture on the Insert menu, then click From File to open the Picture dialog box.

- Navigate to the location in which you store your data files and double-click the wisteria_images folder (Figure 6–50).

Figure 6–50

• Click the swap_image1 file to
  select it, then click the Insert
  button to open the Accessibility
  Properties dialog box.

• **Type** Click here to view this
  week's coupon! in the Alternate
  text text box (Figure 6–51).

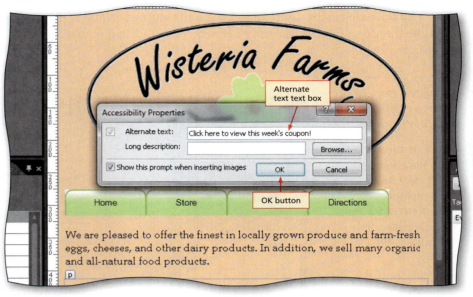

Figure 6–51

4

• Click the OK
  button to close
  the Accessibility
  Properties dialog
  box and insert
  the image.

• Click the image to
  select it, then click
  the Center button
  on the Common
  toolbar to center the
  image on the page
  (Figure 6–52).

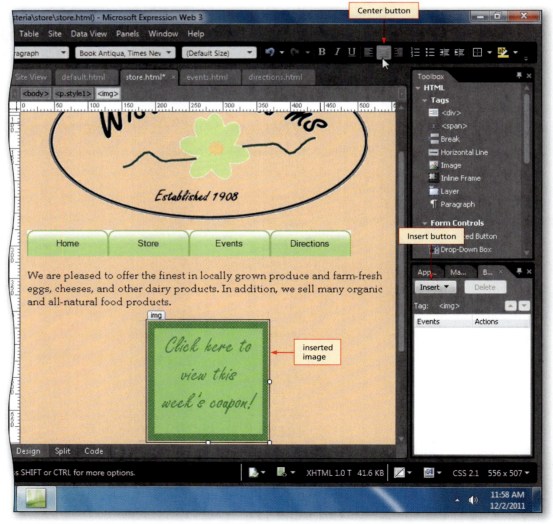

Figure 6–52

5

- Click the Insert button on the Behaviors panel to display the Insert menu, then click Swap Image to open the Swap Images dialog box (Figure 6–53).

Q&A Why is my list of images in the Swap Images dialog box different?

Expression Web suggests images based on recently created or used images from your work session. Clicking the Browse button allows you access to all images in your site or on a computer, drive, or network folder.

Figure 6–53

6

- Click the Browse button to open the Browse dialog box.

- Navigate to the location in which you store your data files, then double-click the wisteria_images folder, if necessary.

- Click the swap_image2 file to select it, then click the OK button to close the Browse dialog box.

- Click the OK button to close the Swap Images dialog box.

- Save the page and embedded files.

- Press F12 to open the page in a browser window. Allow blocked content, if necessary (Figure 6–54).

Figure 6–54

- Position the mouse pointer over the image to swap it (Figure 6–55).

- Click the Expression Web program button on the Windows 7 taskbar to return to Expression Web and leave the browser window open.

Q&A

Why does the image text say to click it, but the image changes when I position the mouse over it?

The default event for a swap image is mouseover. In the next set of steps, you will change the event to onclick to match the text on the image.

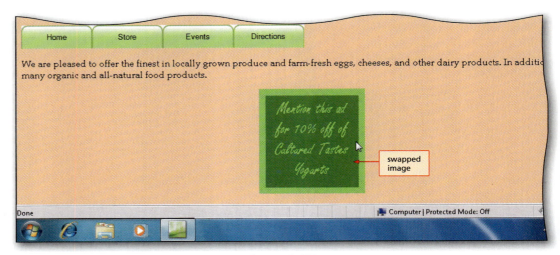

Figure 6–55

To Modify a Swap Image Behavior

The previous set of steps set the image to swap when the user mouses over the image; however, the text on the image specifies that the user should click to see the coupon. The following steps add a restore behavior and change the swap image event so that the user must click the original image to see the second image. The restore behavior event is onmouseout, which means that the original image will reappear when the visitor removes the pointer from the image.

- Click the swap_image1.gif file (the "Click here" image you just added) to select it, if necessary.

- Click the Insert button on the Behaviors panel to display the Insert menu, then click Swap Image Restore to open the Swap Image Restore dialog box (Figure 6–56).

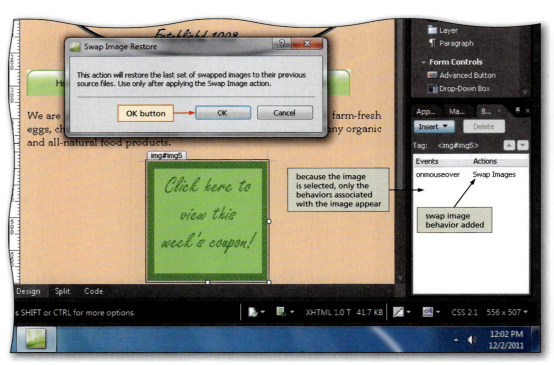

Figure 6–56

2

• Click the OK button to close the Swap Image Restore dialog box and add the swap image restore behavior to the image (Figure 6–57).

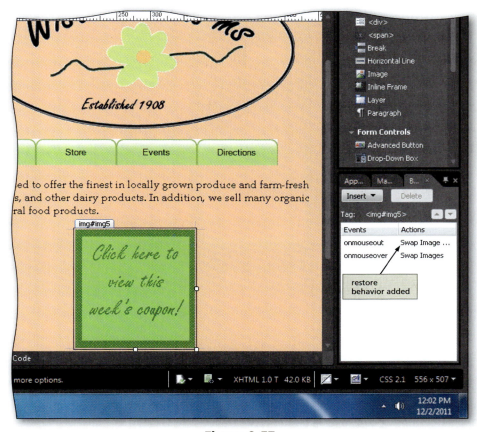

Figure 6–57

3

• Position the mouse pointer over the onmouseover event to display the box arrow, then click the onmouseover event box arrow to open the menu (Figure 6–58).

Figure 6–58

- Click onclick on the menu to make the swap image behavior occur when the user clicks the image (Figure 6–59).

Figure 6–59

- Press CTRL+S to save the store.html page.

- Click the browser program button on the Windows 7 task-bar to return to the browser.

- Press F5 to refresh the page in a browser window.

- Click the image to initiate the swap image behavior (Figure 6–60).

- Click the Close button on the title bar to close the browser window.

 Experiment

- Select other events for the swap image and restore behaviors, and test them in a browser window.

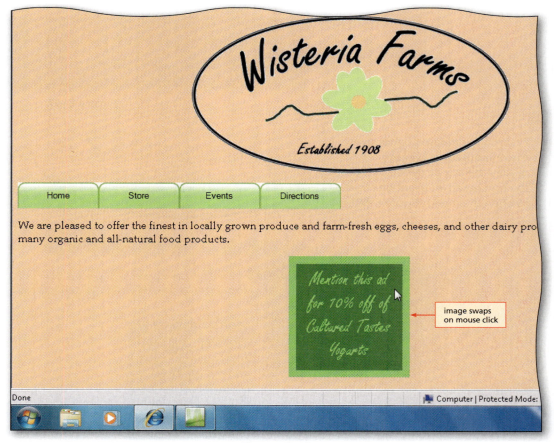

Figure 6–60

Other Ways

1. Double-click a behavior in the Behaviors panel to open the behavior's dialog box

> **Assess how you will provide access to site pages that do not have links in the primary navigation bar.**
> In addition to jump menus, such as the one you previously added in this chapter, image maps are another way to provide links to multiple, related pages. Choose a jump menu to create a list, and an image map to add interactivity and links to a graphical representation of the category of linked pages.

Plan Ahead

Creating Image Maps

Image maps are graphics that are divided into sections. Each section is its own clickable area called a hotspot. Image maps are often used for geographical maps. On a map of Canada, for example, each province can be its own hotspot that, when clicked, displays information such as population, capital, government, or other relevant data for that province. Use image maps when the information you are conveying lends itself to a graphic representation; you would not use an image map to present stock reports, for example.

BTW

Changing Dimensions of a Graphic
You can change aspects of a graphic, such as physical dimensions, using a graphic design program or by changing the formatting of an image in Expression Web.

When creating an image map, you first insert the large image, then use a shape tool to define each area and assign it a link. Not every space on the image needs to be a hotspot; visitors to your site will be able to tell what is clickable by positioning the mouse pointer over the image and waiting until the hand pointer changes to indicate a hyperlink.

A hotspot, like any linked text or element, displays the address of its target page in the status bar when you position the pointer over it. Checking the status bar is another way to test links to be sure of the accuracy of the content of the linked page and to confirm that the linked page contains a method for returning to the current page.

To Add an Image Map

The following steps insert the image of the store layout and create horizontal hotspots linking each store department to a page listing its featured products. You will not create a hotspot for the blank areas or the checkout area, as no additional information is required in those areas. You will close panels so that you can view more of the editing window. You will test the links by viewing the text in the status bar, as you have already viewed these pages when testing the jump menu, so you can be sure of their content and that they contain a navigation element to return to the page.

- Click at the end of the paragraph of text that starts, Click an area, then press ENTER to insert a new paragraph (Figure 6–61).

Figure 6–61

2

• Point to Picture on the Insert menu, then click From File to open the Picture dialog box.

• Navigate to the location in which you save your data files and double-click the wisteria_images folder, if necessary.

• Click the site_map file to select it, then click the Insert button to open the Accessibility Properties dialog box.

• Type `Map displays dairy, dry goods, fruit, vegetables, and greenhouse departments` in the Alternate text text box (Figure 6–62).

Figure 6–62

3

• Click the OK button to close the Accessibility Properties dialog box and insert the image.

• Click the Close button on the Toolbox to close it.

• Click the Close all button on the Behaviors panel to close it and the two Styles panels at once (Figure 6–63).

Figure 6–63

4

- Right-click the Common toolbar to display the Toolbar shortcut menu, then click Pictures to open the Pictures toolbar (Figure 6–64).

Figure 6–64

5

- Scroll to the left, if necessary, to view the left edge of the image, then click the image to select it.

- Click the Rectangular Hotspot button on the Pictures toolbar to change the pointer to a pencil (Figure 6–65).

Figure 6–65

• Drag the pencil to select the green Dairy rectangle and open the Insert Hyperlink dialog box (Figure 6–66).

• Click the Existing File or Web Page button, if necessary, click dairy in the store_pages folder to select it as the link target, then click the OK button to close the Insert Hyperlink dialog box.

Figure 6–66

• Repeat Steps 5 and 6 to create hotspots for the Cereals, grains, and dry goods, Fruits, Vegetables, and Greenhouse sections of the site map with the appropriate links.

• Press CTRL+S to save the store.html page, then click OK to save the embedded image.

• Press F12 to open the page in a browser window, then scroll down to view the image map, if necessary. Allow blocked content, if necessary (Figure 6–67).

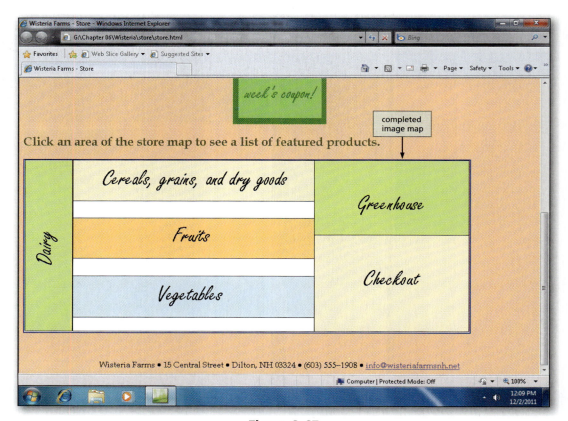

Figure 6–67

8

• Position the pointer over the image map and verify that the hotspots are correct by viewing the path that shows in the status bar (Figure 6–68).

• Click the Close button on the browser title bar to close the browser window.

Click an area of the store map to see a list of featured products.

Cereals, grains, and dry goods

Dairy

Fruits

hand pointer indicates hyperlink

Vegetables

Greenhouse

Checkout

Wisteria Farms • 15 Central Street • Dilton, NH 03324 • (603) 555–1908 • info@wisteriafarmsnh.net

Status bar shows path to linked file

file:///G:/Chapter%2006/Wisteria/store/store_pages/dairy.html

Figure 6–68

To Close a Site and Quit Expression Web

1 On the Site menu, click Close.

2 On the File menu, click Exit.

Chapter Summary

In this chapter, you have learned to create, edit, and test interactive buttons to create a navigation bar that you could paste onto every page. You organized your site by creating folders and moving the button images into them. You learned about behaviors, and created behaviors for a jump menu, a status bar message, and a swap image. You modified the swap image behavior, and also created an image map.

The items listed below include all the new Expression Web skills you have learned in this chapter.

1. Open a Web Site and Web Page (EW 371)
2. Create an Interactive Button (EW 373)
3. Duplicate an Interactive Button (EW 379)
4. Edit an Interactive Button (EW 380)
5. Test Interactive Buttons (EW 382)
6. Copy and Paste the Navigation Bar (EW 385)
7. Organize the Button Images into Folders (EW 387)
8. Add a Jump Menu Behavior (EW 391)
9. Add a Status Bar Behavior (EW 397)
10. Add a Swap Image Behavior (EW 399)
11. Modify a Swap Image Behavior (EW 402)
12. Add an Image Map (EW 405)

For current SAM information, including versions and content details, visit SAM Central (http://samcentral.course.com). If you have a SAM user profile, you may have access to hands-on instruction, practice, and assessment of the skills covered in this chapter. Since various versions of SAM are supported throughout the life of this text, check with your instructor for the correct instructions and URL/Web site for accessing assignments.

Learn It Online

Test your knowledge of chapter content and key terms.

Instructions: To complete the Learn It Online exercises, start your browser, click the Address bar, and then enter the Web address scsite.com/ew3/learn. When the Expression Web Learn It Online page is displayed, click the link for the exercise you want to complete and then read the instructions.

Chapter Reinforcement TF, MC, and SA
A series of true/false, multiple choice, and short answer questions that test your knowledge of the chapter content.

Flash Cards
An interactive learning environment where you identify chapter key terms associated with displayed definitions.

Practice Test
A series of multiple choice questions that test your knowledge of chapter content and key terms.

Who Wants To Be a Computer Genius?
An interactive game that challenges your knowledge of chapter content in the style of a television quiz show.

Wheel of Terms
An interactive game that challenges your knowledge of chapter key terms in the style of the television show *Wheel of Fortune*.

Crossword Puzzle Challenge
A crossword puzzle that challenges your knowledge of key terms presented in the chapter.

Apply Your Knowledge

Reinforce the skills and apply the concepts you learned in this chapter.

Creating an Interactive Navigation Bar and Adding a Behavior
Instructions: Start Expression Web. Create a new one-page Web site, create and attach a new style sheet, then copy the default page to create the other site pages as shown in Figure 6–69. You will create a navigation bar using interactive buttons. You will also create a swap image behavior. You will leave most of the site content blank at this point, but you will add folders and move the pages and interactive buttons into them.

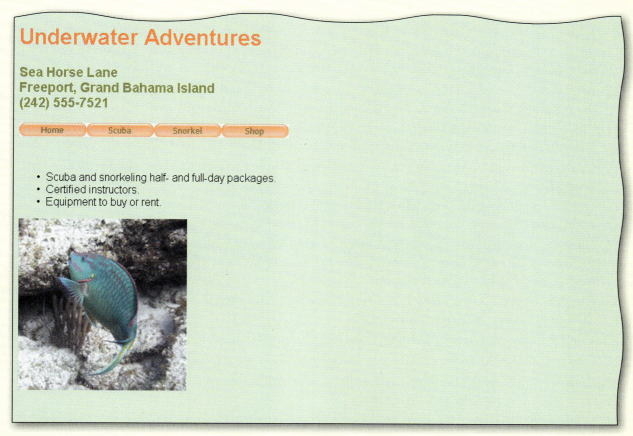

Figure 6–69

Perform the following tasks:

1. Click New Site on the Site menu, then click One Page Site.

2. Click the Browse button, navigate to the drive and folder where you save your data files, open the folder, type `Apply 6-1 Underwater` at the end of the file path in the Location text box, then click the OK button.

3. Point to New on the File menu, then click Page. Click Style Sheets, click the Capsules style sheet type, then click the OK button.

4. Save the new style sheet as `underwater_styles.css`.

5. Open the default.html page, then attach the underwater_styles.css style sheet.

6. Select the Heading 1 <h1> style, then type `Underwater Adventures` as the page heading.

7. Select the Heading 3 <h3> style, then type the following, pressing SHIFT+ENTER at the end of each line:

   `Sea Horse Lane`

   `Freeport, Grand Bahama Island`

   `(242) 555-7521`

8. Press ENTER after the last line to create a new paragraph tag, then save the page.

9. Click the default.html file name in the Folder List to select it, then press CTRL+C to copy the file to the Clipboard.

10. Press CTRL+V to paste a copy of the default.html page in the site folder. Right-click the file name of the copied page, click Rename, type `scuba.html`, then press ENTER.

Continued >

Apply Your Knowledge *continued*

11. Press CTRL+V to paste another copy of the default.html page in the site folder. Click the file name of the copied page to select it, click it again, type snorkel.html, then press ENTER.

12. Press CTRL+V to paste a third copy of the default.html page in the site folder. Click the file name of the copied page to select it, click it again, type shop.html, then press ENTER.

13. Right-click in the Folder List, point to New, click Folder, type scuba as the folder name, then press ENTER. Drag the scuba.html page into the scuba folder.

14. Create folders named snorkel and shop, then drag the snorkel.html and shop.html files into their folders.

15. On the default.html page, click in the paragraph tag below the contact information, then click Interactive Button on the Insert menu to open the Interactive Buttons dialog box.

16. Click the Embossed Capsule 3 option from the Buttons list, type Home in the Text box, then click the Browse button to open the Edit Hyperlink dialog box. Click default, then click the OK button to close the Edit Hyperlink dialog box.

17. Click the Font tab. Click the Original Font Color box arrow, then click Olive. Click the OK button to close the Interactive Buttons dialog box.

18. Click the Home interactive button to select it, then press CTRL+C to copy it to the Clipboard.

19. Click to the right of the button, then press CTRL+V three times to paste three copies of the button.

20. Right-click the second button from the left, then click Button Properties on the shortcut menu to open the Interactive Buttons dialog box.

21. Change the text of the button to Scuba, then change the hyperlink to the scuba page and close all dialog boxes. (*Hint:* The scuba page is in the scuba folder.)

22. Rename the third and fourth buttons Snorkel and Shop, and link the buttons to the appropriate pages.

23. Save the page and all of the image files.

24. In the Folder List, create a new folder called navigation_images, then drag all of the button images into the folder.

25. Click below the navigation bar on the default.html page, press ENTER, click the Bullets button on the Common toolbar, then type:
    - Scuba and snorkeling half- and full-day packages.
    - Certified instructors.
    - Equipment to buy or rent.

26. Press ENTER twice after the last list item, then show the Pictures toolbar if necessary, click the Insert Picture from File button on the Pictures toolbar to open the Picture dialog box. Navigate to the underwater_images folder, select the parrot_fish image, then click the Insert button. Type Rainbow Parrot Fish and Trumpet Fish in the Accessibility Properties dialog box, then click the OK button.

27. Click the image to select it, then click Behaviors on the Panels menu to open the Behaviors panel if necessary.

28. Click the Insert button on the Behaviors panel, then click Swap Image from the menu to open the Swap Images dialog box.

29. Click the Browse button, navigate to the underwater_images folder, click the trumpet_fish image, click OK, click the 'Restore on mouseout event' check box, then click the OK button.

30. Save the file and embedded files, then preview the site in a browser and test the swap images behavior and the buttons.

31. Change the site properties, as specified by your instructor, then save and close the site.

32. Submit the revised site in the format specified by your instructor.

Extend Your Knowledge

Extend the skills you learned in this chapter and experiment with new skills. You may need to use Help to complete the assignment.

Converting Text to a Table

Instructions: Start Expression Web. Open the site, Extend 6-1 Preschool, from the Data Files for Students. See the inside back cover of this book for instructions for downloading the Data Files for Students, or see your instructor for information about accessing the required files.

You will create a navigation bar using a column of interactive buttons to make the default.html page match the one shown in Figure 6–70.

Figure 6–70

Perform the following tasks:

1. Open the default.html page, position the insertion point at the end of the paragraph in the left column, press ENTER, then double-click Paragraph in the Toolbox to insert a new paragraph tag.

2. Click Interactive Button on the Insert menu to open the Interactive Buttons dialog box.

3. Click the Braided Column 3 option in the Buttons list, type home in the Text text box, then click the Browse button to open the Edit Hyperlink dialog box.

4. Click the default file name, then click the OK button to close the Edit Hyperlink dialog box.

5. Click the Font tab, then type Poornut in the Font box to select the font. If the font doesn't appear in the list, then choose another font (such as Matura MT Script Capitals) that resembles the font on the navigation bar in Figure 6–70. Click Bold in the Font Style box, then click 20 in the Size box. Click the Hovered Font Color box arrow, then click Navy from the color palette.

6. Click the Image tab, then type 200 in the Width box. Click the OK button to close the Interactive Buttons dialog box.

7. Click the Home interactive button to select it, then press CTRL+C to copy it to the Clipboard.

8. Press RIGHT ARROW, then press CTRL+V twice to paste two copies of the button.

Continued >

Extend Your Knowledge *continued*

9. Right-click the second button from the top, then click Button Properties on the shortcut menu to open the Interactive Buttons dialog box.

10. Change the text of the button to `registration`, then change the hyperlink to the registration page and close all dialog boxes. If the text doesn't fit on the button, then choose a smaller font size.

11. Rename the third button as `classes` and link the button to the appropriate page.

12. Save the page and all of the image files.

13. In the Folder List, create a new folder called `navigation_images`, then drag all of the button images into the folder.

14. Select the paragraph tag that contains the navigation bar, then press CTRL+C to copy it to the Clipboard.

15. Open the registration.html page, click at the end of the paragraph in the left column, then press ENTER. Press CTRL+V to paste the navigation bar onto the registration.html page.

16. Open the classes.html page, click at the end of the paragraph in the left column, then press ENTER. Press CTRL+V to paste the navigation bar onto the classes.html page.

17. Save all of the pages and image files.

18. In the Folder List, drag all of the button images into the navigation_images folder.

19. Click Behaviors on the Panels menu to open the Behaviors panel if necessary.

20. Click the registration.html tab. Select the word, Applications, in the paragraph under the Application Submission heading.

21. Click the Insert button on the Behaviors panel, then click Popup Message from the menu to open the Popup Message dialog box.

22. Type `Applications will be available starting September 15th.`, then click the OK button to close the dialog box.

23. Save the registration.html page, then preview it in a browser window.

24. Test the navigation bar and drag the pointer over "Applications" to see the pop-up message. Click the OK button to close the pop-up message.

25. Change the site properties, as specified by your instructor, then save and close the site. Using Windows Explorer, change the site folder name to `Extend 6-1 Preschool Site`. Submit the revised site in the format specified by your instructor.

Make It Right

Analyze a site and correct all errors and/or improve the design.

Replacing a Text-Based Navigation Bar with Interactive Buttons

Instructions: Start Expression Web. Open the Web site, Make It Right 6-1 Drama, from the Data Files for Students. See the inside back cover of this book for instructions for downloading the Data Files for Students, or see your instructor for information about accessing the required files.

Create a new navigation bar on the default.html page by replacing the text-based hyperlinks with interactive buttons. Copy and paste the navigation bar to the main site pages, and create folders to store the button images to create the home page shown in Figure 6–71.

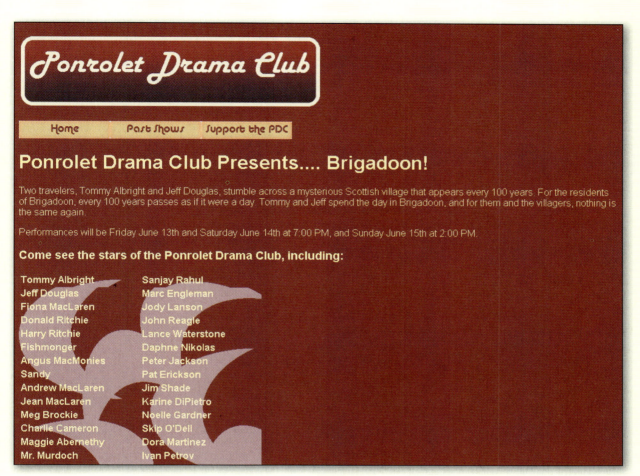

Figure 6–71

In the default.html page delete the content, in the h3 tags, which contains the hyperlinks. Open the Interactive Buttons dialog box. Create a button using the Soft Rectangle 3 button, with Home as the text, that links to the default.html page, with Alba as the font (or a similar font such as Viner Hand ITC), 14-point font size, Maroon as the original font color, and 150 pixels wide. Create two copies of the button in the navigation bar. Edit the second button so that its label is Past Shows and that it links to the past_shows.html page. (*Hint:* the past_shows.html page is in the past_shows folder.) Edit the third button so that its label is Support the PDC and that it links to the support.html page. (*Hint:* the support.html page is in the support folder.) Copy the <h3> tag, with the navigation bar containing the interactive buttons, and paste it over the text-based navigation bars on the support.html and past_shows.html pages. Create folders for the navigation images in the main site folder, the support folder, and the past_shows folder, and move the button image files into them. Change the site properties, as specified by your instructor. Save and close the site. In Windows Explorer change the site folder name to Make It Right 6-1 Drama Site. Submit the revised site in the format specified by your instructor.

In the Lab

Design and/or format a Web site using the guidelines, concepts, and skills presented in this chapter. Labs are listed in order of increasing difficulty.

Lab 1: Adding Interactive Buttons

Problem: Your client, the manager of a senior center, has asked you to create a new multi-page Web site and add an interactive navigation bar. You will create a new one-page site, add a preformatted style sheet, then copy the page twice. You will add interactive buttons to create a navigation bar that includes links to the three site pages, copy it to each page, then create a folder for the buttons to create the page shown in Figure 6–72.

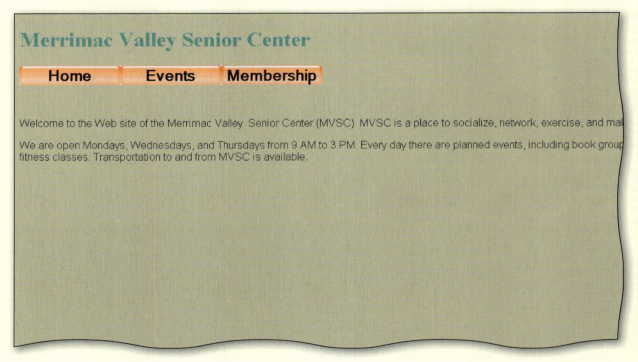

Figure 6–72

Instructions:

1. Start Expression Web.

2. Create a one-page Web site called `Lab 6-1 Senior Site`, then open the default.html page.

3. Create a new style sheet based on the Bars style sheet, save it as `senior_styles.css`, then attach it to the default.html page.

4. Select the Heading 1 <h1> style, then type `Merrimac Valley Senior Center`. Save the page.

5. In the Folder List, click the default.html page, press CTRL+C, then press CTRL+V twice.

6. Rename the two copies of the default.html page so that you have two new pages: events.html and membership.html.

7. Create a paragraph tag on the default.html page under the heading. Type `Welcome to the Web site of the Merrimac Valley Senior Center (MVSC). MVSC is a place to socialize, network, exercise, and make new friends.` Press ENTER, then type `We are open Mondays, Wednesdays, and Thursdays from 9 AM to 3 PM. Every day there are planned events, including book groups, games, and fitness classes. Transportation to and from MVSC is available.`

8. Save the default.html page.

9. Add a new paragraph tag to the default.html page, then click Interactive Button on the Insert menu.

10. Create a button using the Embossed Rectangle 3 button with the text Home that links to the default page. Make the button font bold, use the Tahoma font, set the font size as 14-point, and make the button 150 pixels wide.

11. Copy the button and paste it twice. Edit the two pasted buttons to refer and link to the two other site pages (events and membership), then select the paragraph containing the buttons and copy it to the Clipboard.

12. Copy the navigation bar, then open the events.html and membership.html pages and paste the navigation bar onto each page. Attach the senior_styles.css style sheet to both pages.

13. Save all pages at once and click OK three times to save the embedded images.

14. Create a new folder in the Folder List called navigation_images. Using the Site View pane, move all button images into the folder.

15. Preview the default.html page in a browser.

16. Close the site, then submit the site in the format specified by your instructor.

In the Lab

Lab 2: Adding a Jump Menu

Problem: You want to create a menu of sample worksheets for your math tutoring business. You will add a jump menu and reorder the menu items to create the default.html page, as shown in Figure 6–73.

Figure 6–73

Continued >

In the Lab *continued*

Instructions: Start Expression Web. Open the Web site, Lab 6-2 Tutor Site, from the Data Files for Students. See the inside back cover of this book for instructions for downloading the Data Files for Students, or see your instructor for information about accessing the required files.

Perform the following tasks:

1. Open the default.html page.
2. Create a new paragraph tag above the tag that starts, Contact me. Type `Here are some sample worksheets:`, then press ENTER.
3. Open the Behaviors panel, if necessary, then open the Jump Menu dialog box.
4. Use the table below to create the menu items. The pages shown in the Value column are in the sample_worksheets folder within the main site folder.

Choice	Value
Algebra	algebra_sample.html
AP preparation	AP_preparation_sample.html
Calculus	calculus_sample.html
Geometry	geometry_sample.html
Pre-algebra	prealgebra_sample.html
Trigonometry	trigonometry_sample.html

5. Use the Move Up and Move Down buttons to change the order to: Pre-algebra, Algebra, Geometry, Trigonometry, Calculus, AP preparation.
6. Save the page, preview the site, and test the jump menu.
7. Change the site properties, as specified by your instructor, then save and close the site.
8. In Windows Explorer, rename the site folder as `Lab 6-2 Tutor Site`, then submit the site in the format specified by your instructor.

In the Lab

Lab 3: Creating an Image Map

Problem: You are on your school's fundraising committee and need to show supporters the funds raised this school year. You create a one-page Web site folder and a new style sheet using a preformatted style sheet, and add content and pages. You then insert an image and create an image map to link to the pages to create the page shown in Figure 6–74.

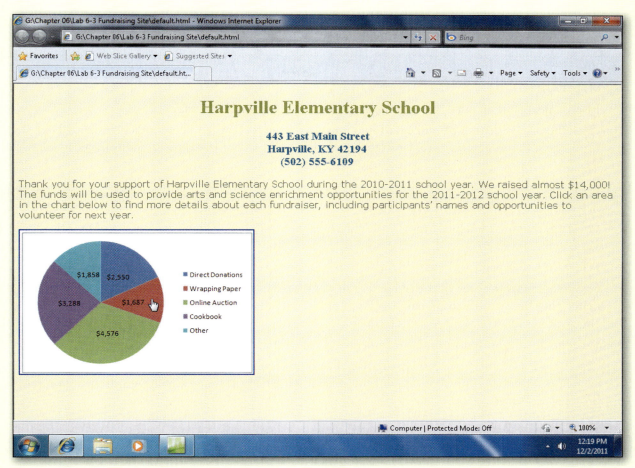

Figure 6–74

Instructions:

1. Start Expression Web.

2. Create a one-page Web site called `Lab 6-3 Fundraising Site`, then open the default.
   html page.

3. Create a new style sheet based on the Arcs style sheet, save it as `fundraising_styles.css`,
   then attach it to the default.html page.

4. Select the Heading 1 <h1> style, type `Harpville Elementary School`, then press ENTER.

5. Select the Heading 3 <h3> style, then type the following, pressing SHIFT+ENTER after each line:

   `443 East Main Street`

   `Harpville, KY 42194`

   `(502) 555-6109`

6. Center the address.

7. Click below the address, then insert a new paragraph tag. Type the following:

   `Thank you for your support of Harpville Elementary School during the`
   `2010-2011 school year. We raised almost $14,000! The funds will be`
   `used to provide arts and science enrichment opportunities for the`
   `2011-2012 school year. Click an area in the chart below to find more`
   `details about each fundraiser, including participants' names and`
   `opportunities to volunteer for next year.`

Continued >

In the Lab *continued*

8. Save the default.html page. Copy and paste the default.html page in the Folder List five times. Rename the copied pages as `direct.html`, `wrapping.html`, `auction.html`, `cookbook.html`, and `other.html`.

9. Insert a new paragraph tag below the paragraph on the default.html page.

10. Click the Insert Picture from File button on the Common toolbar to open the Picture dialog box. From the fundraising_image folder in the Data Files for Students, insert the fundraising_chart file.

11. Type `Pie chart showing donation percentages for 2010-2011 school year` as the alternate text.

12. Select the image, display the Pictures toolbar if necessary, then click the Polygonal Hotspot button.

13. Create a triangular hotspot over the pie slice labeled $1858 by clicking each corner of the slice. When you have connected the first and third corners, the Insert Hyperlink dialog box will open.

14. Select the other page as the target for this hotspot, then close the dialog box.

15. Create hotspots for each of the remaining pie slices, using the legend to the right of the chart to match the slice with the page name. (*Hint:* For larger slices, click multiple times along the rounded edge of the slice to add more sides to the polygon and include more of the slice in the hotspot.)

16. Save the default.html page and the embedded image, then preview the site in a browser.

17. Test each of the hotspots, pressing the Back button to return to the default.html page. Confirm that each hotspot linked to the correct page by checking the text that appears in the address bar on the browser window.

18. Change the site properties, as specified by your instructor, then save and close the site.

19. Submit the site in the format specified by your instructor.

Cases and Places

Apply your creative thinking and problem-solving skills to design and implement a solution.

● EASIER   ●●MORE DIFFICULT

● 1: Creating a Navigation Bar Using Interactive Buttons

Create a new one-page Web site for a car wash. Create a new style sheet based on a preformatted style sheet and attach it to the page. Add a header and div into which you will add a navigation bar. Copy the page using the Folder List to create three other pages, and rename them. Create and test a navigation bar on the default.html page for the home page using the interactive button of your choice. Specify different font colors for original, hovered, and pressed states, then change the vertical or horizontal alignment. Specify the height and width of the button. Copy and paste the button, then modify the text and hyperlink to create navigation for all pages in your site. Save the page and embedded images, then create a folder to store the images. Test the navigation bar in the browser, then copy it to all site pages. Create folders as necessary to store the button images for the navigation bars. Save and close all pages, then quit Expression Web.

• 2: Creating and Modifying a Swap Image

Create a new one-page Web site for a florist. Insert an image using a file from this chapter, a previous chapter, or an image file of your own. Add a swap image behavior using another image of similar size. Accept the defaults in the Swap Images dialog box, then save the page and preview the image in the browser. Return to the default page, then modify the swap image behavior to add a restore behavior and change the event to onclick. Save the page, and refresh the browser window. Test the modified behavior. Return to the default page, then modify the restore image behavior to an event of your choice. Save the page, and refresh the browser window. Test the modified behavior, then save and close the site and the browser window.

•• 3: Adding Behaviors to a Dynamic Web Template

Create a new site for a computer repair shop using a dynamic Web template. Open the default page and preview it in a browser window to see the interactive buttons for the navigation bar. Open the master.dwt page, and set a status bar message. Add a jump menu to the default page that links to at least two site pages. Save all open pages, then refresh your browser to view the status bar message on the default page. Test the jump menu to go to another page and view the status bar message on that page. Close the browser window and the site.

•• 4: Creating a Travel Site

Make It Personal

You want to create a Web site that includes information about a travel spot you have visited or would like to visit. Create a site with at least three pages, using blank pages or a CSS layout and a preformatted style sheet. Enter information on the pages, and create a navigation bar for the site pages using interactive buttons. Create an image swap using two photos from your trip or that you find for public use on the Internet or from the projects in this book. Save the pages and style sheets, then close the site.

•• 5: Planning Navigation for Other Site Pages

Working Together

A department store wants to create a site that has four main site pages: a home page, directions, contact information, and products. Working as a team with several of your classmates, you plan and create the four site pages, and at least four other site pages for store departments. You will focus on creating the pages and navigation, not on creating elaborate content for each page. Each team member should contribute to planning the layout, formatting, and navigation for the site. As a group, decide on the departments for which you will include pages, and decide the best way to include that information on your site. Start by creating a site folder, and add a page using a CSS layout. Create and attach a style sheet using a preformatted style sheet. Copy that page to create additional site pages, and name each of them appropriately. Create a navigation bar using either a column or row format, and add it to each of the main site pages. Create an interactive behavior such as an image map or jump menu to link to the other site pages. Create folders as necessary to keep your site organized. Preview the site, and test the navigation bar and behavior. Save and close the pages and style sheet, then close the site.

E-Commerce Feature
E-Commerce

Objectives

You will have mastered the material in this special feature when you can:

- Define e-commerce and describe the role of e-commerce in today's business environment
- Identify e-commerce business models
- List elements necessary to add e-commerce capability to a Web site
- Describe how to add e-commerce capability to a Web site using third-party payment processing or an all-in-one e-commerce solution

The Role of E-Commerce in Today's Business Environment

Electronic commerce or **e-commerce** (sometimes called **e-business**) encompasses a wide variety of business transactions conducted electronically using the electronic funds transfer (EFT) and electronic data interchange (EDI) systems, corporate **intranets** (private internal networks) and **extranets** (private intranets connected using the Internet), the Internet, and the World Wide Web (Web). For example, e-commerce transactions can include the buying and selling of products and services, customer support activities after the sale, the exchange of data or funds between business partners, and so forth, using electronic communication networks.

E-commerce actually began many years ago with the advent of the EFT system, in which funds are transferred electronically between banks, and EDI systems, in which purchase orders, invoices, and other business documents are exchanged over private communications networks connecting business partners. Access to EFT and EDI systems was generally limited to the banking industry and to large corporations; smaller organizations shared business information and processed payments using traditional mail and telephone connections — methods that were slow, inconvenient, and sometimes costly.

The e-commerce revolution that touches many aspects of our daily lives started with the explosive growth of Internet and Web technologies in the 1990s and continues to be fueled by the expanding availability of high-speed, broadband Internet access to both businesses and consumers around the world. Using high-speed, broadband Internet access, today's individual or business consumer can go online and, in a matter of seconds, shop for and purchase virtually any type of product or service from a business located anywhere in the world.

While individual and business consumers benefit from increased access to products and services, businesses involved in e-commerce enjoy the opportunity to reach more customers, improve customer support, and reduce operating costs by conducting their business transactions online. To learn more about the volume of e-commerce transactions and the overall importance of e-commerce to the United States and the global economy, visit **scsite.com/ew3/websources** and click a link under Special Feature 2, E-Commerce Stats.

A helpful way to look more closely at the types of businesses involved in e-commerce is to identify how the businesses generate their revenues.

E-Commerce Business Models

A **business model** defines how a business generates its revenues. An **e-commerce business model** identifies the revenue-generation processes for a business involved in e-commerce. E-commerce business models can be defined in a number of ways. For example, a business that provides free informational content or services to visitors and generates its revenues by selling advertising space at its site can be defined as following an *advertising business model*. A retailer that sells its products online in addition to or instead of at a physical store can be defined as following a *virtual storefront business model*. An online business that offers information or services to members who pay a monthly or annual subscription fee can be defined as following a *subscription business model*. Many businesses involved in e-commerce combine multiple e-commerce business models to generate revenues. For example, a small business retailer might combine business models, such as advertising and virtual storefront, to generate revenues by selling products directly to consumers and by selling advertising space at its site to other online businesses.

One of the most commonly used ways to broadly categorize businesses involved in e-commerce is to define the seller/buyer relationship in the revenue-generation process.

Business-to-Consumer (B2C)

Online businesses (sellers) that sell products and services — for example, books, tickets to movies and sports events, food items, travel services, and diet and exercise plans — directly to consumers (buyers) are following the general **business-to-consumer** or **B2C** e-commerce business model. Examples of B2C e-commerce sites include:

- Prestogeorge — coffee, tea, specialty gifts (Figure SF 2–1)
- Amazon.com — books and other consumer items
- MyFoodDiary — subscription-based diet and fitness services
- Expedia — travel services

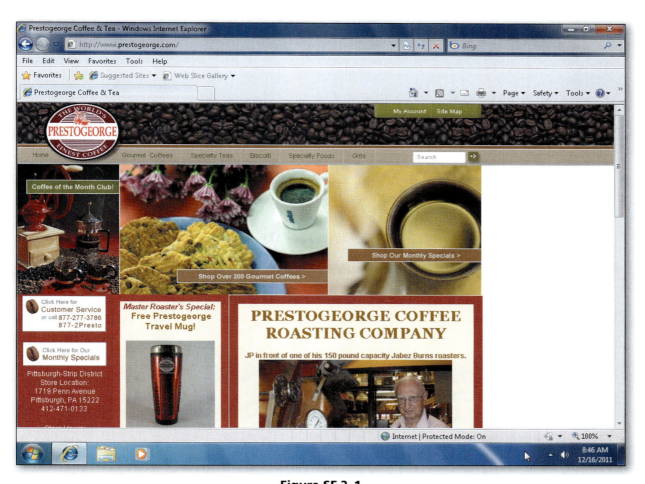

Figure SF 2–1

Business-to-Business (B2B)

Businesses that sell their products or services to other businesses can be described as following the general **business-to-business** or **B2B** e-commerce business model. While you may be more familiar with B2C e-commerce, B2B e-commerce transactions actually dominate the online marketplace. Businesses that sell information technology hardware and software online, virtual stores that sell office supplies coupled with inventory management services, online data backup services, online marketplaces that attract multiple business sellers and buyers in a particular industry, online marketplaces that match suppliers with buyers, and Web site performance analysis and marketing services for online businesses are just a few examples of the wide variety of seller/buyer relationships covered by B2B e-commerce. Real-world B2B e-commerce examples that illustrate these types of seller/buyer relationships include:

- Cisco — IT products and services
- i365 — data backup and recovery products and services
- Dairy.com — marketplace for the dairy industry
- Guru.com — marketplace for freelancers and employers
- Webtrends — Web site performance analysis and marketing services

An extranet is a portion of a company's internal computer network that can be accessed by outsiders, such as business partners, by using an Internet connection. The exchange of business documents, such as requests for quotes (RFQs), purchase orders, receiving reports, and bills of lading, between business partners over Internet-connected extranets is also considered B2B e-commerce.

Consumer-to-Consumer (C2C)

The **consumer-to-consumer** or **C2C** e-commerce business model is being followed when consumers sell items or services directly to other consumers. For example, Web sites that offer online auctions in which consumers bid on items offered for sale by other consumers, online classified ads, and online entertainment or sports venue ticket resale are following the C2C e-commerce business model. eBay, TraderOnline, and StubHub! (Figure SF 2–2) are examples of sites that bring consumers together to sell items to and buy items from each other.

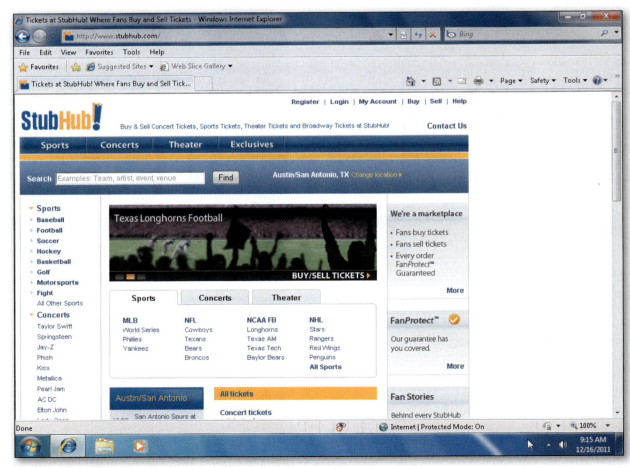

Figure SF 2–2

Consumer-to-Business (C2B)

The **consumer-to-business** or **C2B** e-commerce business model uses a reverse auction process that allows consumers to make binding bids or offers for a product or service, such as airline tickets, hotel rooms, or rental cars. Participating businesses can then choose to accept or decline the consumers' bids. Priceline.com (Figure SF 2–3) is the e-commerce business most often associated with the C2B e-commerce business model.

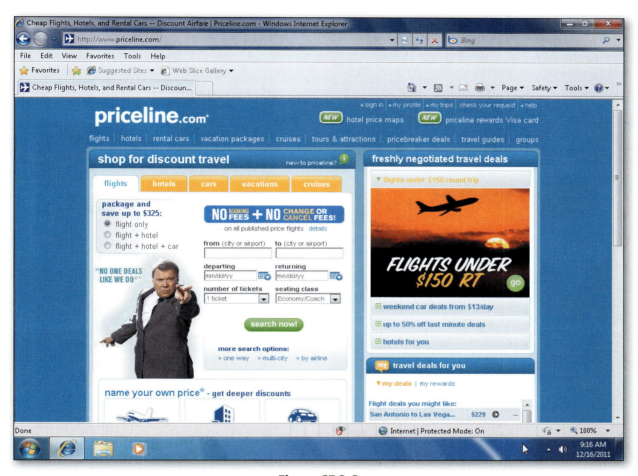

Figure SF 2–3

Business-to-Government (B2G)

Some e-commerce sites create an online marketplace in which businesses with products and services to sell are matched with government agencies that have procurement needs. These online marketplaces are following the general **business-to-government** or **B2G** e-commerce business model. Onvia (Figure SF 2–4), B2GMARKET, and Bidmain are three examples of businesses following the B2G e-commerce business model.

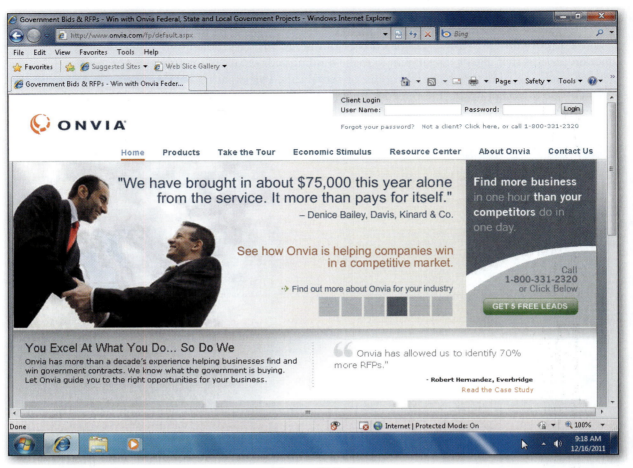

Figure SF 2–4

Business-to-Employee (B2E)

In addition to these general categories based on the seller/buyer relationship, many businesses exploit Internet and Web technologies to connect management and employees over the company intranet. For example, on a company intranet you often find a Web site supported by the company's human resources department (the "seller") that can be accessed by employees (the "buyers"). In this scenario, the human resources department uses its Web site to provide employees with access to important information about employment rules and guidelines, insurance benefits, 401(k) investment management, and more. This electronic connection between management and employees is often called **business-to-employee** or **B2E** e-commerce.

Some online business sites customize their offerings by engaging in multiple types of seller/buyer relationships. For example, Office Depot and Dell offer products and services directly to consumers (B2C) as well as to other businesses (B2B). *The Wall Street Journal* online edition offers subscription services to both individual (B2C) and business (B2B) customers.

To learn more about e-commerce business models, visit **scsite.com/ew3/websources** and click a link under Special Feature 2, E-Commerce Business Models. For a closer look at the Web site examples discussed in this section, visit **scsite.com/ew3/websources** and click a link under Special Feature 2, Business Model Examples.

Web Site E-Commerce Elements

All e-commerce Web sites — regardless of which e-commerce business model or combination of models a business follows — must have in place certain basic elements to support e-commerce transactions, such as:

- a product catalog or information about services offered
- technologies to accept and summarize product orders, including taxes and shipping, if applicable
- technologies to respond to potential customer inquiries about services offered, such as e-mail responses to inquiries or appointment scheduling
- technologies to process orders and payments
- a method for delivering products or services and, for physical products, a method for handling product returns
- a process for providing customer support before and after the sale
- online transaction security policies and procedures

The specific elements required to add e-commerce capability to a business site depend on the needs of the business and its customers. For example, a B2B or B2C company that sells services might require only a catalog of services offered, hours of operation, contact information, and other customer service information at its Web site. However, a B2B or B2C company that sells products will require most, if not all, of the basic elements listed above to add e-commerce capability to its business site.

To illustrate how a combination of basic e-commerce elements can come together to add e-commerce capability to a Web site, assume that you are a small business owner who sells products from a brick-and-mortar store. You now want to add e-commerce capability to your existing Web site.

You will need to add to your site the technologies that allow a customer to select items for purchase, summarize the individual selections into a complete order, and then process the customer's payment for the order. Additionally, you must add to your site options for handling customer questions, complaints, and other feedback. You must also have in place a process for ensuring the security of your site's online transactions and the customer information they generate.

In addition to modifying your Web site, you must also consider the modifications to your **back office operations**—the related internal business activities that take place outside your Web site, such as the process for fulfilling and shipping the customer's order.

Product Catalog

Businesses selling products online must include pages in their Web sites that detail the products site visitors can purchase. These product pages, also called a **product catalog**, should provide the relevant information about each product — a description, a product image, the sale price, the benefits to the buyer, and so forth. Each item in the product catalog should have an option button or box that a visitor can click to select the product for purchase. Figure SF 2–5 illustrates a product page at the WonderBrains.com B2C site.

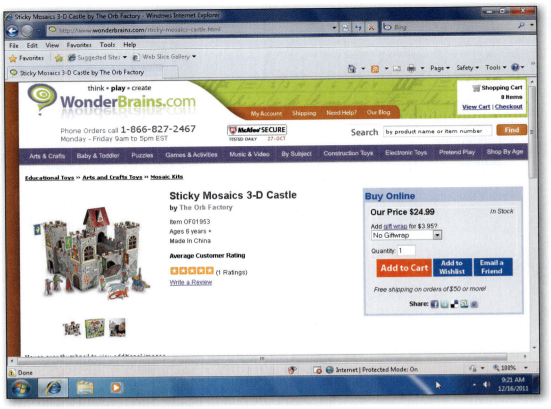

Figure SF 2–5

Shopping Cart

A virtual **shopping cart** is software that records each individual item purchased and then summarizes the purchased items into a single order that includes total item cost, applicable sales tax, applicable coupons or discounts, and shipping costs. You can purchase shopping cart software from a wide variety of vendors and then integrate the software with your product catalog. Virtual shopping carts also generally provide a method for a customer to add or remove items from the cart before he or she finalizes the purchase through the **checkout process**. Figure SF 2–6 illustrates a pre-checkout shopping cart at the Cooking.com site.

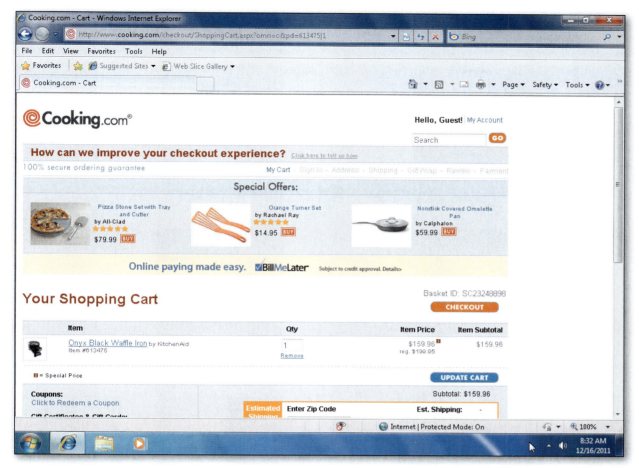

Figure SF 2–6

Completing an online sales order also includes the processing and approval of your customer's payment as well as your shipment of the customer's order. Figure SF 2–7 illustrates the online purchase and payment process from selection to shipment.

BTW

Express Checkout
PayPal Express Checkout and Google Checkout are add-on features to existing shopping cart software used at an e-commerce site. Express checkout features allow online customers to store their name, address, and payment information in a PayPal or Google account, then access that information during the checkout process by clicking a button in a shopping cart.

customer shops at online store

customer adds items to electronic shopping cart

customer enters credit card and other payment information

payment processor authorizes and processes secure credit card payment

order is shipped

order is filled

online store finalizes order

Figure SF 2–7

Payment Processors, Payment Gateways, and Merchant Accounts

During the checkout process, your customer must enter applicable name, address, and payment information. Almost all online purchases in the United States are paid by credit card; to accept credit card payments, an e-commerce site must have in place a method to process and approve credit card payments and receive payment funds from credit card companies. One way to do this is to connect your site to a payment processor and a payment gateway for payment verification and approval. In addition, you must also open a merchant account into which your credit card payment funds can be deposited.

The electronic verification process for an online credit card purchase is performed by a payment processor. An e-commerce **payment processor** is a business that verifies, authorizes, and processes secure credit card transactions in real time over a network, called a **payment gateway**, that connects online stores with credit card companies and financial institutions. Figure SF 2–8 illustrates the verification, authorization, and processing of credit card transactions over a payment gateway.

Figure SF 2–8

A **merchant account** is a business account at a financial institution into which proceeds from credit card payments are automatically deposited. You can apply for a merchant account at a financial institution that specializes in e-commerce transactions by providing information about your online business; for example, business overview, length of time in business, your credit history, and the type of credit cards you will accept. The fees involved with a merchant account can include:

- a one-time setup fee
- a monthly access fee
- a per-transaction fee
- a percentage of each transaction, called the **discount rate**

The financial institution providing the merchant account typically assesses its fees based on an analysis of the business risks associated with the account and its own experience with similar accounts.

A **chargeback** occurs when a financial institution must return funds to a credit card company because the card holder refuses to pay a disputed charge. While the financial institution will deduct the chargeback from the merchant account, there is a risk that the bank might not be able to recover the chargeback if the business owner has already withdrawn the original funds from the account. The chargeback history for similar accounts to the one you open is one factor the financial institution takes into consideration when establishing its fees. The types of products or services you plan to sell at your site can also affect the financial institution's assessment of the chargeback risk on your merchant account because certain products or services historically generate more chargebacks.

An online credit card payment also increases the risk of a chargeback because, unlike a credit card transaction at a brick-and-mortar store, the credit card and the card holder are not physically present during the verification process. This is called the **card not present/card holder not present risk** and typically results in a higher discount rate for e-commerce merchant accounts.

For more information about merchant accounts, payment processors, and payment gateways, visit **scsite.com/ew3/websources** and click a link under Special Feature 2, Credit Card Processing. While most online purchases are paid by credit card, some online sellers also accept person-to-person payment methods, electronic checks, smart cards, or micropayments. For more information about online payment methods, visit **scsite.com/ew3/websources** and click a link under Special Feature 2, Online Payment Methods.

Order Fulfillment

After a customer has made and paid for a purchase at your online store, the item or items purchased must then be delivered to the customer. The process of picking sold items from an inventory, packaging the items, and shipping them to the customer is called **order fulfillment**. A very large online business with a huge volume of product sales might choose to build and staff its own warehouses and manage its own inventory and order fulfillment processes. For your small or medium-sized online store, a more cost-effective choice might be either a virtual inventory system or outsourcing the fulfillment process.

A **virtual inventory** is an online catalog of products that actually are owned and warehoused by third-party manufacturers or wholesalers. An online store that sells from a virtual inventory sends an order and payment for that order to the manufacturer or wholesaler only after the online store's customer has paid for the order. The order fulfillment process is handled by the manufacturer or wholesaler who, upon receipt of payment from the online store, picks the ordered items from its inventory, packages the order for delivery, and ships the order directly to the online store's customer. Selling from a virtual inventory of products is called **drop ship**. Drop ship is one e-commerce choice for small businesses that do not want to tie up cash in an inventory of products or incur additional expenses for order fulfillment.

Before considering a drop ship arrangement, however, do your homework to identify legitimate drop ship opportunities. Some Web sites that advertise drop ship business opportunities or offer to sell lists of manufacturers and wholesalers that participate in drop ship might be business scams. To learn more about drop ship scams, visit **scsite.com/ew3/websources** and click a link under Special Feature 2, Drop Ship Scams.

Another alternative for a small or medium-sized online store is to own your product inventory but outsource the warehousing, inventory management, and order fulfillment processes to a third-party logistics provider. A **third-party logistics provider**, also called a **fulfillment house**, provides inventory management, order picking and packaging, and shipping services. Outsourcing the order fulfillment and inventory control functions gives you much less control over these processes; however, it can substantially reduce the expenses associated with managing an inventory and fulfilling orders. Some third-party logistics providers, such as Shipwire and Webgistix (Figure SF 2–9), focus on e-commerce.

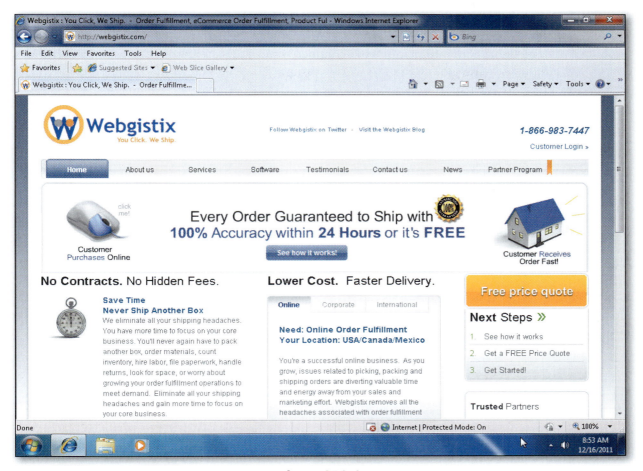

Figure SF 2–9

To learn more about order fulfillment, visit **scsite.com/ew3/websources** and click a link under Special Feature 2, Order Fulfillment.

Customer Support

Quick and efficient communication between buyer and seller is one of the prime advantages of conducting business transactions online. An online store can exploit this communication advantage to both increase sales and increase customer satisfaction by providing online customer support. At minimum, your e-commerce Web site must provide a page with contact information including physical address, phone numbers, and e-mail addresses necessary for customers to contact your business with their questions, comments, complaints, and other feedback. Adding a Frequently Asked Questions (FAQ) page containing answers to commonly asked customer questions can be helpful. Other types of online customer support, such as links to downloadable product user manuals or notifying customers by e-mail of upcoming special sales deals, should be considered depending on customers' needs and expectations.

Transaction Security

Transaction security is also very important for the success of your online store. You must take care to ensure that your customers' personally identifiable and payment information is transmitted securely across a payment gateway and is secure from hackers who might breach the security of your Web site. Additionally, you must look to your own business's financial security by reducing chargebacks and protecting against credit card fraud. For more information on e-commerce security issues for both consumers and your online store, visit **scsite.com/ew3/websources** and click a link under Special Feature 2, E-Commerce Security Issues.

One key to operating a successful online business is to make certain that your site's product catalog, shopping cart, payment approval and processing, and order fulfillment systems are compatible and integrate smoothly. You can choose from a wide variety of e-commerce software and services solutions to make that happen.

Adding E-Commerce Capability to a Web Site

Some businesses involved in e-commerce have all the resources — time, money, accounting and technical staffs, and so forth — necessary to:

- create an online product or services catalog
- get approved for and open a merchant account
- design and develop in-house shopping cart software or purchase existing shopping cart software, customize it, and then integrate it with the Web site
- identify and connect to a payment processor and payment gateway system that is also compatible with the shopping cart software and the merchant account
- tie sales and payment transactions to the business's back office systems, such as order fulfillment and customer support systems

Unfortunately, many owners of small or medium-sized businesses — like the small online store scenario described in this feature — that want to move into e-commerce are likely to find that attempting to identify, purchase or arrange for, and then combine individual e-commerce elements — especially the payment verification, approval, and funding process — into a seamless whole for their Web site can be overwhelming. For many of these businesses, choosing either a third-party payment processor solution or an all-in-one e-commerce solution is a good approach.

Third-Party Payment Processor Solution

In some instances, getting approved for a merchant account might be difficult. For example, a startup online business with an inadequate credit history or a small online store with a low sales volume could have trouble finding an institution willing to establish a merchant account. If you have a limited number of products for sale, you might find opening and maintaining a merchant account is too expensive. Additionally, you might lack the expertise to confidently research and evaluate compatible shopping carts, payment processors, and payment gateways that work with your merchant account. Contracting with a third-party payment processor is one way to resolve these issues.

Using a **third-party payment processor**, such as PayPal Website Payments Standard, 2Checkout.com, and CCNow, allows your customers to shop at your online store and then pay for their purchases at the third-party payment processor's site. A third-party payment processor provides tools for creating a product catalog at your site, including links to the processor's shopping cart. When a customer clicks a product purchase link, such as a Buy Now button, in a product catalog, his or her browser is directed to a shopping cart at the processor's site where the order is summarized and payment information is entered.

The third-party processor handles the payment verification and approval and receives the payment funds, which it then passes back to your online store in a number of ways, including:

- check
- wire transfer
- direct bank account deposit
- account credit with the processor

Fees for a third-party payment processor's services might include a startup fee, transaction fees, a discount rate, and additional fees for accepting other types of payments, such as checks. Figure SF 2–10 illustrates the third-party payment processing option.

customer shops at online store

customer clicks Buy Now link

customer's browser is redirected to a shopping cart at the processor's Web site

customer pays for purchase at the processor's Web site

Buy Now

Payment verification and approval and receipt of funds from credit card company

processor remits funds to online store, which ships order to customer

processor handles payment verification and approval and receives funds

Figure SF 2–10

The primary advantage of an arrangement with a third-party payment processor is simplicity: it is easy for you to get started and offer your customers credit card payment options without the necessity of adding a shopping cart to your online store site, getting approval for a merchant account, and connecting to a payment processor and payment gateway system. The disadvantages include possible higher or unexpected fees, design limitations for your product catalog, and risking unpleasant customer experiences at your site by having your customers leave the site in order to finalize and pay for their order. To learn more about third-party payment processors, visit **scsite.com/ew3/websources** and click a link under Special Feature 2, Third-Party Payment Processors.

Alternatively, you might choose an all-in-one e-commerce package that combines all the essential elements for processing transactions at your online store.

All-in-One E-Commerce Solution

An all-in-one e-commerce solution allows your customers to both shop at your site and then remain at your site to pay for their order. An **all-in-one e-commerce solution** generally includes, at minimum, Web page templates you can use to quickly create your site complete with a product catalog, a shopping cart, and access to the elements needed to verify, approve, and fund payments — a payment processor, access to a payment gateway system, and an account in which to receive funds.

Some all-in-one solutions go further by providing a variety of other features, such as:

- domain name registration
- an option to replace template pages with your own Web pages created in a Web authoring tool, such as Expression Web
- Web site customization and design services
- access to e-commerce Web hosting services
- Web site marketing and promotion services
- an interface to a business's back office operations, such as order fulfillment
- various levels of customer support

Fees associated with all-in-one solutions vary widely by vendor but can include a one-time setup fee, a monthly account fee based on the volume of transactions, and a per-transaction fee. Yahoo! Small Business, Microsoft Office Live Small Business (Figure SF 2–11), Volusion, and Network Solutions are examples of vendors that offer all-in-one e-commerce solutions.

BTW

E-Commerce Web Hosting
Most ISPs that offer Web hosting and companies that specialize in Web hosting offer a different range of services for hosting a Web site involved in e-commerce and charge various fees for those services. Check out Appendix C, Publishing Content to the Web, for more information about selecting a Web hosting alternative.

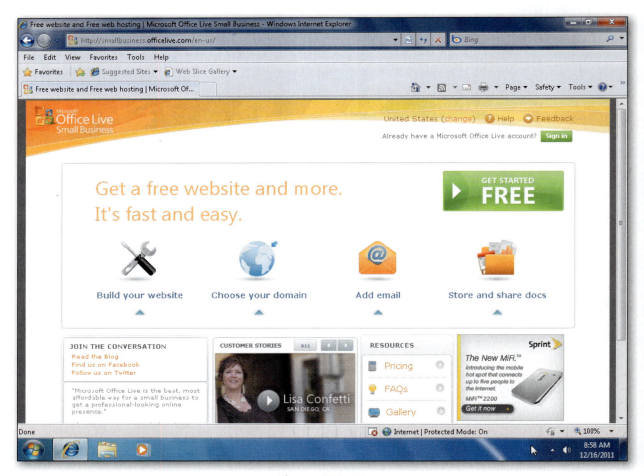

Figure SF 2–11

To learn more about all-in-one e-commerce solutions, visit **scsite.com/ew3/ websources** and click a link under Special Feature 2, All-in-One E-Commerce Solutions.

Feature Summary

In this special feature, you learned how to define e-commerce and to discuss the important role e-commerce plays in today's business environment. You also learned how to classify different types of e-commerce business models based on the relationship between seller and buyer. You learned about the different elements necessary to add e-commerce capability to a Web site, including product or services catalog pages, shopping cart technologies, access to payment approval and processing services, a process for fulfilling orders, a method for providing customer support, and the importance of securing online transactions and customer information.

Finally, you learned about adding e-commerce capability to a site using either a third-party payment processor or an all-in-one e-commerce solution.

In the Lab

Use Bing, Google, or another search tool of your choice to locate relevant Web sites as you work through the following exercises.

Lab 1: Planning for an E-Commerce Site

Problem: You are intrigued by the idea of starting an online business based on your family's long-established coffee roasting business, but are unsure about all the ways that the site could generate revenues. You would like to explore how similar e-commerce sites are generating their revenues.

Instructions: Search the Web for three e-commerce sites offering small-batch roasted coffee beans. Identify, if possible, the ways in which the real-world sites generate their revenues. Then, using what you have learned about similar real-world sites, identify the ways your site might generate revenues.

1. Using word processing or presentation software, create a presentation that summarizes your new e-commerce site, including the products and/or services it will sell. Explain all the ways your site will generate revenues. Note the e-commerce business model or combination of models your online business will follow.

2. Save your presentation as `Lab SF 2-1 Planning an E-Commerce Site`. At the direction of your instructor, print your presentation and give the presentation to your class.

In the Lab

Lab 2: Evaluating Third-Party E-Commerce Solutions

Problem: Your cousin Chris runs a popular surf shop in Venice Beach. Even non-surfers make a special trip to the shop for Chris's unique T-shirt offerings. Chris would like to sell the shirts from his Web site, which currently only provides information on store hours, directions, and surf classes. You need a way to add a product catalog and shopping cart software to his site. You also know that most online payments are made using credit cards; therefore, you need a way to handle online credit card payment and processing. To save time and get Chris's online store up and running, you decide that a third-party payment processor solution would work best for Chris's online store.

Instructions: Search the Web to identify and then review the services and fees provided by at least three third-party payment processors. Then select the processor that you think offers the best combination of cost and services for Chris's new online store.

1. Write a report that summarizes the services provided and costs for those services for each reviewed third-party payment processor. Choose the processor that best meets the needs of the new online store and discuss the reasons for your choice.

Continued >

In the Lab *continued*

2. Include in your report a list of the steps necessary to integrate Chris's existing Web site with the chosen third-party processor. You will find this information at the processor's Web site.

3. Save your report as `Lab SF 2-2 Third-party Payment Processor`. At the direction of your instructor, print the report.

In the Lab

Lab 3: Selecting an All-in-One E-Commerce Solution

Problem: Refer to the Web site you created in Chapter 5 for The Upper Cut. Owners Marcus and Elisa have developed their own brand of custom hair care products. Customers are buying the shampoos, conditioners, and specialty treatments as fast as the salon can stock the shelves. To exploit the popularity of their new products to increase sales, Marcus and Elisa want you to add a product sales component to their existing Web site. You know that you need a way to add a product catalog and shopping cart software to the Web site. You also know that most online payments are made using credit cards; therefore, you need a way to handle online credit card payment and processing. To save time and get the Web site's e-commerce capability up and running, you decide that an all-in-one e-commerce solution would work best for The Upper Cut.

Instructions: Search the Web to identify and then review at least three all-in-one e-commerce solution vendors. Take advantage of any vendor tutorials or demos. Then select the solution that you think offers the best combination of cost and services for the salon's online store.

1. Write a report that summarizes the services provided and costs for those services for each reviewed all-in-one e-commerce solution. Choose the all-in-one e-commerce solution that best meets the needs of The Upper Cut Web site's online store and discuss the reasons for your choice.

2. Include in your report a list of the steps necessary to integrate the salon's existing Web site with the chosen all-in-one e-commerce solution. You will find this information at the vendor's Web site.

3. Save your report as `Lab SF 2-3 All-in-One E-Commerce Solution`. At the direction of your instructor, print the report.

Using the Microsoft Expression Web User Guide

Introduction

You might have a question about how to use a specific Expression Web feature, or perhaps you want to learn more about the different features offered by Expression Web for creating, editing, and publishing Web pages. You can search for information on specific topics, look up a topic in an index, or browse available topics by category in the **Microsoft Expression Web User Guide window**.

To open the Expression Web User Guide window, click the User Guide command on the Help menu. The User Guide window (Figure A–1) contains standard Windows 7 operating system window features, including a title bar and the Minimize, Maximize or Restore Down, and Close buttons. Additionally, the User Guide window contains a **toolbar** with the Hide or Show, Back, Print, and Options buttons; a **tabs pane** containing the Contents, Index, and Search tabs; and a **viewing pane** in which selected Help topics appear. In Figure A–1, the Getting started folder in the Contents tab is selected and the Getting started Help topic page is visible in the viewing pane.

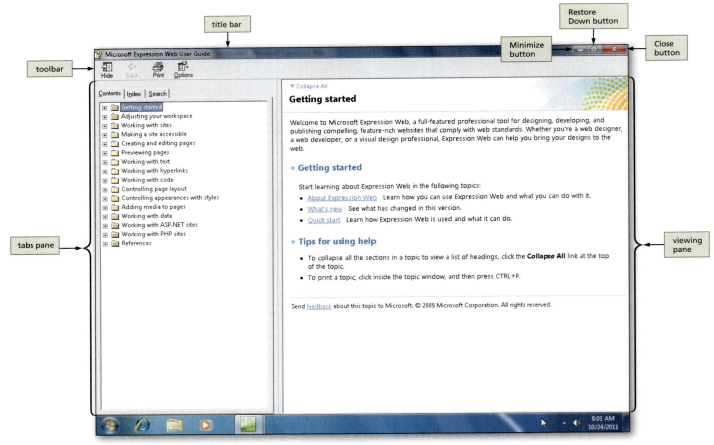

Figure A–1

To Open the Microsoft Expression Web User Guide Window

The following steps open the Microsoft Expression Web User Guide window using a menu command.

1
- Start Expression Web, if necessary. Click Help on the menu bar to open the Help menu (Figure A–2).

Figure A–2

2

- Click the User Guide command to open the Microsoft Expression Web User Guide window (Figure A–3).

Q&A

Can I resize the User Guide window?

You can resize the User Guide window by clicking the Maximize button on the User Guide window title bar to enlarge the window to fill the screen. You can then click the Restore Down button on the User Guide window title bar to restore the window to its previous size. You can also resize the User Guide window using the mouse pointer. If you position the mouse pointer on the left, right, top, bottom boundary, or corner of the User Guide window, when it has been restored to a smaller size, the mouse pointer becomes a sizing pointer. Drag the boundary to resize the window.

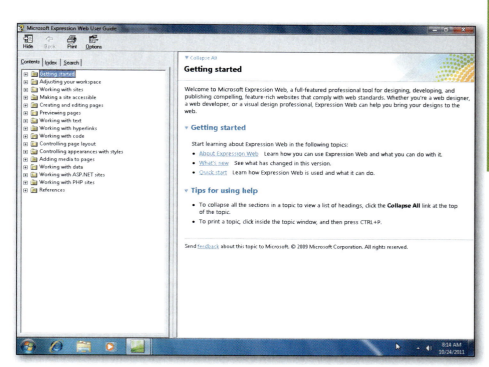

Figure A–3

The Microsoft Expression Web User Guide Window

At the top of the User Guide window is the window's title bar with the name of the window and the Minimize, Restore Down or Maximize, and Close buttons as shown in Figure A–1. Below the title bar are a toolbar, the tabs pane, and the viewing pane.

The Toolbar

The User Guide toolbar, located at the top of the User Guide window below the title bar, contains four buttons, as shown in Figures A–4 and A–5.

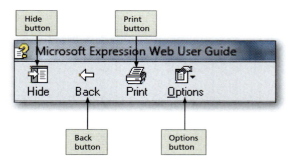

Figure A–4

BTW

Expression Web Online
To learn more about working with Expression Web, click the Microsoft Expression Web Online command on the Help menu to visit the Microsoft Expression Community Web site. On the Expression Community Web site, you will find links to online tutorials, discussion forums, user tips, and other useful information.

- **Hide button** — CLICK the Hide button to hide the tabs pane.
- **Back button** — CLICK the active Back button to revisit a Help topic viewed during this User Guide session.
- **Print button** — CLICK the Print button to open the Print Topics dialog box and set an option for the topic or subtopics to print.
- **Options button** — CLICK the Options button to view a menu of commands for hiding or showing tabs, moving back and forward between previously viewed topics, printing topics, and accessing other User Guide features.

After you click the Hide button to hide the tabs pane, the Hide button is replaced with the Show button you can click to unhide the tabs pane. Figure A–5 illustrates the toolbar with the Show button.

Figure A–5

Finding a Specific Help Topic by Searching the Index Tab

Another quick way to find a specific Help topic is to search the alphabetical index of Help topics available on the Index tab.

Browsing Help Topics by Category Using the Contents Tab

After you open the User Guide window, you can click the Contents tab to view a table of contents or list of general Help topic categories. You can expand a topic category to view a list of individual Help topics or subtopics within the category. Then click an individual Help topic to view the topic details in the viewing pane on the right side of the window.

To Browse Help Topics by Category

The following steps expand and collapse a Help topic category in the Contents tab and display a specific Help topic in the viewing pane.

1

• Click the Contents tab, if necessary. Click the Expand icon to the left of the 'Adding media to pages' category to display a list of the individual topics and subtopics in that category (Figure A–6). The Expand icon becomes the Collapse icon.

Figure A–6

2

• Click the Adding Silverlight applications topic to view the specific Help topic in the viewing pane (Figure A–7).

Figure A–7

● Drag the Scroll box in the viewing pane to view the entire Adding Silverlight applications topic, if necessary.

● Click the Collapse icon to the left of the 'Adding media to pages' topic in the Contents tab to collapse the topic category (Figure A–8).

Figure A–8

To Search for a Help Topic Using the Index Tab

The following steps show the Index tab and search the alphabetic topic index by keyword to display a specific Help topic.

● Click the Index tab in the tabs pane to view the alphabetic topic index (Figure A–9).

Figure A–9

• Type data tables in the 'Type in the keyword to find' text box to scroll the index and select the data tables topic (Figure A–10).

Figure A–10

• Double-click the data tables topic in the Index tab to open the Topics Found dialog box (Figure A–11).

Figure A–11

- Click 'Using data tables' in the Topics Found dialog box to select a specific topic.

- Click the Display button in the dialog box to view the topic in the viewing pane (Figure A–12).

Figure A–12

Searching for a Specific Help Topic Using the Search Tab

You can search for a specific Help topic by performing a keyword search using the Search tab. Like the Index tab, the Search tab contains the 'Type in the keyword to find' text box in which you type your search keywords or phrases. You then click the List Topics button to perform the keyword search.

To Search for a Specific Help Topic Using the Search Tab

The following steps search for a specific Help topic by typing keywords in the 'Type in the keyword to find' text box in the Search tab and then clicking the List Topics button.

1

- Click the Search tab in the tabs pane.

- Type CSS in the 'Type in the keyword to find' text box.

- Click the List Topics button in the Search tab to list Help topics related to the CSS keyword (Figure A–13).

Figure A–13

2

- Double-click Apply a style in the 'Select Topic to display' list to view the topic in the viewing pane (Figure A–14).

- Click the Close button on the User Guide window title bar to close the User Guide window.

- Close Expression Web.

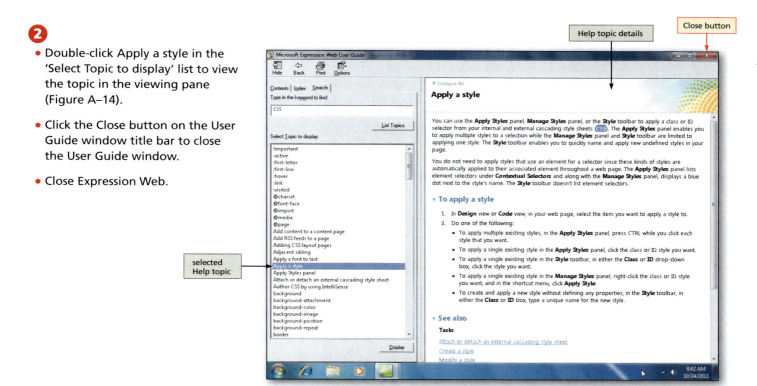

Figure A–14

Other Ways

1. Press ALT+F4 to close the User Guide window

Getting Help with the User Guide

1 Browsing Help Topics Using the Contents Tab

Instructions: Use the User Guide window Contents tab to browse for specific Help topics. Print individual Help topics at the direction of your instructor.

1. Press the F1 keyboard shortcut key to open the User Guide window. Using the Contents tab, find three Help topics about publishing a Web site. Review the Help topics and create a brief outline you can use to explain Web site publishing issues covered by the Help topics. Close the User Guide window.

2. Open the User Guide window using the method of your choice. Use the Contents tab to browse the Help topics for information on selecting and pasting text. Review the Help topics and then write down the step-by-step instructions you can use to explain to another student how to select and paste text. Then close the User Guide window using the ALT+F4 keyboard shortcut keys.

2 Using the Index Tab and the Toolbar

Instructions: Use the Index tab to search for specific Help topics using the alphabetic Help topic index. Print individual Help topics at the direction of your instructor.

1. Open the User Guide window using the method of your choice and view three help topics of your choice by searching the Index tab.

2. Click the Back button on the toolbar to move back to view the recently viewed Help topics.

3. Click the Hide and Show buttons on the User Guide toolbar to hide and show the tabs pane.

4. Click the Options button on the User Guide toolbar to explore using menu commands to work in the User Guide window. Close the User Guide window.

3 Searching for Specific Help Topics Using the Search Tab

Instructions: Use the Search tab and keywords to search for specific Help topics. Print individual Help topics at the direction of your instructor.

1. Open the User Guide using the method of your choice. Search the User Guide using the keyword phrase `attaching a style sheet` and then list the relevant Help topics. Review the specific Help topic of your choice. Close the User Guide window.

2. Open the User Guide window using the method of your choice and then use keywords and the Search tab to search for Help topics about bulleted or numbered lists. Review at least two specific Help topics related to bulleted or numbered lists. Be prepared to discuss the topics with your classmates. Close the User Guide window.

3. Open the User Guide window and, using the key phrase `keyboard shortcuts` and the Search tab, display the Keyboard shortcuts Help topic. Write down 10 keyboard shortcuts you think will be most useful to you. Close the User Guide window.

Appendix B
Web Standards and Accessibility

Introduction

The application of Web standards and accessibility guidelines in the development and creation of your Web pages can enhance your Web pages' usability and cross-browser compatibility. Additionally, it can make your pages' content accessible by visitors with disabilities.

Web Standards

A **standard** is a generally accepted principle, rule, guideline, or technology that defines how to perform a task or measures the quality and consistency of the task's output. Industries from electrical engineering to accounting use standards, rules, and guidelines to ensure consistent high-quality output or technological performance. Two examples of **technology standards** include the IEEE 802.20 standard for deploying mobile broadband wireless across networks and the Hypertext Transfer Protocol (HTTP) standard for transmitting Web pages over the Internet.

  Web standards encompass the guidelines and technologies developed to ensure the cross-browser compatibility of Web pages and the general usability and accessibility of those pages. Since the mid-1990s, the World Wide Web Consortium, or W3C (Figure B–1), has been establishing Web standards while coalitions such as the Web Standards Project and the Web Standards Group promote the use of those standards across the Web development community.

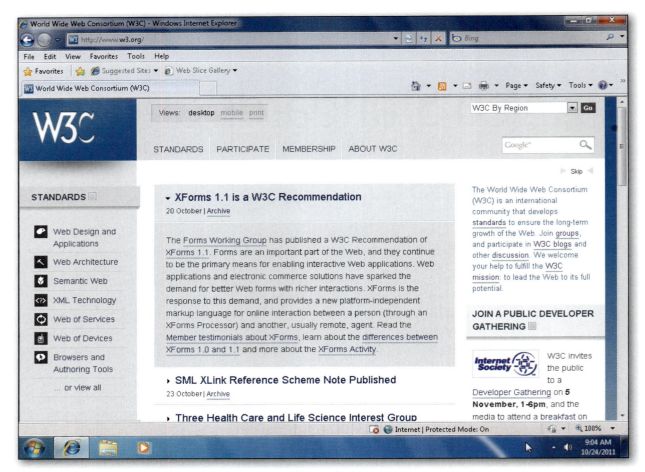

Figure B–1

Current Web technology standards developed by the W3C include the markup languages that define the arrangement and content of Web page elements (HTML 4.01, XHTML 1.1, XML) and Cascading Style Sheets (CSS) that control the layout and formatting of Web page elements. The development of Web standards is an ongoing process. For example, the W3C and related interested groups are currently working on the standards for HTML 5, the fifth major revision of the HTML standard, and the XHTML 2.0 standard.

To create standards-compliant Web pages, you should create your Web pages using valid HTML or XHTML markup and use CSS to lay out and format Web page content. Expression Web contains features such as CSS compatibility reporting that help you create standards-compliant Web pages. Ensuring that your Web pages comply with standards can be beneficial in many ways. For example, standards-compliant Web pages are easier to maintain, are compatible with current and future browser technologies, download faster, and provide content that is accessible by all users, including those with disabilities.

For more information about the W3C, the Web Standards Project, the Web Standards Group, or other Web standards topics, visit **scsite.com/ew3/websources** and click a link under Appendix B, Web Standards.

Web Accessibility

The goal of **Web accessibility guidelines** is to ensure that all Web page content is available to people with disabilities; for example, people with visual impairments who typically use assistive technologies, such as screen readers, to access Web pages.

The W3C **Web Accessibility Initiative** (Figure B–2) and **Section 508** of the U.S. Rehabilitation Act of 1973 define current Web accessibility guidelines. Two examples of Web accessibility guidelines are: (1) always add a text equivalent for a non-text element, such as a picture; and (2) never use color alone to identify a hyperlink.

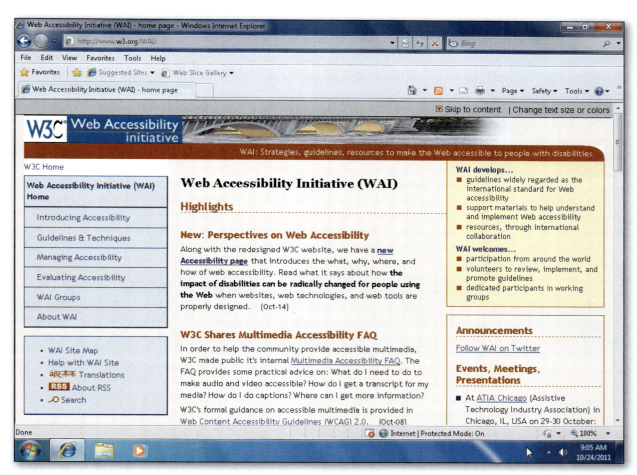

Figure B–2

Expression Web has features, such as the Accessibility Checker (Figure B–3), to help you find and solve accessibility problems with your Web pages. The Accessibility Checker can be launched by clicking Accessibility Reports on the Tools menu or by clicking Run Accessibility Checker on the Accessibility Panel.

Figure B–3

Although the terms *Web usability* and *Web accessibility* are sometimes used interchangeably, incorporating all aspects of good Web design — structure, layout, color, and so forth — with Web standards to create your Web pages improves the usability of those pages for everyone who visits them. Web accessibility issues focus on making Web content accessible to visitors with disabilities. For more information about the Web Accessibility Initiative, Section 508, and other Web accessibility topics, visit **scsite.com/ew3/websources** and click a link under Appendix B, Web Accessibility.

Appendix C
Publishing Content to the Web

Introduction

Publishing, or copying, your Web site's files — Web pages, graphics, and other related files — to a Web server allows you to share your site with others. In order to publish your Web site so that others can access it, you need a domain name for your site and access to space on a Web server.

A **domain name** identifies your Web site and is part of the Uniform Resource Locator (URL) that a visitor types in his or her Web browser's address bar to download your site's pages. For example, the domain name for the Microsoft Web site is *microsoft.com* and the site's URL is *www.microsoft.com*. You can register your site's domain name with an **accredited registrar**, such as GoDaddy, Network Solutions (Figure C–1), or Register.com, for a small annual fee.

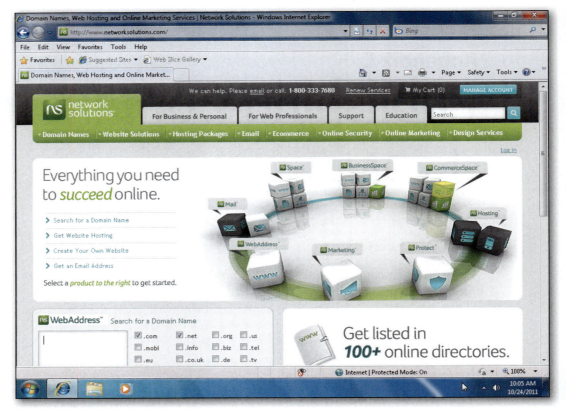

Figure C–1

For more information about the Domain Name System (DNS) and registering domain names, visit **scsite.com/ew3/websources** and click a link under Appendix C, Domain Name System.

A **Web server** is a computer (and its software) that stores Web pages and then "serves up" the pages upon request from a Web browser. **Web server space** is available from a variety of sources. For example, your school might make Web server space available for students and faculty, or you might be able to acquire server space from your **Internet service provider (ISP)**, either as part of your Internet connection service or for an additional fee. Additionally, thousands of companies, such as Yahoo! Small Business (Figure C–2), BlueHost, Microsoft Office Live Small Business, and Rackspace offer **Web hosting services** for all types of Web sites — from small one- or two-page personal sites to large, multipage e-commerce sites. Some Web hosting providers might also offer a number of additional services, such as e-mail accounts, shopping cart add-ons, Web site marketing services, and so forth.

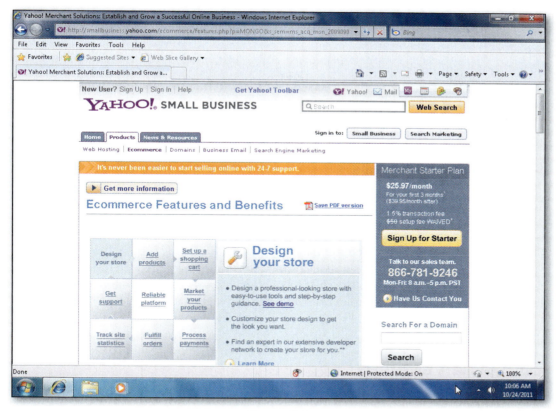

Figure C–2

Web hosting fees vary depending on a number of factors, such as the:

- Type of site (personal or business)
- Amount of server space required
- Number of pages at the site
- Number of e-mail accounts
- Anticipated level of traffic to the site
- Level of customer support you need

Many Web hosting companies also offer domain name registration services. Some Web hosting companies that cater to personal or small business Web sites might offer free Web hosting in exchange for posting advertising banners on the site's pages.

Before selecting a Web hosting service provider, you should first identify the amount of server space and bandwidth required for your Web site, plus the number of e-mail accounts and the types of services you require. Next, you should evaluate a number of service providers to compare prices for those services that you require. Other important considerations in your evaluation include comparing the service providers' server types and the availability of server-side functions, such as the ASP.NET Framework for Web pages built using ASP.NET tools or FrontPage Server Extensions for existing FrontPage sites updated in Expression Web. Additionally, you should consider how each service provider handles customer support, server backup, and downtime, and whether disaster recovery plans and procedures are in place.

BTW

Server-Side Web Technologies
The ASP.NET Framework for Web pages is a set of Microsoft technologies used to create dynamic Web sites. FrontPage Server Extensions is an old Microsoft server-side technology required to enable certain features, such as dynamic content, in Web pages created using the Microsoft FrontPage Web page authoring software.

Finally, before publishing your site's files to a Web server, you should contact the network system administrator or technical support staff at your service provider (school, ISP, or Web hosting company) for specific instructions on how to upload your files, including the path to the server, your username, and your password.

To explore service providers that offer a variety of services and different levels of customer support, visit **scsite.com/ew3/websources** and click a link under Appendix C, Web Hosting Services.

Publishing Your Site Using Expression Web

Expression Web provides features that allow you to copy your Web site files to or from a variety of sources and destinations, such as a **temporary staging server**, a **live Web server**, a folder on your computer's hard drive, or a storage device on your local network. Copying or publishing your Web site files to a temporary staging server allows you to test your site before it goes "live." As noted earlier, publishing your tested Web site files to a live or production server makes the site accessible by visitors using a Web browser. Publishing your Web site files to a folder on your hard drive, to a removable storage device, or to a network storage device allows you to create a backup of your site's files.

Connection Settings

The first time you publish your Web site files using Expression Web, you must specify a publishing destination; for example, a remote Web server, including the connection type and location. To do this, open the site and click the Publishing command on the Site menu to open Publishing view. Then click the 'Add a publishing destination' link to open the Connection Settings dialog box.

The Connection Settings dialog box (Figure C–3) provides options for naming the site, selecting the server-supported technology to be used in publishing site files, specifying the destination location's Internet address including directory, and specifying the username and password necessary to log on to the server. The six server-supported technologies (connection types) are:

- **FTP (File Transfer Protocol)** — the most commonly used technology for transferring files over the Internet
- **SFTP (Secure or SSH File Transfer Protocol)** — a secure protocol for file transfer over the Internet
- **FTPS [FTP over Secure Sockets Layer (SSL)]** — a secure protocol for file transfer over the Internet
- **FrontPage Server Extensions** — server-side software that uses the HTTP or HTTPS protocol to transmit Web pages over the Internet and enables interactive Web page features for pages originally created using Microsoft FrontPage
- **WebDAV (Web-based Distributed Authoring and Versioning)** — an extension of the HTTP protocol that allows individuals within a workgroup to check in and check out Web site files for editing
- **File System** — a method of publishing between storage devices on the same computer or network

Figure C–3 illustrates the Connection Settings dialog box with the FTP option selected and a remote server as the destination location.

Figure C–3

After specifying the server type and location and setting any additional options in the Connection Settings dialog box, click Add to close the dialog box and view the open site's folders and files in Publishing view (Figure C–4).

Figure C–4

You can then publish your Web site files to the remote server by clicking the blue 'Publish files to the destination site' arrow. After your files are published, Publishing view shows both your local files and the files on the remote server, as shown in Figure C–5. While the site is publishing, the Publishing Status panel opens and shows the status of the upload.

Figure C–5

Publishing View

Publishing view allows you to see the local Web site folders and files in the view's left pane and the remote or published Web site files at the destination location in the view's right pane. You may be tempted to think of a local Web site as a site stored on your computer or network server, and the remote Web site as a site stored on a hosting company's or ISP's Web server. However, the terms *local Web site* and *remote Web site* refer only to the source and destination of the Web site files to be published and not the physical location of the storage devices involved.

The *local Web site* is always the Web site you opened in Expression Web, no matter where the site's files are physically stored; for example, the local Web site files might be physically located on your local computer's hard drive, a network storage device, a staging Web server, or a live Web server. The *remote Web site* is always the destination for the published files, which also might be a staging Web server, a live Web server, a folder on your hard drive, a network storage device, or a removable storage device.

For example, in the Publishing view shown in Figure C–6, the local Web site files and folders (the source) are stored on a computer's hard drive, and the remote Web site (the destination) is a CD in a CD drive on the same computer on which a backup copy of the Web site's files and folders is stored.

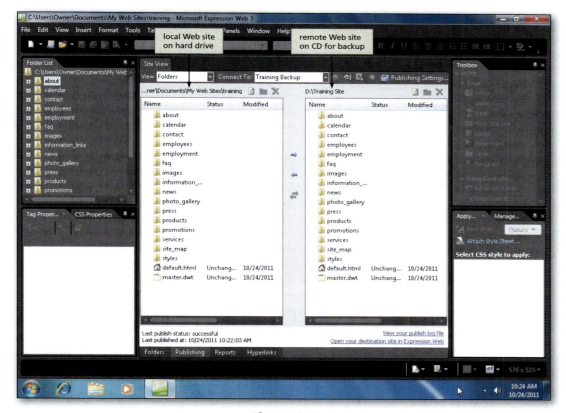

Figure C–6

You can choose to publish all files, selected files, or changed files by using drag and drop, using commands on the shortcut menu, or setting file publishing options using the View drop-down menu on the Site View tab. You can also synchronize local and remote files or exclude files from the publishing process using commands on the shortcut menu.

As you learned in the previous section, the File Transfer Protocol (FTP) is a commonly used technology for copying files from one location to another over the Internet. While FTP is a server type option in the Connection Settings dialog box, some Web developers might prefer to use FTP client software, rather than Expression Web, to publish their files.

Publishing Your Site Using FTP Client Software

Another convenient way to publish your Web site is to use an FTP client to copy the site's files from one location to another. **FTP client software** provides a familiar graphical user interface of menu commands and toolbar buttons to help you quickly publish your Web site's files using FTP. FTP client examples include CuteFTP (Figure C–7), FileZilla, and SmartFTP.

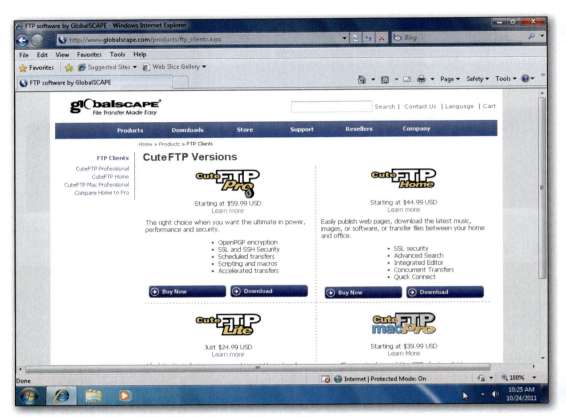

Figure C–7

Before using an FTP client to publish to a remote Web server, you must set up the location, username, and password to access the server using the FTP client's site manager feature. Then you open the remote Web site and view the local and remote Web sites' folders and files at the same time in side-by-side panes, as shown in Figure C–8. Figure C–8 illustrates a Web site's folders and files stored on a computer's hard drive and published to a remote Web server using CuteFTP client software. CuteFTP client software allows you to select and then copy one or more folders and files to or from the local and the remote Web sites using a menu command, a toolbar button, or drag and drop.

Figure C–8

Appendix D
Microsoft Expression Studio 3

Introduction

Microsoft Expression Studio 3 is a family of related software products — Expression Web 3, Expression Design 3, Expression Blend 3 plus SketchFlow, and Expression Encoder 3 — used by Web developers to create standards-compliant Web pages. In addition to creating Web pages, the Expression Studio products help developers import, create, and edit vector and bitmap graphics; create interactive Web-based applications; create user interface prototypes; and produce audio and video content for Web-based applications.

Expression Web

A **WYSIWYG (What You See Is What You Get) editor** is software that automatically inserts markup language tags as you work with the software's graphical interface, including menu commands, toolbar buttons, and task panes, to create and edit a Web page. **Expression Web**, which you learn about in the chapters of this text, is a WYSIWYG editor used by both novice and professional Web developers to create standards-compliant Web pages. Expression Web is the replacement software for Microsoft FrontPage, which is no longer supported by Microsoft.

Expression Web provides easy-to-use Web site and page templates for the beginner while also delivering more sophisticated tools required by Web development professionals, such as Cascading Style Sheets for layout and formatting, the SuperPreview feature that allows you to see how a page will look in different browsers and browser versions, and a feature for Web standards compliance testing.

Expression Design

Vector graphics are images created by drawing shapes and lines, while **raster graphics**, also called **bitmaps**, are images created one pixel at a time. An example of a vector graphic is a company logo created by combining different drawing shapes and lines. Examples of bitmaps include animated images and photographs.

Expression Design (Figure D–1) is software you can use to import, create, and edit vector graphics and bitmaps. Expression Design includes features that let you apply special effects to graphics, combine vector graphics with bitmaps, and convert bitmaps into vector graphics and vice versa. Expression Design also offers tools for exporting graphics into Expression Web and Expression Blend.

Figure D–1

Expression Blend

Expression Blend is software designed for professional developers who need to create graphical user interfaces (GUIs) for Windows desktop applications using the Microsoft .NET Framework platform.

Expression Blend can also be used to create GUIs for rich interactive applications using XAML (Extensible Application Markup Language) and the Microsoft Silverlight plug-in technologies. A **rich interactive application**, or **RIA**, is a Web-based application with multimedia content. Silverlight is a browser plug-in that works with different browsers and different operating systems to display the multimedia content included in RIAs. For more information on Silverlight, check out the Silverlight appendix.

Blend (Figure D–2) provides tools for professional developers to combine images, animation, video, audio, text, and controls, such as buttons, list boxes, and scroll bars, in creating rich content for desktop or Web-based applications. **SketchFlow** (Figure D–3), a feature of Expression Blend, is a set of tools a developer can use to mock-up a prototype for the user interface for an application or Web project in development, such as a series of interactive Web pages.

Figure D–2

Figure D–3

For more information about the Microsoft .NET Framework, XAML, Microsoft Silverlight, or SketchFlow, visit **scsite.com/ew3/websources** and click a link under Appendix D, Microsoft Platforms.

Expression Encoder

Encoding software is used to compress audio and video files and output the files in a specific audio or video format. **Expression Encoder** (Figure D–4) is encoding software designed specifically to work with Silverlight technologies.

A variety of audio and video file formats can be imported into Expression Encoder, including AVI, WMV, WMA, MPEG, and QuickTime files. The encoded files can be output as WMV or WMA files or encoded using a Silverlight output template. Expression Encoder also contains the Screen Capture feature that allows you to capture on-screen actions, Webcam video, and sound.

Figure D–4

For more information about the individual software products that make up Expression Studio, visit **scsite.com/ew3/websources** and click a link under Appendix D, Expression Studio 3.

Appendix E
Using Expression Web in Windows XP

The step-by-step instructions and illustrations in this text are based on Expression Web running on the Windows 7 operating system. If you are running Expression Web on the Windows XP operating system, your instructor might modify certain step-by-step instructions as necessary to perform tasks.

You also will see some variances between the desktop, the Windows taskbar and Start menu, the Expression Web window, and Expression Web dialog boxes on your screen with the illustrations in this text, including the:

- Default Windows color scheme and desktop background
- Size and color of the Minimize, Maximize, Restore Down, and Close buttons on the Expression Web title bar
- Program's title text color on the title bar
- Taskbar color and the Start button size and shape
- Start menu colors, arrangement, contents, and style
- Dialog box colors, boundary style, and, in some instances, dialog box content

This appendix illustrates examples of these differences by showing how to start Expression Web and then open and close an existing Web site.

To Start Expression Web

The following steps, which assume Windows XP is running, start Expression Web based on a typical installation. Your instructor might provide alternate instructions for starting Expression Web on your computer.

1
- Click the Start button on the Windows XP taskbar to display the Start menu.

- Point to All Programs on the Start menu to display the All Programs submenu.

- Point to Microsoft Expression on the All Programs submenu to display the Microsoft Expression Web 3 command (Figure E–1).

Figure E–1

2
- Click Microsoft Expression Web 3 to start Expression Web.

- If the Expression Web window is not maximized, click the Maximize button to the left of the Close button on the Expression Web title bar to maximize the window (Figure E–2).

Figure E–2

Other Ways

1. Double-click the Microsoft Expression Web 3 icon on the desktop, if one is present
2. Click Microsoft Expression Web 3 on the Start menu, if present

To Open an Existing Web Site

The following steps close the Untitled_1.html page, if necessary, and open the Boon Mountain Resort Web site data file from the USB flash drive where you save your data files. When you open a Web site, you will see two Open Site dialog boxes. The first Open Site dialog box allows you to select a site from a list of recently opened sites or key the path to a site. You can click the Browse button in this Open Site dialog box to open the second Open Site dialog box and use your computer's drive and folder structure to browse for a site. Your drive and folder information will likely differ from what is shown in the Open Site dialog box figures.

1

- Click File on the menu bar.

- Click Close to close the Untitled_1. html page (Figure E–3).

Figure E–3

2

- With your USB flash drive connected to one of the computer's USB ports, click Site on the menu bar.

- Point to Open Site on the Site menu (Figure E–4).

Figure E–4

- Click Open Site to display the first Open Site dialog box (Figure E–5).

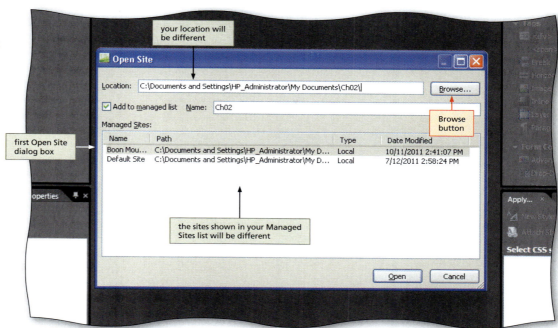

Figure E–5

4

- Click the Browse button to open the second Open Site dialog box and browse for the location of your data files.

- Click the Look in box arrow to view the list of available drives.

- Click the USB flash drive to select it and view its contents.

Q&A

How do I locate the site to open if I am not using a USB flash drive?

Use the same process, but select your device or network folder from the Look in list.

- Double-click the data file folder, if necessary, to open it.

- Click Boon Mountain Resort_final to select the site name (Figure E–6).

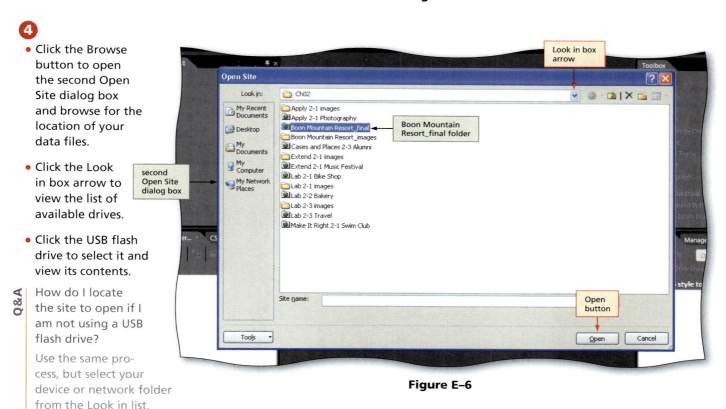

Figure E–6

5
- Click the Open button twice to close both dialog boxes. The site and all of its files and folders open in the Expression Web window (Figure E–7).

Figure E–7

To Close a Web Site

The following steps close the Boon Mountain Resort Web site and the Expression Web program.

1
- Click Site on the menu bar to open the Site menu.

- Point to Close to highlight the command (Figure E–8).

- Click the Close command to close the Boon Mountain Resort_final Web site.

- Click the Close button on the Expression Web title bar to close Expression Web.

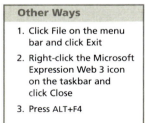

Other Ways

1. Click File on the menu bar and click Exit
2. Right-click the Microsoft Expression Web 3 icon on the taskbar and click Close
3. Press ALT+F4

Figure E–8

Using Expression Web in Windows Vista

The step-by-step instructions and illustrations in this text are based on Expression Web running in the Windows 7 operating system environment. If you are running Expression Web in the Windows Vista operating system environment, your instructor might modify certain step-by-step instructions as necessary to perform tasks.

You also will see some variances between the desktop, the Windows taskbar and Start menu, the Expression Web window, and Expression Web dialog boxes on your screen with the illustrations in this text, including the:

- Default Windows color scheme and desktop background
- Size, shape, and color of buttons on the taskbar
- Taskbar color and contents
- Start button size and shape
- Start menu colors, arrangement, contents, and style
- Dialog box colors, boundary style, and, in some instances, dialog box content

This appendix illustrates examples of these differences by showing how to start Expression Web and then open and close an existing Web site.

To Start Expression Web

The following steps, which assume Windows Vista is running, start Expression Web based on a typical installation. Your instructor might provide alternate instructions for starting Expression Web on your computer.

- Click the Start button on the Windows Vista taskbar to display the Start menu.

- Click All Programs on the Start menu to display the All Programs list.

- Click Microsoft Expression on the All Programs list to display the Microsoft Expression Web 3 command (Figure F–1).

Figure F–1

- Click Microsoft Expression Web 3 to start Expression Web.

- If the Expression Web window is not maximized, click the Maximize button to the left of the Close button on the Expression Web title bar to maximize the window (Figure F–2).

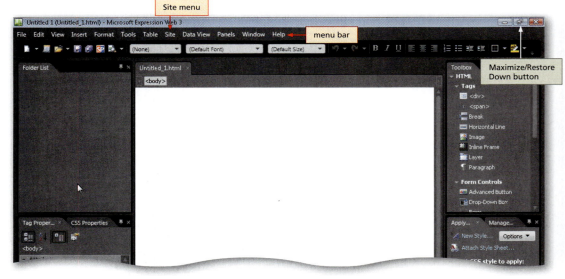

Figure F–2

Other Ways	
1. Double-click Expression Web icon on desktop, if present	2. Click Microsoft Expression Web 3 on Start menu, if present

To Open an Existing Web Site

The following steps close the Untitled_1.html page, if necessary, and open the Boon Mountain Resort Web site data file from the USB flash drive where you save your data files. Your drive and folder information will likely differ from what is shown in the figure.

1

- Click File on the menu bar (Figure F–3).

- Click Close to close the Untitled_1.html page.

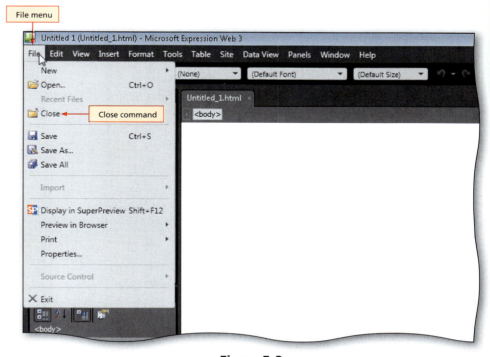

Figure F–3

2

- With your USB flash drive connected to one of the computer's USB ports, click Site on the menu bar (Figure F–4).

Figure F–4

3

- Click Open Site to display the Open Site dialog box.

- Click the Browse button to view the list of available drives.

- Click the Computer link in the Open Site dialog box to display the contents of the computer.

- Double-click the USB flash drive to select it and view its contents.

Q&A How do I locate the site to open if I am not using a USB flash drive?

Use the same process, but navigate to your desired location from the Computer folder window.

- Double-click the data file folder, if necessary, to open it.

- Click Boon Mountain Resort_final to select the site name (Figure F–5).

Figure F–5

4

- Click the Open button to display another Open Site dialog box.

- Click the Open button to open the site and all of its files and folders in the Microsoft Expression Web 3 window (Figure F–6).

Figure F–6

To Close a Web Site

The following steps close the Boon Mountain Resort Web site and the Expression Web program.

- Click Site on the menu bar to open the Site menu (Figure F–7).

- Click Close to close the Boon Mountain Resort_final Web site.

- Click the Close button on the Expression Web 3 title bar.

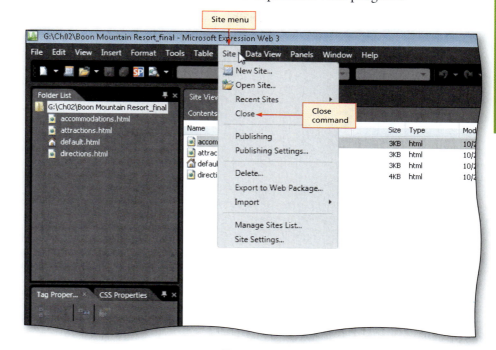

Figure F–7

Other Ways

1. Click File on menu bar, click Exit

2. Right-click Microsoft Expression Web 3 icon on taskbar, click Close

3. Press ALT+F4

Appendix G
Changing Screen Resolution

A **pixel** (short for picture element) is a single point of light on a computer screen. **Screen resolution** is a setting that determines the number of pixels necessary to display the program windows, pictures, text, and icons you see on your screen. Screen resolution usually is stated as the two numbers that represent the width and height of the pixels. For example, a screen with a 1024 × 768 screen resolution, the most common resolution used today, displays 1,024 pixels in width and 768 pixels in height; the screen illustrations in this book were created using the 1024 × 768 screen resolution. Other less common screen resolutions include the 800 × 600, 1152 × 720, 1280 × 768, and 1440 × 900 screen resolutions.

When you increase the screen resolution, you see more information on the screen, but the size of the information (text characters, toolbar buttons, dialog boxes, icons, pictures, and so forth) decreases; this might make the information more difficult to see for certain users. Alternatively, if you decrease the screen resolution, the size of the information increases, resulting in less visible area in which to view the information. Decreasing the screen resolution might, therefore, cause desktop icons to overlap or program toolbar buttons to be hidden.

Toolbars, buttons, and other elements can look different or appear in various locations in the program window when viewed at different screen resolutions. Variations in monitor shapes and sizes can also cause two screens set at the same resolution to look slightly different.

To Change the Screen Resolution

The following steps change your screen resolution to 1024 × 768 to match the illustrations in this text.

- Minimize all open windows so that the Windows 7 desktop appears.

- Right-click the Windows 7 desktop to display the Windows 7 desktop shortcut menu (Figure G–1). Your shortcut menu might have additional commands.

Figure G–1

- Click the Screen resolution command on the shortcut menu to open the Screen Resolution window (Figure G–2).

Figure G–2

3

- Click the Resolution button and drag the slider in the Resolution pane to the 1024 × 768 position (Figure G–3).

- Press the ESC key to close the Resolution pane.

Figure G–3

4

- Click OK to open the Display Settings dialog box (Figure G–4).

- Click Keep changes to change the resolution to 1024 × 768.

- Click the Close button on the title bar to close the Screen Resolution window.

Figure G–4

Index

Note: **Boldface** entries include definitions.

2Checkout.com, EW 436

A

about_artist file, EW 277
accessibility, EW 320, EW 398
Accessibility Checker, APP 14
accessibility properties, EW 75–76
Accessibility Properties dialog box, EW 306, EW 327, EW 332, EW 400, EW 406
accredited registrar, **APP 15**
Add Choice dialog box, EW 393, EW 394
advertising business model, EW 424
aligning images, EW 94
alignment, **EW 233**
all-in-one e-commerce solution, **EW 437–438**
alternate text, **EW 75–76**, EW 236
alternative fonts, EW 262
Amazon.com Web site, EW 425
animated GIFs or images, EW 236
Apple Safari, EW 54
Apply Styles panel, EW 31, EW 84, EW 195, EW 249, EW 252, EW 254, EW 256
artist.html page
  adding content and link to, EW 276–280
  attaching multiple style sheets, EW 280–282
  attaching style sheets, EW 274–276
  links, EW 283–284
artist_image style, EW 254, EW 256
artist_styles.css file, EW 273
aspect ratio, **EW 89**
ASP.NET Framework for Web pages, APP 17
assistive technology, EW 320
asymmetric arrangement, EW 232
Attach Style Sheet dialog box, EW 280–281, EW 313–315
attached, **EW 242**
audio, EW 236
audio files, compressing, APP 27
AutoFormat, EW 340, EW 346–348
AutoFormat dialog box, EW 347–348
avatars, EW 236
AVI file format, APP 27

B

B2B (business-to-business) e-commerce business models, **EW 425–426**
B2C (business-to-consumer) e-commerce business models, **EW 425**
B2C e-commerce sites, EW 425
B2E (business-to-employee) e-commerce, **EW 428**
B2G (business-to-government) e-commerce business models, **EW 427**
B2GMARKET Web site, EW 427
Back button, **APP 4**
back office operations, **EW 429**
background colors, EW 228, EW 230
background images and tables, EW 316
backing up Web site files, APP 18
BACKSPACE key, editing text with, EW 183
balance, **EW 232**
behaviors, **EW 368**
  defining, EW 390
  improving site visitors' experiences, EW 370
Behaviors panel, EW 392
Bidmain Web site, EW 427
bills of lading, EW 426
bitmaps, **APP 24**, EW 236
BlueHost, APP 16
bookmarks, **EW 120**, EW 134–136
borders, **EW 95–96**
box-like divs, EW 154
breadcrumb trail, **EW 224**, EW 226
Browse dialog box, EW 401
browsers, **EW 48**
  ActiveX content restricted, EW 378
  automatically blocking interactive sites, EW 372–373
  bookmarks, EW 120
  CSS (Cascading Style Sheets), EW 194
  interactivity, EW 372–373
  previewing in, EW 54–55, EW 203
  security, EW 372–373
  unable to *see* status bar, EW 398
bulleted list, **EW 25–27**
business documents, exchange of, EW 426
business models, **EW 424**

business-to-business. *See* B2B (business to business) e-commerce business models
business-to-consumer. *See* B2C (business-to-consumer) e-commerce business models
business-to-employee e-commerce. *See* B2E (business-to-employee) e-commerce
business-to-government. *See* B2G (business-to-government) e-commerce business models
button file names, EW 379
buttons
  image files for each state, EW 372
  organizing images into folders, EW 387–390

C

C2B (consumer-to-business) e-commerce business models, **EW 427**
C2C (consumer-to-consumer) e-commerce business models, **EW 426**
Call Script behavior, EW 390
captions, **EW 316**, EW 317–319, EW 336
card not present/card holder not present risk, **EW 434**
cascading, **EW 193**
Cascading Style Sheets. *See* CSS (Cascading Style Sheets)
CCNow, EW 436
cells, **EW 302**, EW 316, EW 337
  combining, EW 304
  content on two lines, EW 323
  entering text, EW 323–326
  images, EW 326–329
  line breaks, EW 323
  margins, EW 320
  merging, **EW 336–337**
  properties, EW 319–322
  splitting, **EW 336**, EW 338–339
centering text, EW 36
Change Property/Restore behavior, EW 390
chargebacks, **EW 433–434**, EW 436
Check Browser behavior, EW 390
Check Plug-in behavior, EW 390
checkout process, **EW 430**
Cisco Web site, EW 426

class-based style
  positioning content, EW 254–256
  rules, **EW 245**, EW 246
class of element, EW 244
clickable hot spot, EW 226
Clipboard, **EW 103**
closing
  Expression Web, EW 57–58
  panels, EW 84, EW 85–87
Code view, **EW 48**, EW 49–51
  modifying Web pages, EW 266–268
code, viewing and entering, EW 2
color schemes, EW 227–230
colors
  background, EW 228, EW 230
  fonts, EW 37–38, EW 228
  foreground, EW 230
  images, EW 236
  links, EW 226
  storing information, EW 246
  Web-safe palette, EW 230
columns, **EW 302**, EW 316,
    EW 317–319
  adding, EW 329–333
  deleting, EW 304
  distributing, **EW 345**
  filling, EW 333–336
  selecting, EW 320, EW 334
  width, EW 320, EW 323
commands
  Help topics, APP 4
  toggle, EW 52
Common toolbar, **EW 7**, EW 8
compressing, **EW 75**
  audio or video files, APP 27
compression, lossy or lossless, **EW 75**
Confirm Rename dialog box, EW 388,
    EW 389
connection settings, APP 18–20
Connection Settings dialog box,
    APP 18–19, APP 21
consumer-to-business. *See* C2B
    (consumer-to-business)
    e-commerce business models
consumer-to-consumer. *See* C2C
    (consumer-to-consumer)
    e-commerce business models
contact information, EW 435
content, positioning, EW 254–256
content elements, EW 230–233
Convert Text to Table dialog box,
    EW 343
Cooking.com Web site, EW 430
copying
  elements, EW 274–276

images, EW 103–105
  internal links, EW 127–129
credit card fraud, EW 436
cropped images, **EW 106–111**
cropping handles, EW 106
CSS (Cascading Style Sheets), APP 12,
    EW 2, EW 193, **EW 242**
  browsers and, EW 194
  formatting Web sites, EW 244
  positioning elements, EW 254–256
  syntax, EW 244–245
  tables, EW 316
  text styles in tables, EW 340–341
  user-defined style sheets, EW 260
  versions, EW 194
  viewing and modifying code, EW 2
CSS code, entering, EW 265
.css extension, EW 260, EW 261
CSS files, comments in, EW 265
CSS layouts, pre-built, EW 271–274
CSS Properties panel, EW 256–259
CSS reports, EW 244
  creation, EW 286–287
CSS Reports dialog box, EW 287
CSS rules, EW 244
  prioritizing, EW 246
cursive (or script) fonts, EW 262
customer support, EW 435
CuteFTP, APP 22

D

Dairy.com Web site, EW 426
data tables, **EW 302**
  creation, **EW 316–322**
  inserting, EW 317–319
  width, EW 320
declaration, **EW 194**
default
  browser, EW 54
  fonts, EW 262
default.html page, EW 280, EW 371,
    EW 382, EW 384–385, EW 391,
    EW 396–397
  creation, EW 305–309
  formatting table on, EW 347–348
  links, EW 283–284
default toolbar, EW 8
DELETE key, editing text with, EW 183
delineated, **EW 342**
Dell, EW 428
design basics, EW 217, EW 237
  alignment, **EW 233**
  balance, **EW 232**
  color schemes, EW 227, EW 228–230

content positioning, EW 230–231
focal point, **EW 233**
guidelines for links, EW 226
multimedia, EW 236
navigation system, **EW 224–226**
page layout, EW 227
page length, EW 230–231
proximity, **EW 233**
target audience, EW 218, **EW 220**
text, EW 234–235
Web page types, EW 220
Web-ready images, EW 236
Web site purpose, EW 218, EW 219
Web site structure, EW 218,
    EW 222–223
design interface, EW 2
Design view, EW 2, **EW 48**
desktop applications and rich content,
    APP 25
dialog boxes, EW 2
direct formatting, EW 246
directions.html page, EW 384–386
discount rate, **EW 433**
distribute, **EW 345**
division-based layout, **EW 20**
divs (<div> tag), **EW 20–22**
  box-like, EW 154
  CSS layout, EW 271–274
  nesting, EW 154
div#top_nav visual aid, EW 385,
    EW 386
DNS (Domain Name System), APP 16
docking panels, EW 84
documents, extra line breaks in,
    EW 177
domain name, **APP 15–16**
Domain Name System (DNS), APP 16
downloading Web pages faster, EW 20
drop ship, **EW 434–435**
dynamic Web sites, APP 17
dynamic Web templates, **EW 152**
  creation, EW 189–193
  interactive buttons, EW 372

E

eBay Web site, EW 426
e-business, **EW 424**
e-commerce, **EW 424**
  adding capability to Web site,
    EW 436–438
  Web site elements, EW 429
e-commerce business models, **EW 424**
  B2B (business-to-business),
    EW 425–426

B2C (business-to-consumer),
    EW 425, **EW 425**
B2E (business-to-employee), **EW 428**
B2G (business-to-government),
    EW 427
C2B (consumer-to-business), **EW 427**
C2C (consumer-to-consumer), **EW 426**
e-commerce Web sites, EW 429
  card not present/card holder not
    present risk, **EW 434**
  chargebacks, **EW 433–434**, EW 436
  communication between buyer and
    seller, EW 435
  contact information, EW 435
  credit card fraud, EW 436
  credit card payments, EW 432–434
  customer support, EW 435
  discount rate, **EW 433**
  drop ship, **EW 434–435**
  FAQs (Frequently Asked Questions)
    page, EW 435
  fulfillment house, **EW 434–435**
  hackers, EW 435–436
  hosting, EW 438
  merchant accounts, **EW 433**
  order fulfillment, **EW 434–435**
  payment gateways, EW 435
  payment processors, **EW 432**
  third-party logistics provider,
    EW 434–435
  transaction security, EW 435
  virtual inventory, **EW 434–435**
EDI (electronic data interchange)
    systems, EW 424
Edit Hyperlink dialog box, EW 375,
    EW 381–382, EW 393–394
editable regions, **EW 172**
editing
  master page information, EW 189
  text, EW 182–189
editing window, **EW 8**
EFT (electronic funds transfer)
    systems, EW 424
electronic commerce, **EW 424**
electronic data interchange systems.
    See EDI (electronic data
    interchange) systems
electronic funds transfer systems. See
    EFT (electronic funds transfer)
    systems
element-based style rules, **EW 245**
  multiple selectors, EW 266
elements
  copying, EW 274–276, EW 370,
    EW 378

  interactive, EW 368
  pasting, EW 274–276
  restoring to original state, EW 390
  reusing, EW 370, EW 378
  style rules, EW 259
  styles, EW 242
e-mail links, EW 120
  forms vs., EW 136
embedded, **EW 74**
embedded style sheets, EW 244
encoding software, **APP 27**
enhancing images, **EW 98–111**
entry page, **EW 222**
events, behaviors of, EW 390
events.html page, EW 384–386
Expedia Web site, EW 425
Expression Blend, **APP 25–27**
Expression Design, **APP 24**
Expression Encoder, **APP 27**
Expression Web, **APP 24**
  closing, EW 57–58
  connection settings, APP 18–20
  editing window, EW 6
  Publishing view, **APP 20–21**
  publishing Web sites, APP 18–21
  quitting, EW 58, EW 204
  starting, EW 5–6, EW 77, EW 156,
    EW 246
  Windows Vista, APP 33–37
  Windows XP, APP 28–32
  workspace, EW 7–9
Expression Web Help, EW 43,
    EW 193
Expression Web 3 Quick Reference
    Web page, EW 38, EW 390
Expression Web templates, EW 227.
    See also templates
Expression Web User Guide,
    EW 373
Extensible Application Markup
    Language (XAML), APP 25,
    APP 27
Extensible Hypertext Markup
    Language (XHTML), **EW 48**
Extensible Stylesheet Language.
    See XSL (Extensible Stylesheet
    Language)
external links, **EW 120**
  adding, EW 129–132
  testing, EW 132–133
external style sheets, **EW 194**, EW 244
  creation, EW 260–261
external styles, EW 194
extra line breaks, EW 177
extranets, **EW 424**, EW 426

F
fantasy fonts, EW 262
file extensions, EW 5
file formats, **EW 75**
File System, **APP 18**
File Transfer Protocol (FTP), **APP 18**,
    APP 21
files
  choosing types, EW 74
  closing, EW 182
  file naming conventions, EW 5
  folder structure and location, EW 5
  naming, EW 10
  order of, EW 284
FileZilla, APP 22
filling columns or rows,
    EW 333–336
Find and Replace tools, EW 183
finding and replacing text,
    EW 186–189
finding Help topics, APP 4
Flash movies, EW 236
flowchart of site structure, EW 223
focal point, **EW 233**
Folder List, EW 385
Folder List panel, EW 84, EW 167
folders, EW 284–286
  adding, EW 167–168
  deleting, EW 166
  images, EW 116–120, EW 160
  naming, EW 10
  organizing button images,
    EW 387–390
  renaming, EW 161–162
  subfolders, EW 160
  templates, EW 160
Folders view, EW 8
font families, EW 43, **EW 262**
  availability, EW 265
  creation, EW 262–265
fonts, EW 235
  alternative, EW 262
  changing, EW 44–45
  characteristics, EW 36
  choosing, EW 43
  color, EW 37–38, EW 228
  cursive (or script), EW 262
  default, EW 262
  fantasy, EW 262
  generic sans-serif, EW 262
  interactive buttons, EW 372
  monospace, **EW 262**
  mood of site, EW 36
  previewing, EW 263

resizing, EW 38–40
sans serif, **EW 262**
serif, EW 235, **EW 262**
unavailable, EW 264
Web-safe, EW 262
font styles, EW 262
foreground colors, EW 230
formatting, EW 244
applying, **EW 30–32**
defining with styles, EW 246
direct, EW 246
individual HTML pages, EW 259
Quick Tag Selector, EW 31–32
removing, EW 177
separating Web page content from, EW 193
table text, EW 340–341
Web pages, EW 5
Web sites, EW 244
forms *vs.* e-mail links, EW 136
frames, EW 233, EW 354
framesets, **EW 354**
Frequently Asked Questions. *See* FAQs (Frequently Asked Questions) page
FrontPage, APP 24
FrontPage Server Extensions, APP 17, **APP 18**
FTP client software, **APP 22–23**
FTP (File Transfer Protocol), **APP 18**, APP 21
FTPS [FTP over Secure Sockets Layer (SSL)], **APP 18**
fulfillment house, **EW 434–435**

G

gadgets, EW 236
galisteo_styles.css style sheet, EW 254, EW 280, EW 282
generic sans-serif font type, EW 262
.gif (Graphics Interchange Format) file format, EW 75
global changes to templates, EW 190–193
Go To URL behavior, EW 390
GoDaddy, APP 15
Google Checkout, EW 431
Google Chrome, EW 54
graphic link, text equivalent for, EW 226
graphical user interfaces (GUIs), APP 25
graphics, **EW 72**. *See also* images
resizing, EW 405
grouping styles, EW 260
Guru.com Web site, EW 426

H

hackers, EW 435–436
headers, **EW 320–322**
heading styles, **EW 30**, EW 33–35
Help topics
alphabetic index by keyword, APP 6–8
browsing by category, APP 4–6
commands, APP 4
finding, APP 4
printing, APP 4
revisiting, APP 4
searching for specific, APP 8–9
hidden navigational elements, EW 226
Hide button, **APP 4**
hierarchical structure, **EW 223**
high resolution (high res), **EW 74**
home page, **EW 10**, EW 220
masthead, **EW 20**
navigation area, **EW 20**
opening, EW 14
Who?, What?, and Where? questions, EW 220
Home Page link, EW 226
hosting e-commerce Web sites, EW 438
hotspots, **EW 368**, EW 405
hover image, EW 383
hovering state, EW 373
.htm (<.html>) file extension, EW 5, EW 162
HTML 4.01, APP 12
HTML files
creating and editing, EW 2
embedding HTML files in, EW 348
file extensions, EW 5
HTML (Hypertext Markup Language), **EW 48**
HTML tags, **EW 48**
HTML/XHTML editor, EW 2
HTTP (Hypertext Transfer Protocol) standard, APP 11
hyperlinks (links), **EW 72**. *See also* links
Hyperlinks view, EW 8
Hypertext Markup Language (HTML), **EW 48**

I

icons and style sheets, EW 269
ID-based style rules, **EW 245**, EW 246
ID-based styles, EW 271
defining, EW 249–253
ID selector, EW 244
IEEE 802.20 standard, APP 11

I-frames (inline frames), **EW 302**, EW 304, EW 348
creation, EW 349–351
displaying Web page from, EW 349
embedding stylist_table.html file, EW 352–353
increasing height, EW 351
placement, EW 349
security, EW 348
target links in, EW 352–353
image creation and editing software, EW 236
image files
controlling, EW 111–120
interactive buttons, EW 387
pixels, **EW 74**
technical considerations for, EW 74–75
thumbnails, **EW 111–116**
image links, **EW 224**
image maps, EW 226, **EW 368**, EW 370, EW 405–410
hotspots, **EW 368**, EW 405
images, **EW 72**
aligning, EW 94
alternate text, EW 236
animated, EW 236
aspect ratio, **EW 89**
borders, **EW 95–96**
cells, EW 326–329
choosing, EW 74
colors, EW 236
copying, EW 103–105
cropped, **EW 106–111**
embedded, **EW 74**
enhancing, **EW 98–111**
file formats, **EW 75**
file sizes, EW 74
folders, EW 116–120, EW 160
from external devices, EW 75
high resolution (high res), **EW 74**
inserting, EW 76, EW 80–83
low resolution (low res), EW 74
margins, **EW 95**, EW 97–98
padding, **EW 95**
pixilated, **EW 74**
poorly chosen, EW 236
positioning, EW 87, EW 93–94
proportions, **EW 89**
resample, **EW 89**
resizing, EW 89–93
resolution, **EW 74**
sizing, EW 87
sloppily edited, EW 236
sources, EW 74

tables, EW 326–329
templates, EW 154
text wrapping, **EW 93**
transparency, EW 99–103
Web-ready, EW 236
wrapping text around, EW 76, EW 94
inactive state, EW 373
indenting text, **EW 41**
inheritance, **EW 245**
inline frames. *See* I-frames
    (inline frames)
inline styles, **EW 194**, EW 244
Insert Hyperlink dialog box,
    EW 283–284, EW 352, EW 408
Insert menu, EW 392
Insert Table dialog box, EW 317
IntelliSense, **EW 265**
IntelliSense shortcut menus, EW 266
interactive buttons, **EW 368**, EW 370,
    EW 372
  creation, EW 373–378
  duplicating, EW 379
  editing, EW 379–382
  fonts, EW 372
  hovering state, EW 373
  image files, EW 387
  inactive state, EW 373
  organizing, EW 379–382
  placement on page, EW 378
  pressing state, EW 373
  testing, EW 382–384
Interactive Buttons dialog box,
    EW 372–377, EW 380–381
interactive contents, EW 383
interactive elements, EW 368
interactive games, EW 236
interactive navigation bar, EW 372
interactive tools, EW 368
interactivity, **EW 368**
  preloading Web pages, EW 372
  Web browsers, EW 372–373
  Web sites, EW 370
internal links
  adding, EW 121–125
  copying and pasting, EW 127–129
  testing, EW 125–127
internal style sheets, **EW 194**, EW 244
internal styles, EW 194
Internet, EW 424
Internet connection speed, EW 111
Internet Explorer, previewing Web
    sites, EW 54–55
intranets, **EW 424**, EW 428
ISP (Internet service provider),
    APP 16

italicizing text, **EW 42–43**
i365 Web site, EW 426

J

JavaScript, **EW 368**
.jpg (Joint Photographic Experts Group)
    file format, EW 75
Jump Menu command, EW 392
Jump Menu dialog box, EW 393,
    EW 395
Jump Menu/Go behavior, EW 390
jump menus, **EW 368**, EW 370
  creation and behaviors, EW 391–396

K

keyboards, editing text, EW 183–186
keywords, **EW 15**

L

layout, EW 5, EW 244
  defining with styles, EW 246
layout frames, EW 354
layout tables, EW 233, **EW 354**
Layout Tables panel, EW 354
line breaks, EW 183, EW 323
  cells, EW 323
  removing extra, EW 177
linear structure, **EW 222**
  Next page or Previous Page links,
    EW 226
links, **EW 72**, EW 276–280,
    EW 283–284
  checking, EW 288–289
  guidelines for positioning and
    creating, EW 226
live Web server, **APP 18**
local Web sites, APP 20
logos and transparency, EW 99–103
lossless compression, **EW 75**
lossy compression, **EW 75**
low resolution (low res), EW 74

M

mailto links, **EW 120**
main image, EW 254
Manage Styles panel, EW 195
margins
  cells, EW 320–322
  defining, EW 254
  images, **EW 95**
  modifying, EW 97–98

positioning, EW 87
  sizing, EW 87
master page, editing information on,
    EW 189
masthead, **EW 20**
maximizing panels, EW 84
menu bar, **EW 7**
menus, EW 226
merchant accounts, **EW 433**,
    EW 436, EW 437
merging cells, **EW 336–337**
metadata, EW 160
Microsoft Expression Community
    Web site, APP 3
Microsoft Expression Studio 3, **EW 2**
  Expression Blend, **APP 25–27**
  Expression Design, **APP 24**
  Expression Encoder, **APP 27**
  Expression Web, **APP 24**
Microsoft Expression Web 3, **EW 2**.
    See also Expression Web
Microsoft Expression Web User
    Guide, APP 1–10
Microsoft Expression Web User Guide
    window, **APP 1–3**
Microsoft FrontPage, APP 24
Microsoft .NET Framework, APP 25,
    APP 27
Microsoft Office Live Small Business,
    APP 16, EW 438
Microsoft Silverlight, APP 25, APP 27
minimizing panels, EW 84
Modify Style dialog box, EW 249,
    EW 251, EW 252–253
monospace fonts, **EW 262**
mouse, selecting text with,
    EW 183–186
Mozilla Firefox, EW 54
MPEG file format, APP 27
multimedia, EW 236
MyFoodDiary Web site, EW 425

N

naming styles, EW 198
navigation area, **EW 20**
navigation bar, EW 120, **EW 224**,
    EW 226
  changing style, EW 195–197
  copying and pasting, EW 385–386
  interactive, EW 372
  primary and secondary, EW 370
  small caps, EW 256–259
  space at top, EW 256–259
  text-based hyperlinks, EW 372

updating, EW 163
  Web pages with no links on, EW 370
navigation_buttons folder, EW 388,
    EW 389
navigation div, selecting entire, EW 385
Navigation menu, **EW 224**
navigation system, **EW 224–226**
navigation tabs, **EW 224**
navigational elements, EW 226
navigational links, EW 120–140
  bookmarks, **EW 120**, EW 134–136
  e-mail links, EW 137–138
  external links, **EW 120**, EW 129–133
  internal links, EW 121–129
  mailto links, **EW 120**
nested tables, EW 309
nesting divs (<div> tag), EW 154
Network Solutions, APP 15, EW 438
New dialog box, EW 271–272,
    EW 305–306, EW 354
New Site Location dialog box,
    EW 306
New Style dialog box, EW 254–256,
    EW 259, EW 260
Next Page link, EW 226

O

Office Depot, EW 428
online businesses and B2C
    (business-to-consumer), **EW 425**
onmouseout event, EW 402
onmouseover event, EW 403
on-screen actions, capturing, APP 27
Open Browser Window behavior,
    EW 390
Open dialog box, EW 277
Open Site dialog box, EW 371
Opera, EW 54
Options button, **APP 4**
order fulfillment, **EW 434–435**

P

padding, **EW 95**
page description, **EW 15**
page layout, EW 227
page length, EW 230–231
page_styles.css style sheet, EW 261,
    EW 266, EW 268–270, EW 280
page templates, EW 155
page title, **EW 15**
panels, EW 2, **EW 8**, EW 84
  closing, EW 85–87
  rearranging, EW 9

paragraph (<p>) tag, EW 23–25
  containing image, EW 76
paragraphs, inserting text,
    EW 183–186
Paste Text dialog box, EW 279
pasting
  elements, EW 274–276
  internal links, EW 127–129
  text, EW 177–182
payment gateways, **EW 432**,
    EW 435–438
payment processors, **EW 432**,
    EW 436–437
PayPal Express Checkout, EW 431
PayPal Website Payments Standard,
    EW 436
personal information, securing, EW 152
photographs and lossless compression,
    EW 75
Picture dialog box, EW 306, EW 332,
    EW 399, EW 406
Picture Properties dialog box,
    EW 328, EW 332
Pictures toolbar, EW 407
pixels, **APP 38**, **EW 74**
pixilated, **EW 74**
placeholders, **EW 76**
  replacing text, EW 172–176
  templates, EW 156–159
planning Web sites, EW 2
Play Sound behavior, EW 390
Popup Message behavior, EW 390
portfolios, **EW 152**
positioning
  content, EW 254–256
  images, EW 93–94
.png (Portable Network Graphics) file
    format, EW 75
pre- and post-publishing testing, EW 237
pre-built CSS layouts, EW 271–274
preformatted style sheets, EW 309–316
Preload Images behavior, EW 390
pressing state, EW 373
Prestogeorge Web site, EW 425
Preview box, blank, EW 250
previewing
  in browsers, EW 54–55
  fonts, EW 263
  Web sites, EW 54–55, EW 139–140,
    EW 203, EW 288–289
Previous Page link, EW 226
Priceline.com Web site, EW 427
primary goal, **EW 219**
primary navigation bar, EW 370
Print button, **APP 4**

Print Preview feature, EW 56
Print Topics dialog box, APP 4
printing
  Help topics, APP 4
  Web pages, EW 55–56
product catalog, **EW 429**, EW 438
programs, quitting, EW 182
project planning guidelines, EW 2
properties
  accessibility, EW 75–76
  cells, EW 319–322
  CSS rules, EW 244
  styles, **EW 194**
  tables, EW 319–322
  Web pages, EW 14–20
proportions, **EW 89**
proximity, **EW 233**
publishing destination, APP 18
Publishing Status panel, APP 20
Publishing view, **APP 20–21**,
    EW 8
publishing Web sites, **APP 15–18**,
    EW 54
  connection settings, APP 18–20
  Expression Web, APP 18–21
  FTP client software, **APP 22–23**
  local Web site, APP 20
  Publishing view, **APP 20–21**
  remote Web site, APP 20
purchase orders, EW 426

Q

Quick Reference Summary, EW 38,
    EW 390
Quick Tag Selector, **EW 8**, EW 52,
    EW 340
  formatting, EW 31–32
Quick tags, **EW 52**
QuickTime file format, APP 27
quitting Expression Web, EW 58,
    EW 204

R

Rackspace, APP 16
raster graphics, **APP 24**
receiving reports, EW 426
Register.com, APP 15
registering domain name,
    APP 15–16
Rehabilitation Act of 1973, Section
    508, **APP 13**
remote Web sites, APP 20
removing formatting, EW 177

renaming
  folders, EW 161–162
  Web pages, EW 161, EW 162–163
replacing text. *See* finding and
    replacing text
Reports view, EW 8
requests for quotes. *See* RFQs
    (requests for quotes)
resample, **EW 89**
resizing
  fonts, EW 38–40
  images, EW 89–93
resolution, **EW 74**, EW 231
restore behavior, EW 398, EW 402
Restore command, EW 390
RFQs (requests for quotes), EW 426
RIA (rich interactive application),
    APP 25
rich interactive application (RIA),
    APP 25
rollover buttons, **EW 368**
rollover links, EW 226
rows, **EW 302**, EW 316, EW 317–319
  adding, EW 329–333
  deleting, EW 304
  distributing, EW 345–346
  filling, EW 333–336
  height, EW 320
  selecting, EW 320
rulers, displaying, EW 87–88

S

SAM and current information, EW 204
sans serif fonts, EW 235, **EW 262**
Save As dialog box, EW 273
Save Embedded Files dialog box,
    EW 377
saving
  Web pages, EW 30
  Web sites, EW 10
screen resolution, **APP 38–40**, EW 231
ScreenTips
  adding, EW 138–139
  viewing and testing, EW 139–140
scsite.com/ew3/websources Web site,
    APP 12, APP 14, APP 16, APP 18,
    APP 27, EW 230–231,
    EW 235–237, EW 424, EW 428,
    EW 434–437
search boxes, EW 120
search engines, **EW 15**
secondary goals, **EW 219**
secondary navigation bar, EW 370
secondary navigation element, EW 370

Secure or SSH File Transfer Protocol
    (SFTP), **APP 18**
security
  I-frames (inline frames), EW 348
  personal information, EW 152
  Web browsers, EW 372–373
Select Style Sheet dialog box,
    EW 315–316
selectors, **EW 194**, EW 244
serif fonts, **EW 235**, **EW 262**
server-side technology, APP 17
Set Text behavior, EW 390
Set Text of Status Bar dialog box,
    EW 397
SFTP (Secure or SSH File Transfer
    Protocol), **APP 18**
Shipwire Web site, EW 434
shopping cart, **EW 430–431**,
    EW 436–438
Show button, APP 4
site map, **EW 224**
site navigation, **EW 368**, EW 370
site search feature, **EW 224**
site templates, EW 155
Site View tab, APP 21, EW 8
SketchFlow, **APP 25**, APP 27
small caps, EW 256–259
SmartFTP, APP 22
Snapshot panel, EW 51
Snapshot view, **EW 48**, EW 51,
    EW 54
sound, capturing, APP 27
specificity, **EW 193**
spell checker, **EW 45–47**
splash page, **EW 222**
Split Cells dialog box, EW 338
Split view, **EW 48**, EW 49–51
splitting cells, **EW 336**
standard elements, EW 154
standards, **APP 11**
standards-compliant Web pages,
    APP 12
status bar, **EW 8**
  unable to see, EW 398
status bar behavior, **EW 396–398**
store.html page, EW 383,
    EW 385–386, EW 399, EW 404,
    EW 408
store_pages folder, EW 393, EW 408
striping, **EW 340**
structure, **EW 222–223**
structure of Web sites, EW 160
  adding folders, EW 167–168
  adding Web pages, EW 169–171
  deleting folders, EW 166

deleting Web pages, EW 164–165
modifying, EW 163–171
updating navigation bar, EW 163
StubHub! Web site, EW 426
style rules, EW 280
  class-based, **EW 245**
  element-based, **EW 245**
  elements, EW 259
  ID-based, **EW 245**
  prioritizing, EW 246
  selectors, EW 244
  semicolons (;) separating, EW 194
style sheets, **EW 193**, **EW 242**,
    EW 244
  attaching, **EW 242**, EW 259,
    EW 268–270, EW 274–276,
    EW 315–316
  cascading style sheet (CSS), EW 193
  creation, EW 259, EW 310–314
  defining, EW 193
  embedding, EW 244
  entering code, EW 259, EW 265
  evaluating, EW 244, EW 286
  external, **EW 194**, EW 244
  grouping styles, EW 260
  icons, EW 269
  ID-based styles, EW 271
  internal, **EW 194**, EW 244
  multiple, EW 280–282
  number of, EW 260
  organizing, EW 260, EW 284–286
  preformatted, EW 309–316
  separating content from formatting,
    EW 193
  style creations, EW 198–201
  tables, EW 304
  types, EW 194
  user-defined, EW 260
style templates, EW 155
styles, EW 30, EW 242
  applying, EW 201–202
  conflicts, EW 194
  consistency, EW 193
  creation, EW 31, EW 198–201
  declaration, **EW 194**
  defining, EW 193
  defining formatting and layout,
    EW 244
  external, EW 194
  grouping, EW 260
  headings, **EW 30**, EW 33–35
  inline, **EW 194**, EW 244
  internal, EW 194
  modifying, EW 195–197,
    EW 256–259

naming, EW 198
prioritizing, EW 193, EW 260
property, **EW 194**
punctuation, EW 194
purpose of, EW 244
saving, EW 244
selectors, **EW 194**
storing rules, EW 242
subheading, EW 30
syntax, **EW 194**
tables, EW 340–341
text, EW 340–341
value, **EW 194**
Styles panel, EW 256
stylist_table.html file, EW 316,
   EW 333, EW 341
  embedding in I-frame (inline frames),
   EW 352
subfolders, EW 160
subheading styles, EW 30
subscription business model, EW 424
subsidiary pages, **EW 221**
swap image behavior, **EW 398**
 adding, EW 399–402
 initiating, EW 404
 modifying, EW 402–403
swap_image1.gif file, EW 400, EW 402
Swap Image/Restore behavior, EW 390
Swap Image Restore dialog box,
   EW 398, EW 402–403
swap images, EW 398, EW 402
Swap Images dialog box, EW 401
switching views, EW 48–51
symmetric arrangement, EW 232
syntax, **EW 194**

T

Table AutoFormat, **EW 346–348**
Table Fill command, **EW 333–336**
Table menu, EW 329
Table Properties dialog box, EW 316,
   EW 320–322, EW 345
<table> tag, EW 316
tables, EW 302, EW 354
 adding to Web page, EW 304
 background image, EW 316
 borders, EW 318
 captions, **EW 316**, EW 317–319,
   EW 336, EW 353
 cells, EW 304, EW 316–317
 columns, EW 316, EW 317–319,
   EW 329–333
 content, EW 304, EW 323
 converting text to, EW 342–344

creation, EW 316–322
 CSS text styles, EW 340–341
 default settings, EW 316
 designing, EW 304, EW 340
 distributing rows and columns,
   EW 345–346
 entering text, EW 323–326
 filling columns or rows, EW 333–336
 formatting text, EW 340–341
 headers, EW 304, **EW 320–323**
 HTML tags, EW 316
 images, EW 326–329
 inserting, EW 317–319
 items and characteristics, EW 316
 merging cells, EW 336–337
 nested, EW 309
 organizing existing content into,
   EW 304
 planning structure, EW 309
 predetermined formatting options,
   EW 346–348
 properties, EW 302, EW 319–322
 rows, EW 316, EW 317–319,
   EW 329–333
 splitting cells, EW 336–339
 striping, **EW 340**
 structure, EW 304
 style sheets, EW 304
 styles, EW 340–341
 title row, **EW 336**
 width, EW 320
Tables toolbar, EW 329–333,
   EW 337–338, EW 347
tabs pane, **APP 1**, APP 4
Tag Properties panel, EW 84, EW 256
target audience, EW 218, **EW 220**,
   EW 224
<tc> tag, EW 316
<td> tag, EW 316
technology standards, **APP 11**
templates, EW 152, EW 227
 dynamic Web pages template,
   EW 189–193
 embedded styles, EW 193
 folders, EW 160
 global changes to, EW 190–193
 images, EW 154
 placeholders, EW 156–159
 replacing placeholder text,
   EW 172–176
 starting new Web site with,
   EW 154–159
 types, EW 155
 Web site creation, EW 157–159
 XHTML-based, EW 152

temporary staging server, **APP 18**
testing
 external links, EW 132–133
 internal links, EW 125–127
 pre- or post-publishing, EW 237
 Web sites, APP 18
text, EW 233, EW 234–235
 alternate text, **EW 75–76**
 bulleted list, **EW 25–27**
 capitalizing, EW 38–40
 centering, EW 36, EW 337
 converting to tables, EW 342–344
 delineated, **EW 342**
 entering and editing, EW 20–27,
   EW 172–176, EW 182–189
 finding and replacing, EW 186–189
 font families, **EW 262**
 formatting tables, EW 340–341
 images and, EW 326
 indenting, **EW 41**
 italicizing, **EW 42–43**
 paragraphs <p> tag, EW 23–25
 pasting, EW 177–182
 readability, EW 235
 removing formatting, EW 177
 replacing in placeholder,
   EW 172–176
 resizing, EW 38–40
 styles, EW 242, EW 340–341
 tables, EW 323–326
 wrapping around images, EW 76,
   EW 94
text attributes, EW 36
text-based hyperlinks, EW 372
text links, **EW 224**, EW 226
text wrapping, **EW 93**
<th> HTML tag, EW 320
<th> tag, EW 316, EW 340
third-party logistics provider,
   EW 434–435
third-party payment processors,
   EW 436–437
thumbnails, **EW 111–116**
title bar, **EW 7**
title row, **EW 336**
toggle commands, EW 52
Toolbar shortcut menu, EW 407
toolbars, **APP 1**, EW 8–9
Toolbox panel, EW 84
<tr> tag, EW 316
tracer lines, **EW 317**
TraderOnline Web site, EW 426
transaction security, EW 435
transparency of images,
   EW 99–103

U

undocking panels, EW 84
Upper Cut Web site folder,
EW 305–309
uppercut_styles.css file, EW 310–315
URL (Uniform Resource Locator),
APP 15
usability testing, EW 226, EW 237
user-defined style sheets, EW 260
User Guide toolbar, APP 3–4
User Guide window
Contents tab, APP 4–6
Index tab, APP 4, APP 6–8
Search tab, APP 8–9
tabs pane, **APP 1**
toolbar, **APP 1**
User Guide toolbar, APP 3–4
viewing pane, **APP 1**
Windows 7 operating system window
features, APP 1

V

valign attribute, EW 353
value, **EW 194**
vector graphics, **APP 24**
vegetables.html page, EW 396
video, EW 236
video files, compressing, APP 27
view buttons, **EW 8**
viewing pane, **APP 1**
views, switching, EW 48–51
virtual inventory, **EW 434–435**
virtual storefront business model,
EW 424
visitors with disabilities, APP 14
visual aids, **EW 52**
hiding and displaying, EW 52–54
Quick tags, **EW 52**
table borders, EW 318
Volusion, EW 438

W

W3C (World Wide Web Consortium),
APP 11–12
Wall Street Journal online edition,
EW 428
Web Accessibility Initiative, **APP 13**
Web. *See* World Wide Web
Web accessibility, EW 320
Web accessibility guidelines,
APP 13–14
Web Accessibility Initiative,
APP 13

Web-based applications and rich
content, APP 25
Web-based Distributed Authoring and
Versioning (WebDAV), **APP 18**
Web browsers. *See* browsers
Web hosting fees, APP 17
Web hosting services, **APP 16**, APP 17
Web page tab, **EW 8**
Web pages, EW 2
accessibility problems, APP 14
adding, EW 169–171
adding content, EW 276–280
automatically saving, EW 30
closing, EW 57
completing content, EW 41–42
content positioning, EW 230–231
copying images, EW 103–105
creation, EW 305–309, EW 315–316
CSS (Cascading Style Sheets),
EW 259
deleting, EW 164–165
division-based layout, **EW 20**
download speed, EW 20, EW 259
dynamic Web page template,
EW 189–193
editable regions, **EW 172**
entering text, EW 20–27
entry page, **EW 222**
folders, EW 160
formatting, EW 5
frames and tables, EW 354
graphics, **EW 72**
Home Page link, EW 226
hyperlinks (links), **EW 72**,
EW 276–280, EW 283–284
images, **EW 72**
interactive buttons, EW 378
keywords, **EW 15**
layout, EW 5
modifying in Code View, EW 266–268
navigation bar, EW 120
opening, EW 14, EW 247–248
page description, **EW 15**
page length, EW 230–231
page title, **EW 15**
preloading, EW 372
primary navigation bar, EW 370
printing, EW 55–56
properties, EW 5, EW 14–20
reloading, EW 372
renaming, EW 161, EW 162–163
saving, EW 30
screen resolution, EW 231
separating content from formatting,
EW 193

spell checking, EW 45–47
splash page, **EW 222**
standards-compliant, APP 12
status bar behavior, **EW 396–398**
style creations, EW 198–201
style sheets, EW 315–316
subsidiary pages, **EW 221**
tables, EW 304, EW 317–319
text, EW 5, EW 234–235
types, EW 220–222
viewing, EW 48–51
Web accessibility guidelines,
APP 13–14
Web-ready images, EW 236
Web-safe fonts, EW 262
Web-safe palette, EW 230
Web server, **APP 16**
Web server space, **APP 16**
Web site goals, EW 2, EW 218–219
Web site objectives, **EW 219**
Web sites, **EW 2**
all-in-one e-commerce solution,
EW 437–438
balance, **EW 232**
checking links, EW 288–289
closing, EW 204
color schemes, EW 228–230
combination structure, EW 223
communicating message, EW 218
creation, EW 10–13, EW 305–309
credit card payments, EW 432–434
dynamic, APP 17
e-commerce capability, EW 436–438
e-commerce elements, EW 429
entry page, EW 222
folders, EW 166, EW 167–168
formatting, EW 244
guidelines, EW 5
hierarchical structure, **EW 223**
home page, **EW 10**, EW 220
interactivity, **EW 368**, EW 370
linear structure, **EW 222**
local, APP 20
navigating, EW 370, EW 373
navigation system, **EW 224–226**
navigational links, EW 120–140
objectives, EW 218
online purchase and payment process,
EW 431
opening, EW 77–80, EW 247–248
organizing, EW 284–286
planning, EW 2
previewing, EW 54–55, EW 139–140,
EW 203, EW 288–289
primary goal, **EW 219**

product catalog, **EW 429**
publishing, **APP 15–18**, EW 54–55
purpose, EW 5, EW 218–219
remote, APP 20
saving, EW 10
search boxes, EW 120
secondary goals, **EW 219**
shopping cart, **EW 430–431**
source and destination of files, APP 20
splash page, EW 222
standard elements, EW 154
statement of purpose, EW 219
structure, EW 10, EW 160, EW 218,
    EW 222–223
subsidiary pages, **EW 221**
target audience, EW 2, EW 218,
    EW 220
templates, EW 154–159, EW 157
testing, APP 18
third-party payment processors,
    EW 436–437
types, EW 2
Web pages, EW 164–165, EW 169–171,
    EW 220–222
webbed structure, **EW 223**
Web standards, **APP 11–12**, EW 193
Web Standards Group, APP 11
Web Standards Project, APP 11, APP 12
Web templates, **EW 152**, EW 227
Web usability, APP 14
webbed structure, **EW 223**
Webcam video, capturing, APP 27
WebDAV (Web-based Distributed
    Authoring and Versioning), **APP 18**

Webgistix Web site, EW 434
Webtrends Web site, EW 426
What You *See* Is What You Get
    (WYSIWYG) design interface,
    EW 2
What You *See* Is What You Get
    (WYSIWYG) editor, **APP 24**
Windows desktop applications graphi-
    cal user interfaces (GUIs), APP 25
Windows Explorer, widening column,
    EW 247
Windows Internet Explorer, EW 54
Windows Vista
  closing Web site, APP 37
  Expression Web, APP 33–37
  opening existing Web site, APP 35–36
  starting Expression Web, APP 34
Windows XP
  closing Web site, APP 32
  Expression Web, APP 28–32
  opening existing Web site, APP 30–32
  starting Expression Web, APP 29
Wisteria Farms Web site, EW 371
wisteria_images folder, EW 399,
    EW 401, EW 406
WMA file format, APP 27
WMV file format, APP 27
WonderBrains.com Web site, EW 429
Word
  closing, EW 182
  copying and pasting text from,
    EW 276–280
  versions, EW 276
workspace, **EW 7**

adjusting layout, EW 84–88
resetting layout, EW 9, EW 156,
    EW 246, EW 371
toolbars, EW 8
workspace window, EW 7–8
World Wide Web (Web), EW 424
World Wide Web Consortium (W3C),
    APP 11–12
wrapping text around images, EW 76,
    EW 94
WYSIWYG (What You *See* Is What
    You Get) design interface, **EW 2**
WYSIWYG (What You *See* Is
    What You Get) editor,
    APP 24, EW 233

X

XAML (Extensible Application
    Markup Language), APP 25,
    APP 27
XHTML 1.1, APP 12
XHTML-based templates,
    EW 152
XHTML (Extensible Hypertext
    Markup Language), **EW 48**
XML, APP 12
XSL (Extensible Stylesheet Language),
    EW 244

Y

Yahoo! Small Business, APP 16,
    EW 438

Quick Reference Summary

In the Microsoft Expression Web 3 program, you can accomplish a task in a number of ways. The following table provides a quick reference to each task presented in this textbook. The first column identifies the task. The second column indicates the page number on which the task is discussed in the book. The subsequent four columns list the different ways the task in column one can be carried out.

Microsoft Expression Web Quick Reference Summary

Task	Page Number	Mouse	Menu Bar	Shortcut Menu	Keyboard Shortcut
Add Folder	EW 167		File | New | Folder	New | Folder	
Behavior, Insert	EW 391	Click the Insert button in the Behaviors panel, then click the behavior to add			
Behavior, Modify	EW 402	Double-click behavior in Behaviors panel to open *behavior* dialog box			
Bold	EW 30	Bold button on Common toolbar or Formatting toolbar	Format | Font	Font	CTRL+B
Bookmark, Insert	EW 134		Insert | Bookmark		CTRL+G
Bullets	EW 25	Bullets button on Common toolbar or Formatting toolbar	Format | Bullets and Numbering		
Caption, Add to Table	EW 317		Table | Insert | Caption	Insert | Caption	
Cell Properties, Change	EW 320		Table | Table Properties | Cell	Cell Properties	
Cell, Split	EW 338	Split Cells button on Tables toolbar	Table | Modify | Split Cells	Modify | Split Cells	
Cells, Merge	EW 337	Merge Cells button on Tables toolbar or Formatting toolbar	Table | Modify | Merge Cells	Modify | Merge Cells	
Center Text	EW 36	Center button on Common toolbar or Formatting toolbar	Format | Paragraph		CTRL+E
Close Page	EW 57	Close button on editing window	File | Close	Close	CTRL+W
Close Site	EW 57		Site | Close		
Copy	EW 103		Edit | Copy	Copy	CTRL+C
Crop an Image	EW 106	Crop button on Pictures toolbar | drag cropping handles | Crop button on Pictures toolbar again			
CSS Layout Page, New	EW 271		File | New | Page | CSS Layouts		
CSS Report, Run	EW 286		Tools | CSS Reports		

Microsoft Expression Web Quick Reference Summary *(continued)*

Task	Page Number	Mouse	Menu Bar	Shortcut Menu	Keyboard Shortcut
Delete File or Folder	EW 166		Edit | Delete	Delete	DELETE
Delete Text (Left of Insertion Point)	EW 183				BACKSPACE
Delete Text (Right of Insertion Point)	EW 183				DELETE
E-mail Link, Add	EW 137	Insert Hyperlink button on Common toolbar	Insert | Hyperlink	Hyperlink	CTRL+K
Find Text	EW 186		Edit | Find		CTRL+F
Font	EW 44	Font box arrow on Common toolbar or Formatting toolbar	Format | Font	Font	
Font Color	EW 37	Font Color arrow on Common toolbar or Formatting toolbar	Format | Font	Font	
Font Family, Create	EW 262		Tools | Page Editor Options | Font Families tab		
Font Size	EW 39	Font Size box arrow on Common toolbar or Formatting toolbar	Format | Font	Font	
Heading Style, Add	EW 33	Style box arrow on Common toolbar or Formatting toolbar			
Hotspot, Add	EW 405	*Shape* Hotspot button on the Pictures toolbar | draw hotspot shape			
Hyperlink, Insert	EW 122	Insert Hyperlink button on Common or Standard toolbar	Insert | Hyperlink	Hyperlink	CTRL+K
Image, Align	EW 94	Double-click image to open Picture Properties dialog box	Format | Properties | Appearance tab	Picture Properties | Appearance tab	
Image, Insert	EW 80	Insert Picture from File button on Common toolbar, Formatting toolbar, or Pictures toolbar	Insert | Picture | From File		
Image Margins, Modify	EW 97	Drag margin border Or Double-click image to open the Picture Properties dialog box	Format | Properties | Appearance tab	Picture Properties | Appearance tab	
Image, Resize	EW 89	Drag corner resize Or Double-click image to open Picture Properties dialog box	Format | Properties | Appearance tab	Picture Properties | Appearance tab	
Images, Borders and Padding	EW 95	Borders button arrow on Common or Formatting toolbar	Format | Borders and Shading		Hold SHIFT | drag blue lines around graphic
Indent Text	EW 41	Increase Indent Position button on Common or Formatting toolbar	Format | Paragraph		CTRL+M
Inline Frame, Add Link	EW 352	Set Initial Page button in I-frame			
Inline Frame, Insert	EW 349	Double-click Inline Frame button in Toolbox	Insert | HTML | Inline Frame		
Interactive Button, Create	EW 373		Insert | Interactive Button		
Interactive Button, Edit	EW 380	Double-click to open Interactive Buttons dialog box		Button Properties	

Microsoft Expression Web Quick Reference Summary *(continued)*

Task	Page Number	Mouse	Menu Bar	Shortcut Menu	Keyboard Shortcut
Italicize	EW 42	Italic button on Common or Formatting toolbar	Format | Font	Font	CTRL+I
New Folder, Create	EW 116		File | New | Folder	New | Folder	
New Web Page	EW 169	New Document arrow on the Common toolbar | Page	File | New | Page	New | HTML Or New | ASPX Or New | ASP Or New | PHP Or New | CSS	CTRL+N
Page Properties, Set	EW 15		File | Properties	Page Properties	
Panel, Close	EW 85	Close button on panel title bar	Panels | panel name		
Panel, Dock	EW 84	Drag panel title bar to edge of window			
Panel, Maximize	EW 84	Turn off AutoHide button on panel title bar			
Panel, Minimize	EW 84	Turn on AutoHide button on panel title bar			
Panel, Open	EW 84		Panels | panel name		ALT+F1
Panel, Undock	EW 84	Drag title bar to blank area			
Paste	EW 103		Edit | Paste	Paste	CTRL+V
Paste Formatted Text	EW 177		Edit | Paste		CTRL+V
Paste Unformatted Text	EW 177		Edit | Paste Text		
Preview Site	EW 54	Preview in *browser* button arrow on Common toolbar | *browser*	File | Preview in Browser | *browser*		F12
Print	EW 56		File | Print | Print Or File | Print | Print Preview | Print		CTRL+P
Quick Tag Selector, Use	EW 31	Tag on Quick Tag Selector			
Quit Expression Web	EW 58	Close button on program window title bar	File | Exit		ALT+F4
Remove Formatting	EW 177	Paste Options button below pasted text | Remove Formatting	Format | Remove Formatting		CTRL+SHIFT+Z
Rename File or Folder	EW 161	Click file or folder name | click file or folder name again | type new name		Rename	
Replace Template Text	EW 172	Select tag on Quick Tag Selector | type replacement text Or Select tag tab | type replacement text			
Replace Text	EW 186		Edit | Replace		CTRL+H
Reset Workspace Layout	EW 9		Panels | Reset Workspace Layout		

Microsoft Expression Web Quick Reference Summary *(continued)*

Task	Page Number	Mouse	Menu Bar	Shortcut Menu	Keyboard Shortcut
Rulers, Show or Hide	EW 87		View | Ruler and Grid | Show Ruler	Show Ruler	
Save Web Page	EW 30	Save button on Common toolbar	File | Save	Save	CTRL+S
ScreenTip, Add to Hyperlink	EW 138		Insert | Hyperlink Or Format | Properties	Hyperlink Properties	CTRL+K
Select Paragraph	EW 183	Triple-click paragraph			
Select Text (One Character at a Time)	EW 183				SHIFT | left or right arrow
Select Text (One Word at a Time)	EW 183				CTRL+SHIFT | left or right arrow
Select Word	EW 183	Double-click word			
Snapshot View	EW 49		Panels | Snapshot		
Spell Check	EW 46		Tools | Spelling | Spelling		F7
Style, Apply	EW 201	*Style* button in Apply Styles panel			
Style, Create Code	EW 266	Type first letter(s) of selector name or value, then double-click selector from shortcut menu		Type first letter(s) of selector name or value, then press down arrow and ENTER	
Style, Create New	EW 198	New Style link in Apply Styles panel	Format | New Style	New Style	
Style, Modify	EW 195	*Style* button arrow in Apply Styles panel | Modify Style		Modify Style	
Style, New	EW 254	New Style link in Apply Styles panel	Format | New Style		
Style Sheet, Attach	EW 268	Attach Style Sheet link in Apply Styles panel	Format | CSS Styles | Attach Style Sheet		
Style Sheet, New	EW 260		File | New | CSS	New | CSS	
Style Sheet, New from Preformatted	EW 310		File | New | Page | Style Sheets		
Switch Views	EW 49	Show *view type* View button at bottom of editing window	View | Page | *view*		CTRL+PAGE DOWN Or CTRL+PAGE UP
Table AutoFormat	EW 347	Table AutoFormat button on Tables toolbar	Table | Modify | Table AutoFormat	Modify | Table AutoFormat	
Table Column, Add	EW 330	Column to the Left button on Tables toolbar Or Column to the Right button on Tables toolbar	Table | Insert | Column to the Left Or Table | Insert | Column to the Right	Insert | Column to the Left Or Insert | Column to the Right	
Table Column, Delete	EW 330	Delete Cells button on Tables toolbar	Table | Delete | Delete Columns	Delete | Delete Columns	CTRL+X
Table, Convert to Text	EW 342		Table | Convert | Table to Text		
Table, Fill	EW 334		Table | Fill | Down Or Table | Fill | Right		

Microsoft Expression Web Quick Reference Summary *(continued)*

Task	Page Number	Mouse	Menu Bar	Shortcut Menu	Keyboard Shortcut
Table, New	EW 316	Insert Table button on Common toolbar	Table | Insert Table		
Table, New from Text	EW 342		Table | Convert | Text to Table		
Table Properties, Change	EW 320		Table | Table Properties	Table Properties	
Table Row, Add	EW 330	Row Above button on Tables toolbar Or Row Below button on Tables toolbar	Table | Insert | Row Above Or Table | Insert | Row Below	Insert | Row Above Or Insert | Row Below	
Table Row, Delete	EW 330	Delete Cells button on Tables toolbar	Table | Delete | Delete Rows	Delete | Delete Rows	CTRL+X
Tag, Add	EW 20	Double-click tag in Toolbox Or Drag tag from Toolbox to desired location Or *tag* button on Common toolbar	Insert | HTML | *tag*		
Thumbnail, Create	EW 113	Auto Thumbnail button on Pictures toolbar		Auto Thumbnail	CTRL+T
Transparency, Set Around an Image	EW 99	Set Transparent Color button on Pictures toolbar			
Undo Action	EW 21	Undo button on Common toolbar	Edit | Undo		CTRL+Z
Visual Aids, Show or Hide	EW 52	Visual Aids button on status bar | Show	View | Visual Aids | Show		CTRL+/
Web Page, Delete	EW 164		Edit | Delete	Delete	DELETE
Web Page, Open	EW 14	Open button arrow on Common toolbar | Open Or Double-click page in Folder List or Site View tab	File | Open		CTRL+O
Web Page, Rename (Folder List)	EW 162	Click file name in Folder List | click file name in Folder List again | type new name		Rename	F2
Web Site, Create from Template	EW 157		Site | New Site		
Web Site, Open	EW 77	Open button arrow on Common toolbar | Open Site	Site | Open Site		